Yin Yu Tang

Nancy Berliner

Yin Yu Tang

The Architecture and Daily Life
of a Chinese House

TUTTLE PUBLISHING

Boston • Rutland, Vermont • Tokyo

First published in 2003 by Tuttle Publishing, an imprint of Periplus Editions (HK) Ltd., with editorial offices at 153 Milk Street, Boston, Massachusetts 02109.

Printed in Singapore
Design: Mind, London

Library of Congress Cataloging-in-Publication Data

Berliner, Nancy Zeng, 1958-
　Yin Yu Tang : the architecture and daily life of a Chinese house / Nancy Berliner.
　　p. cm.
　Yin Yu Tang will open to the public in the Peabody Essex Museum, June 2003.
　Included bibliographical references and index.
　ISBN 0-8048-3487-3
　1. Architecture, Domestic--China--Huizhou Diqu. 2. Vernacular architrecture--China--Huizhou Diqu. 3. Huizhou Diqu (China)--Social life and customs. 4. Huang family. I. Title: Architecture and Daily Life of a Chinese house. II. Peabody Essex Museum. III. Title.

NA7449.H85B47 2003
728'.372'0951222--dc21　　　2002041621

Distributors

North America, Latin America and Europe:
Tuttle Publishing, Distribution Center, Airport Industrial Park
364 Innovation Drive, North Clarendon, VT 05759-9436
Tel: (802) 773-8930; Fax: (802) 773-6993
info@tuttlepublishing.com

Japan:
Tuttle Publishing, Yaekari Bldg., 3F
5-4-12 Ōsaki, Shinagawa-ku, Tokyo 141 0032, Japan
Tel: 81-35-437-0171; Fax: 81-35-437-0755
tuttle-sales@gol.com

Asia Pacific:
Berkeley Books Pte. Ltd.
130 Joo Seng Road, #06-01/03, Singapore 368357
Tel: (65) 6280-3320; Fax: (65) 6280-6290
inquiries@periplus.com.sg

Front cover: The skywell of Yin Yu Tang, from the second floor and (inset) cousins of the 34th generation dressed in their best clothes and gathered around Huang Zhenzhi, circa 1926. From left to right: Huang Zhenzhi's cousin Huang Zhenxin, his yonger half sister Huang Aizhu, Huang Zhenzhi, his younger female cousin Huang Xianying, and Huang Zhenxian.

Front flap: Yin Yu Tang's *tianjing*, "sky well," courtyard with fish pools.

Spine: The front gate of Yin Yu Tang, looking into the forecourt.

Back cover: (from left to right) Front facade and entryway of Yin Yu Tang while still located in Huang Cun; a small porcelain teapot with overglaze design of bamboo and rocks, given as a present to Huang Zizhi by his cousin in 1902, when he was nineteen years old; Huang Zixian, 1910s.

Title page: Front facade and entryway of Yin Yu Tang while still located in Huang Cun.

Photo Credits

Unless otherwise noted, all photographs and artworks courtesy of the Peabody Essex Museum.

Front cover (skywell), front flap, spine, frontispiece, back cover (facade), and Figs. 35, 37, 39, 164, 175, 180, 187, 190, 210: Photograph by Cheng Shouqi; Figs. 2, 3, 15, 21, 22, 31, 98, 108, 124, 181, 182, 195: Photographs by Nancy Berliner; Figs. 6, 8, 45, 167: Photographs by Richard Gordon; Figs. 10, 11; Photographs by Hedda Morrison, courtesy of Harvard University; Figs. 12, 54: Photographs by Jeff Dykes; Fig. 16: The Metropolitan Museum of Art, Bequest of John M. Crawford, Jr., 1988. (1989.363.39) Photograph by Malcolm Varon. Photograph ©1990 The Metropolitan Museum of Art; Fig. 17: Collection of Rev. Richard Fabian, San Francisco. Photograph by Donald J. Felton; Fig. 23: Photograph courtesy of the Huang family; Figs. 25, 53, 65, 83, 84, 92, 95, 120, 166, 170, 197: Photographs by Mark Sexton; Fig. 36: architectural students of Dong Nan University; Figs. 119, 132, 142, 143, 144, 145, 146, 151, 152, 155, 156, 158, 159, 160, 165, 172, 191, 192, 193, 201, 206: © John G. Waite Associates, Architects PLLC; Fig. 129 and maps pages xi and xiv: © Bohoy Design/Michael Yurkew; Figs. 134, 135, 136, 137: Photographs by Richard Howard; Fig. 140: Photograph by Mark Sexton/Jeffrey Dykes

Contents

Foreword

Chinese civilization spans more than 4,000 years, and its accomplishments in literature, science, technology, the arts, architecture, and many other endeavors stand among the finest and most significant in human history. China is now re-emerging as a nation of world influence. Yet many people in America and elsewhere have a relatively limited understanding of China's past and present. The Yin Yu Tang project, and this publication, create unique opportunities to help illuminate a part of China's rich and complex heritage as revealed through a merchant's home built in the Qing dynasty and the lives of the family who inhabited it over many generations into the late twentieth century.

The Peabody Essex Museum has many reasons for undertaking the unprecedented endeavor of acquiring a historic Chinese house and many of its furnishings, carefully dismantling the house, transporting it from Huang Cun in southern China's Anhui Province to Salem, and preserving, re-erecting, and interpreting it to the public.

This project represents a perfect convergence of PEM's longstanding interests and commitments to Asian art and to architecture. The museum began collecting Asian art in 1799, the year it was founded. Our Asian collections, acquired over more than two centuries, include more than eighty thousand works of art and culture, both domestic and export, representing China, Korea, Japan, India, Bhutan, and other Asian nations.

PEM also has a long and distinguished commitment to architecture. The Museum helped to pioneer the historic preservation movement in America, starting in the nineteenth century. Today the Museum possesses more than twenty-three historic buildings, including four National Historic Landmark buildings and eight others on the National Register of Historic Places representing five centuries of New England architecture.

The Yin Yu Tang house and its associated interpretive galleries open to the public in June 2003. The project is part of a complete transformation of the Peabody Essex Museum that features more than 250,000 square feet of galleries and a public spaces; entirely new installations of the museum's collections of Asian, Oceanic, African, Native American, Maritime, Asian export, and American decorative art; and a dramatic new addition designed by internationally acclaimed architect Moshe Safdie. Like the Yin Yu Tang project, the transformed museum reflects our conviction that art and culture are inextricably interconnected and that the museum should present and interpret art and the world in which it was made.

Successfully meeting the logistical and interpretive challenges involved in the Yin Yu Tang project required exceptional leadership on the part of many people. Ms. Nancy Berliner, Curator of Chinese Art at PEM, played a central role in making this project and this publication a reality. Mr. Wang Shukai, also a member of the Chinese Art Department, served as a stable and effective bridge between the museum and our colleagues and officials in China. Ms. Vas Prabhu, Deputy Director for Interpretation at PEM, played a key role in developing the interpretive program. John G. Waite Associates, Architects, one of America's leading historic preservation architecture firms, provided outstanding guidance to a complex architectural preservation program. Tuttle Publishing has produced a compelling book, and the Longbow Film Group did exceptional film work. I also wish to thank for their support the many members of the museum's staff and the numerous consultants and advisory groups with whom we have worked.

We owe a tremendous debt to our colleagues and other leaders in China who made this project and publication possible. I especially wish to thank Mr. Yang Jiechi, the Chinese Ambassador to the United States; Mr. Bi Pumin, the Xiuning County Magistrate; Mr. Luo Zhewen, one of China's preeminent architectural historians; and Mr. Wang Xiang, Director of the Huangshan Museum. I also wish to thank the many other officials and friends in China who have strongly supported this endeavor, including the people of Huang Cun. Finally, I wish to express my deepest appreciation to the members of the Huang family for their exceptional commitment to this pioneering project and publication.

—Dan L. Monroe, Executive Director
Peabody Essex Museum

Introduction

Fig. 1 **The Chinese character *jia*, written with the symbol for "roof" over the symbol for "pig," means "house, hometown, and family."**

If you love the house, you also love the crow on its roof.

The purpose of this book is to examine a Chinese house from the village of Huang Cun, called by its inhabitants "Yin Yu Tang."

Like many Chinese verbal expressions, the name of this house lends itself to many levels of poetic interpretation. The three words can be translated simply as *Shade/Shelter*, *Abundance*, and *Hall*. They imply an aspiration for sons who will become high officials—and the desire that the building will shelter the builder's descendants for many generations.

While still standing in Huang Cun, Yin Yu Tang sheltered eight generations of Huang family descendants. Over the past years it has been relocated from China—dismantled, crated, uncrated, conserved and then re-erected—to the Peabody Essex Museum, of Salem, Massachusetts, in the United States.

In exploring the house called Yin Yu Tang, it is clear that a home is made up of much more than the lines, the designs and the wood that frame the building's spaces.

The examination of this two-hundred-year-old house led to an examination of its home village of Huang Cun, through each and every one of the timbers which made up its walls, floors, and ceilings, through its rooms, through the lives and memories of the many people who occupied them, and through the history of their decoration and modification of their personal spaces.

The term "archiculture" describes this more expansive way of looking at architecture. Archiculture can be defined as "the culture inherent in the creation, the use, the decoration and the history of an architectural space." Considering the many physical, temporal and human facades that are contained by Yin Yu Tang, this archicultural approach includes both the house and the crow on the roof.

This all-encompassing approach to examining a home is particularly appropriate when considering the Chinese regional domestic architecture on exhibit in Yin Yu Tang.

The Chinese word *jia* can mean family, hometown, and home. The high value that traditional Chinese culture places on parents and family also extends to devotion to hometown and the physical family home.

In China, deceased ancestors are considered part of a family. At regular ceremonies, living descendants hung portraits of their ancestors in their reception hall, visited their graves, and offered them food, clothing and utensils for their use in the spirit world.

This loyalty to, and worship of, the family's ancestors stems from the traditional understanding that ancestors and preceding generations are intimately linked with the success and longevity of the present and future generations.

The hometown, of course, is where the ancestors are buried, and where they receive offerings, and where all members of the family line are to be buried.

The physical home is a haven for both the spirits of the ancestors and their living descendants. Though the crow may have flown off, and generations passed away, the ancestors' imprint on their family, their home, and their hometown remain—and are part of the living realm.

In this sense, a house incorporates and cannot be separated from the family that inhabits it. Because of this indivisible nature of the *jia*, the chapters that follow discuss not only the physical structure of Yin Yu Tang, and not only its original design, but also the ancestral village that surrounded it and the family who lived within it, molding and remaking it over time.

Given the antiquity of Chinese culture, and the dramatic sweep of its history over the past few hundred years, it is as important to place Yin Yu Tang in time as it is to locate it geographically. In the time line below, the small circle represents the moment in time when Yin Yu Tang, was created. During the hundreds, even thousands, of years leading up to that point, different styles of domestic housing developed, including the regional Huizhou architecture.

During the years directly before the creation of Yin Yu Tang, the man who commissioned the house, influenced by his fellow Huizhou merchants, may have saved as much of his income as he could in anticipation of building a grand home for himself and his descendants. In the years directly following its construction, the descendants of the original builder were born, lived, produced heirs and then died in this house. Throughout the years of their lives, they were formed by the "archiculture" of their house, and dutifully left their own mark on it.

"If you love the house, you also love the crow on its roof." This Chinese saying recognizes the importance of acknowledging the totality—the entirety of an object or person.

According to the guidelines created for the preservation of Yin Yu Tang, its re-erection at the Peabody Essex Museum was designed to preserve the entirety of the house's history, including the impact of time and people on the house.

A well-worn threshold and the remains of a fine brick carving smashed during the Cultural Revolution are as much a part of the house and its history as one of the untouched brick tile ornaments on the façade. Likewise, the use of the reception hall for playing mahjong in the 1920s and the occupation of a room by a poor peasant family after land reform in 1950 are as much a part of the of the house's archiculture as are the bases of the stone columns. Every aspect of the house—no matter how common or ephemeral —was to be preserved in the process.

This book considers the geographical, economic and historical circumstances that determined the development of the family who built the house, as well as the physical construction of the house, and the lives of many of the individual members of the Huang family who lived, laughed and cried, who cooked and ate, who pasted up wallpapers and occasionally tore down traditions, within the high walls of Yin Yu Tang.

At its new location in the United States, Yin Yu Tang will open its doors to embrace non-Huang family members, visitors from all corners of the earth. These new occupants, temporary though their stay may be, will be welcome to explore all aspects of Yin Yu Tang— and experience and learn from both the house and the lives of the people who inhabited it.

c. 1800 construction of YYT

YYT in Salem

development of vernacular housing forms

lives and changes in YYT

Chronology

c. 1210
Cheng Keyuan is adopted by the Huang family, changes his name to Huang Keyuan and, in time, becomes the originating ancestor of the Huang family clan in Huang Cun.

c. 1400
Huang Yueqi (d. 1413) writes the first *jiapu*, a genealogy of the Huang Cun Huang family.

1760
Guangzhou (Canton) is established as sole official site of legal trade with foreign nations.

1785
November 28. The *Grand Turk* sails out of Salem Harbor for Guangzhou (Canton), the first trade ship to travel from New England to China. Salem becomes one of the biggest ports in New England in the nineteenth century.

1799
East India Marine Society, the forebear of the Peabody Essex Museum, is founded by sea captains in Salem, Massachusetts.

c. 1800
Construction of Yin Yu Tang in Huang Cun

1820–50
A pavilion is constructed in the forecourt of Yin Yu Tang.

1839–42
Opium Wars. Chinese defeated by British and cede Hong Kong.

1850–1864
Taiping Rebellion

1851
Local Xiuning county fine green tea is exported to Europe and America.[1]

Chinese immigrants begin coming to the United States to join the California gold rush.

1856
Taiping Army enters Xiuning County.

1857
Huang Yangxian (1857–1885) is born.

1860s
Chinese immigrants come to the U.S. to participate in building the transcontinental railroad.

1875
Native Xiuning child, Wu Jingrong, at age eleven, is selected to study abroad in America.

1876
First railroad constructed in China.

c. 1878
Birth of Huang Zixian, son of Huang Yangxian.

1882
Chinese Exclusion Act in the United States prohibits Chinese workers from entering the U.S.

1883
Birth of Huang Zizhi, son of Huang Yangxian.

1885
Death of Huang Yangxian while traveling. The young father's boat was attacked by pirates.

1887
French missionaries begin building a Catholic church in Xiuning County town.

1900
Boxer Rebellion

c. 1900
Huang Yangxian's widow forced to sell four rooms in Yin Yu Tang to distant relative.

c. 1909
Birth of Huang Zhenzhi, son of Huang Zixian

1910
Huang Su establishes the Huang Clan Primary School in Huang Cun.[2]

1912
Establishment of the Republic of China. End of the imperial monarchy. Qing County official flees Xiuning.

1915
Xiuning County's native products, Wang

Shengchao tea and Hu Kaiwen ink, are selected to be exhibited in the Panama-Pacific World Exposition.[3]

Madame Cheng, mother of Huang Zixian and Huang Zizhi, dies.

1919
Chinese Communist Party (CCP) is established.

c. 1920
Huang Zixian becomes manager of kerosene shop in Tunxi.

1926
November. The warlord Sun Chuanfang, with a total of more than 40,000 soldiers, retreats to occupy Xiuning for several months, wreaking havoc.[4] Huang family is forced to flee Yin Yu Tang and live for a time in the neighboring village of Gewu.

c. 1926–27
Huang Zhenzhi marries Wang Yaozhen. Redecorates bedroom with imported wallpaper.

1928
Huang Zizhi opens pawnshop in Hankou with two partners. His oldest son, Huang Zhenxin, apprentices there.

Birth of Huang Xilin, son of Huang Zhenzhi and Wang Yaozhen.

1934–35
Long March

1934
Great drought in Xiuning County, relief care for 94,000 refugee victims[5]

Hankou pawnshop closes because of conflict among partners. Huang Zizhi plans to open new shop in Shanghai. At the steamship pier in Hankou, he refuses to allow porters to carry bags and is struck by porter. Later dies from injuries.

1935
Mao becomes primary leader of the CCP.

Huang Zhenxin marries Miss Chou Lijuan, moves to Shanghai and opens charcoal shop.

May. Red Army establishes a base in Xiuning County.[6]

1937
Rape of Nanjing

1937–1945
Japan occupies Shanghai.

1939–45
World War II

1940
October 28. Japanese army planes bomb Huizhou High School in Xiuning County killing one student and injuring three.[7]

1941
Birth of Huang Xiqi, son of Huang Zhenzhi.

Huang Zhenzhi, father of Huang Xiqi and Huang Xilin, dies.

1946–49
Civil war between Nationalists and Chinese Communist Party. CCP is victorious. Chiang Kai-shek and Nationalists flee to Taiwan.

1949
April 28. The People's Liberation Army enters and liberates Xiuning County.[8]

Students from Huang Cun follow the People's Liberation Army to Shanghai. Huang Xilin joins People's Liberation Army.

People's Republic of China is established.

Establishment of the Agrarian Reform Law (redistribution of landlords' holdings) and New Marriage Law (rights to women).

1950–53
Korean War: Chinese in conflict with U.S.

1951
October. Land reform campaign for Xiuning County begins, and is completed in November 1951; 392 square miles (101,493 ha) are divided among 19,046 poor peasant households.[9]

c. 1951
During land reform, two rooms in Yin Yu Tang, belonging to Huang Zhengang, are confiscated and assigned to poor peasants.

1957
Anti-capitalist and rightist struggles begin in China and Xiuning County.[10]

1958
Creation of People's Communes

October. The entire Xiuning County is organized into six communes, which were further broken down to 343 production teams.[11] Public cafeterias are arranged for all the villages of the entire county. Xiuning's peasant population of 185,000 eat daily in 1,219 cafeterias.[12]

The two Huang Clan ancestral halls in Huang Cun are torn down. Building materials are donated to Country Reservoir Project.

1958–61
Great Leap Forward

1959–61
Famines throughout China result in at least 30 million deaths. About 15,000 people in Xiuning County appear to have died of starvation.[13]

1959
Conflicts over administration of Tibet

1966–76
Cultural Revolution

Demonstrations of Party loyalty at Yin Yu Tang: carved tile decorations on house facade are battered, a heart inscribed with the character "loyalty" is placed on an entrance.

1966
Red Guards climb Qiyun Mountain in Xiuning County, a sacred Taoist mountain, to destroy the "Four Olds," smashing more than 2,000 statues of deities.[14]

1968
Urban youth are sent to the countryside.

Huang Xiqi returns to Huang Cun and becomes a teacher under the requirement that intellectuals return to their own villages.

Many of Huang family ancestors' graves dug up

1971
U.S. table-tennis team is invited to China.

1972
President Richard Nixon visits China.

1976
Premier Zhou Enlai dies.

September 9. Mao Zedong dies; 155,000 people in Xiuning County hear the official broadcast for "the Entire Party, the Entire Army and the Entire People of the Nation."[15]

Gang of Four is arrested. End of Cultural Revolution

October 24. Ten thousand people demonstrate in Xiuning to celebrate the crushing of the Gang of Four.[16]

Front pavilion and kitchens of Yin Yu Tang collapse and are dismantled.

1978
Four Modernizations campaign begins: governmental effort to develop agriculture, industry, national defense, and science and technology.

1979
Beginning of one-child-only policy

Deng Xiaoping visits U.S.

Economic reforms. Communes are phased out.

1981
Electricity comes to Huang Cun. Two lightbulbs are installed in Yin Yu Tang.

Wang Yaozhen leaves Yin Yu Tang and Huang Cun to join her son Huang Xilin in Shanghai.

1982
Huang Xiqi leaves Huang Cun to teach at Longwan Grade School in Xiuning County.

1983
Communes are reconfigured into villages, and land is assigned to villagers.[17]

1990
Several pieces of furniture and paintings stolen from Yin Yu Tang.

1996
Huang Binggen, Huang Zhenxin, Huang Xiqi, and their families return to visit Yin Yu Tang and the family graves, and decide to sell house.

1997
Death of Deng Xiaoping

Yin Yu Tang Cross Cultural Agreement signed with Huangshan Municipality.

Huang Family Timeline

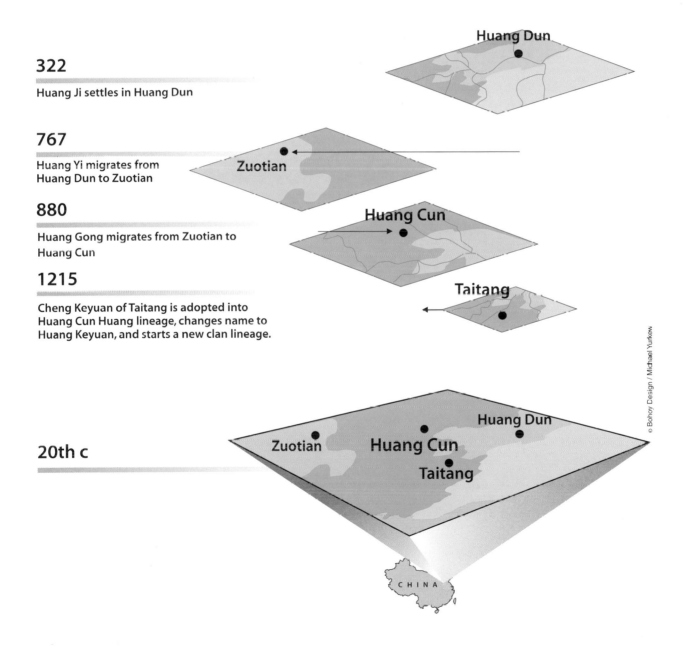

322

Huang Ji settles in Huang Dun

767

Huang Yi migrates from
Huang Dun to Zuotian

880

Huang Gong migrates from Zuotian to
Huang Cun

1215

Cheng Keyuan of Taitang is adopted into
Huang Cun Huang lineage, changes name to
Huang Keyuan, and starts a new clan lineage.

20th c

Huang Dun

Zuotian

Huang Cun

Taitang

Huang Dun

Zuotian   Huang Cun

Taitang

CHINA

© Bohoy Design / Michael Yurkew

The Huang Family

Huang Family Voices

Throughout the research process for this book and the Yin Yu Tang house project, Huang family members contributed many hours and days, detailing and describing their routine lives and special moments in their home village of Huang Cun and in their ancestral home, Yin Yu Tang. Their voices appear throughout this text.

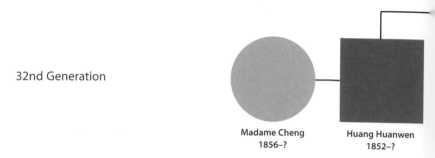

32nd Generation

Madame Cheng
1856–?

Huang Huanwen
1852–?

Huang Zhenxin (b. 1914) was born and raised in Yin Yu Tang. At the age of 14, as was customary for boys in this region, he left his home to apprentice as a merchant in the distant city of Hankou. After his father, also a merchant, passed away in 1934, he returned home to marry, but soon moved to Shanghai to start a small business. He has lived there ever since.

33rd Generation

Huang Xianying (1921-2000) was born and raised in Yin Yu Tang. She attended the local village primary school, studied at a normal school and became a schoolteacher. She married a merchant from the nearby village of Yuetan and moved with him to Shanghai. She remained there for the rest of her life.

Huang Xiqi (b. 1941) was born and raised in Yin Yu Tang. After attending the village primary school, he went on to middle school and normal school, and became a primary school teacher. For many years, he taught at the Huang Cun Primary School. In 1982, he was assigned to teach at a large school in another town and, at that time, moved out of Yin Yu Tang. He has now retired and lives with his grown children in a new home in the county town of Xiuning.

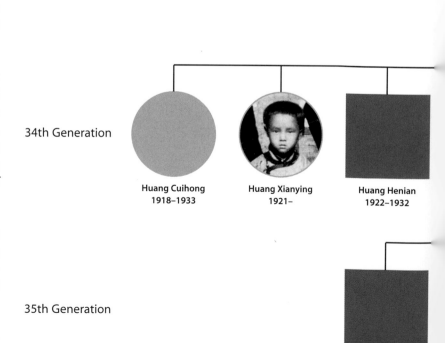

34th Generation

Huang Cuihong
1918–1933

Huang Xianying
1921–

Huang Henian
1922–1932

Huang Cui'e (b. 1904) was born and raised in Huang Cun, but is not a member of the Yin Yu Tang branch of the Huang family. She is the oldest living person born in Huang Cun. Like Huang Xianying, she married a merchant from the village of Yuetan and moved with him to Shanghai, where they have lived for over sixty years.

35th Generation

Note: This project is indebted to Carma Hinton and Richard Gordon for the energy and devotion they contribute in making these video recordings.

Huang Xiren
1940–1941

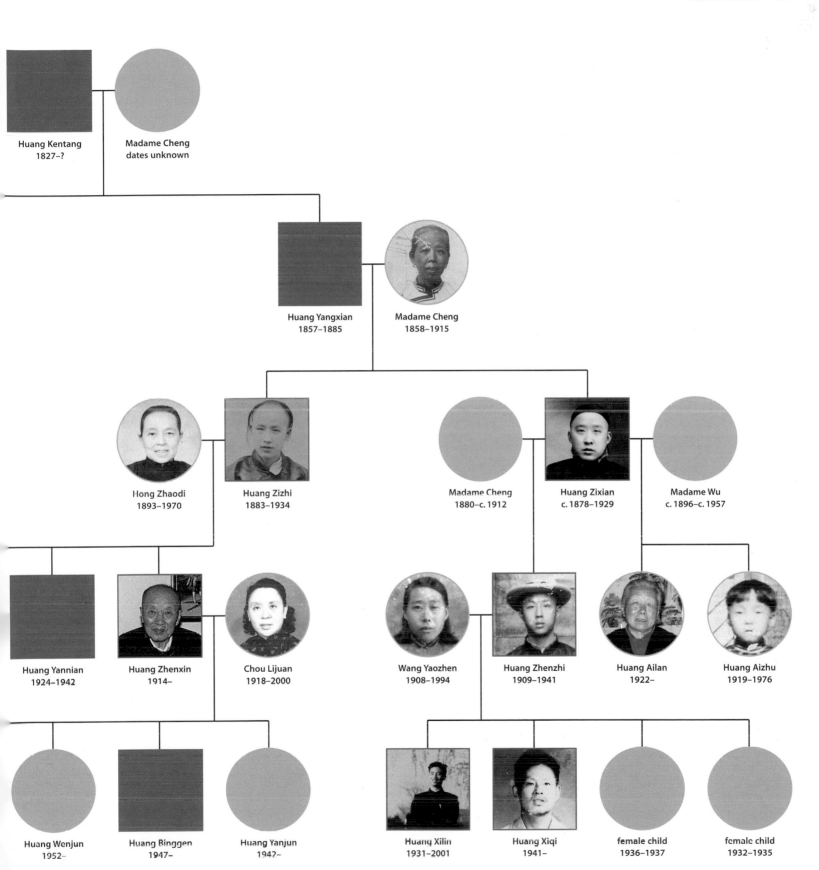

Maps and Names

Names and Pronunciation Guide

Chinese personal and place names in this text are written in *pinyin* (literally "spelled sound"), a transliteration system developed in the 1950s to romanize the sounds of Chinese characters as they are pronounced in the national Chinese language, known as *putonghua*. The people of Huizhou speak putonghua, as well as their own regional dialect, as do the populations of each area in China. The pinyin pronunciations provided in this text all accord with the nationally accepted, putonghua pronunciations of the characters. Certain conventions of this system are unexpected to the English speaker, such as:

x is pronounced like *sh* in she
q is pronounced like *ch* in cheese
c is pronounced like *ts* in cheats
zh is pronounced like *j* in Joe.

The name Huang Xianying is pronounced *Hwong Shyen-ying*, rhyming with "wrong hen sing"

Huang Zhenxin is pronounced *Hwang Jun-sheen*, rhyming with "wrong bun bean"

Huang Zizhi is pronounced *Hwang Dze-dje*, rhyming with "wrong uh uh"

Huang Xiqi is pronounced *Hwang Shee-chee*, rhyming with "wrong she tea"

Huang Cun, Huang Village, the home town of the Huang family, is pronounced *Hwang Tsoon*, rhyming with "wrong ruin"

Chinese personal names are conventionally written and spoken with the surname, or family name, first, followed by the given name.

Dynasties and Time Periods

During the past four millennia, the region known today as China was ruled over by a series of dynasties, each representing a familial lineage of emperors, and, in the last century, republics. The exact boundaries of the ruled land varied from era to era. This list includes only the major time periods and dynasties, and the reign periods for the last two dynasties.

Next page: Fig. 2 **The village of Nanping. Yixian County.**

Neolithic Cultures	c. 5000 – 2000 B.C.E.
Yellow Emperor Huang Di (legendary)	c. 2700 B.C.E.
Xia Dynasty (legendary)	2100 B.C.E. – c. 1600 B.C.E.
Shang Dynasty	c. 1600 – c.1050 B.C.E.
Zhou Dynasty	c. 1050 – 256 B.C.E.
Qin Dynasty	221 – 207 B.C.E.
Han Dynasty	
Western Han	206 B.C.E.–8 C.E.
Eastern Han	25–220 C.E.
Three Kingdoms period	220 – 280
Jin Dynasty	265 – 420
Six Dynasties period (in south)	265 – 589
Sixteen Kingdoms period (in north)	316 – 589
Sui Dynasty	581 – 618
Tang Dynasty	618 – 906
Five Dynasties period	907 – 960
Northern Song Dynasty	960 – 1127
Southern Song Dynasty	1127 – 1279
Yuan Dynasty	1279 – 1368

Ming Dynasty	**1368 – 1644**
Hongwu	1368–1398
Jianwen	1399–1402
Yongli	1403–1424
Hongxi	1425
Xuande	1426–1435
Zhengtong	1436–1449
Jingtai	1450 1456
Tianshun	1457–1464
Chenghua	1465–1487
Hongzhi	1488–1505
Zhengde	1506–1521
Jiajing	1522–1566
Longqing	1567–1572
Wanli	1573–1620
Taichang	1620
Tianqi	1621–1627
Chongzhen	1628–1644
Qing Dynasty	**1644 – 1911**
Shunzhi	1644–1661
Kangxi	1662–1722
Yongzheng	1723–1735
Qianlong	1736–1795
Jiaqing	1796–1820
Daoguang	1821–1850
Xianfeng	1851–1861
Tongzhi	1862–1874
Guangxu	1875–1908
Xuantong (Puyi)	1909–1911
Republic of China	**1912 – 1949**
Republic of China (in Taiwan)	**1949 – present**
People's Republic of China	**1949 – present**

1 | Huizhou: Mountains and Merchants

. . . Xiuning County, as a southern region of Anhui, is located in the upper reaches of the Zhe River. It rests among thousands of mountains and hills and is therefore difficult to get access from outside and geographically stable inside. It covers a region with a diameter of 300 li. . . .[1]

When we got fairly inside the Hwuy-chow [Huizhou] district I was able to ramble about in the country as before. The river became not only shallow, but in many parts so full of rocks and stones that it was next to impossible to pick out a passage for the boat. It still wound through a hilly and mountainous country. The hills, however, became gradually more fertile as we proceeded, and in many parts they were cultivated to their summits. Crops of millet and Indian corn were growing amongst the tea-bushes, which were now observed in large quantities on the sides of the hills.[2]

[Be] born in Hangzhou, marry in Suzhou, die in Yangzhou and [be] buried in Huizhou.[3]

Huizhou is the traditional name, dating back to the Song dynasty (960–1279), of a prefecture in the southeastern corner of Anhui Province 223.7 miles (360 km) southwest of Shanghai. During various time periods in the past, the Huizhou prefecture, once called Xin'an, encompassed numerous counties, including Shexian, Xiuning, Qimen, Yixian, Jixi, Taiping, Ningguo, and Wuyuan. Today, because of border changes, Huizhou, or Huangshan Municipality as it was renamed in the 1980s, is made up of four counties and four districts, in a landmass of 3,786 square miles (9,807 sq km). The subject of this book, Yin Yu Tang, is a house from a small village, Huang Cun, in one of these four Huizhou counties, Xiuning.

The region of Huizhou, with its myriad mountains and extensive rivers, nurtured a unique culture and population that eventually gave rise to the building of Yin Yu Tang. An exploration of the physical region and the culture of the inhabitants—a culture that developed as they found distinctive ways to manage and inhabit their environment—will sketch a picture of the land that embraced the Huang clan and the foundation on which one Huang family member came to construct a home for generations of his descendants.

For centuries the most prominent feature of Huizhou has been its mountains, which cover a large percentage of the region's land. In Xiuning County, mountains and hills cover 76.6 percent of the 824.3 square miles (2,135 sq km) of land. The high mountain peaks generally range between 328 to 1,969 feet (100 and 600 m), with individual peaks reaching as high as 6,040 feet (1,841 m) in the Huang Shan range.

Until the 1949 revolution, the second most outstanding trait of Huizhou, heard repetitively in references to the region, was the vast number of traveling merchants. These Huizhou men became ubiquitous features of the urban landscape all over China.

Testimony from travelers, inhabitants, and scholars—Chinese and non-Chinese alike, from the thirteenth century through the twentieth century—confirms, over and over, the widespread knowledge of these Huizhou features: mountains and merchants.

Fig. 3 **Threshing rice in a village surrounded by hills and mountains. Xiuning County.**

Without Hui [people], nothing [in business] can be accomplished.[4]

These two facets of Huizhou are intimately linked. The predominance of the hills and mountains of Huizhou made self-sufficiency, in terms of rice consumption, impossible. Rice needs to be grown on flat spaces. The steep geographic formations covering such a large percentage of the land excluded the possibility of abundant rice harvests. Since a reliable source of food for consumption is essential for the continued inhabitance of a place, the situation forced the people of Huizhou to become merchants, trading their local resources for rice from neighboring regions. A Ming dynasty (1368–1644) gazetteer of Xiuning County—where only 7 percent of the land is arable, 90 percent of which is necessarily dedicated to rice cultivation[5]—clearly noted the mountains and lack of agricultural land as the root behind the Huizhou merchants.

The district is [set] among 10,000 mountains. Its land is difficult and not flat. Its earth is tough and unchanging. . . . Though the people are industrious and use all their strength, the harvest is only enough to provide for half [the population.][6]

Because [agriculture] is not sufficient to feed the people of the county, most people are engaged in commerce as their constant business. As early as the Eastern Jin dynasty, the people of Xiuning had started to do business outside their hometown. They traveled to the south and the north. Some were peddlers and some set up their shops. They consider what is abundant and what is in shortage, and buy or sell out according to the trend of demand and supply.[7]

Abundant riverways, particularly the Xin'an River, which flows east from Huizhou all the way to the metropolis of Hangzhou, allowed this trade to flourish. The proficiency and renown of Huizhou people as merchants developed and blossomed over the years, and the name *Huizhou* became inexorably linked with the word *merchant*.

[As I have] observed in private, in my prefecture of Xin'an, where there are six urban centers within the prefecture, for every ten families there are nine in business, who have had to travel widely for their businesses.[8]

A unique regional culture and lifestyle evolved in this largely merchant society, where men, busy selling their wares throughout China, were often absent from households; where these same prospering merchants endeavored to imitate the more respected lifestyles of scholars, literati, and urbanites; and where the growing wealth of these merchants was funneled into building grand homes for their wives, children, and descendants, and magnificent clan halls for their ancestors. Though the merchant way of life brought prosperity to the individuals, their families, and their clan, being so far from home, for such long stretches of time, was not a desirable existence. A Huizhou saying, muttered often, underscores the sense of resignation accorded such an ill fate: "[In your] previous life you must not have cultivated yourself enough, so [you] were born in Huizhou. At the age of twelve or thirteen, you are tossed out [of your home.]" And yet, for those for whom Huizhou was home and for whom home was supremely important, traveling as merchants was inevitably the only way to carry on their

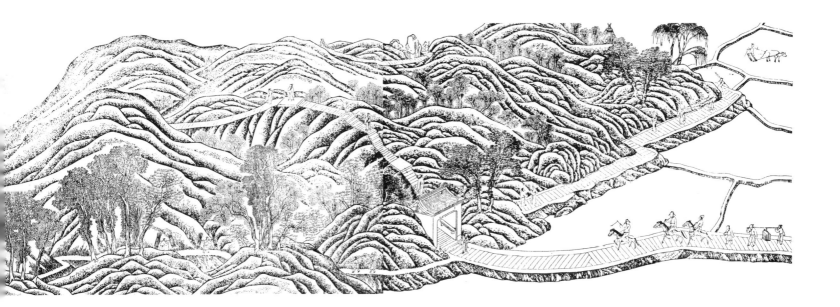

filial duties to their families and homes: "Those like us leave our villages and towns, leave our wives and blood relations, to travel thousands of miles. And for what? For no other purpose but to support our families."[9]

The painful sentiment of the unavoidability of this lifestyle is reflected in a local Huizhou folksong:

Green bamboo leaves, young green one. Send a letter up to Huizhou. Tell Pa not to be anxious, tell Ma not to worry, their son is in Suzhou, working as a clerk. One day three meals of crispy rice, one dish of two salted fish heads. The hands of the son are like chicken claws, the two feet of the son are like charcoal kindling. Oh heaven, oh earth, old man and woman, the son is away and eating bitterness. Green bamboo leaves, young green one. Send a letter up to Huizhou. Tell Pa not to be anxious, tell Ma not to worry, their son is in Suzhou, working as a clerk. The son is away learning business, remember your parents words: "With fennel [a pun on the word huixiang, to return to the hometown] and dried beancurd, you can't maintain yourself. The bitterness you are eating is what makes a man into a man." After I have finished learning business, I will return again to Huizhou. Oh, heaven, oh earth. Old man and woman, if I don't have any promise, I won't return home again.[10]

Fig. 4 (opposite) **An early twentieth-century photograph of a village in Wuyuan County.**

Fig. 5 (above) **The mountains of Xiuning County as depicted in the c. 1605 woodblock-printed handscroll *Huan Cui Tang Yuan Jing Tu*, commissioned by the Ming publisher of fine illustrated books, Wang Tingna (c. 1569–after 1628), who was a native and resident of Xiuning County.**

Fig. 6 (right) **Ming dynasty official's home. Huang Cun, Xiuning County.**

Fig. 7 (far right) **Interior courtyard of a Ming merchant's home. Qiankou Museum, Huizhou District.**

Commercial Resources

The people [of Huizhou] take tea, lacquer, paper, and wood along the river to Jiangxi in exchange for rice with which to feed themselves.[11]

Pioneers first came to settle in Huizhou during the Qin (221–207 B.C.E.) and Han (206 B.C.E.–220 C.E.) dynasties. The population of the region increased dramatically in the early years of the Tang (618–907) and Song (960–1279) dynasties, as ordinary people were trying to escape from war-torn or bandit-ridden areas to the north and south. Both war and banditry interrupted daily lives, and the mountains of Huizhou offered some protection and an opportunity to carry on the tasks of farming and eating in a more settled manner. But as their settlements coalesced the necessity of trade with other regions became apparent.

While the predominance of trading as an occupation stayed a constant until the 1949 Communist revolution, the primary businesses and products of Huizhou men varied over the centuries as the country and the region changed. From early trading in regional resources and products—such as lumber and tea—the Huizhou merchants expanded into other trades. Many set up small shops in urban areas around the country, returning to their ancestral homes to marry and continue the family line, pay reverence to their ancestors, and die and be buried. The Huizhou merchant was so prevalent in the rest of China that shopping streets in many towns far from Huizhou were called the Huizhou Merchant Street, and the merchants in Ming short stories inevitably hailed from Huizhou.

County gazetteers, produced under imperial directive throughout the country, include—in addition to sections on geography, history, important men, and virtuous women—a large section on the products of the region, including both agricultural products for local consumption as well as more crafted products for sale and export. The 1815 Xiuning County gazetteer's local product category lists various types of grains, such as glutinous and nonglutinous rice and barley; beans and sesame; vegetables such as ginger, turnip, scallions, garlic, bamboo shoots, rape, wood ear fungi, squashes, eggplant, and mustard; and fruits such as peaches, walnuts, loquats, watermelon, papaya, peanuts, and haws. Under "Wood and Bamboo," the gazetteer includes *nanmu* (cedar), pine, fir, cypress, tung, elm, cassia, willow, poplar, mulberry, plantain, and wide variety of bamboos. Medicinal herbs are listed, as well as flowers, fowl, marine life, and many domestic and wild animals. Lastly, the gazetteer enumerates the more crafted products of the region that were exported to the rest of the country. First and foremost among this group in 1815 was tea. A lengthy explanation in the gazetteer includes the legend that the first place of tea leaf cul-

tivation in China was at Song Luo Mountain in Xiuning County and an acknowledgment of the profitability of the tea trade in Xiuning. The other products given mention are ink, fans (which by 1815 were no longer in production), indigo (for dying fabric), and in small amounts, linen, honey, wax, lacquer, tung oil, vegetable oil, and mother-of-pearl inlaid lacquer dishes.[12] Although tea was an important export in 1815, it was not the first, the last, or the only commodity to support the families of Huizhou.

Timber

During the earlier years of settlement as the Huizhou population grew, the problem of the lack of cultivatable land became apparent. Given the abundance of timber, the settlers began trading wood to nearby regions in exchange for rice, the staple of their diet. In the seventh, eighth, and ninth centuries, lumber became a primary source of income for the region. Among the timber exported were pine, cryptomeria, catalpa, and bamboo. Wood products such as tung oil, lacquer, and ink, and fruits such as oranges and pears were also exported.[13]

The Song dynasty saw the beginning of Huizhou's true flourishing as an origin of traveling merchants. In 1126 the Jin captured Kaifeng (the capital of the Song dynasty) and kidnapped the emperor. What remained of the imperial government fled south and established a new capital. This elegant new capital, Lin'an (Hangzhou today), was settled on West Lake, 124 miles (200 km) east of Huizhou. With Huizhou's accessibility to Lin'an via riverways, Huizhou merchants were able to quickly begin supplying timber and carpenters for the new capital's palaces and other needed buildings.[14]

Tea

Even without seeing [the mountain of] Huangshan, you can smell the tea scent ten miles away.

—Local Huizhou saying

During the first week of April in Huizhou, young women and men scramble up the hills, baskets on their backs, to pick the prized early-budding leaves of the tea bushes. The leaves are dried and processed into aromatic bundles to be exported all over China, where they are among the most favored of teas.

By the Song dynasty, tea had become a beverage popular all over China, drunk not just within Buddhist monasteries (where the custom started), but also among the elite and eventually all classes of China. Fine tea leaves are grown most successfully on high mountains. Again, one of Huizhou's drawbacks—the mountains—became an advantage, and the inhabitants of Huizhou were able to diversify the range of income-producing products beyond timber. According to an early record, "[in Huizhou] . . . where there is land lacking, those who support [themselves] by tea-growing are seventy to eighty percent. From this they clothe and feed themselves and pay their land and labor taxes."[15]

Legends claim that Song Luo Mountain, in Xiuning County of the Huizhou region, was the origin of all tea bushes in China. A poem by the Ming dynasty (1368–1644) poet Cheng Songyan expresses his reverie on drinking Song Luo Mountain tea:

Drawing up the famous spring water, I come to boil the Song peak tea. Plucking the leaves from among the clouds, selecting the sprouts from before the rains . . . seven bowls [of the tea] are just perfectly lavish.[16]

In the mid-nineteenth century, a British traveler to Huizhou described his visit to the revered, but by then neglected, Song Luo Mountain:

Our chairs being ready, we got into them, and, passing through the town, crossed the river and took the road for Sung-lo [Song Lou] and Hieu-ning [Xiuning]. We reached our destination a little before dark, and I had the first view of the far-famed Sung-lo-shan, the hill where green tea is said to have been first discovered . . . and where green tea was first manufactured.

Sung-lo-shan appears to be between two and three thousand feet above the level of the plains. It is very barren, and, whatever may have formerly been the case, it certainly produces but little tea now;

indeed, far from all I could learn, the tea that grows on it is quite neglected, as far as cultivation goes, and is only gathered to supply the wants of the priests of Fo, who have many temples amongst these rugged wilds.[17]

Despite the nineteenth-century demise of Songluoshan tea, Huizhou tea was, and continues to be, one of the most prized teas in the country. An eighteenth-century imperial painting—*Nanxun Tu*, "The Journey to the South," detailing the Qianlong emperor's journey from the capital of Beijing to the commercial cities of the south—depicts a main shopping district in Beijing. A prominent shop sign alerts consumers to a store owned by a Huizhou merchant selling Huizhou tea.

By the first year of the Xianfeng emperor's reign (1851), green tea was exported from Xiuning County to Europe and the United States, and foreigners interested in tea were traveling to this remote district to understand the mysteries and production of the leaf. All remarked on the enormity of tea business carried out in the region. In the mid-nineteenth century, Robert Fortune wrote down his observations and his reactions to seeing the vast amounts of tea during a visit to Xiuning:

The great article of trade is green tea. There are a large number of dealers who buy this article from the farmers and priests, refine and sort it, form it into chops, and forward it on to Shanghae [sic] or Canton, where it is sold to the foreign merchant. Seven or eight hundred chops are said to be sent out of this town annually. I observed also a great number of carpenters' shops for the manufacture of chests, a

Fig. 8 **Tea bushes covering hills with a decorated gravesite among them. Hongli, Xiuning County.**

trade itself which must employ a large number of men. In fact, this town and the surrounding populous district may be said to be supported by the foreign tea-trade.

Nearly all the way from Yen-chow-foo the river was bounded by high hills on each side. Now, however, they seemed, as it were, to fall back, and left an extensive and beautiful valley, through the middle of which the river flowed. Nearly all this low land is under tea cultivation, the soil is rich and fertile, and the bushes grow most luxuriantly. I had never before seen the tea-plant in such a flourishing condition, and this convinced me that soil had much to do with the superiority of Hwuy-chow [Huizhou] green teas.[18]

Fortune was not alone in his astonishment. Another European traveler, Walter Henry Medhurst, had been equally impressed with the region and its tea production:

In the town, there are not only large house of business in the green tea line, but also every kind of handicraft is practiced that is in any way connected with the packing and transporting of the teas; together with the host of shop-keepers who live by disposing of eatables and wearing-apparel to the traders and mechanics thus engaged. Seven or eight hundred chops of tea are annually sent from Tun-k'he [Tunxi]. . . .[19]

Along with Chinese connoisseurs and European travelers, the government of China also recognized the importance of Huizhou tea. In 1915, the fourth year of the Republic of China, just after the fall of the imperial government, tea from Xiuning was one of thirty-four native Chinese products chosen to represent China at the Panama-Pacific International Exposition in San Francisco. Today, tea is still one of the major profitable industry in the region, and almost as much land is dedicated to tea bushes (175,100 *mu*; 1 mu=733.5 sq yds) as to rice cultivation (192,100 mu).

Salt

Lumber and tea had been mainstays of the Huizhou economy through the Song (960–1279), Yuan (1279–1368), and early Ming (1368–1644) periods. But in the mid-Ming, Huizhou merchants began a deep involvement in the trade of an age-old product, salt. The new trade brought an even more expansive wealth to the Huizhou region. Its success not dependent on a local product or natural resource, the salt trade among Huizhou merchants was a result of their well-developed trading networks, their trading savvy and skills built upon generations of experience, and the cash they had available to invest in the trade. The high rate of literacy among Huizhou men also gave them an advantage as merchants.[20]

Fig. 9 **Ming dynasty pagoda, Qiankou, Huizhou District.**

But in addition to the Huizhou people's own talents, changes coming from the imperial capital also prompted their success in the salt trade. During the Jiajing emperor's reign (1522–66), new, extraordinarily heavy taxes were suddenly levied on Huizhou people. Owning land for production was no longer a great profit-bearing enterprise because of the tax burdens.[21] Suddenly, many landowners turned from their agricultural-based income-bearing occupations—which included tea and lumber—to other trades. The scholar Gu Yenwu notes that "not until the late Zhengde (1506–1521) and early Jiajing did things begin to change. Merchants and traders became numerous and ownership of land was no longer esteemed. . . . By the end of the Jiajing period (1522–1566) and during the Longqing (1567–1572), things changed even more rapidly than before. The number of those who gained wealth from trade increased, and the number of those who gained wealth from land decreased."[22]

Beyond the tax situation, in the mid-Ming dynasty, the imperial government additionally altered its salt-trade regulations and unknowingly created a great opportunity for Huizhou merchants to prosper. In the momentous year of 1492, the Chinese government, under the official Ye Ji, instituted reforms of the salt trading regulations.[23] Previously, the government, which had had a monopoly on the salt trade, obligated all salt traders to first earn their right to trade in salt by bringing provisions to the frontier, to feed the army. There a chit would be given to the trader, who could then exchange it for a predetermined amount of salt to sell on the market. The long-distance travel to the border inhibited those who were in agicultural production. In the sixteenth century, a new regulation allowed the chits to be purchased directly. Much of the salt was produced in the Lianghuai region, where salt had been produced in the greatest quantities since the Tang dynasty and in increasing amounts in the Ming. The proximity of Huizhou to the Lianghuai region offered the Huizhou merchants further advantages. For the Huizhou merchants, with their readily available cash, often pooled from family members, the salt trade was a viable and potentially profitable new commodity.[24] Soon they were among the principal traders in salt.

The result of the salt reforms was enormous wealth infiltrating into the hands of Huizhou merchants. As in the past, many of the merchants based themselves in larger cities—particularly Yangzhou, the great transportation crossroads where the north–south–flowing Grand Canal intersected the Yangzi River—while their wives, children, and ancestors remained in Huizhou. With their wealth, the salt merchants built exquisite gardens and homes in their temporary bases, and large dwellings and ancestral halls in their hometowns. They additionally built pagodas, schools, bridges, and roads in Huizhou to improve transportation and do good works for the home region to which they were so devoted.

Fig. 10 **A merchant with abacus.**

Pawnshops

The pawnshop of the eighteenth century was an important monetary resource in China. Moneylending banks did not yet exist, so the pawnshops, which lent cash by holding collateral and charging interest, served as nascent financial institutions. During the eighteenth century, with the country under the relatively peaceful and prosperous reign of the Qianlong emperor (1736–1795), pawnshops flourished in China. Even the imperial government invested its money in them.

With a decline in the salt trade, Huizhou merchants, again advantaged by surplus cash, began investing in pawnshops. A change in social and agricultural structures, which no longer allowed peasants to be "enserfed" when they were in debt, forced many more people to turn to pawnshops for temporary loans and permitted business to thrive.

Pawnbroking was not new in China. Begun as early as the fifth century, pawning was first based in Buddhist monasteries, many of which had superfluous funds from donations that they could loan without charging interest. The loans were considered good deeds to aid members of society. The loaning of money as an act of pure benevolence was only temporary. By the late Tang (618–907), the monasteries had begun charging interest, and soon non-Buddhists were developing the concern into a moneymaking operation. By the Yuan dynasty (1279–1368), monasteries were no longer involved in moneylending, and it became a purely entrepreneurial pursuit.[25]

By the eighteenth century, investing or working in pawnshops had become particularly prevalent in Xiuning County. Common sayings, repeated in local gazetteers, held that nine out of ten men in Xiuning were pawnbrokers and that by 1900 all the pawnshops in China were owned by Huizhou merchants.[26] A Xiuning adage— "Pawnshop students [can only] piss in tin pots"—maintained that the pawnbrokers were incapable of any other occupation than pawnbroking.[27]

The Xiuning pawnbrokers created their establishments in larger urban areas, often quite far from Huizhou. In Shanghai, Hankou (in modern-day Wuhan), and Hangzhou, the pawnbrokers found many ready customers: "By the years of the Guangxu reign [1875–1909], one could hardly find a pawnbroker who was not from Huizhou, there was 'no place too far for Huizhou merchants to expand.' They pressed eastward to the north of Jiangsu, westward to Yunnan, Guizhou, and Gansu, northward to the east and south of Liaoning, and southward to Fujian and Guangdong, and further south they sailed to Japan, Thailand, and other Southeast Asian countries, their footmarks left on 'almost half of the globe.'"[28]

Essential Information for Pawnshop Operation [29]
(author unknown)

My family practices the pawnshop business. It has been in the business for several generations up to my time. I am ashamed that I am but a man of mediocre ability, one who has expended my time in vain. In my time of leisure, as I sat quietly, thinking about the past, about my mistakes and my ineptitude, wishing to cover my previous mistakes, and to supplement my own inadequacy, I proposed this project on the Pawnshop business (which, of course, has fallen short of my original intention), and made it into a volume, to advise others in the future....

One ought to pay particular attention to [this]: whenever one retrieves a guest's bundles, when one takes in the ticket at the counter, one should first register it, then go upstairs to retrieve the package. You must clearly record the numbers and the words on the retrieval ticket—the numbers for each of the digits (how many ten thousands, how many thousands, how many hundreds, etc.), their surnames, what the pawned objects are, and how many packages. You must carefully check each piece of information before you can take the items out. Do not be rash and careless! ... It is better to wear coarse clothes and be prepared to endure hardship—and at times to let others use you as a stepping stone. After the goods have been sought, be sure to pack the resulting space well, for fear that the other bundles might drop down and spread open on the floor. Once they spread open and create a chaotic mess, then it is not only difficult to look for the goods, but it is also likely that one would get a tongue-lashing from the customers at the counters looking for their goods.... When students wake up in the morning, they should add water to the ink well, grind down the ink stick to make ink, help tidy up the pawnshop counters, pick up trash papers and broken string, and sweep the floors and throw out the dust. When all chores are done, everyone should wait respectfully behind the counter to await the opening of the store.

At night, one needs to learn to take out the retrieval ticket and calculate the entire sum, and to run through the output of the day again. In all, one has to excel in the abacus, calligraphy, and accounting skills. Each one of these skills needs to be refined and honed. If any one of these skills [is] lacking, then one would suffer from a serious disadvantage.... In wrapping the bundles, you must be careful, and be sure to appraise their values. In order to climb the ladder of success in this pawnshop business, you must harbor a good conscience toward the goods and clothing that come into your hands. You should view the goods that enter the shop as your own possessions. When you encounter fine silk clothing, be sure to fold these carefully. If there are items that need to be interleaved with paper, do so; and if there are those that need to be wrapped with paper, wrap them. Do not ever ruin the objects! Whether one is depositing or withdrawing the goods, the process should be smooth, without a disturbance or a blemish.

Your parents bore and raised you; you need to know that you should acquire glory for your parents' sake. If you do such lowly things, then not only would your parents be ashamed, but also your own name will be spoiled for life. If you wait until after that time to return [to goodness], then the regret might have come too late. It is better to wear crude clothes, and fill your stomach with vegetables and rice, and save a few pennies to send home [to your parents]. On the one hand it will comfort your parents; on the other hand it can prevent yourself from being wasteful.

During your leisure time in the evening, further ask your elders for guidance on the abacus. You need to study it diligently yourself. For an abacus is the basis of a person—one definitely should be able to handle it with great skill and experience. After being fully acquainted with the abacus and the cursive script, one should study the standard script. Then, there is the art of correspondence—one also needs to learn it well and have it in one's heart. In writing the characters, one needs to be flawless and exact. You surely need to write your future correspondences yourself—how can you ask others to write for you? Further, since writing is the exterior of a man, it should always be orderly. If the writing were to dance about wildly and cannot be deciphered, then when others see it, though they may not say anything in their mouths, in their hearts they will harbor criticisms....

- The main gate in the pawnshop should be shut and locked by dinner time, nine o'clock at night. If there are colleagues who are out taking a bath, or chatting with friends, they need to let the guards know, so that the guards can lock the gates a bit later. If you do not let them know, and do not return early enough, then you will be locked outside the gate, and would have to be interrogated for it.
- Smoking opium inside the shop is strictly forbidden. Once discovered, you will be immediately dismissed and will not be pardoned. This holds true even if you were smoking opium outside.
- The colleagues of the pawnshop are not permitted to pawn clothing or objects in this shop. When discovered, they will be immediately dismissed.
- When pawning out an item, especially those bundles that are already packed full, you need to bring the original packaging downstairs. You cannot secretly rip it open upstairs to examine it, and to exchange the items with your own clothing, etc. Once found out, you will be immediately dismissed.
- Gambling items are not permitted to enter the pawnshop. Even during the New Year's period, one is not allowed to gamble for money.
- Each time during the holidays, every table will be given four kilos of wine, and no more. This is because alcohol is capable of disturbing one's disposition, and it can also make one overly courageous. One should not drink too much!
- My fellow colleagues, please don't wander outside aimlessly! Do not seek the flowers and willows [i.e., prostitutes]! When discovered, you will be discharged immediately. It is difficult to enumerate on all the bad habits in the pawnshop. In short, a mishap is the result of human will. If you have a bad habit, it is in truth because you have consciously willed yourself to do so. All those who teach each other the bad habits, should all be dismissed.
- All the colleagues can take off two months every year to return home and visit with their families. One must not extend beyond this limit.
- You fellow gentlemen, do not ever harm your own reputations. With a bad reputation, others will naturally look down on you. Then you would not be able to achieve any status in high or low grounds—and in the future it would be difficult for even you to not be embarrassed of yourself!

Fig 11 Pawnshop sign.

When one sees the freedom allowed every clerk in the establishment to roam as he will and notices that the rooms containing even the silver ornaments are closed with only an old Chinese padlock that anyone can open with a chopstick, the question instantly arises how pilfering by these clerks is prevented. But no matter how often the question is presented the answer is no more satisfactory than the first one given—"they do not steal." When asked how such honest clerks are found, the answer in a surprised tone is, "Why how could it be otherwise if we are to run our business?" How such men are obtained, or how they are trained after they enter the shop, is a mystery, but some of the rules of the shop may help in the solution. Not one local man is employed. . . . Not one, even the manager, is allowed to bring wife or family, or contract a marriage here. The idea is that no man can give full heart to his business if burdened or demoralized by family cares or pleasures. They are brought in on three years' term and at the end have a full year's furlough, after which they come back to their old jobs. They eat and sleep within the pawnshop walls and with rare exceptions never go outside. . . . For pure loyalty to the shop whose rice they eat it would be difficult to find their superiors the world over.[30]

Four Treasures of the Scholar's Studio

In addition to the major trades in which the Huizhou merchants engaged, Huizhou entrepreneurs also came to manufacture specialty items, thereby elevating the reputation of the region within China. Among these items produced with fine local resources were the principal instruments used in the highest of art forms, calligraphy. Those instruments, known as the *wen fang si bao*, the Four Treasures of the Scholar's Studio, were the brush, the ink stick, the paper, and the ink slab, upon which the ink stick was ground. The fabrication of these treasures in Huizhou provided the remote, mountainous, and commercial district with a literary and artistic association.

As early as the Tang, a fine paper was being manufactured in Huizhou for painting and calligraphy. It was praised for its luminous and smooth nature. Emperor Li Houzhu of the Southern Tang dynasty (937–975) was so enamored of the paper that, having purchased great amounts, he built a pavilion to store it, which he call the Cheng Xin Tang (The Hall of Pure Heart). The paper then adopted the new name, Cheng Xin Tang paper. By the Ming dynasty, the original paper was already considered such a treasured rarity that the great painter and calligrapher Dong Qichang said upon seeing an early sheet, "I don't dare write on this paper." The Ming poet Zhuan Ruojin wrote a poem praising the paper of the region, beginning with the line, "The water of the Xin'an River is so clear, the bottom is visible. The paper made by the water's edge is as bright as the water."[31]

The prevalence of working in the pawnshop trade in Huizhou inspired at least one experienced Huizhou native to pen a book on the business for young apprentices. In his book, *Essential Information for Pawnshop Operation*, an anonymous writer encourages his readers to be morally upright, hardworking, and diligent. Making friends with the bad elements of society, smoking opium, and succumbing to laziness would not be tolerated in a well-run establishment.

The reputed lack of theft and the orderliness of pawnshop warehouses, massive brick structures filled with valuable goods, is testimony that the apprentices and personnel generally followed these strict precepts. Indeed, the success of the Huizhou pawnshops was often attributed to the family, clan, and Confucian bonds—values instilled in Huizhou merchants in their hometowns and nurtured in the distant towns of their workplaces. An astounded correspondent for the *North China Herald* wrote in 1914 of the extraordinarily high morals in China's pawnshops:

Huizhou paper production also figured into the poems of the Qing poet Zhao Yanhun:

The mountain people are constantly busy
In droves moving stones to build their new walls.
The piles of paper along the river,
All around the sound of threshing shakes the setting sun.[32]

To this day there are fine papers produced in Huizhou and the surrounding area, but the quality is not considered to equal the papers made 1,000 years ago.

In 1915, along with tea, Hu Kaiwen ink from Xiuning County was also chosen to represent China at the Panama-Pacific International Exposition. Like tea, ink had been one of the famed products of the Huizhou region since as early as the Tang. According to legend, at the end of the Tang dynasty, a Hebei Province inkmaker, Xi Zhao, and his sons saw the large, ancient, and dense pine trees at the foot of Huangshan, knew that they would be excellent for fine ink, and decided to settle there. Chinese ink is made from the soot of burning pine trees, fused together with a natural glue (often made from the antlers of young deer), formed in a wooden mold into a stick shape, and then dried until it is hard. When he is about to begin work, the painter or calligrapher—or an assistant—grinds the ink stick on a stone ink slab, mixing it with water, to create liquid ink.

The ink produced by the Xi family was said to have the luster of lacquer, and its reputation spread quickly. The secret of Huizhou inks, produced later by many other families, was indeed, as Xi Zhao had presumed, said to be the fine pine trees growing in the mountains. Like the Cheng Xin Tang paper, this Huizhou ink reached the Southern Tang Emperor Li Houzhu. He was so appreciative of the ink, that he gave the ink maker's family his imperial surname Li.

Among the more famed ink makers over the centuries were Fan Yulu and Cheng Dayue of the late Ming dynasty, both of whom created stunning manuals recording the fine incised molded images on their ink sticks. In Cheng's manual, he included European Bible images that he had seen in etchings brought to China

Fig. 12 (below, left) Ink stick depicting the world produced by the Xiuning County Hu Kaiwen ink stick workshop for the Panama-Pacific International Exposition in 1915.

Fig.13 (left) A scholar sits at his desk with the four treasures of the scholar's studio in a woodblock print design for an ink stick, published in the *Chengshi Moyuan* (*Cheng Family Garden of Inksticks*) in 1606 by the Shexian County ink manufacturer Cheng Dayue.

by his acquaintance, the Italian Jesuit Matteo Ricci (1552–1610). A later famed ink maker was Hu Kaiwen, and even today, Hu Kaiwen ink is considered one of the finest in China. In 1915, the company produced a special round ink stick in the shape of the world for the Panama-Pacific International Exposition. This work won a gold medal at the exposition. Again, the natural resources of Huizhou's geography that had also thrust the inhabitants into merchant profession tendered great benefits and fame for Huizhou.

Below the trees, the earth of Huizhou yielded another treasure for scholars. The best type of stone for an ink slab, on which to grind the ink stick into liquid ink, is one that is dense enough not to absorb the water, but abrasive enough for the hard ink stick to be ground down. The She ink-slab stone, quarried in Huizhou and named for the Huizhou county of Shexian, was ideal for grinding ink. Along with ink, the stone, finely carved into ink slabs, became a cherished piece of equipment for the scholar's desk.

Together with Wang Boli brushes, also produced in She County, the inks, paper, and ink slabs of Huizhou made the region a renowned source of quality utensils for scholars. Though not a significant source of currency for the entire region, the production of these treasures in Huizhou had by the twelfth century already begun to give the region's reputation a scholarly flavor.

Cultural Resources

Education and Scholarship

In Chinese Confucian tradition, the hierarchy of occupations located merchants on the bottom rung. Highest were the educated scholars and government officials, thus the pride of the merchants of Huizhou in having literary accoutrements associated with their region. The scholars' and officials' high rank was based on their responsibility to watch over the entire society. Just below the scholars and officials were the peasants—who provided the materials to feed and clothe the people of the nation—and below them, but above the merchants, were the artisans, who refined the natural resources into functional and socially beneficial products. The merchants were placed last, as they made their profits only off the labors of others.

The system elevated the masses of peasants and downgraded the wealthy and potentially powerful merchants. But the propounded ideal in Confucian society was also that any son—like the popular symbol of a carp leaping over the rocks to become a dragon—could become, through studying hard and passing civil examinations, a scholar and government official.

In an effort to make the hurdle from merchant to official, wealthy Huizhou merchants as early as the Tang dynasty subsidized the creation of schools and academies (*shuyuan*) in their hometowns. These endeavors to educate young men were quite successful. During the Northern Song (960–1126), Huizhou families produced 130 *jinshi*, that is, men who had passed the highest level of national civil examinations, allowing them to become officials of the state. During the Southern Song (1127–1279), 188 men of this remote, mountainous, but increasingly wealthy region became jinshi. These numbers represent the second-highest number of jinshi of all regions in China at that time. The rate of accomplishment of Huizhou men in the national civil examinations remarkably continued throughout the Ming and Qing dynasties. Many of the jinshi came from wealthy families and clans, who, analysis by Harriet Zurndorfer has shown, were large landowners, selling tea and lumber, and therefore had the financial luxury to pool money and educate the most promising of their sons.[33] The great sixteenth-century scholar Wang Daokun, a native of Huizhou, noted that for every three merchants in Huizhou, there was one scholar.[34] The glory and power accorded to officials and their families in Chinese society made the struggle to pass these exams a worthy investment for those who could afford the exhaustive time and funds to study.[35] The glory of success in the civil examination would shine not only on an official's immediate family but on the clan, the lineage, and all the future descendants.

Fig. 14 **Man carrying paper-and-bamboo figure of a *zhuangyuan*, the scholar who achieves the highest marks on the civil examination in imperial times. In the Huizhou region it is customary for a father to give a *zhuangyuan* figure to his married daughter on New Year's, in hopes that she will give birth to a son who will become a high official. Wucheng, Xiuning County.**

The veneration for those who passed these exams is apparent from one example in the town where Yin Yu Tang originated. A native of that small and remote village of Huang Cun, Huang Fu first passed the provincial civil examination in the first year of the Jiajing reign (1522) and succeeded in the far more difficult, and prestigious, feat of passing the national civil examination in the eighth year of the Jiajing reign (1529) of the Ming dynasty. In passing this exam, the scholar received the respected title of jinshi. This accomplishment did not go unnoticed in the halls of the imperial palace, in the annals of regional history, or in the landscape of Huang Cun. The Jiajing emperor in 1531 ordered that a grand hall be built in honor of Huang Fu in his native home. The grand building, called Jin Shi Di (the Jin Shi Residence), which is still standing, has three courtyards and a second story in the rear section, beyond the second courtyard. Its columns, made of rot-resistant cypress and gingko woods, are more than forty inches in diameter in some places, and some of the major beams measure twenty-seven feet in length. The *Xiuning County Gazetteer* (*Xiuning Xianzhi*) dedicated a section to the biography of this local hero:

Huang Fu, whose pen name was Ziqian, was a native of the Huang Village. He succeeded in the National Imperial Examination and was appointed a chief officer of the Ministry of Defense and then promoted to the position of the Officer in Charge of Military Recruits. . . . In Zhejiang, he led projects digging canals around the cities and dredging the waterways of the region. His work there left many ben-efits for the people. Because of it, he was promoted to the Advisor to Hunan and Canton. After his death, he was worshipped as a worthy of his hometown.[36]

The respect accorded to Huang Fu and his rise to officialdom in his own village is evident not only by the building originally built in his honor but also by the continual reverence accorded to him and the continual maintenance and endurance of Jin Shi Di. Today, it stands in the center of the village and is the most-tended building in the village.

The continued emphasis and interest in education in Huang Cun is also evidenced by the pride residents have in their village school, the Huang Cun Primary School, opened by the local Huang lineage during the first years of the twentieth century to prepare their children, girls and boys, for the modern, urban world.

Art and Collecting

During the Ming and Qing dynasties, so many of the Huizhou merchants maintained residence in the Yangzhou and Jiangnan regions, centers of literati culture, while doing business that they absorbed and adopted the glorified literati values of the scholars and officials they so esteemed. These scholarly mannerisms—which put a premium on fine homes and gardens, education, and sophisticated art collecting—came to be reflected in the lifestyle of many Huizhou merchants, both in the Jiangnan region and in

Fig. 15 (left) **Ink painting on house exterior. Shexian County.**

Fig. 16 (opposite above) **Ni Zan (1301–1374)** *Wind Among the Trees on the River-bank.* **Hanging scroll; ink on paper. The Metropolitan Museum of Art, Bequest of John M. Crawford, Jr. 1988.**

Fig. 17 (opposite below) **Hongren (1610–1664)** *Land-scape,* **album leaf mounted as a hanging scroll; ink on paper. Reverend Richard Fabian Collection, San Francisco, CA.**

Huizhou. A late Ming commentator, Shen Defu, described how the penchant for early Ming art first spread to "the fashion-concious gentry of Jiangnan, and [then] spread to the easily persuadable great merchants of Anhui."[37] In their hometowns they built themselves elegant gardens, wrote and published chess manuals, constructed libraries, and soon became the preeminent collectors of literati-style paintings.

A seventeenth-century Huizhou observer, Wu Qizhen (active 1635–77), quoted by Sandi Chin and Ginger Hsu in their article on Huizhou merchants, recalled in an essay the zeal for collecting among the Huizhou merchants: "I remember the past splendours of the collections in our Huizhou area—there was no place that could compare with Xiuning and Shexian. Moreover, the difference between refinement and vulgarity [of a person] was thought to depend on whether or not he owned antiquities. Accordingly, people fought to acquire things, without concern for price. The antique dealers all rushed to the area. Those who were doing business outside the area collected antiques eagerly and brought them more. Thus, extensive collections came into being."[38]

Literati-style paintings tended to be primarily ink on paper, created in manner that would exhibit the movement of the brush rather than depict reality in minute or colorful representation. The revered early artists of this style were men such as the Yuan artist Ni Zan, whose quiet dry lines express his inner perspective. During the Ming dynasty many artists were pursuing this subtle, elegant, and elevated style. The Huizhou merchants recognized the cachet in scholarly society of owning such works and, with their prosperity, could afford to become the major collectors of the time.

During the seventeenth century a Hui style of painting developed, perhaps encouraged or patronized by the Huizhou merchants, that reflected an strong interest in the literati style of painting. In this school of painting, which became known as the Xin'an Hua Pai (Xin'an painting school), there was an emphasis on ink, line, and brush, and little or no interest in color or naturalistic details. As early as the Kangxi reign period (1662–1722), a writer, Zhang Geng, noted the strong relationship between these artists' works and the style of the Yuan painter Ni Zan. Among the painters from Huizhou who rose to fame during the late Ming and early Qing period were Cheng Jiasui, Zha Shibiao, and Ding Yunpeng, of Xiuning County.

The emergence of the Huizhou style of painting is still reflected today on the walls of many Huizhou houses. Masons, when they finish putting the white lime plaster coat on the outer walls of houses, do small paintings above the doorways and windows. Though some paintings depict opera figures, many are ink landscapes or birds and flower paintings reminiscent of the Huizhou painting style.

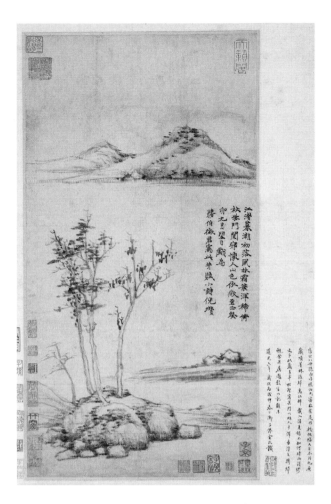

The Culture of Home and Family

Sayings about home and hometowns abound among native Huizhou people. The most common—and one that is used all over China—is *luo ye gui gen*, "falling leaves drop toward their roots," implying that as people age or die, they always return to their hometown.

Lineage and ancestral devotion in Huizhou is particularly strong and, interestingly, stronger than in many regions of China. The abundance of ancestral halls and the profusion of genealogical records are testimony to the profound commitment in Huizhou to family, lineage, and ancestors. There are more family genealogies from Huizhou in archives than from almost any other region in China. And even today, magnificent ancestral halls mark many towns and villages.

This unusual focus on family may have been a result of the merchant basis of the society. The men were spread across the land, but close family ties bound them to their homes, enforced their dedication to their homes and family, and re-enforced mutual assistance among lineage members.

Genealogies

The careful attention paid to family genealogies is one example of this focus. Periodically, in the history of a lineage, one or several members compile the birth and death records of each branch of the family, producing a massive volume—either hand-scribed or printed—tracing all of the male members (and their mothers, but rarely their daughters) back to one common ancestor.

Writing genealogies, because of the importance of families and ancestor worship and the intimate bond between the living and the deceased, is traditionally considered a virtuous act of filial piety. The genealogy ensured not only the continuation of the knowledge but also the reverence and care of the ancestors. In a preface to the Huang Chuan [i.e., Huang Cun] Huang Family Genealogy, a writer praises Huang Yihui, its compiler and editor:

Alas! Genealogy is the deed to which a descendant should give priority in his agenda. Yihui keeps this in his mind and this is why he is high above others. Here he shows his flawless filial piety and reverence and profound moral merits. . . . Those who are the grandsons of Yihui should have the same will as Yihui. Then, people will naturally be moved to protect the tombs of the ancestors, to pay respect to the ancestors, and to use proper addresses to distinguish the near from afar.

The lineage, the bond to the lineage of all the family individuals, the continuation into the future of the family line, and the accounting of the many previous generations was considered an essential and fundamental source of proper social relationships, particularly filial piety, and therefore social harmony. This thought is echoed repeatedly from the fifteenth century through the twentieth century as a primary purpose behind the genealogical histories. The preface to a 1485 Huang family genealogy exclaimed this as the driving force behind genealogies:

Fig. 18 (left) **Qing ancestral hall later converted into a general store. Bei An, Shexian County.**

Fig. 19 (opposite) **Ancestral tablets, each carved with an ancestor's name, which traditionally would have been kept in a lineage ancestral hall. From Xiuning County.**

A family genealogy is a book to record the source and the later development, and to collect information of the clan members. Without the edition of the family tree, one will not be able to know his roots and his source. Nor will he be able to exalt the filial piety to the ancestors and to pay respect to them for their widespread benefits to the descendants. When the edition is completed, the root and source will no longer be in darkness, and one will know his ancestors better. In this way, the filial piety is exalted and the respect to the ancestors will spread wider. The Huang clan at Huangchuan, a renown[ed] family with good virtues, will be getting even greater in the future, bringing more glories to their ancestors, keeping the family name appreciated for thousands of years, and getting even more prosperous with the passage of time. This is what I want to say in the preface.[39]

Rituals That Bind a Lineage

Before the 1949 Communist revolution (today called "the liberation" in China), lineage bonds were refortified each year at New Year's with ceremonies at the ancestral hall. The ancestral hall, called the *citang*, usually one of the largest and most celebrated buildings in a village, contained the ancestral tablets of all lineage members from the village who had died. Native daughters, who, of course, were married out of the family, never had their tablets placed in the ancestral hall of their father's lineage. A separate section of the hall—or occasionally, as was the case in Huang Cun, a separate building—was reserved for tablets of the matriarchs of the lineage. The wives of the men, who had married into the family, were decidedly important and worthy of worship, as they gave birth to the heirs of the next generation in the family line.

Death was another fundamental step. It transformed a family member into an ancestor and a spirit, worthy of continued respect and devotion. Funerals and funerary rituals, therefore, were significant events, performed with great pomp and serious adherence to ritual.

We didn't hang up the ancestor portraits constantly. We would hang them up only during the first month. Before we ate, we would spread out the chicken, the fish, and the meat, etc., on the table, light the candles and burn incense, and receive the ancestors as they returned home. Then we would send them off. Only after we sent them off would we eat.

[In the ancestors' portraits] the clothes were red, some were blue. The hats looked like Qing dynasty hats. . . . There was one painting with many people, in a pyramid shape. There were two, then three. . . . All were the sons and grandsons of the Huang family. . . . They were hung in the upper hall, in the central hall, against the back wall.

—Huang Xiqi

Awareness of the names of ancestors and lineage history through genealogies allows the relationship between the deceased and their descendants to be a living and fluid relationship. This relationship between the living and the ancestors—whether with their portraits at home, with the whole clan and the ancestral tablets at the ancestral hall, or with ancestors' souls at gravesite—is reinforced periodically with ceremonies and rituals. The rituals traditionally involved offerings to the deceased in the form of food, incense, and symbolic houses, servants, clothes, money, and various home appliances made of paper and bamboo to make life more comfortable for those in the netherworld. Beyond proffering objects to the deceased ancestors, the living members of the family also impart verbal praise and verbal requests to the powerful spirits. Traditional beliefs hold that the deceased have closer contacts with the control of spiritual forces and, therefore, the winds of fortune. Treating ancestors well could thereby sway them to assist with the challenges faced by their living descendants, and encourage good fortune, longevity, and the birth of sons to carry on the family line.

Fig. 20 **Uncompleted bamboo-and-paper servants to be burned at a funeral, Qimen County, 1999.**

Offerings and Requests for the Ancestors

A Huang lineage genealogy book from Yin Yu Tang provides, in its first section, a series of prescribed entreaties for family members to make to their deceased ancestors on specific ceremonial days. The inclusion of this type of text is not unusual in a genealogy.[40] The list of ancestors exists so that they can be remembered and offerings can be made to them. The accompanying text to be recited provides the acceptable sentiments and appropriate prayers for those ancestors. These front pages of the genealogy, which are not complete, include extensive addresses for the family to make at the graves of the ancestors on the spring festival of Qing Ming, on the fifteenth day of the seventh month and on the twenty-fourth day of the twelfth month, to welcome the ancestors back for New Year. There is also a prayer to the nearby mountain deities to be presented at Qing Ming to thank them for allowing the presence of the graves at their auspicious geomantic site.

The appeals are an apt reflection of the understood, mutually supportive relationship between ancestors and descendants, as well as clear expressions of the desirable aspirations of the living. In the entreaty to be made on Qing Ming, for instance, the speaker expresses a desire for the wealth, glory, success in the civil examinations to become officials, a multitude of sons, and, for those who choose to follow along the merchant route, success in business. The prayer notes that this way, "there will never be a shortage of the wealth used in the ceremonies for the dead, and the money will be used to improve the offerings [to ancestors]." The entreaties therefore reinforce the cycles of ancestor worship and family bonds.

The presence of the standardized rituals in the genealogical history of the family echoes the integral relationship of the genealogy and ancestor worship. Whereas in many cultures a genealogical tree may exist for tracing history or connecting living individuals to heroic ancestors, in China, the link to one's ancestors is part of a vital self-perpetuating cycle of the life of a family. Presenting offerings and gratitude to the ancestors can result in wealth and fertility for the living, ensuring that the ancestors will thereby be continuously receiving offerings and that the living, when they become ancestors, will also be worshipped and nurtured.

The tradition of worshipping ancestors at their graves on Qing Ming continued until the 1950s and 1960s. Huang Xiqi of Yin Yu Tang remembers the ceremonies from his childhood: "Our ancestral graves were very exquisitely built. I still have the impression of how they looked in the fifties and sixties. They were all made of stone, the base, the railings, and the dome. There was a hole in the middle for hanging [ritual paper] money. I remember that there was grave after grave in the cemetery. Oh, it was bright and beautiful [in] springtime, the ancestor worshipping crowds were quite lively—and much money was burnt."

Burial at Home

In all parts of China, the importance of home and lineage traditionally dictated that people be buried in their hometowns. Being buried in one's own hometown ensured that later descendants would care for the spirit's soul and all its needs. For Huizhou merchants, whose lives were often at risk as they traveled, this custom

Speech to Memorialize the Ancestors on Qing Ming (excerpted)

Being prostrate [in front of the tombs of the ancestors, I state]:

The season of late Spring has come. How could one not come to consider filial piety at this time? The benefits from our ancestors to us are truly deep, all of us want to express our respectful sincerity....

Please enjoy this banquet and accept the offerings we provide.

Being prostrate [in front of the tombs of the ancestors, I am] aware that it is from the souls [of our ancestors] that our good fortune has come, and it is they who make the offspring more and more prosperous with the passage of time. We, the descendants, feel guilty for accepting the virtue of our ancestors in an imperfect way. Thus, we want to express the intention that even the wolves and beavers may have [to memorialize their forefathers] and to present the sincere [thanks to ancestors] that even ants may have.

Being prostrate [in front of the tombs of the ancestors, I] wish your frozen souls will stay clear and your jadelike spirits will be as active as when you were alive, so that you will benefit your sons and prosper your grandsons and so that they may inherit the good fortunes you had before. Every one of your offspring will be noble and famous, and they will have gold and jade piled up. From generation to generation, the family will ever remain glorious and wealthy. The fame that the family holds will spread as melons' vines do, and the fortunes we enjoy will develop as crickets reproduce. Whenever [the people of this family] try to obtain something, [they] shall achieve it. When [they] engage in trade, their business will be prosperous. When [they] engage in farming, the sunshine and rain will alternate in a perfect way. When [they] devote [themselves] to learning, [they] will be successful in examinations and receive high official posts thereby. In every season of the year, [they] will enjoy hundreds of good fortunes. In this way, there will never be a shortage of the wealth used in the ceremonies for the

dead, and they will use their money to improve the offerings [to ancestors and deities as well]. Please consider this and accept our offerings.

Statement in the Ceremony of Offering Sacrifice to Ancestors on the Fifteenth Day of the Seventh Month (excerpted)

Being prostrate [in front of the tombs of the ancestors, I state]:

At the time when the breezes start, [we] want to express our sincere desire to repay the root from which our family grows. When for the first time during this year we taste the new crop of snow-white rice, it is proper to enact the ceremony to offer new grains [to our ancestors]. Sweeping and cleaning both inside and outside of our house, we in this divine way welcome the presence of the souls of our forefathers.

The third round of wine now is poured onto the ground. Being prostrate [in front of the tombs of the ancestors, we] wish the souls of the ancestors will [accept it] as if they were here. Their virtues will give us boundless benefits: They will make the four seasons in good harmony so that we may have good harvest. [They will help us] to obtain fantastic wealth each year. We wish that in this way our family will be wealthy and each will have enough to spend, that we will enjoy good harvest every year, that both the main stem and the branches [of the family tree] will be favored and the family will increase its population, and that both the persons and the properties of the family will be guarded [by the souls of ancestors] so that the family will be prosperous. In this way, the cultural and ritual excellence of the family will be handed down from generation to generation, and its future accomplishments will not be inferior to the previous ones. In farming, the five grains will grow well and achieve good harvest. In learning, [the students from this family] will achieve quick success. Since whatever we do relies on the blessings [from you, our ancestors], we burn the money used in the other world for you. Please look down on us and accept our offerings.

meant that even if they died on the road, descendants had to do all they could to bring the body back home.

In 1853 Robert Fortune, a British botanist who visited Huizhou and other tea-growing regions in China, had a surprise encounter with the bodies of deceased Huizhou merchants en- route home:

A circumstance now occurred which astonished me not a little at the time, although it must be a common thing in the country. When the second boat was brought alongside, and the floor of our cabin taken up to get at the cargo, I found that we had some fellow-passengers which I had never calculated upon. Two enormous coffins, each containing the body of a Chinaman [sic], had been lying directly under my bed for the last three weeks without my having the least suspicion of the fact. It was, perhaps, just as well that this was the case, for the

knowledge of the circumstance would not have added to my comfort, and might have made me sleep less soundly. These coffins were now removed to the other boat, in which they were taken onwards to their last resting-place. On inquiring, I found that the deceased were natives of Hwuy-chow-foo, and had left their native country some years before to reside at Hang-chow, where they had died. Their friends were now taking their remains back to their own land, to be buried in the graves of their ancestors.[41]

In the Yin Yu Tang household, full of merchants, the occurrence of death on the road was not infrequent, and the family always tried their utmost to transport the elders' bodies home to be buried.

Huang Yangxian, born in 1857, a merchant of the Yin Yu Tang Huang family, died in 1885 when a boat he was traveling on was

Fig. 21 (right) **Paper-and-bamboo mansion to be burned for deceased ancestors. Huang Cun, Xiuning County.**

Fig. 22 (far right) **Paper-and-bamboo mansion being burned. The smoke will carry the structure to the deceased ancestors in the spirit world.**

Fig. 23 (opposite) **The Huang family descendants of Yin Yu Tang worship the recently repaired graves of their ancestors in the forest on the Qing Ming holiday 2002.**

attacked by pirates. Almost 45 years later, his son, Huang Zizhi, also died away from home in Shanghai. For years his coffin was stored temporarily in Shanghai, at the Huizhou Merchants' Association Hall (*huiguan*), until there was an appropriate time to bring it back to Huang Cun. Huang Zhenxin, Huang Zizhi's son, who followed in his father's steps as a merchant, recalls how his father's encoffined body was kept in Shanghai for over a decade until there was an opportunity to send it home for burial:

My father died in Shanghai, but his coffin [was not moved back home immediately and] remained at the Huizhou Merchants' Association Hall for many years. Perhaps until 1947 or 1948. Not until the eve of the liberation of Shanghai was it moved back to Huang Village. [Father] stayed in Shanghai for several decades, so his funeral was held in Shanghai. Because the situation was tense on the eve of Shanghai's liberation, the association moved a group of coffins back to Anhui. My father was then buried at Huang Cun.

There was never any consideration of burying Huang Zizhi in Shanghai, as that might have resulted in the unfortunate circumstance of what in China is referred to as a "wandering soul." These lonesome spirits of the dead, buried away from their hometowns, have no descendants to make food offerings to them and, hungry, may threaten to cause havoc in their surroundings. Moreover, they are unable to watch over and attend to their own descendants in their hometown.

Ancestral devotion and lineage bonds were so strong that they were, at certain times in history, seen as a threat to greater social loyalties by ruling parties. When the brash army of the Taiping

Heavenly Kingdom—a rebellious movement with utopian ideals that attempted to conquer China through violence—came through Huizhou in the 1850s, they destroyed many of the ancestral halls, which they felt drew away allegiance to their authority, and burned many family genealogies.

Huang Zhenduo, who was born about 1897 and whose parents or grandparents certainly witnessed the Taipings' invasion of Huang Cun, notes that "when the Taiping Army was besieged in Huizhou, the sufferings [of the clan] were great and the old clan histories and documents were either partially destroyed or totally lost."

Likewise, the Communist government, after 1949, encouraged the destruction of these lineage structures and discouraged the devotion and worship of ancestors. Such devotion was considered feudal, "old," and potentially obstructing of progress in the country.

In Huang Cun, the village in which Yin Yu Tang was located, the ancestral halls were taken down in 1958 so that the building materials could be used to construct a reservoir. Huang Xiqi recalls that during the Cultural Revolution, in the campaign against the Four Olds, families had to destroy all their ancestors' tablets. Some villagers burned them for cooking fuel; others used the wooden boards as soles for sandals.

Despite the occasional interruptions and massive destruction of the physical apparatus of ancestral worship, the devotion to family and lineage has continued in Huizhou. With the relaxation of the "anti-feudal" atmosphere, many families are once again caring for their ancestors and their family graves. Symbolic paper money is being burned for the deceased to spend; foods are offered at gravesites; and symbolic paper and bamboo houses, clothes, servants, and other accoutrements are burned for their enjoyment in

the spirit world. The paper houses are reminiscent of fine Huizhou houses—multiple stories high, with formal reception halls, characteristic white exterior walls, hams drying on beams, and, on the altar tables, as is frequently seen in houses today, a cassette player and a clock. The offerings allow the descendents to pass their days in what is known in China as their "yin residence," a structure that is often far more luxurious than the home they inhabited in life, the "yang residence."

In 1999 the Yin Yu Tang Huang family commissioned a large paper-and-bamboo mansion to be constructed and then burned for their ancestors. In 2001 the family restored their ancestors' graves and made offerings to their predecessors in the family line.

A Huizhou folk song relates that "in a person's life, the most painful [part] is traveling on business; abandoning the wife, forsaking your sons, and leaving your hometown."[42] However, returning home at the end of their lives—and even more important, in the time beyond that—the Huizhou merchants are well pampered.

Bringing the Outside World Home

Women and children living in the village were connected to their merchant husbands and fathers in the large cities of China by private and later public postal systems. This and the periodic return visits of Huizhou men made their rural home villages far more cosmopolitan than an average provincial Chinese village.

Letters written between members of the Huang family aptly demonstrate how the phenomenon of the traveling merchants created a great flow of money and goods into the remote villages of Huizhou:

My father was in Hangkou. Each month he would send my mother 5 "dollars." Our home didn't have any other income. We completely depended on my father sending us money. There was always plenty of money.

—Huang Xianying

Missives noting the receipt of funds often came with requests for specific items from family members back home. About 1910 Huang Zixian, working in a pawnshop in Hankou, remarked in a letter to his younger brother Zizhi, working in Jiangxi, that "Aunt Yunfa's mother asked me to buy her a sleeveless leather vest. There are few leather clothes here in the pawnshop and [of those that are here] none are good. The price of lambskin this year is too high. Perhaps I will have to buy it [for her] next year."

That same year the mother of these two merchants, Madame Cheng, wrote to her younger son, Huang Zizhi, in a large city with what might have seemed like a simple request: "Please order one salted large-sized carp for your uncle, one for the mother of Dan, and one for Aunt Yunfa. In total, have 3 pieces salted. The mother of Guo also asked you to order one for her."

And a cousin on his mother's side, Cheng Jinhe, also wanted to take advantage of his relative in a metropolis with easily available products: "Kesui came to my place to ask you to buy a fan with a gold covering for him. Please do him the favor at your earliest convenience." Other letters ask for calligraphy, paintings, porcelain, and cloth.

When the men returned, they often brought with them knowledge, goods, and specialty foods. Among the ephemera pasted on the bedroom walls of Yin Yu Tang, in remote Huang Cun, were European wallpaper from the 1920s, advertisements from Shanghai-manufactured products, English teaching books with an Isaac Babel short story (translated from Russian into English and Chinese), a large map from a newspaper depicting the progress of World War I, and another 1918 newspaper photograph of English navy officers in front of a mosque in Jerusalem.

This internationalism was a result of a proprietal obligation merchants had to bring presents home for their relatives. The *Xiuning Gazeteer* notes this obligatory gift-giving in a section entitled "Local Customs": "When a merchant comes back home from outside, he should present his relatives and neighbors with such things as scissors, towels, cloth for making shoes, bedding, and clothes. This is called 'Presents for Human Relations.'"[43] Huang Zizhi kept fastidious records of all the presents he bought home from one trip to Shanghai in 1929. The list (see pages 80–81) included cans of biscuits, dried shrimp, handkerchiefs, perfume, liquor, fermented bean curd, and towels.

The moment of a returning father was always welcomed because

Fig. 24 (right) **Paper packaging labels for dyes, professing that the products will "never fade," pasted on a cabinet in Yin Yu Tang.**

Fig. 25 (below) **Label from tin can of hash pork made in a Shanghai factory during the first half of the twentieth century. The label was found among papers and debris while dismantling Yin Yu Tang.**

of the exciting presents he might bring home. Huang Zhenxin recalls: "When my father came back, he would bring many delicious things to eat. We kids would be really happy. Sometimes he would bring us candy to eat. At that time one couldn't buy candy in the countryside. He also brought back a great deal of porcelain from Leping [located near the the great porcelain kilns of Jingdezhen]. It was very precious and unavailable in the countryside."

The Huizhou merchants were probably also responsible for the introduction and popularity of photography in Huizhou and Huang Cun. Though photography came to China as early as the 1850s, and studios were already established in large coastal cities by the 1860s, there were few Chinese photographers in rural areas at that time. The Yin Yu Tang Huang family members had numerous photographs taken of themselves in Huang Cun by itinerant photographers, with painted backdrops of Western-style interiors. Photographs, some on glass plates, from as early as 1900 and many more in the next couple of decades were found in the house. The male merchant members of the family may have carried these reminders of their families on their journeys away from home.

Women's Lives

The absence of many adult men from the villages and their intermittent return visits created a unique culture in Huizhou. While the lives of women there were in some ways very similar to women's lives in the rest of China—for years the custom of bound feet and restricting education were just as prevalent in Huizhou—in other manners, their routines differed greatly from those of their sisters in other regions. The primary distinction was that the husbands of Huizhou wives were rarely at home. The situation resulted in the anomalistic circumstance in China of households being run primarily by women.

Traditional Confucian ideology and Confucian hierarchal practices were the rule in Huizhou. Sons carried the family line, and daughters were considered financial burdens who had to be fed until they could be married off to another family. Once married, a woman was no longer part of her parents' household. Marriage rituals in Huizhou include a ceremony to demonstrate that a woman will not carry even a speck of dust from her parents' house to her new in-laws' home. As she is about to leave her parents' home, a bride must first stand on a chair, don new shoes, and then be carried out of the house on the back of her new husband guaranteeing that she will not bring the dust from her parents' house's floor into her new household.

As in other parts of the country, marriages are arranged by matchmakers. Negotiations are made between the parents of the groom and the parents of the bride regarding the bride's trousseau. The groom's family makes a gift to the bride's parents to lighten the cost of the new furniture, fabrics, and clothing the bride will bring into her new home.

Grooms and brides traditionally would not meet before they married. Women would enter their new homes with a cloth over their heads, which when removed would reveal to them their new surroundings and the strangers among whom they would live and

serve the rest of their lives. The morning after her wedding, the new daughter-in-law would be expected to do all the cooking, serving, caring for her in-laws, and all the house and clothes cleaning. The burden of being a young bride was not an easy one to bear:

In the past, brides rode in a sedan chair. It was painful to ride in a sedan chair. I had to wear layers and layers of clothes. The sedan looked big from the outside but was actually very small inside. There was a rooster, a hen, and bottle gourd underneath. Four people carried the sedan. It was my first time in a sedan. I got dizzy and wanted to throw up. There was a kerchief covering my head. I had a hard time. Outside they blew their trumpets and beat their drums. That was how it was when we got married. If you were marrying off your daughter, the sedan came to your house, departing at midnight, arriving at the husband's house at dawn. There were firecrackers and we had to bow to his ancestors. . . .

I wore red clothes . . . a red dress, a red top, a phoenix coronet just like the ones they wore in operas. The coronet on my head made my head hurt. It was so heavy. . . . The chickens stank, and there was chicken shit. I was miserable. The rooster belonged to the man's family and came with the sedan to take a hen home. They were mating chickens. . . . I cried a lot. A lot of people cried: my aunt, my sister-in-law, my mother. . . . The bride was going out to be judged. Making shoes, farming, cooking, if you didn't know how to do any one of those tasks people looked down on you. . . .

Marriages were arranged by parents. I never saw my husband until the wedding night. Now kids can date in school. . . . When I first arrived I didn't know anyone. There was a bridesmaid who took me from one place to another, offering wine and tea and all kinds of things. It made me very dizzy. I had to close my eyes and walk and be the bride. I couldn't eat for three days and nights. I didn't have an appetite. Now things are changed. There are no more sedan chairs. . . .

—Huang Cui'e

Despite the almost inevitably rude entrance into a husband's home, and perhaps having to cope with a demanding mother-in-law, most Huizhou women did have one luxury: the absence of a domineering male figure ruling their lives or their homes. Unlike their fellow wives in other regions, Huizhou merchant wives spent much of their lives without their husbands' daily presence.

After perhaps six or seven years away apprenticing in a shop, men would have come home to marry the wife chosen by their parents and matchmakers. The marriage ceremonies completed, they would quickly return to the distant job. In the following years, they might return home only every three or four or even six years. One elderly resident of Huang Cun remembered going to Shanghai, where his father worked, as a young teenager to become

Fig. 26 (top) **Women having their photograph taken, illustrated in the Shanghai lithographed pictorial *Dian Shi Zhai Huabao* published from 1884 to 1898.**

Fig. 27 (above) **An unidentified female member of the Yin Yu Tang Huang family photographed in the early twentieth century.**

Fig. 28 (right) **Bedroom of a couple about to be married decorated with trousseau and dowry items provided by the bride and groom's parents. Xiuning County, 1999.**

Fig. 29 (far right, top) **Groom as he sets out with gifts to fetch his bride. Xiuning County, 1999.**

Fig. 30 (far right, bottom) **Reception hall in bride's home, celebrating her marriage. Xiuning County, 1999.**

an apprentice: "I didn't recognize my father when I met him at the age of thirteen. I had only seen him twice before. Someone had to point him out to me."

Huang Zhenxin recalled the tension in Yin Yu Tang when his strict father returned for one of his periodic home visits. The children would have to stay quiet and the women were petrified to play mahjong. Kneeling for hours was a common punishment for children who dared annoy their stern father.

Spousal relations in Huizhou were rarely sentimental. Walter Henry Medhurst, in the first half of the nineteenth century, traveled through tea-growing regions in China, including Huizhou, and had the opportunity to see less dramatic, less romantic, and probably more common emotional expressions of separated spouses. He describes, in his book, the arrival home of a Huizhou tea merchant after two years of traveling:

After traveling 40 li, we arrived at the dwelling of my fellow-traveler. He had been nearly two years away, and I was curious to see, under such circumstances, what sort of reception a Chinese father of a family would meet with on his return home; on arriving at the village, one or two persons recognized him, but without stopping to converse, he passed on to his own dwelling. Entering this, he found his younger

brother, who had been left in temporary charge of his abode, and to whom was entrusted the out-door work connected to this little farm, sitting in the front room, engaged in shelling some beans. This man, on recognizing his brother, merely gave him a nod, after which he rose up, cleared away the beans, and proceeded to sweep the floor, which much needed it. The wife then came in, and without any salutation proceeded to wipe the table, and spread the tea-cups. The daughter, a young woman of eighteen, was equally indifferent; and both she and her mother seemed only anxious to know what fine things he had brought with him. His baggage not having arrived, they were obliged to wait for the gratification of their curiosity.[44]

Fig. 31 **Huang Cui'e (left), with her husband Zhu Mingmo, born and raised in Huang Cun, in her present Shanghai home.**

The usual absence of husbands made for a different type of household and a different type of relationships. Although married Huizhou women were theoretically intended to be only part of their husband's household and lineage, they often retained strong bonds with their own brothers, who could assist in times of need when there was no male presence in the sister's household. In Chinese, a mother's brother—whether younger or older—is distinguished by the appellation *jiujiu*, while a father's older brother is a *bofu*, and a father's younger brother is a *shushu*. The jiujiu often plays an important role throughout a Huizhou man or woman's life. At marriage in Huizhou, it is the mother's brother who is most significant in her children's lives. During a house construction, the jiujiu likewise takes an honored position in seating arrangements. Letters between members of the Huang family and their mother's brothers further confirm the importance of this relationship. Mother's brothers would traditionally be called into negotiate in any quarrels between a man and his wife or in the division of family property. This unusual relationship is exemplified in the lyric novella written by Wang Yaozhen, a daughter-in-law in the Yin Yu Tang household. In it, the wife writes to her husband, a merchant in a far-off town, about the lavish gifts she has bought for her own brother's birthday:

The seventh day of the ninth month was my brother's birthday.
According to custom, I am obligated to present him with gifts.
So, I had to pawn three fur coats.
I bought a pair of pigs' heads,
Ten packages of longevity peaches and longevity noodles,
And a fruit box as well as candles.
In all, I spent a tael of silver.[45]

In addition to enjoying the unusual circumstance of maintaining a close relationship with their maiden families, the Huizhou women living alone and responsible for their husbands' households wielded more power than women who lived daily under their husbands' eyes. Huizhou husbands usually sent monthly stipends back to their wives or mothers, with extra cash for New Year's celebrations. The women had to know how to manage these funds and the daily household expenses. In the same novella by Wang Yaozhen, the wife writes to her husband about the home finances:

As long as you continue to earn money,
Be sure to mail funds back here for our daily expenses.
Last month you mentioned in your letter [that you mailed back]
5 taels of silver,
But in my weighing, I discovered there was a shortage of 8 li.

I returned the 2 taels to our neighbor,
And took out the rectangle-shaped hairpin,
The rest was all used for shopping.
I entrusted the Old Pi who lives opposite from our house to assist me.
He bought a load of oil, salt, and other goods.
I calculated and discovered that the goods he bought for me were not
*   as low-priced [as he promised.]*
And by false accounting, he made 260 cents of profit for himself.

Her husband is impressed by her abilities to manage the household and writes back:

Your letter is long, comprehensive and clear,
And you describe everything so vividly.
It demonstrates how bright my wife is,
A successful housewife managing the family and a successful person.[46]

The circumstances of happily independent women managing family households—long separated from husbands of pre-arranged marriages—would not ordinarily encourage romantic relationships, and probably did not. However, poems and songs of women yearning for their distant husbands did develop in the Huizhou region.

One Huizhou folk song expresses a wife's regrets that she did not marry a farmer who would have been home on a daily basis.

"I would rather be married to a farmer"

Regrets, oh regrets
I should never have married a boy who leaves home.
Two of every three years, I must watch over an empty house.
For what am I planning a tall house?
Why am I impoverished for a large hall?
Night after night, my solitary body sleeps on an empty bed.
I knew early that today I would be embittered a thousand times over.
I'd rather have been married to a farmer.
In the day, he's in the fields, in the evenings he sits in the house.
During the days I'd sit and accompany my mother- and father-in-law
*   in front of the hall,*
In the evenings, I'd be with my man on the flowered bed.[47]

The theme of women longing for distant men is an ancient one in China, and male poets, whether describing reality or just their personal desires for pining women, penned numerous poems on the subject. The Tang dynasty poet Li Bai (701–762), for instance, wrote one such poem in a woman's voice:

"Yearning"

I yearn for one
Who's in Chang'an
In autumn, crickets wail beside the golden rail:
The first frost, although light, invades the bed's delight.
The lonely lamp burns dull, of longing I may die;
Rolling up screens to view the moon, in vain I sigh.
My flowerlike beauty's high
As the cloud in the sky.
Above, the boundless heaven blue is seen;
Below, the endless river rolls its billows green.
My soul can't fly over the sky so vast or the earth so wide;
In dreams I can't go through the mountain pass to his side
We are so far apart,
The yearning breaks my heart.[48]

This poem expresses a sorrowful separation of a woman and her husband, which may or may not have been a common situation.

In "The Pearl Sewn Shirt," a late Ming short story by Feng Meng-long (1574–1646), the author offers yet another perspective as he tells the story of woman left alone while her husband, a merchant, goes traveling. The two had deep affection for each other, and the husband, so delighted with his bride, had stayed home for three years after his marriage. Realizing he must take up his money-earning lifestyle again, he goes back on the road. She pines for him for a year and a half, but through the clever manipulations of an elderly woman, is persuaded that perhaps her husband has made off with another woman:

"What I want to know," said the old woman, "is this: what's so precious even about a fortune in gold and jade, if to acquire it means neglecting such a lovely lady as yourself?" And she continued, "It's the same with all these merchants who roam up and down the country. They treat their lodgings as their home and their home as their lodgings. Take my fourth daughter's husband, for instance, Manager Chu Eight—now he's found himself this concubine he's happy from dawn to dusk. Never thinks about his home—goes back once every three or four years, and before he's been there more than a month or two, off he starts again. His first wife lives like a widow bringing up orphan children. . . . It's a common saying, 'if you can't be an official, a merchant's the next best thing.' A traveling merchant can find romance anywhere he goes, but the one who suffers is the wife he leaves behind."[49]

Eventually, the memory of her husband fading, the young wife takes on a lover, another traveling merchant. By the end of the story, the original couple is blissfully reunited, and as in most Chinese short stories, everyone lives happily ever after.

The possibility of a traveling merchant taking on a second wife or concubine in his town of business was indeed not preposterous, but the situation did not always resolve harmoniously. While Huang Zhenxin, who grew up Yin Yu Tang during the early twentieth century, the thirty-fourth generation of the Huang family, notes that his father did not take a second wife, he does describe how a close friend of his father's, Huang Shaoqing, also from Huang Cun, did take a "small wife" in Leping, the town where they both worked. Huang Shaoqing was so enamored of this second wife that he rarely returned home to Huang Cun to visit his first wife. Instead of building her and their children a home of their own in Huang Cun, he installed her and their children in Yin Yu Tang, paying rent to Huang Zizhi and helping to pay for upkeep of Yin Yu Tang. She lived in Yin Yu Tang for many years, as another resident of the house recalled, "an angry and bitter woman."

An interesting irony of the merchant's home in Huizhou is that while the male ancestral line and the living men were considered the foundation and the roots of the family, it was primarily women and children who occupied the hometown home. Mothers-in-law, daughters-in-law, daughters until they married, and sons until they left to be apprentices at age thirteen or fourteen were the constant residents of the household. And these women, who came as strangers to the house and to one another, were responsible for caring for the spirits of the ancestors of their husbands as well as responsible for producing and raising the next male generation of their husbands' family.

Virtuous Women

Here are to be seen a number of commemorative arches, intended to keep alive the recollection of the various virtuous females who have adorned the city of Hwuy-chow [Huizhou]; these arches are such in numbers, and so lavishly adorned, as to lead a stranger to think that all the feminine virtue in the empire has been congregated in Hwuy-chow.[50]

The women of Huizhou were, on occasions, bestowed with great public honors for the sacrifices they made for their husbands' families. Textual records of virtuous women in Chinese history originated at least two thousand years ago. Books such as *Lie Nu Zhuan, Biographies of Exemplary Women*, by Liu Xiang, composed during the Han dynasty, were reprinted innumerable times through the following millennia. The *Biographies* documented women who were exemplary for their intelligence as well as those whose chastity or devotion to their husbands' family outshone others. *Nu Jie*, written by the female writer Ban Zhao, also of the Han, espoused to women the concept of *bei ruo xia ren* (always think of yourself as a lower person) and heralded the custom of a woman submitting to a man.

Stone archways were a means of commemorating people of high standards in China. Men who had become high officials were often rewarded with an honorary stone archway by the government, and honorable women occasionally also received these positive and public affirmations of their behavior. In order to receive the status of *jiefu*, a chaste widow, a woman had to have been widowed before the age of thirty and continued to live, without remarrying, in her husband's home, until the age of fifty.[51] While the recording and recognition of virtuous women was a cultural phenomenon all over China, the practice seems to have flourished in Huizhou. Even today when most of the archways have vanished, along with ancestral halls and temples, as symbols of feudalism during the more zealous days following the Communist revolution encounters with stone archways in the middle of rice fields or by the side of the road for men who passed high levels of exams, as well as chaste widows, are not uncommon in Huizhou.

Despite the high respect paid to women with these archways, they were still not afforded as high regard as men. In Huizhou, the word *paifang* is used to designate an archway for a man, and the word *pailou* is used to indicate one for a woman. According to custom, roads were constructed to lead under a paifang, as a man could be "below" another man in rank. However, a road approaching a pailou would circumnavigate the structure so a man would not find himself "below" a woman.

The prevalence of these archways commemorating women is congruous with the emphasis on clan relations and ancestral worship so evident in Huizhou. If a woman was encouraged by the possibility of such a posthumous title to stay devoted to her husband's clan, even if her husband has passed away, she could assist in maintaining the continuity of the family line. A widow would take care of her in-laws, take care of the ancestors, and more important, raise up a son (or sons) to carry on the family. Even if a husband died before his wife became pregnant, a widow would often adopt a son into her husband's family so as to sustain the family's continuity.

In 1815 the *Xiuning Gazetteer* printed the records of all the women of the county who had received honorary titles, including, for instance, a woman from Huang Cun: "Madame Huang, the Wife of Dai Ying. A native of the Huang Village, she married Dai Ying of Yaoxi and became a widow at the age of twenty-six. She then adopted a son to continue the family line and has kept her integrity for thirty years now."[52] Though the system did not necessarily promote the happiness of women, it did support the more important Huizhou virtue of continuing the family.

The more apparent presence of women in Huizhou society—and their greater responsibilities and resourcefulness due to the absence of men away on business—may have also influenced the preponderance of the memorials for women. Though women certainly could not have petitioned the local officials for titles, their sons (who were primarily raised by their mothers) might have felt stronger emotional ties to their mothers than to their absent fathers. A successful son could petition the government for the right to build an archway in honor of his mother, thereby bringing glory not only to his mother but on the whole family and their descendents as well.

The myriad mountains are the first immediately apparent significant topological feature of the Huizhou region, and their presence had a deep impact on the generations who came to live among them. Over and over, those inhabitants have murmured that the mountains prompted their ancestors to become traveling merchants. These filial and family-devoted merchants always returned home to their mountains and there made their own indelible marks on the unique cultural landscape that came to be called Huizhou. The following parts explore the roots and sprouts of one family that developed out of that distinctive Huizhou history and landscape.

Fig. 32 **The virtous heroine Madame Hua Rui depicted in the Ming dynasty Wanli period (1573–1620) woodblock-print edition of the Han dynasty work** *Lie Nu Zhuan, Biographies of Exemplary Women,* **included in** *Huipai Banhua Yishu* (*The Art of Hui-style Woodblock Prints*), **Zhang Guoji, editor, Hefei, Anhui Meishu Chubanshe, 1995.**

Next page: Fig. 33 **Cousins of the thirty-fourth generation dressed in their best clothes and gathered around the eldest of their generation, Huang Zhenzhi, circa 1926. From left to right are: Huang Zhenzhi's cousin Huang Zhenxin, his younger half sister Huang Aizhu, Huang Zhenzhi, his younger female cousin Huang Xianying, all of whom who lived in Yin Yu Tang, and a nonfamily member who lived in Yin Yu Tang, Huang Zhenxian. The background depicts a "modern" room. The table on the right holds an electric lamp—not yet seen in Huang Cun, as electricity did not arrive there for 50 more years.**

2 | *Jia*: Hometown and Family

Ancestors are the roots of a tree, and the source of a river.
— Huang Lineage Genealogy (1485)[1]

The word *jia* in Chinese has multiple meanings—"home," "family," and "hometown"—and like all roots, home, family, and hometown can become inextricably and emotionally intertwined. For descendants of the [Huang Village] Huang lineage, Huang Cun is *jia*, their hometown. It is home to each individual, to immediate family members, to all the ancestors and all future descendants. A family line in China means membership in an endless chain of human links, through time and across space; it is a set of human links with a set of values and mutual loyalties. Membership in a lineage gives each individual a place, a home, and a significant role in carrying on the line with dignity.

The Huang lineage that was born in Huang Cun, sowed their land, strode to far-off cities to carry wealth back to that land, constructed proud homes on that earth, buried and worshipped their respected ancestors there, and passionately and continuously came back to this village, and to this lineage, that they called home. Yin Yu Tang, and the lives within, sprouted directly from its root in the physical and cultural environs of Huang Cun and from its footing in the temporal environs of the generations of Huang lineage ancestors.

Huang Cun—The Hometown

Today, on this small plain of flat land, two kilometers down a dirt path from a main county road, lying between hills and spilling into a narrow, ravinelike extension, are a cluster of white houses, occasionally punctuated by a new modern concrete or colored-tiled structure. The characteristic horse-head walls of the houses and the dark tile roofs contrasting with the bright white exterior walls provide a visually and texturally striking mass among the green bamboo-covered hills and the surrounding rice paddies.

At one time Huang Cun, the hometown of Yin Yu Tang, was on an important travel route, a stone-paved pathway leading through the county, journeyed by merchants and officials. The route made the village a common resting place, and there were several inns that served travelers. The travelers and the multitude of merchants who called Huang Cun home, as well as the several prominent officials who hailed from there, contributed to the small, remote village being an up-to-date town with constant news and goods from large cities. It was a town that its people were, and still are, rightly proud of.

For the members of the Huang family, neither the picturesque qualities of the village nor its history is what identifies or ties them to this place. A tight familial bond, strengthened over generations among the living and between the living and the dead, has held the people to their place. It is here that the Huangs literally planted

Fig. 34 **Huang Cun, circa 1900. In this photograph, found among papers in Yin Yu Tang, the villagers are gathered on the large open lawn in the center of Huang Cun and along the walkway in front of the grand hall of Jin Shi Di (on the right side of the photograph) and neighboring residences. The entrance to Yin Yu Tang is visible on the far left of the photograph.**

their roots, bury and make offerings to their ancestors, and continue to give birth to their descendants.

My idea about the old home is that we were born there, and spent our childhood with our relatives and friends there. We were very attached to it. . . . Everyone felt warm and loved. Every year, the New Year's, weddings, and funerals bound us together. There was a kind of emotion going on underneath.

—Huang Zhenxin

In Their Words

Through the generations, several inhabitants of Huang Cun have felt compelled to delineate or describe their hometown. These descriptions begin to give a physical framework within which to further explore the world and people of Huang Cun.

Huang Sisheng, a fifteenth-century native of Huang Cun, took a poetic approach in his description of his hometown and composed a series of odes on Huang Chuan[2] (meaning Huang River, an earlier name of the village). He portrayed the place by pointing out eight scenic locations:

The round-shaped hill rising up in the East with a mirror-like flat rock is [the first scenic point] and is called East Hill Tossing up the Moon.

A beautiful hill coming from the south is of the shape of an upside-down dipper. It is [the second scenic point] and is called South Hill Raising Up a Dipper.

A mountain with multiple peaks ranging for several miles, connecting to Wang Brook, has a dynamic look, like flying or dancing. It is [the third scenic point] and is called Far Away Dragon Screen. This is the "life-line" mountain of Huang Chuan.

The place where springs and brooks come together, like bends and ropes circling round several times, and connect to the Flowing Pond is [the fourth scenic point] and is called Big Pond with Jades. This is the most splendid scene of the waters of Huang Chuan.

[The fifth scenic point is called] the Sacred Summit, and this name is derived directly from its shape. This is the place where Huang Puzhou was born.

[The sixth scenic point is called] the Bells of Rock Hill. It is famous for the temple on it. Gods worshipped there bless the people of the place. The temple and the hill look very like the one where King Xuan of Zhou stayed.

In the north, there are numerous tall pine trees withstanding snow and frost. Cranes of white-black colors with red crests often rest on these trees. This [is the seventh scenic point] and is called Pine Woods with Crane Nests.

In the south, there are the most fertile farmlands of Huang Chuan. Each [field] looks like a piece of scale. With Spring showers and Fall clouds, there will always be good harvest. Viewing this place from afar, it looks like a turtle. [This is the eighth scenic point] and is called Farmland with Hidden Turtle.

Conjuring up a picture of a village from a quick read of Huang Sisheng's assembled words is not an easy task. A slow, close reading reveals a lush panorama of hills, mountains, brooks, ponds, temples, pine trees, birds, and terraced rice paddies. Evident is the passion the author held for this intimate patch of land, hills, streams, and buildings that he and his relations called home.

The next glimpse we get of Huang Cun in the historical record occurs several dynasties later, under Qing rule. Down a path, among the hills of Huang Cun and its surrounding terrain, came an itinerant photographer, most likely carrying the tools of his trade at either end of a pole over his shoulder. Whether it was a celebratory occasion or just a chance arrival, the villagers gathered to visually record themselves and their hometown. Across the center of the selected view for the photograph is a swath of white lime-plastered buildings. Beyond the buildings is the auspiciously located tree-covered hill and before the structures is a wide, open lawn of grass. The inhabitants, who appear quite small in the image, are proudly scattered among the grass and along the path in front of the buildings. The most compelling entity of the photograph is Jin Shi Di, the grand sixteenth-century shrine built to honor one of the village's most successful scholars. Unlike the odes, which focus on the natural scenery of Huang Cun, the villagers chose to portray their hometown with an image of themselves and a representation of a glorious ancestor. Off to the far left of the photograph, a person leans in a doorway that leads to a private house behind the high white wall. That home—Qi Fang, the Seventh Branch—was formally called Yin Yu Tang by the villagers.

A couple of decades later, in the early twentieth century, Huang Zizhi (1883–1934)—a descendant of the odes' author, Huang Sisheng—born and raised among the same hills and waterways of Huang Cun, a son of the Yin Yu Tang household, a businessman with some worldly knowledge, and a prolific note-taker—recorded for posterity the exact borders of the same village. His description includes both legal county plot registration numbers (in accordance with the official county regulations), and the local, more colorful designations and descriptions of the elements of the landscape:

Fig. 35 **Looking across the fields and paddies on the outskirts of Huang Cun.**

The Boundaries of Huang Village

The boundary starts from Dongkeng Tai (Terrace of East Depression), and runs through the hill which is at the right of the back of Huang Family School (previously the Water Deity Temple³ of Shang Huang Cun [Upper Huang Village]). The location of this hill is called Dong Keng, and its shape is like a drum. Then it runs to the wall of the school and goes through the road to Lailong Shan (Arriving Dragon Hill) of Xia Cun (Lower Village), which is also called Zeshu Men (Gate of Choosing Trees). Then it runs across the hill and goes down to the house of Dongjiu family. Then it runs through the house of Guanjiu family, and goes to Shifang Wu (Cubic Stone House), that is, from the road between Qian Wu (Front Village) to Shang Men (Upper Gate) to the road to Xia Fang (Lower Direction). Then on this road, it runs from the Xiang Shan (Elephant Hill), which is on the right, through Wu Chang Miao (Temple of Five Animals), down to such places as the house of Xiafang Kou and Qinglong Shan (Green Dragon Hill). When the boundary reaches Xiawu (Lower Village), it goes back to the opposite bank of the brook, a place called Sanmu Qiu. Then, it goes across the brook again and reaches the wall of the main house of the "Great Gate" of Tianman Futan. Then, it turns to the right and reaches Huangbai Tan (Yellow Cedar Terrace), the Deep Depression of Baihu Shan (White Tiger Hill), and the hill of the Deep

Depression Hill, i.e., the rolling cave. Out of the rolling cave, it runs as far as to the Shitou Chang (Lion-head Square) of Chen Tang (Chen's Pond). Then, it goes back again, straight to the hill that is opposite the hill at the right of the Shiling Dian (Palace of the Stone Hill). After that point, it goes back to the rolling cave. From Gaozhong Yingshan (Tall Bell Lake Mountain) it goes to Houdi Shan (Back Bottom Hill). Then, it leaves Xiangxian Li (the Lane of the Village Worthies) and reaches the Ancestral Hall, whose location is called Ganzi Bing. After that, it goes to the "Elephant Nose," and enters Chang Wu (the Long Village). Then, it enters Xingshun Tang, i.e., the back of the Windy Hill.

Huang Sisheng, perhaps influenced by the poets and writers of his time, focused on the natural elements of Huang Cun: the hills, the waters, the trees, the birds. He mentions only one temple among the sights of Huang Cun. By the time the anonymous photographer was arranging his subjects and Huang Zizhi was writing, the man-made structures were as incorporated into the village's landscape and appearance as the rolling forms of the land. Huang Zizhi refers to the school, the homes of specific families, and the ancestral hall as markers among the knolls and valleys of the village.

When Huang Xiqi, a school teacher, who was born and raised in Yin Yu Tang during the second half of the twentieth century, describes his vivid and warm memories of the Huang Cun in which he grew up, details of the landscape again come to the forefront:

In my memory, things were like this when I was a kid: there was a huge green grass lawn stretching from the entrance of the village to the back way of the village. It was so green, just like a green carpet. At the very front of the lawn, there was a big piece of land. And in front of the land, there was a small brook with clear water. On the two banks of the brook, there were trees of various kinds planted. They bloomed at all seasons. There was a road paved with flagstones leading into the village. As soon as you reached the area lined with trees, you would be able to see this village. And the first thing you saw in the village was my house. By the area lined with trees, there was a rounded gate built with stones. When we were passing [by], we could take a break there on a hot day or when we were tired. That gate deteriorated gradually and collapsed in the fifties. So it's gone now, leaving behind only a flagstone-paved road into the village.

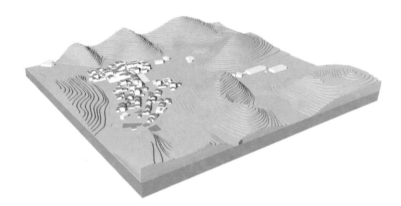

Fig. 36 (above) **Topological survey of Huang Cun, created by architectural students of Dong Nan University.**

Fig. 37 (right) **Yin Yu Tang, in Huang Cun, backed by a tree-covered hill, with an open expanse in front, and houses clustered on either side.**

Common Areas

The expanse of Huang Cun as described by Huang Zizhi's boundaries encompasses primarily buildings and land owned by private families—most of whom were Huangs—and land, institutions, or buildings owned or operated communally by the Huang family lineage group. Additionally, there were several other smaller communal shrines supported by donations from the public. The descriptions of Huang Cun written by disparate generations of inhabitants all mention the shared properties that clearly were partially responsible for forming (and were themselves formed by) the identity of the village. After the 1949 Communist revolution, with the redistribution of property, many of these communal assets took on new functions, but they continue to represent a shared ancestral history and form a fundamental bonding base for the village.

Before the 1949 revolution, five primary common buildings defined the social parameters of Huang Cun: two ancestral temples (one for the men and one for the women); Jin Shi Di (featured in the circa 1900 village photograph); a temple to the deity Guan Di; and the Huang Cun Primary School. All these buildings, with the exception of the Guan Di temple, were restricted to Huang lineage members and excluded non-Huang villagers. In addition, a large open lawn (also featured in the photograph) filled the center of the town; there, children could play, chickens could ramble, and laundry could be dried.

The Ancestral Halls

Ancestral halls, common all over China, are the communal buildings for lineage members to worship and pay homage to their ancestors. In Huizhou, where lineage and family bonds are so fundamental, ancestral halls are usually the most prominent structures in a village. These halls housed the ancestral tablets of the Huang lineage and were the site of communal ancestral worship at specific times of the year. The two ancestral halls of Huang Cun were located in a section of the village called Xiangbi, "Elephant's Trunk," a name included in Huang Zizhi's boundary descriptions. Xiangbi is a narrow strip of land that stretches between a steep hill and a waterway, west of the village's center. The two ancestral halls were on the northern bank of the stream and faced south. There is no known date recorded regarding the first construction of the Huang ancestral halls. The early-nineteenth-century edition of the *Xiuning County Gazetteer* makes note of a Huang ancestral hall in Huang Cun but does not mention a date of construction.

Older Huang Cun villagers often remark that their women's ancestral hall was far more elaborate than the men's. Moreover,

they add, the women's chamber was located to the east, the more auspicious side, of the men's hall. "The women's hall was on the big side, and the men's was on the small side," explained Huang Cui'e, who was born in Huang Cun in 1904, and was raised there. The women's hall, according to local villagers, was built with funds donated by a wealthy widow who was intent on celebrating the women of the village. Legend holds that she contributed 100 pieces of gold for its construction. The men's hall was possibly built earlier, and the highly decorative ornamentation of the women's hall may have been at least partially due to its later construction, when more ornate architecture was fashionable. Siting the building on the east may have been a matter of convenient open space.

Though the traditional ceremonies have not been performed in the Huang Cun ancestral halls for over four decades, memories of that austere space and the momentous annual events are still sharp in the memories of those who attended:

The most magnificent building of the village was the ancestral hall, which was divided into two parts: the hall for gentlemen and the hall for ladies. The building was located alongside the brook running from the Huang Village to the village of Elephant's Trunk. In front of the building there are many stone bases on which flagpoles are set. Each stone base was as high as a man and its diameter was about four feet. Two gray stone lions guarded the gate of the building. And two door gods were painted on the gate. Flowers, including a tall camellia, were planted on both sides of the road between the gate and hall.

I heard that it [the ancestral hall] was built in the Ming dynasty. It was very grand, just like an emperor's palace, with a succession of entrances and steps. There were many ancestral memorial tablets. Villagers with the Huang surname from both the Upper and Lower Huang Village would go to that ancestral hall to worship their ancestors.

Pancakes, what we call here kao bing, *were distributed at the ceremony of ancestral worshipping. Depending on men's ages, pancakes of different sizes were given out.*

—Huang Xiqi

The gravity of the ancestral halls was even remembered by those who were not allowed in them. Jiang Xiuqing is a resident of Huang Cun, but not a member of the Huang lineage. His grandfather first moved to the village over a hundred years ago, settled there, and married a daughter of the Huang family, but the family has, naturally, retained the surname of their male ancestors. "My name is not in the ancestral hall here. . . . [When I was a child], we could only looked from the doorway. We were scared. Ghosts reside there. . . . We would have to go back to Jiangxi to pay respects to our own ancestors."

Members of the Huang lineage made annual contributions to fund the upkeep of the ancestral halls and the ceremonies. Additional money and grain flowed into the lineage's accounts from renting lineage-owned farmland to local peasants. The lineage and their hall developed, therefore, not only into a familial and spiritual group but also into a financial entity.

With the institution of Communist ideology, the worship and reverence of ancestors was highly discouraged. In the government's eyes, the tradition fell under the rubrics of superstition and feudalism. Since loyalty to family and ancestors could compete with allegiance to the government, ancestral worship was to be slowly eliminated from the new China. In 1958 the Huang Cun village leaders agreed to the county's request to donate the building materials from the ancestral halls to a reservoir project for the county. All villages in the area were asked to contribute to the massive project. The stones, wood, and bricks of the no-longer-functioning ancestral halls seemed a more than presentable bequest. The villagers dismantled the halls and sent the materials off to the reservoir construction site:

It was really a shame. It must have been very difficult to build what we pulled down. But the secretary of the production brigade handed you the task, so the production team [the villagers] had to do it. We pried up tiles, took away bricks, and pulled down the beams by tying ropes around them. . . . We dared not speak our opinions. If you did, then the Party secretary would say you were sabotaging the irrigation project, and that was a crime. . . . If you looted some bricks, you could use them for building a pigsty. Roof beams and columns could be used as firewood.

—Jiang Xiuqing

Fig. 38 **One of two stone drums that once stood at the entrance of Huang Cun's ancestral hall.**

The ancestral tablets, again said to be representing feudal and backward superstitions, were also recycled for their material value. Some were used for firewood; others, according to local villagers, were used as soles for sandals.

Today all that remains of the ancestral halls is one entrance stone, of which there certainly was once a pair, representing a drum. The same type of stone drums still stand at the entrance of Jin Shi Di. New residences have been built on the sites.

Jin Shi Di

Over the stream from Xiangbi, past a few homes, and down narrow walkways, to the present center of Huang Cun, the grand shrine Jin Shi Di still dominates the space. The name emblazoned at the entrance of the structure, *Jin Shi Di*, translates as the "residence of the Jin Shi" (one who passes the highest level of civil examination, becoming eligible for an official government appointment). When a gentleman named Huang Fu, a native of Huang Cun, passed the highest level of civil examination in 1531, the emperor issued an edict that a hall be built in the village to honor his feat. It was then that this impressive, three-courtyard structure, covering 945 square yards (790 sq m), was erected. The colossal 102 gingko and cypress columns, many of which are 1.75 yards (1.6 m) in circumference, and the massive beams (some of which are 9.8 yards [9 m] long) would have necessitated a great amount of large lumber and labor. The fine workmanship in the wood and stone carvings demonstrates an insistence on hiring the finest of artisans to produce this edifice.

Elderly living villagers all recall that before the revolution, Jin Shi Di was used by the Huang family members as a location to hold their weddings and funerals. Wedding celebrations were held in the front part of the building and funerals were held in the back section.

Huang family members could use the upstairs altar to keep their family ancestral tablets for worship. Placing the ancestral tablets at the ancestral hall incurred annual fees, but keeping them at Jin Shi Di was free to all Huang family members. Jin Shi Di was also available as a storage space for living Huang family members to store their coffins. Having a coffin made long before death is a common custom in the Huizhou region. With a completed coffin the elderly can avoid worrying that a lack of funds after their death might prevent a proper burial.

The ancestral tablets in Jin Shi Di were, like those of the ancestral hall, burned for firewood or made into sandals after the 1949 revolution. The coffins were sent back to their owners to be kept at home. By the time of the campaigns of the Great Leap Forward (1958) and the Cultural Revolution (1966–76), Jin Shi Di was

Fig. 39 (far left) **Front entrance of Jin Shi Di, a 1531 shrine built in Huang Cun to honor Huang Fu, a Ming dynasty native of Huang Cun who passed the highest level of the civil examinations and became a government official.**

Fig. 40 (left) **An interior column of Jin Shi Di.**

being used for village meetings and political-struggle sessions. For a time, the village kept their communally owned water buffaloes in Jin Shi Di. Remains of political movements can still be seen in Jin Shi Di. Posters from the Great Leap Forward still decorate some walls, and written exclamations of "Long Live Chairman Mao" embellish entrances to various rooms within the building.

In 1981 the county again asked the village to donate building materials, this time for an electric generating plant. Dismantling Jin Shi Di, with its massive timbers, was suggested, but resistance grew among the villagers. A relative of one villager, a professor of architecture in Beijing, heard about the situation and composed a letter recommending that the building be preserved. At the last moment, county officials halted their plans, and the building was put under the protection of the Anhui Provincial Cultural Relics authorities.

The Guan Di Temple

A fourth significant communal building in Huang Cun was the temple dedicated to the deity Guan Di. A deity of war and prosperity, Guan Di, also often called Guan Gong, was the second most worshipped deity in China (after the Buddhist bodhisattva and deity of mercy, Guanyin). In life, Guan Gong had been a loyal and powerful military general during the Three Kingdoms period (220–80). After his death, he came to be worshipped particularly by those interested in military affairs, commerce, and giving birth to sons. Guan Di temples were common in the Huizhou region and were often located at the entrance to a village, to protect the community. The small temple building is located at the *shuikou*, "the water entrance," where the water of a stream poured into the plain of the village. (Huang Zizhi, in his description of the village, referred to this building as a temple to the water deity. No county documents have yet been able to definitively identify the deity of this building, but elderly villagers all call it the Guan Di temple.) The temple literally straddled the stream, which today still flows under the building.

In addition to the temple for Guan Di, Huang Zizhi mentions a smaller temple dedicated to the Wu Chang, the five animals. This may have been a temple to aid in protecting of the village's livestock.

The religious and moral underpinnings of Huang Cun, with the Confucian ancestral halls and the temples for the Taoist deities, were at one time rounded out by a Buddhist nunnery located east of the ancestral halls. There is little trace left today of the nunnery but a small bridge crossing a stream, a bridge that villagers note was the entrance to the Buddhist sanctuary and today leads to a flourishing vegetable patch.

Huang Clan Primary School

With whisperings of new lifestyles traveling with the merchants from larger metropolises, a new use was found for the Guan Di temple in the early years of the twentieth century. Just before the overthrow of the Qing dynasty in Beijing, a village leader named Huang Su established a Huang lineage school in Huang Cun, on the second floor of the Guan Di temple. The school was created as a "modern" institution and was the first such school in the county. Instead of studying the traditional Confucian classics, which had been taught to young boys by private tutors for centuries, the children of Huang Cun's school learned math, Chinese, sports, arts, and English. In the thirst for modernity and modern education, as Huang Cui'e, born in Huang Cun in 1904 and now in her nineties, has noted, the deities from the temple were all thrown into the streambed when the school was established.

Huang Su established the Huang Clan Primary School, applauded as the first modern primary school in the county, in Huang Cun in the second year of the Xuantong reign period (1910),[4] the year before the imperial Qing government was overthrown. The school began as a clan school, open to members of the Huang lineage and supported by the ancestral hall. Though there were non-Huang families in the village, the school was not officially open to them. Some villagers note today that non-Huang clan members could attend, but they had to pay extra: "Huang family members paid 1.2 yuan tuition, and non-Huang family members paid 2.4 yuan."[5] If Huang family children could not afford to pay tuition, the ancestral hall had a fund to subsidize them.

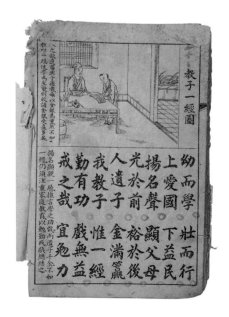

Fig. 41 **Page from the** *San Zi Jing*, **a time-honored Chinese primer in which all lines are three characters long, depicting a traditional study session of a master and student. This lithograph copy of the book, published circa 1912, was found among papers and documents in Yin Yu Tang.**

The tuition paid by the students went toward the upkeep of the building and purchasing the desks and benches. The ancestral hall paid the schoolteacher, not in cash but in grain. Most attendees remember that the teacher, before the revolution, was paid 100 *jin* of unhusked rice per month, which amounted to about seventy pounds of rice and was considered a low salary.

Both boys and girls, despite some parents' disapproval, were welcomed at the school. Huang Cui'e, living today in Shanghai, was in the first class of the school and recalls her family's reaction to her education: "My mother did not want me to go to school. She wanted me to stay home and learn to sew. [It] was a good elementary school, a revolutionary and progressive school. We didn't have to read the *San Zi Jing* [a classical Chinese primer]. We wore the same clothes as the boys at school, played soccer and everything. . . . Everybody was afraid of violating the rules. We couldn't spit. The county praised our environmental sanitation."

Huang Zhenxin (b. 1914), another early student of the school, also has strong memories of the "modernity" of their small but impressive institution of learning: "At school, we had to speak standard [Mandarin] Chinese. We also sang and played together. In addition, we were required to learn English. Therefore, our school was called a 'foreign school.' I can now still remember the [English] alphabet we learned when I was very young. That was an excellent school. There were even animal specimens, such as pangolin and eagle. We broke some traditions and we did not have queues."

The official motto of the school was "Diligence and Frugality." Under this guiding principle, the school developed over the years and its fame grew. In 1920, the ninth year of the Republic, the village was honored by a visit from a national education official. The well-known educator from Beijing, Huang Yanpei (not a relative of the Huang Cun Huang family) came to Huang Cun to inspect the Huang Clan Primary School. Village legend holds that he was standing outside the school and overheard the teacher conducting a class. He was so impressed that there could be such fine teachers in a small village that he wrote a calligraphic couplet.[6] The couplet reads: "To know that which a gentleman has learned, as the years progress; It is necessary that I travel to southern Wan [southern Anhui]."[7] The calligraphy proudly hung on the walls of the school for many years, until they were destroyed after the revolution. One proud Huang Clan Primary School attendee still has copies of this and other couplets hanging in his home.

An unknown writer in a partial letter found among the ephemera in Yin Yu Tang, most likely written shortly after Huang Yanpei's visit, reveled in the admiration for the school: "As for our clan school, it has been progressing since it was set up. Its success has been completely due to Mr. Houji's proper management and excellent instruction. Now the great educationists of the

Education Department all treat our lineage's school as the number one school of the highest category. I hope from now on the students will make even greater efforts and graduate with practical knowledge. If so, the glory of our lineage will become even greater!"

A New School Building

By the 1940s, the Guan Di temple building was deteriorating. The members of the lineage gathered enough donations from villagers to build a new school building. While the new school was being constructed across the path from the Guan Di temple, classes were held in one of the other communally owned structures, Jin Shi Di. Once the school was completed and had moved into its new quarters, in 1948, the Guan Di temple did not revert to its original sectarian function. Instead, the building became a small shop selling daily necessities, which it still is today.

After the 1949 revolution, the school's stewardship was taken over from the Huang lineage by the county government. The county changed the name of the school from Huang Shi Xiao Xue Huang Clan Primary School to the Huang Cun [Village] Primary School. The disparity in tuition between Huang and non-Huang children was also abolished. Teachers now followed the curricula and content dictated by the local county education administration.

A report card, dated July 1977, of a Yin Yu Tang Huang child studying at the Huang Village Primary School provides a sense of the educational parameters of the time. The front of the report exhibited a quote from Mao: "The focus of our education should be that those who receive an education will all obtain development

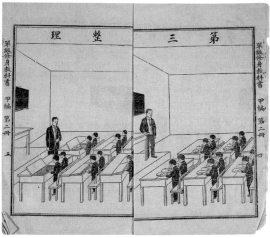

Figs. 42 & 43 (above) **Illustrations from a book for children on good morals and behavior,** *Xiushen Jiaocai Shu,* **"Teaching Materials for Self-Cultivation", depicting a modern style school, first published in 1912 (reprinted in 1916), by the Shanghai Commercial Press.**

Fig. 44 (left) **Children at Huang Cun Primary School, Huang Cun, Xiuning County.**

Huang Cun Today

The appearance of Huang Cun differs today somewhat from its earlier self. The paifang were razed in the mid-twentieth century. The grand lawn is gone and has been replaced by a concrete slab, a more convenient surface for villagers to dry their rice and other crops.

The stone pathways have almost all disappeared, replaced by dirt. Most of the old stones were taken up after the revolution by local villagers to use as building materials for new homes. Some villagers lament the loss of the old stone pathways. One man daily sweeps a remaining strip of the stones that passes by his house. Another shakes his head at the disregard for the few enduring old stones by those who insist on driving their tractors over the stones, often breaking them.

When new houses are built, they incorporate more contemporary building styles. Houses from the fifties, sixties, and seventies feature large windows on the first-floor facades—something never seen in earlier Huizhou houses, which let light in only through central skywells and small exterior windows on the second floor. Unable to afford the stone or brick carvings that decorated the exteriors of older houses, owners of newly built houses hired masons to paint images inspired by China's revolutionary era above their entranceways. Traditional methods of siting and orienting buildings—for example, fengshui—are now considered "old-fashioned" and "superstitious." As a result, many of the new houses have been built on sites that for centuries had been considered unusable. A large percentage of the new houses face south, changing the layout but not the emotional focus of the entire village.

of morality, knowledge, and athletics, and all become cultured laborers in realizing socialism. Education must serve the proletariat and must unite with production." The preprinted card also contained a message to the parents urging that they help their children during the summer to conscientiously study Marxism, Leninism, and the works of Chairman Mao; to study comrade Lei Feng [a popular 1960s model comrade]; and to struggle deeply against the Gang of Four. Seven-year-old Huang Zhaofeng (b. 1970) received an 80 in politics, a 90 in language, a 90 in math, and an Excellent in singing and sports. The teacher's handwritten note remarks that he "enthusiastically loves the Party and Chairman Mao, enthusiastically loves Chairman Hua [Guofeng], hates the Gang of Four, conscientiously studies socialism and cultural classes, and his homework is completed punctually. Through his study of Lei Feng, he has made improvements."

Fig. 45 (above) **Post-1949 painted decoration above an entranceway depicting Mao Zedong with slogans reading "Respectfully wishing Chairman Mao ten thousand years of longevity." Xiuning County.**

Fig. 46 (right) **A recently constructed house stands aside a mid-twentieth-century traditional-style house. Xiuning County.**

Fig. 47 (far right) **A traditional house being dismantled and replaced with a newer-style home. Xiuning County.**

The Huang Family

Alas! Everyone has his parents who have given birth to him, and everyone has his ancestors. Since there was a common ancestor, there is a clan. Ancestors are the roots of a tree, and the source of a river.
—Huang Lineage Genealogy (1485)[8]

Huang Cun is primarily populated by members of the Huang Cun Huang lineage, all of whom are surnamed Huang. According to local tradition, daughters of Huang fathers are almost always married to families from other villages, who are not surnamed Huang, and go to live with those families. Likewise, parents choose girls from other villages, not surnamed Huang, to marry the Huang sons and move into the Huang Cun Huang family homes. In this manner, the Huang-surnamed sons, the mothers of their sons, and their sons all remain in the village, and the houses and property continue to be maintained within the Huang lineage.

In addition to the Huang families, there are also some families in Huang Cun with other surnames, such as Jiang or Shao. These families call themselves *kejiaren* (guest family people), as Huang Cun is not their hometown, the home of their ancestors. Most of the kejia ren have lived in the village for only two or three generations, migrating there as artisans or farm laborers.

Most intimately integrated into the landscape, natural and man-made, of the village Huang Cun are the Huang families. A large part of each individual lineage member's identity is defined not only by his or her role within the immediate family—as father or daughter-in-law, grandparent or eldest son—but by the personal links to his or her ancestry and ancestors. The immediate links to ancestors are evident by the graves scattered about the surrounding landscape and, even more distinctly, by genealogical records. Because of the importance of being part of a family and lineage, the ability to trace one's ancestral line is important. Moreover, an understanding of one's ancestry was believed to instill greater social ethics. These records individually serve to allow individuals to know the great and small deeds of their predecessors in the long and strong chain of a lineage; together they offer a dynamic history of the people of Huang Cun.

The Huang Cun Genealogies

In considering a family's history, the living may trace a path to their immediate family and in turn to yet more distant ancestors, and even to mythological legends. What results is a series of individuals linked by birth (and, occasionally, adoption) and family pride, with occasional blanks. In the course of almost one thousand years, the Huang Cun inhabitants have made multiple attempts to record,

in full, their clan's history. While there is no known published and printed version of a Huang Cun Huang lineage genealogy, there are a number of handwritten manuscripts from a variety of time periods that demonstrate the surprisingly difficult process of piecing together a long and complex history of related individuals. Below is first an exploration of these manuscripts, then a narrative of the histories they tell.

Three primary genealogies and several death anniversary lists have been uncovered and consulted for the present Huang Cun Huang lineage history: a handwritten genealogy recording the first twenty generations of the Huang Cun Huang family preserved by the Yin Yu Tang family, which, as it is missing its first page, is untitled and which I shall call the YYT Genealogy; a 1963 handwritten genealogy by Huang Zhenduo (1898–1977), a Huang Cun native whose son is still living in Huang Cun, titled "The Compiled Family Records," which I shall call the HZD Genealogy; a 1572 handwritten manuscript in the Shanghai Library titled "Huang Chuan Huang Lineage Genealogy," which I shall call the Chenghua Genealogy; a handwritten wooden plaque that hung on the wall of Yin Yu Tang, recording the twenty-eighth through the thirty-fourth generations of the Yin Yu Tang ancestors only; a handwritten paper pasted on the wall of Yin Yu Tang, listing the tenth through seventeenth generations; and several unfinished miscellaneous lists of ancestors and gravesites found among the papers of Yin Yu Tang.

The three full genealogies primarily trace the male descendants of the family. Daughters were married out of the family and therefore were not essentially part of the family. Men's full given names are included in the genealogies. Wives—and often there were multiple wives for one man—are usually identified by their maiden surnames.

These were not the only genealogies that had ever been written for the lineage. According to Huang Zhenduo's 1963 preface, between the fifteenth century and the early-twentieth century, there were at least seven previous genealogies compiled on the Huang Cun Huang family lineage.[9]

The earliest known genealogy of the Huang Cun Huang lineage, compiled by Huang Yueqi of the seventh generation, less than two hundred years after the birth of the first generation, is no longer extant. The Chenghua Genealogy offers a brief biography of the lineage's first genealogist:

Yue
The eldest son of Mr. Heng, he had a literary name: Yueqi. He was born in the kuimao *[cyclical] Year of the Zhizheng Period of the Yuan dynasty (1363) and passed away on the seventh day of the first month of the* kuiyi *Year of the Yongle Period of the Ming dynasty (1413). He was buried at Licun [inner village], and his grave is in the shape of a flag.*

His wife's maiden name was Wang. She was buried at the Huang Family Cemetery Woods.

They had four sons—Youqing, Fuzhen, Zhi'ang, and Jian'an —and two daughters. The elder daughter married Mr. Wang of the Bi Village, and the younger daughter married Mr. Wu of Jiangtan.

Mr. Yue was generous and open-minded. He pursued righteousness and rituals, and was very modest. He was successful in managing the family, establishing a solid foundation, and influencing the later generations. He was the first man to edit the Huang family tree of the Huang lineage at Huang Chuan.

Before considering the history of the lineage, the content of each of the extant genealogies is worth exploring.

Yin Yu Tang Genealogy

The Yin Yu Tang (YYT) Genealogy is a handwritten manuscript of a total of fifty-six pages with two distinct sections. Shen Jing, librarian of Rare Books at Harvard Yenching Library, determined that the paper and ink of this manuscript dated from the mid-nineteenth century, and was more than likely copied from an earlier work at that time.[10] The first pages of the manuscript were separated from the work and have been lost. Therefore, it lacks a title and prefaces.

The first extant section is a series of ritualized prayers to be recited to ancestors at their graves, or to other deities, on specific occasions during the year. The second section—which, Shen Jing has noted, was most likely penned at a slightly later time by a different hand on different paper and with different ink—is a recording of twenty generations of the Huang Cun Huang lineage, beginning with the first ancestor, the first generation, a man named Huang Keyuan. Perhaps the most encompassing of the genealogies, particularly of the tenth through twentieth generations, this manuscript names 322 men, 377 wives of those men (though many of the men did not live to adulthood, there were also many who had two or three wives, resulting in more female ancestors than male), and nine daughters. Daughters, not considered part of a family line, were usually not worthy of mention.

For each of the first nine generations, the YYT Genealogy lists only one ancestor, who was the direct ancestor of the following generation. The genealogy disregards early branches, such as three of Huang Keyuan's four sons and their descendants, that eventually died out.

However, for the subsequent eleven generations—from the tenth through the twentieth—the genealogy recounts all male offspring. For each male, a compendium of facts, when known, is offered. These facts try to include what was considered the most vital information: given name, literary name, number of sons, place of burial, the surnames of wives and concubines, and their places of burial. If known, the given name of the wife is also mentioned. When relevant, an official post is also recorded. The genealogy does not make note of the dates, or even years, of births or deaths of the subjects. A typical entry is that of Huang Zhouqi of the ninth generation:

Son of Youqing. His literary name was Shiqi. He was buried at Xiazhuang (Lower Village), and his tomb is the shape of a dragon,[11] [situated] minus 30 degrees to the right, in the North-South direction.

His wife's maiden name was Wang Man. She was buried at Tingzi Shan (Pavilion Hill), and her tomb is in the shape of a vigorous tiger jumping over a wall, [situated in the] West-East direction.

The inclusion of daughters was less imperative than the mention of sons. For a daughter, the name of the family and village to which she was married was only rarely supplied. The entry for Huang Siyi of the seventeenth generation, whose daughters perhaps married men of prominent families, did not exclude his female offspring:

The eldest son of Renjian. His literary name was Zhifu. He had three sons and three daughters. The eldest daughter married Mr. Wang of Upper Stream. The second daughter married Mr. Dai of Yaoxi. The youngest daughter married Mr. Wang of Lower Stream. He [Huang Siyi] was buried at the Baqi Cemetery in Calamus Depression.

His wives' maiden names were Wu Runhua and Xu Kuaidi.

Among the many fascinating facets of Chinese life that can be analyzed by reading this genealogy is the subject of women's names. Through the many generations of the Huang lineage, beginning as early as the eleventh generation and continuing through the twentieth century, the wives' names reflect their parents' desire for sons. Women's names such as Zhuandi, sounding like "rotating to little brother," or Zhaodi, "beckoning little brother," appear over and over in this genealogy, indicating the parents' wish that their next child be a son.

The genealogy does not avoid noting a litany of other known facts about specific ancestors when they are known. Of most interest are subjects regarding high official status, unusual death situations, and adoption of sons to carry on the family line. If a son, or a even widow, migrated away from Huang Cun, the genealogy makes note of it. If a person died away from home, the genealogy reports this important fact, as the ancestor's spirit cannot conveniently be worshipped at his grave. If a widow, in her filial devotion, kills herself at her husband's death, the genealogy records the courageous deed. Such, for instance, was the case for Huang Mu of the twelfth generation:

Mu
The eldest son of Tianjuan.
    His wife's maiden name was Wang Haodi. Her husband died during travel. When his coffin was brought back home, she committed suicide to follow her husband.

The early twenty-first-century members of the Yin Yu Tang branch of the Huang lineage belong to the thirty-third, thirty-fourth, and thirty-fifth generations. During the mid-nineteenth century, when the extant YYT Genealogy was penned on its present paper, the living members would have been of at least the thirtieth generation, yet oddly, only members up to the twentieth were recorded.

Huang Zhenduo Genealogy

The Huang Zhenduo (HZD) Genealogy is a handwritten booklet of ten pages with an introduction by Huang Zhenduo dated Qing Ming, 1963; followed by a section titled "Outline of the Sources and Developments of the Huang Lineage"; and a section titled "The History of the Huang Lineage at Huang Village."
    Qing Ming, the Festival of Pure Brightness, celebrated on the 106th day after the winter solstice,[12] is one of the important days of the year for worshipping ancestors and therefore was an appropriate time for Huang Zhenduo to compose the preface to his arduously compiled genealogy. In Huang Zhenduo's preface, he relates the deep significance of knowing one's ancestors and recording a genealogy, dangerously criticizes the Communist era's lack of respect for traditional reverence for ancestors, gives a brief synopsis of the history of Huang Cun genealogies, and describes the political upheavals in which they were lost:

When the Taiping Army was besieged in Huizhou, the sufferings [of the lineage] were great and the old lineage histories and documents were either partially destroyed or totally lost. My clan brother Diyuan (Kaixiang) searched the remaining documents and collected lineage-wide the lists of memorial days of all families as reference. In this way, he continued the job of compiling and re-editing of the lineage history. Because too many years had passed and too many great changes had taken place, he felt so sad for not being able to include some important details.
    At that time, I was only thirteen years old, and I participated in the project [c. 1910]. Scarcely before the work had been completed, Brother Diyuan passed away. In the following fifty years, Yuan Shikai

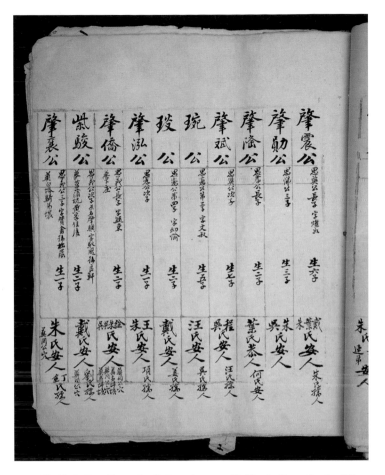

Fig. 48 **The Yin Yu Tang Huang Family Genealogy, provided by the Huang family of Yin Yu Tang, traces the family from the first generation through to the twentieth.**

and Jiang Jieshi [Chiang Kai-shek] in turn committed treason, the warlords seized areas in their own feuds and fought against each other, and the barbarian Japanese invaded China. The nation fell to the verge of extinction. In 1949, the revolution turned everything between Heaven and Earth upside down. As a result, the authentic re-edited version by Diyuan disappeared along with many other documents.

Huang Zhenduo's passionate discussion bemoans the lack of knowledge of family ancestry that proliferated in the 1960s, when many long-held traditions were criticized as feudal and counter-revolutionary. While protesting the current situation, he also articulates why he believes in the essentiality of genealogies:

Men of today often fail at being able to recite the names of their ancestors beyond three generations. They live in such an ignorant way that they do not know whence they are from, let alone the achievements their ancestors had made. Isn't it a great pity?

Those who have their ears [but do not have brains] only heard that [they should cut off] the poisonous remains of the feudal society, and they confused the feudal system with clans. In this way, they fail to understand the significance of the root to a tree and the source to a river. Without remote ancestors, how can there be close relatives? With the destruction of the knowledge of a clan, how could the filial piety and the respect of a younger brother to an older brother be preserved and deepened? How could human morals and ethics be maintained? The clan consciousness is fundamentally different from the ideas of those who arrogantly boast of their noble origins and enjoy a life of luxury on others' labor without doing anything themselves. Since the [Communist] Land Reform, [the principle has been established that] one will be given nothing to eat if he/she does not contribute his/her own labor. Then why should we worry about [what we are doing to restore the feudal customs]?

Furthermore, there are still national funerals and ceremonies in order to exalt those of high virtue and to pay respect to those of great achievements. This kind of practice will never change no matter what racial group one may belong to and what period of time one may live in. Throughout the world, all the nations are devoted to recording and re-editing their histories. The family history or family tree is similar to the history of a nation. They all aim at encouraging and inspiring the future generations by recording the rise and fall with the passage of history as well as the cultural achievements. How could this practice be abolished?

In the first section of his genealogy, Huang Zhenduo, unlike the writer of the YYT Genealogy, traces the Huang Cun Huang lineage back many millennia, all the way to the sixth-generation descendants of the legendary first emperor of China, the Yellow Emperor, who, having feuded in a region called Huang, took that place name as their surname. He continues on (using information, he explains, from previous genealogies) and notes that the thirty-third generation descending from the Yellow Emperor was a Huang Liangze who served King Wu of the Zhou dynasty in the eleventh century B.C.E. Huang Zhenduo follows these Huangs through the various ancient dynasties up to the fourth century, when the first Huang is said to have moved to the Huizhou area, then known as Xin'an. Huang Ji was appointed governor of Xin'an in the year 322 C.E., during the Western Jin dynasty, and settled in the town of Huang Dun, a small city located in the northeastern section of the Tunxi district, 14.3 miles (23 km) northeast of Huang Cun. (The name of this town was originally Jia Dun, but was changed to Huang Dun by the son of Huang Ji. The *huang* character in the name Huang Dun, however, is a different character than the surname Huang.)[13]

According to Huang Zhenduo, one branch of these Huang Dun Huangs moved from Huang Dun to the village of Zuotian in Qimen County in the year 767 and created a new Huang lineage there. In the late-ninth century, one member of this Qimen lineage, fleeing strife during a rebellion, migrated to Huang Chuan, present-day Huang Cun, in neighboring Xiuning County. (See Huang migration map.) This next Huang Chuan lineage continued for another ten generations, until in the early thirteenth century one couple found themselves childless and decided to adopt "a son to expand and continue the achievements and business and so that the family line would go on forever without an end." This boy, originally named Cheng Keyuan, a son of Cheng Ye of the town of Taitang, changed his surname to Huang and became the same Huang Keyuan who is listed, without any further historical explanation, as the first ancestor in the YYT Genealogy.

In his second section, "The History of the Huang Clan at Huang Cun," Huang Zhenduo, beginning with Huang Keyuan as the first generation, traces the family through the twenty-seventh generation. He offers far longer descriptions of the individuals than are available in the YYT Genealogy, including specific birth and death years, but lists only one male per generation. He registers only the direct ancestors of his own line, rather than listing all the descendants of each generation. An example of Huang Zhenduo's description in comparison to the YYT Genealogy's record can be made with the instance of a member of the fifteenth generation, Huang Kuihuan. The YYT Genealogy merely states that he was "the eldest son of Zhengchen. He had three sons. His daughter Xizhu married to certain Cheng at Shandou. His wife's maiden name was Cheng." Huang Zhengduo's entry is far more extensive, giving a solid sense of this seventeenth-century man's personality, his righteous preference for the simple rustic life, his trustworthiness in the business world, and his conscientious upholding of Confucian principles:

Kuihuan

The eldest son of Zhengchen. His literary name was Xiangming, and another literary name was Mengjiu. He was born on the first [day] of the eleventh month of the dingwei *year of the Wanli reign Period of the Ming dynasty and passed away on the twelfth day of the seventh month of the* renchen *year of the Shunzhi reign Period of the Qing dynasty (1607–52). His wife's maiden name was Cheng and she was from Fanggan. She was born on the first [day] of the eleventh month of the* dingwei *year of the Wanli reign Period of the Ming dynasty and passed away on the twentieth day of the third month of* wuzi *year of the Shunzhi reign Period of the Qing dynasty (1607–48). They were buried together at Chentang (Sinking Pond). They had three sons: Renji, Renbao, and Rentang, and a daughter who was married to Mr. Cheng at Shandou.*

Mr. Kuihuan was outstanding in his talents and his knowledge.

He was good-hearted and modest. Devoted to his parents and loyal to his friends, he was extraordinarily selective in taking and giving. A lady of the Cheng family at Anqi married Mr. Wang of Hongfang. Mr. Wang was, thus, the husband of Mr. Kuihuan's niece. Mr. Kuaihuan and Mr. Wang were also business colleagues working in Chu (Hubei). At the end of the Chongzhen period, there were many rebellions in that region. Mr. Wang returned home first, and he asked Mr. Kuihuan to bring back home twenty thousand liang of gold. Mr. Kuihuan did so without any loss. When he returned home, he led a simple and rustic life. After a while, Mr. Wang invested the funds in [a] salt business in Zhejiang Province and suffered such a great loss that his capital almost completely disappeared. A fellow clan member whose name was Wang Zongyou told him that [he] had entrusted the wrong person to do the business, saying, "Why did you not entrust your relative who brought back your funds for you?" Mr. Wang had heard some slander regarding Mr. Kuihuan and replied that he was afraid that Mr. Kuihuan would appropriate the money. Mr. Zongyou said, "Is there such a person who is not greedy for money during a chaotic period and enjoys a simple and rustic life, but in a time of peace he becomes a person who wants to appropriate others' money?" Mr. Wang then became conscious of the truth and invited Mr. Kuihuan to manage his business. Mr. Kuihuan traveled between his home and Jiangsu and Zhejiang Provinces, and finally passed away in a guest house when away from home. On his dying bed, he passed away while reciting a sentence of the Golden Mean [translator's note: one of the four basic classics of Confucius]: "One should never feel shame and regret even in the deepest room of one's private residence."

Huang Zhenduo's genealogy not only records events of the distant past but also includes updates by a later generation to document more recent historical events, such as the Cultural Revolution:

Shengyuan
During the so called Great Proletarian Cultural Revolution (1966-67 [perhaps a misprint for 1976]), enduring the ten years [of] severe disasters, [the family was criticized] groundlessly and wrongly blamed. The residence was twice searched with properties confiscated. All the clothes and goods for daily use were looted. It was really unbearable!

Despite the confiscation and harassment, Huang Zhenduo's genealogy managed to avoid destruction.

Many historical documents, such as this genealogy, trace family roots even further back to mythological and ancient historical times. These surname legends were developed at much later dates. Though genealogies like to quote them, in actuality, direct blood relations to these ancestors can rarely be drawn, as will be apparent below. Lineages of less distant times, however, are more verifiable.

Just as the YYT Genealogy ends at the twentieth generation, Huang Zhenduo's pauses after the nineteenth, is blank for the twentieth, twenty-first, and the twenty-second, and only picks up with names and descriptions at the twenty-third generation.

The Huang Chuan Huang Lineage Genealogy

The Huang Chuan Huang Lineage (Chenghua) Genealogy, a handwritten manuscript now in the Shanghai Library, is dated by its last inscription a later supplemental afterword to the genealogy— written in the sixth year of the Chenghua reign period during the Ming dynasty (1368–1644)—1572. The prefaces and other afterwords are dated 1485 and 1486, and the last sons entered in the genealogy were born in the 1480s. The bound manuscript of pages covers the first through the eleventh generations of the Huang lineage of Huang Cun. With both prose paragraphs and family trees, it offers detailed information on the descendants and lineages of all four of Huang Keyuan's sons. As all but one of these lines died out, the two later genealogies dispensed with them entirely.

The most unusual aspect of this genealogy, in comparison to the other two, is the emphasis the editors put on the Huang lineage's connection to Huang Keyuan's biological ancestors, the Chengs of the town of Taitang. The Huang family member, Huang Yihui, who researched and assembled the genealogy, apparently requested prominent members of the Tai Tang Cheng family to provide prefaces to the book. Among them was Cheng Bian of Taitang, who had participated in the national civil examination and referred to himself with the stately title of "Confucian scholar." He also appealed to a Mr. Yu Rui, a grand scholar at the Imperial Hanlin Academy in Nanjing to write an additional preface.

Many family genealogies in China, particularly in the Ming, were written in hopes of demonstrating family connections to high officials or important personages. The Cheng family produced far more high-ranking descendants, and this edition of the Huang genealogy may have been an attempt to link the Huang family with such accomplished individuals.

In his preface, Cheng Bian adamantly declares that the purpose of the genealogy was not to raise the status of the family by exhibiting familial connections to eminent members of society: "Alas! The purpose of editing a genealogy should be to remember the ancestors, and to distinguish the closer relatives from others. It should not be a practice to show off the achievements and prosperity of a clan. The current genealogy of the Huang family is properly based on loyalty and sincerity. Therefore, it is simple without ostentatious decorations, and it is detailed but not all-inclusive. The ancestors who were poor were not excluded, and the family history is in good order. The current work is far superior to many genealogies of the

Fig. 49 (above) **Memorial archway in Taitang Village, Xiuning County.**

Fig. 50 (opposite) **Farmer in Taitang Village, Xiuning County, winnowing rice. Characters on the side of the winnowing machine indicate that the wooden winnower belongs to the Cheng family, 2001.**

one who received the highest merits in defending our dynasty, Mr. Hukang, who was bestowed the rank of earl. As for those who devoted themselves in learning and maintained integrity in their virtues without any intentions of boasting, there was never a shortage for each generation."

Mr. Yu Rui, in his preface, offers more details on this valiant Huang Hukang, "whose excellent military skills earned him an appointment of the commander of 100 soldiers in the Yangzi River and Huai River regions." Yu Rui also notes that the Huangs' reputation was further enhanced by the virtues of their wives and widows, many of whom continued to maintain their loyalty to the family even when their husbands died at a young age. "There were many ladies of chastity from the Huang family who kept their integrity without any reluctance."

As this genealogy does not restrain itself from mentioning, the most noteworthy among the ancestors of the Huang Cun Huang clan was the officially ranked father of Huang Keyuan, Cheng Ye. The genealogy seems indeed to have been written in an attempt to demonstrate this link to the illustrious Cheng family. Cheng Bian clearly considers the forebearers of Huang Keyuan to be the Cheng family and not the Huangs. In discussing the history before Cheng Keyuan, he notes that it is not necessary to record "the part before

world that improperly include big names although they were not close to the clan, and exclude the poor although they were in the direct line."

Despite his protestations, Cheng Bian cannot help but call attention, in his preface, to one of the more accomplished members of the clan, a certain Huang Cang of the eighth generation, who passed the civil examinations: "During the Yongle reign period [1403–1424] of the Ming dynasty, Mr. Cang, the grandson of eighth generation of Keyuan became a candidate of national examination and was appointed the governor of Luzhou and Puzhou. His much appreciated governing had many great achievements and was known both near and far. The family established a tradition of poetry and rites, and its prosperity came to a climax then, setting an excellent standard for families of other clans." At some point, Huang Cang's descendants must have not produced sons, as his line did not continue to be preserved in later genealogies.

Another contributor of a preface, a Mr. Yu Yun, also unabashedly points out the most renowned ancestors of the Huang clan: "After Mr. Keyuan, the most famous personages of the family in terms of the achievement in the national examination and excellence in government were Mr. Cang, the regional governor, and

Mr. Keyuan. . . . Nothing was included in this new edition because the Family Tree of Taitang already exists." Descendency from the Huang Clan of Huang Dun, so emphasized in the HZD Genealogy, is entirely ignored in this earlier edition.

Though today neither Huang Cun nor Taitang natives are aware of their connections to each other, Cheng family members have continued to live in Taitang to the present and through the years have continued to produce officials and important personages. A large four-column archway in Taitang known as the "Imperial Honor Archway" still stands at the entrance of the village. It was built during the Wanli Period (1573–1620) of the Ming dynasty, in honor of a native of the village, Cheng Yuanhua. Below the archway, one autumn day in the year 2000, a man was refining his rice harvest in a thresher distinctly inscribed with his family name, "Made for the Cheng Family," testimony to the continuation of that family line in the village.

The Story of the Huang Cun Huang Lineage's Origins

Together these genealogies reveal far more than a list of names and a few accomplishments. They reveal a rich history of the Huang lineage at Huang Cun. Huang Zhenduo denotes 1210 as the year when the accepted first generation ancestor of the Huang Cun Huang lineage arrived at Huang Cun. That year was about eighty years after the establishment of the southern Song government in Lin'an (modern Hangzhou), after the Jin had overthrown the northern capital of Kaifeng. As noted earlier, the establishment of the capital in Lin'an, just 124 miles (200 km) from Huang Cun and accessible from Huizhou by waterways, had enabled the Huizhou merchants to make excellent profits from selling Huizhou timber to the ever-expanding new capital. The abacus was just coming into use, and paper currency was becoming a means of financial exchange. In Huizhou, merchants were prospering, young scholars were passing civil examinations in record numbers, and in one small village people were worried about carrying on the Huang family line.

For almost three hundred years, the small Huang lineage had carried on among the hills and streams of Huang Cun. In the *jiashen* year of the Longxing reign of the Song, a year that translates to 1164 in the Gregorian calendar, a son named Huang Wan was born, a descendant of the twelfth generation from that first settler of Huang Cun. Huang Zhenduo gives accolades to Huang Wan and his clan, praising their learning and their respect for Confucian knowledge. "For several generations, Wan's family had engaged in both agriculture and reading [Confucian classics] as a family tradition." In time, Huang Wan married a woman surnamed Qian, and together they had a son whose given name was Qi.

For an unknown reason, this only son of the late-twelfth-century descendant Huang Wan fled and disappeared, leaving the family line in an apparent heirless lurch. Had he committed a crime? Or been murdered while traveling on business? The genealogies offer no explanation. The loss of the son may have come, though, at a time when his mother was already too old to give birth, and his father—conceivably already forty-six years old—could not rely on having enough years left to take a chance on a second, younger wife's ability to produce a male heir. The couple turned to other means to resolve their lack of a successor. It was at this juncture that Huang Wan decided to adopt a son "to expand the achievements and to continue the business so that the family line would go forever without an end."[14]

The Chenghua Genealogy explains the younger sister of the wife of Huang Wan had married into the Cheng family of Taitang, a small village in eastern Xiuning. She had married Cheng Ye, a man who would eventually, and significantly, become a county magistrate of Xuancheng, several counties north of Xiuning. In Taitang the young wife had given birth to first one and then another son. The family of Huang Wan requested to adopt this second son, named Cheng Keyuan, and the Cheng family agreed. Upon adoption, Cheng Keyuan's surname was changed to that of his adopted family.

Adoption of an unknown orphan was a rare occasion in China. However, this practice of adopting from within an extended family to enable a lineage to continue on was not at all unusual. Huang Zhenduo remarks on the legitimacy of this adoption in his genealogy: "His mother was the sister of Mr. Huang Wan's wife, so he, as a nephew, a relative within the level three circle according to the rites, could be adopted." In reviewing the Huang family genealogy, the practice was repeated at various critical moments to ensure the continuation of the family line. For instance, the genealogy noted that Huang Zi of the twelfth generation had three sons, and the third he allowed to be adopted by a relative in another village:

Zi

The second son of Tian'an. He had three sons. The third son was Xiyuan, with a literary name Gongcong and a literary title Mengsuo. He then was adopted by Huang Zhulong of Donggou (East Valley), and renamed Zhiyuan.

His wife's maiden name was Cheng Landi.
His concubine was Qiuxi.

In the next generation, Huang Ruqi adopted Huang Benzhi, the second son of a Huang Cun cousin, to continue his own line. Huang Benzhi himself, of the thirteenth generation, did fulfill his obligation and continued the family line. He had three sons. The eldest did not produce any heirs, but the second did have a son to carry on the name:

Ruqi

The eldest son of Jin. He adopted the second son of Daoxian as his son to continue the family line.

Benzhi

The second son of Daoxian. Later he became the adopted son of Ruqi and had three sons. His eldest son was Rizhao, who had no sons. His second son was Rijie, [who] had one son, Zuzhi, who migrated to Suzhou.
His wives' maiden names were Hu and Cheng.

Among the three genealogies, there is only one mention of the adoption of a girl. In Zhenduo's genealogy, he mentions that during the early part of the twentieth century, the second wife of twenty-third generation Huang Shengyuan gave birth to two sons, and then adopted a girl named Yazi:

His literary name was Buying, and his wife's maiden name was Yao Feng, who gave birth to four sons and a daughter. . . . His second wife was Nanjinglao who gave birth to two sons: Dongmin and Liumin. She also adopted a daughter whose name was Yazi. Dongmin as the fifth son died before adulthood. . . .

Mr. Shengyuan passed away (1876–1937). . . . Mr. Shengyuan was the manager of Dasheng Company at Tunxi. He led a frugal life and saved a lot of money. He built a two story building for his children with the money.

The name Yazi means "servant girl," and she was most probably adopted (possibly even purchased) in order to assist as a servant in the well-off household and later become, as was not an uncommon practice, a less-expensive wife of their son. The wife of Zhenduo's second son, who is still alive, in fact, entered into marriage in this manner.

Huang Keyuan

The adopted boy Huang Keyuan developed into an important personage who merited much praise and respect from his descendants. Because of the revered position given to this Huang Keyuan by all following generations, a brief examination of him here is worthwhile.

None of the biographies in the genealogies provide much substantial information about him other than his childhood adoption. He was said to be learned and virtuous. Perhaps by the time any of the extant genealogies were written down, too much time had passed and there was no extensive data available. However, he must have had excellent leadership qualities, scholarship, and wisdom to have acquired the lofty status of first ancestor.

Together the genealogies offer an outline of a man who married a woman surnamed Jin and had four sons. Reviewing the later generations of the line reveals that probably only one of these branches, the descendants of his son Zongren, continued for more than fifteen generations, and it is to Zongren that all the surviving Huang Cun Huang family members trace their lineage. Below are the biographies of Huang Keyuan provided by the three genealogies:

Keyuan (YYT Genealogy)

His literary name was Tingguang, and another literary name was Shouxin. He was buried at Xiazhuang, and his tomb is in the shape of a yellow dragon rushing in a great river. A hill is at its left, and it faces south. He had four sons. The eldest was Zongqi, whose offspring discontinued after six generations;[15] the second son was Zongren; the third son was Zongyi, who resided in Licun close to Qingshan gate; the youngest son was Zongli.

His wife's maiden name was Jin, buried together with him.

Keyuan (HZD Genealogy)

His literary name was Shouxin, and another literary name was Tingguang. He was born in the gengwu *year of the Jiading Period of the Emperor Ning of the Song dynasty (1210) and passed away in the* yihai *year of the Deyou Period of the Emperor Xian of the Song dynasty (1275). His wife's maiden name was Jin. Together they were buried at Xiazhuang, and their grave is in the shape of a yellow dragon rushing up a hill. He had four sons: Zongqi, Zongren, Zongli, and Zongyi. Ancestor Keyuan was the second son of Mr. Cheng Ye at Taitang. At the age of five, he was sent to Huang Chuan as the adopted son of Mr. Huang Wan to continue the family line. His mother was the sister of Mr. Huang Wan's wife, so he, as a nephew, a relative within the level three circle according to the rites, was adopted. His character was steadfast and unyielding, and he was endowed [with] a nature of loftiness and brightness. Day in and day out, he was engaged in doing good deeds and studying hard. And he served his adopted parents as his own. He established a solid foundation for later generations, and his achievements are still inspiring people of the current generation. The family line will go on forever without an end.*

Keyuan (Chenghua Genealogy)

According to the genealogy, Mr. Keyuan was the second son of Mr. Cheng Ye of Taitang. He was born in the gengwu *year of the Jiading Period of the Emperor Ning [1210] of the Southern Song dynasty. His nature was decisive and unyielding, and he had an endowment of brightness. He was good at learning and studied very hard day in and day out. Therefore, he could lay a virtuous foundation for the Huang clan at Huangchuan and blessed his offspring to*

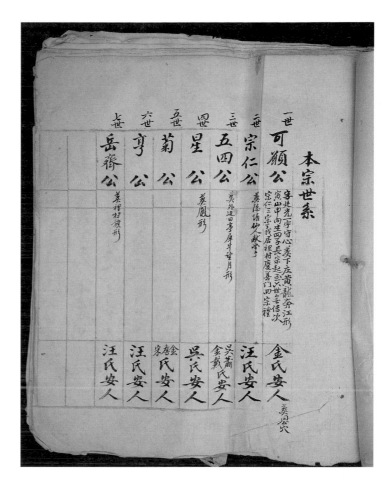

Fig. 51 **The first page of the Yin Yu Tang Genealogy providing the names of the first seven generations of the Huang Cun Huang lineage. For the first nine generations, only the names of the direct ancestors are provided in this genealogy.**

continue the family line forever. He was buried at Xialin. The hill at the back of the tomb is to the northeast, and the tomb itself faces southwest.

His wife's maiden name was Jin, and she was buried at the same place.

They had four sons: Zongqi, Zongren, Zongyi, and Zongli.

While Huang Keyuan is considered the patriarch of the Huang Cun Huang family, careful reading of the genealogies makes it clear that descendants of the original Huang clan who settled in Huang Cun in the ninth century continued to live in and around Huang Cun. The last entry of the Chenghua Genealogy, a 1572 copy of a mid-fifteenth-century postscript by Huang Juan (probably the son of Maozong), records a dispute over rights to burial land. The dispute regarded land said to be inherited from Huang family members, but, the writer supposes, not from the Keyuan branch:

It has long been said that there are no subdivisions of the Grave Grove of the Huang Clan within its members. In the twelfth year (1533) of Jiajing Period, when the members of our branch went there to repair the tombs, we saw that others had also gone there to set up gravestones. We argued with them so that they left without having erected the gravestones. Then both sides came together to discuss the subdivisions. They said their subdivision was the property of Huang Yuanfu. Huang Yuanfu was the uncle of Mr. Rushan. The land was the property under his management. Through later investigation, we found that Huang Yuanfu was a descendant of old Huang family, not a descendant of Mr. Keyuan.

Huang Keyuan's Descendants

Following through the many subsequent generations and Huang Keyuan's many descendants, the YYT Genealogy is perhaps the most encompassing.

Several interesting characteristics stand out in reviewing this group of men and women. The first twenty generations of the Huang Cun Huang clan, as recorded in the three genealogies, did not produce many luminaries by classical Chinese standards. Descriptions do include such glorious personalities as Huang Youqing, who "was generous and honest, and both resolute and thoughtful. He was also very skillful and efficient when doing business. Three times his business was destroyed by fire. Each time he managed to rebuild it within a year." However, there were few nationally recognized heroes from Huang Cun. The Chenghua Genealogy boasts of Huang Cang and Huang Hukang, but these branches presumably died out, and their names, oddly, do not appear in genealogies written at later dates.

Huang Maozong, of the tenth generation, also known as Huang Yihui, the editor of the Chenghua Genealogy, was conferred an official position with full official hat and clothes of the seventh level. His sons were also—not surprisingly, being influenced by their learned father—high achievers. His second son, Tianyi, was "appointed adviser to the Prince of Anhui," and his fourth son, Tianjuan, became a "vice prefect of Tai'an." There are, however, no records or notations that any of these men passed examinations, and it is possible that they acquired their ranks through other means. Only one ancestor mentioned in the HZD Genealogy, Huang Renbao, of the sixteenth generation, reached proper official status. According to the document, he "participated in the national examination and was accepted by the Imperial Academy. From there he received the appointment of a lieutenant district governor." (Though his name is included in the YYT Genealogy, no mention is made there of his achievements.)

Huang Cun's most distinctive celebrity was Huang Fu, who oddly appears in none of the genealogies. His achievements and their veracity, however, are confirmed by the official county gazetteer and by the building, Jin Shi Di, constructed in his honor. Huang Fu, a native of Huang Cun during the mid-Ming dynasty, also passed the national civil examinations and became an official. His name appears under "Personages" in the *Xiuning County Gazetteer*, with a lengthy description of his career. His absence in the present genealogies may be attributed to his being a descendant of the "old" Huang family, that is, not of the Keyuan branch. Or he may have been a post-Chenghua descendant of one of Keyuan's sons' lines that eventually died out and was not recorded for posterity.

Beyond these recorded men, the virtuous women from Huang Cun may have received more glories than their husbands. There are twenty-three women from Huang Cun (including daughters of Huang families who were born in Huang Cun and married into other villages, as well as wives of Huang men who married into the village) listed in the *Xiuning County Gazeteer* of the Daoguang reign Period (1815). They are primarily praised for their dedication to their husband's family and determination to remain chaste as widows. Among the women from the seventeenth century was one native daughter of a Huang Cun Huang family, who married a Mr. Shao Yuanzuo of Minkou Village: "In the second year of Emperor Shunzhi, there was a rebellion of some hill bandits. She was afraid that she would be raped by the bandits and dropped herself from a high building and died. At that year, she was only twenty-three years old and was five months' pregnant." But most were elevated to their revered status for remaining devoted to their husband's family after his death, even if they were still very young brides, raising the husband's heirs, and never marrying again.

One woman, the wife of Huang Chengyin, who lived during the eighteenth century, is a typical example of this adulation. She is noted with great respect in the HZD Genealogy:

His [Chengyin's] wife's maiden name was Dai, and she was born on the seventh day of sixth month of bingyin *year of the Qianlong reign Period (1736–95) and passed away on the seventeenth day of the eighth month of* kuiwei *year of the Daoguang reign Period (1796–1823). They had a son: Qizheng. . . . When Qizheng was just a month old, Chengyin passed away. At that time the lineage had become very large and there were many men of the same generation. Mrs. Dai was a young lady and she endured the hardship of keeping her chastity. She stayed at home and took care of her son. She enjoyed a long life without any gossip against her. Her behavior was praised by fellow villagers.*

As can be seen from many entries, in addition to the name of the male ancestor, the place of burial was also judged crucial information to be noted. This was important because descendants were obligated to make offerings to the ancestors, and the site of the burial, determined according to fengshui principles, was essential for ensuring good fortune for future generations. The description of Huang Zongren, who lived in the thirteenth century, notes that ". . . he was buried at Huangmulin (Huang Family's Cemetery Woods) at Yin Tang (Hidden Pond) . . . a hill that the fengshui experts appreciated as a fortunate site and called it the shape of An Immortal Demonstrating His Boxing."

Describing particular individuals, the genealogy mentions interesting facts that would have been meaningful to readers. It deliberately notes the men who, probably being merchants, migrated from Huang Cun to larger trading towns. These included a certain number of men (including Rijing of the fifteenth generation, the second son of Benshan) who migrated to the South Bridge of Songjiang, and his cousin Rijie of the same generation and Weicheng of the nineteenth generation, who migrated to the city of Suzhou, in Jiangsu Province:

Rijing
The second son of Benshan. He migrated to the South Bridge of Songjiang.
   His wife's maiden name was Jin.

Rijie
The second son of Benzhi. He migrated to Suzhou.
   His wives' maiden names were Cheng and Wang.

The region encompassing Suzhou and Songjiang was particularly prosperous during the late Ming period, when the fifteenth generation was busy working, and innumerable Huizhou merchants were based there. The presence of Huang Cun Huangs in Suzhou, and some deciding to settle there, is not surprising.

Not only were such emigrants settling in the literary and financial center of China during the latter half of the Ming dynasty, they were also leaving their hometown and their lineage. Their names, and the names of their descendants, do not reappear on the genealogy. They would begin in their new homes as their ancestor Huang Keyuan did, a new branch and a new family line.

The Twenty-first Generation and Beyond

The three genealogies from Huang Cun offer much detailed information about the family. But even if they are read together, questions about the heritage of the Huang clan remain unanswered. The most glaring unresolved matter is the lack of information about the twenty-first, twenty-second, and twenty-third generations.

The Chenghua Genealogy describes the generations of the Huang family in detail up to the eleventh generation. The YYT Genealogy is less detailed but lists a greater number of people through the twentieth generation. The YYT plaque picks up at the twenty-eighth generation. The HZD Genealogy goes up to the present day but notes an informational lapse that occurred at the twentieth generation. There are in this edition no names for the twentieth, twenty-first, or twenty-second generations. The HZD picks up with names at the twenty-third. However, the question arises: how did the twenty-third generation know they were the twenty-third generation? And then a more important question crops up—what happened after the twentieth generation?

If one generation is approximately twenty-five years long (that is, men are having their first son at twenty-five years of age), twenty generations would equal 500 years. If the first generation was, as noted, approximately 1210, the twentieth generation would have lived during the early eighteenth century. If one generation is twenty years, twenty generations would be 400 years, and the twentieth generation would have been living during the early-seventeenth century. According to Huang Zhenduo's calculations, the nineteenth generation lived during the mid-eighteenth century. Placing the twentieth generation at the end of the eighteenth century.

Huang Zhenduo was also clearly perplexed by the events of the twentieth and twenty-first generations. In his confusion, he lays the blame entirely on the invasion of the Taiping Heavenly Kingdom in the 1850s and 1860s. This army of rebels had conquered a great deal of southern China by the time it had reached Xiuning County in 1852. The ideology of the Taipings called for a more communal society, equality of men and women, and the annihilation of Confucian customs and ancestral worship. Hong Xiuquan, the leader of the Taipings, is said to have remarked to the masses: "When you bow down to lumps of clay, to wood and stone, I ask when did you lose your mind?"[16] Ancestral halls, along with ancestral tablets, private homes, genealogies, and histories were destroyed as the Taipings swept through towns.

Huang Zhenduo's description of the impact of the Taipings' presence in Huizhou is in keeping with many Huang Cun villagers' descriptions of the thirteen years (1851–64) during which the "Long Haireds," as the Chinese population called them (because of their unplaited, loose hairstyles), ravaged the Chinese countryside:

I heard about the Taiping Heavenly Kingdom from my grandmother . . . [who] passed away in her nineties. . . . [She said] people escaped from the village, some hid in caves, some in ditches. Houses were burned down. It was a mess. . . . My grandmother said that our house was a ruin. The house used to extend all the way to the open space by the tea garden, but it was destroyed during the Taiping Heavenly Kingdom.

The Taipings almost certainly came through Huang Cun. The *Xiuning County Gazetteer* of 1990 records their entrance into the county in 1852 and notes their presence in and out of the county over the following decade. In addition to Mr. Huang's account above from his grandmother, a small piece of evidence from the Taipings was uncovered inside a cabinet from Yin Yu Tang. Doors on most Chinese cabinets, and houses, pivot on a round dowel that fits into a hole on the cabinet sill. Inside the hole on one particular cabinet was a coin from the Taiping Heavenly Kingdom. The hole at the center of the coin may have helped the door pivot.

The Taiping Rebellion does not completely solve the question of the twenty-first generation, however. The rebellion occurred too many years after the twentieth generation. Speculation can offer a few more far-fetched theories. Could the only surviving branch of the Huang Cun Huang family have been excommunicated from the lineage for a grave crime and, as custom held, been banished from the records? Seeing that there were so many family members of the twentieth generation, this theory does not seem plausible.

The twentieth generation, according to calculations, may have occurred during the transition from the Ming to the Qing Period. Violence and upheaval in the region may have prevented lineage members from focusing on recording their newly born heirs. Or, they were recorded, but the destruction during the Taiping Rebellion obliterated any newer records that had been kept in the ancestral hall. The rediscovery at a later date of only the older

genealogies would have allowed those to be re-recorded, but perhaps enough time had passed that names of the twenty-first and twenty-second generations were forgotten and lost.

According to Huang Zhenduo, there were lineage histories written around 1400, 1500, 1540, 1660, and 1710. For an unknown reason, no clan member for the next two hundred years attempted to edit an updated version of the genealogy. Events in Xiuning, as evinced from the *Xiuning County Gazetteer*, during the years from the mid-seventeenth century through the mid-nineteenth century followed an occasionally smooth and occasionally rough course. During the early-seventeenth century, the successes of the Xiuning merchants continued to bring prosperity to the region. In 1645 Qing troops invaded the county, in their bid to overthrow the country. Once the Ming were defeated and the new government officials in place, the county continued in its monetary comfort. The multitude of still-standing seventeenth- and eighteenth-century homes, ancestral halls, bridges, and pagodas is testimony to the funds that were flowing into the hands of Xiuning residents. The *Gazetteer* makes note of droughts, floods, earthquakes, and even tiger attacks. But behind the disasters, there were also stunning accomplishments by local residents. In the year 1777, for instance, seven men from Xiuning all passed the national civil examinations, demonstrating the continued dedication to education and striving for officialdom among the merchant families. A few years later, a man from Xiuning finished at the top of all his countrymen taking those national exams. The *Gazeteer* also makes note of individuals from Huang Cun who were passing exams and women who were being extolled for their chastity. No known specific disaster, except the Taiping Rebellion, seems to have struck Huang Cun and been accountable for the loss of records of several generations of the Huang clan.

With the same filial fervor as his ancestors, a Huang Cun villager, Huang Diyuan, began to edit a new genealogy in about 1910. The memorial days he collected would have been similar to the plaque kept in Yin Yu Tang (see page 53). If the latter genealogies, from 1710, had vanished, all that may have been available to Huang Diyuan were the early, still preserved genealogies listing family members up to the twentieth generation. Thus, his inability to account for the post-twentieth generations.

Unfortunately, the courageous researcher Huang Diyuan, trying to reconstruct two hundred years of a lineage's history, passed away soon after he had completed his work and was not there to protect it as calamities fell again upon China and Huang Cun. Huang Zhenduo, who as a child assisted in Huang Diyuan in his original research work, fortunately managed to find Diyuan's draft and, probably with as least as much zeal as his predecessors, worked to re-edit a new genealogy in 1963.

The Ancestors of Yin Yu Tang

Huang Zhenduo's home, built by his father and still inhabited by his son, a daughter-in-law, and a grandson, is just down the path and around the corner from their Huang relatives in Yin Yu Tang. The Huang household of Yin Yu Tang has often been called by local villagers *Qi Fang*, "the Seventh Room, or the Seventh Branch." A *fang* (branch or room) is a family line that distinguishes itself by separate physical living quarters from its parental line. The patriarch who began Qi Fang would have been the seventh son of a family who established his own home. The occupants of Yin Yu Tang often note that the Fifth Branch lived just to the east of Yin Yu Tang, and the Sixth Branch lived directly behind. The houses of these brothers literally abutted one another.

Huang Zixian (c.1878–1929) of Qi Fang, like Huang Zhenduo and many of his common ancestors, attempted in the 1920s to trace their lineage's genealogy. He was not as successful as Huang Zhenduo. Huang Zixian left a series of pages with the names of the Huang Dun and Zuotian lineages, and lists of several people's birth days, death anniversaries, and burial places, but no completed, edited genealogy. However, it may have been Huang Zixian, the eldest son of his generation, who, in his determination to pay homage to his family's history, created the Yin Yu Tang Death Anniversary plaque, which for many years hung in the Yin Yu Tang courtyard. The last entry in the handwriting of the first twenty entries is for Madame Cheng, Huang Zixian's first wife. The following entry, in a different handwriting, records the death of Huang Zixian himself.

The lack of a full genealogy after the twentieth generation for the Huang lineage is somewhat balanced by the presence of this plaque and the information it provides.

The plaque, written in black ink on a white board, begins with the twenty-eighth generation. Since the ancestors referred to here are specifically delineated as the "Yin Yu Tang Ancestors," it is presumed that all these people resided in Yin Yu Tang. The translation of the plaque is on the following pages.

Like the genealogies, the plaque offers innumerable tidbits of information and cultural customs. While the genealogies in book form often record the births and occasionally the marriages of daughters, the plaque does not record the deaths (or births) of any daughters. Even on this intimate family level, girls were not embraced by the family's history. Young, unmarried daughters of Huang Zizhi definitely died before he did, yet their names are not recorded. Nor, however, are two of Zizhi's sons who died before they married. The only ancestors who qualified to have their names on the list were those who themselves produced heirs, and therefore had descendants to worship them and be concerned about the

Fig. 52 **Huang Yangxian as depicted in a painting by his son Huang Zizhi. Huang Zizhi was just two years old when his father died and must have painted this likeness either from a photograph or from a decription given by his mother.**

anniversaries of their deaths. The absence of these heirless family members on the plaque underscores the continuous determination among most individuals in China to have sons. Those without sons literally vanish from written history.

The plaque does not mention the years of the births or deaths of the ancestors. What is most important is the month and day, on the lunar calendar, of death, so that it can be respectfully observed, by sacrifices and by not holding weddings or other festivals. Cyclical years of important birth anniversaries, such as the deceased's sixtieth birthday, are additionally noted for some individuals so that they can be properly celebrated.

A noticeably absent individual from the plaque is an heir of Huang Huanwen of the thirty-second generation. Huang Huanwen was the eldest son of Huang Kentang. There is no available information about these individuals except what is presented on this plaque. Huang Huanwen's birth year was approximately 1851, the year before the army of the Taiping Heavenly Kingdom entered Xiuning. He and his wife most likely lived for at least sixty years, as the notation regarding the seventieth anniversary of his birth was a reminder for descendants to observe the date. Being the eldest son, had he had heirs, they would have had priority in the living arrangements in Yin Yu Tang. The absence of their names on

Death Anniversaries of Yin Yu Tang Ancestors

The Ancestors of the 28th Generation	Master Zanyu [his wives:]	the nineteenth day of the ninth month
	Mother Madame Zhu	the ninth day of the fourth month
	Mother Madame Ding	the sixteenth day of the tenth month
	Mother Madame Jin	the fourth day of the first month
The Ancestors of the 29th Generation	Master Runqing [his wives:]	the third day of the sixth month
	Mother Madame Cheng	the third day of the second month
	Mother Madame Li	the thirtieth day of the third month
The Ancestors of the 30th Generation	Master Weichuan	the twenty-eighth day of the eighth month
	[his wife:] Mother Madame Wu	the first day of the tenth month
	Second Uncle Ancestor Master Peizhi [his wives:]	the twenty-first day of the fourth month
	Mother Madame Zhu	the sixth day of the sixth month
	Mother Madame Cheng	the thirtieth day of the eleventh month
	Third Uncle Ancestor Master Dongmei	the seventh day of the seventh month
The Ancestors of the 31st Generation	Master Kentang The centenary anniversary of his birthday: [his wife:]	the twenty-seventh day of the eleventh month the fifteenth day of the first month of the *dingmao* year [1927]
	Mother Madame Cheng The centenary anniversary of her birthday:	the nineteenth day of the ninth month the nineteenth day of the first month of the *yichou* year [1925]
The Ancestors of the 32nd Generation	Uncle Master Huanwen His seventieth birthday: [his wife:]	the first day of the eleventh month the tenth day of the first month of the *xinyou* year [1921]
	Mother Madame Cheng Her seventieth birthday:	the twentieth day of the third month the fifth day of the first month of the *yichou* year [1925]
	Direct Ancestor Master Yangxian His seventieth birthday: [his wife:]	the thirtieth day of the fourth month the seventeenth day of the sixth month of the *dingmao* year [1927]
	Mother Madame Cheng Her seventieth birthday:	the tenth day of the fifth month the fourteenth day of the third month of the *wuchen* year [1928]
The First Wife of the 33rd Generation	Miss Cheng Her fortieth birthday:	the twenty-third day of the tenth month the third day of the fifth month of the *gengshen* year [1920]
The Ancestors of the 33rd Generation	Direct Ancestor Master Huang Zixian	the thirteenth day of the seventh month
	Uncle Master Huang Zizhi He was buried at Jiulong Shan together with Zhenying[17]	the sixteenth day of the second month
The Ancestors of the 34th Generation	Direct Ancestor Master Nian	the nineteenth day of the seventh month
The Additional Ancestor Mother of the 33rd Generation	Miss Wu	the thirteenth day of the second month

the plaque and in the memories of all who lived in the house indicates either that Huang Huanwen had no sons or that the sons themselves died childless, leaving the house to the sons of Yangxian, the younger son of Kentang.

The plaque was hung on a staircase wall facing into the courtyard where it could be observed and read on a daily basis for as long as anyone still alive can remember. Beyond the plaque, there were other annual reminders within Yin Yu Tang of the all-important ancestors.

Each year, as all who lived in the house vividly remember, on the twenty-fourth day of the twelfth month, the portraits of the ancestors were taken out of their wooden boxes and hung on the walls of the first-floor reception hall:

At New Year's, we would make offerings to the ancestors' portraits. From the oldest, first generation, the figures were arranged in a pyramid shape [on the painting]. . . . At the top row was one person, then two, then three. . . . They were all Huang family sons and grandsons. . . . Some wore red robes, some wore blue. Their hats looked like Qing dynasty hats. We hung them in the first floor reception hall. Before dinner, we would pray, burn incense, put out wine and food. On the evening of the thirtieth [of the twelfth month] it was always like this. . . . The ancestor portraits were not hung regularly, only during the

first month. Before we ate, chicken, fish, meat, and other things were laid out on the table, candles were lit, and incense was burned. First we would receive the ancestors back home and then we would send them off. We could eat only after they had been sent off.

—Huang Xiqi

During the Cultural Revolution, many families burned their ancestor portraits to prove their loyalty to the Communist Party. The Yin Yu Tang ancestor portraits seemed to have survived this period. However, after the Cultural Revolution, when new economic reforms were instituted there was an overly exuberant focus on wealth—and the burglary of valuables increased drastically. The Yin Yu Tang ancestor portraits were stolen from the house, leaving a vacuum in the family's home. Huang Zhenxin (b. 1914), who grew up in Yin Yu Tang, recalls the ancestors:

In the past, during every Lunar New Year, the twenty-fourth day of the twelfth month was set aside to worship ancestors. All the portraits of ancestors would be hung up. Everyone had to worship ancestors in an orderly way. The worshipping would continue on New Year's Eve and the Lantern Festival, ending only on the eighteenth day of the first lunar month. The main change about the house is that all ancestors' portraits, which we used to lock in a wardrobe, are gone.

Fig. 53 **This wooden plaque, titled "Death Anniversaries of the Yin Yu Tang Ancestors," listed the names and death dates of the matriarchs and patriarchs of the twenty-eighth through the thirty-fourth generation and their death anniversaries. "Alas, genealogy is the priority to which a descendant should keep highest in his agenda,"** said Yu Rui, in his preface to the Huang Family Genealogy, 1468.

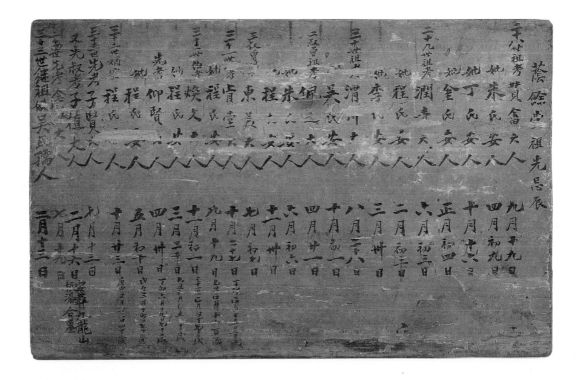

Fig. 54 A Huizhou ancestal portrait of an unidentified wife and husband. As is typical of ancestral portraits of couples, the woman is always seated on the left, and the husband on the right, as propriety demands that the hierarchally superior person sit on the conceptual east side of the painting, determined by assuming that the subjects are facing south.

Generation after Generation

During this century and a half, from the 1850s to the 1980s, the fortunes of the Huang family of Yin Yu Tang waxed and waned. Individuals' personal assets or tragic fates as well as the vicissitudes of politics and history had powerful impacts on the lives of the inhabitants of Yin Yu Tang. Despite the absence of the ancestors' images, the living family members, with the assistance of photographs and documents, are able to recount full descriptions and stories of generations of Yin Yu Tang residents over the past one hundred and fifty years. In the spirit of lineage genealogies, of recording lives for future generations to further understand the place and family they call home, and as well to understand how both the passage of history and the winds of fortune have affected individual lives in one small town, the following segments provide biographies of the recent Huang family generations who occupied Yin Yu Tang—from the thirty-second generation to the thirty-fifth generation.

The 32nd Generation

The first generation covered here came of age during one of the most tumultuous periods in the history of Xiuning County.

Huang Yangxian and Madame Cheng: Eight Pounds and Eight Pounds' Wife

By 1858, when a child was born to the not insubstantial Cheng family, descendants of a successful candidate in the provincial exams of the town of Fanggan (near Huang Cun in the county of Xiuning) the fierce troops of the Taiping Heavenly Kingdom had already invaded and occupied the county for over two years.

A local magistrate in Anhui had written a description of the arrival of the Taipings that was soon translated into English and published by a British commander. His account reflects the total devastation that was said to have been wreaked by the rebels and that reportedly led to the deaths of more than thirty million people across the country:

On the appearance of the Kwang-tung outlaws (Taepings) in the third year of Hien-Fung (1853) the local vagabonds dwelling on the common boundary of Honan and Ngan-hwui [Anhui] rose in swarms. . . . They have slain the authorities and harassed the people, trampling them under foot at their good pleasure. From Ngan-hwui [Anhui], westward, into Honan, throughout a region measuring some three hundred li in length, and one thousand li in circumference, the villages are in ruins, and dead bodies are lying in all directions.[18]

Fig. 55 & 56 **For much of Chinese history, the deeds of the Taiping Heavenly Kingdom were condemned. But, because it was considered a peasant uprising and many of the ideals—such as equality between men and women, and communal life—were similar to those raised by Mao, the Communist government was far more sympathetic in their judgment of these rebels. The images from this 1956 children's book (*Taiping Tianguo Shihua*, the illustrated history of the Taiping Heavenly Kingdom, edited by Luo Ergang, and published by Jiangsu Renmin Chubanshe, Nanjing) on the Taiping Rebellion depicts "struggles with members of the landlord class" and the burning of Nanjing, the "Heavenly Capital" as it was called by the Taipings when they occupied it, as it was being retaken by Qing imperial troops.**

Fig. 57 **A nineteenth-century photograph of a wedding procession.**

The local Xiuning County gazetteer recounting local history, also reported on the events:

In the fifth year of the Xianfeng reign Period [1856] on the twenty-third day of the third month, the Taiping Army entered Xiuning County. They engaged in battle with the Qing Imperial Army; casualties on both sides were heavy. In total, the Taiping occupied Xiuning County for over nine months, but they were not completely defeated here for six years, until the fourth month of the eleventh year of the Xianfeng reign Period [1862].[19]

Despite the war whirling about, Xiuning's economy and society was experiencing some encouraging moments. In 1851 local county fine green tea began to be exported, under the name of Green Tun, to Europe and America.[20] While the landscape and lives were being devastated by the occupation of the Taiping Heavenly Kingdom and the whole country's economy was certainly drained by the recent Opium War, contacts between Xiuning and the outside world continued to develop. In the thirteenth year of the Tongzhi emperor's reign (1875) a native Xiuning child, Wu Jingrong, at age eleven, was selected to study abroad in America.[21] He was one of 172 students sent from China to study in the United States between 1872 and 1875.[22] And in 1887 French missionaries established a Catholic mission in the county seat. But opportunities to study abroad would not have been available to the young Cheng girl, and the presence of the Frenchmen may have barely brushed her daily life.

Though there are no records or memories of her childhood among her living descendants—even her given name and premarital nickname are lost to history, a common fate for women—we can speculate that the first child of the Cheng family was trained, as most other girls of her generation, to sew and embroider, grow vegetables, and experience the pain, trauma, and possible pride of having her small feet bound in bandages to keep them at a minute size. Small feet and good embroidery skills, in addition to a proper family background, would improve the chances for a girl's marriage into a good family.

Like almost all girls of the era, the Cheng girl most likely had never seen the man who would become her husband. Nor is it likely that she would have visited Huang Cun or Yin Yu Tang, the home in which she would live for the next four decades.

Fellow women villagers have described a bride's exhausting ride in the sedan chair on the day of her marriage, carried aloft by four men, who often shook and swayed the their heavy load as they meandered along the hills and paths to the bride's new home, a red head cloth and covered windows obstructing her vision of the outside world and the man who would become her companion for life.

Perhaps, though, the young Cheng girl had heard about Yin Yu Tang and the Huang family. Men in the Yin Yu Tang Huang family had been marrying women surnamed Cheng for at least four generations. The brother, father, grand-uncle, and great-grandfather of the man she would marry—the twenty-nineth, thirtieth, thirty-first, and thirty-second generations of the Huang family—had all married women surnamed Cheng. Whether all the young ladies came from Fanggan, or from the same family as this Cheng girl, is unknown. The propensity for Cheng women in the Huang family of Huang Cun is apparent, and not only in these later generations. During the first through the twentieth generations of the Huang family, sixty women surnamed Cheng married into the Huang family of Huang Cun, representing more than 15 percent of the wives of Huang men. (Some of these men, of course, had multiple wives.) Though the Yin Yu Tang genealogy, more focused on the male heirs, makes note of only nine Huang daughters, three of those married Cheng men.[23] The constant intermarrying with the Chengs may have been a maneuver to solidify ties with the clan in which the ancestor Keyuan was born and from whom he was adopted by the Huangs. Despite her predecessors, this Cheng girl most probably, like the majority of brides, felt like a complete stranger when she arrived for the first time at Yin Yu Tang and the cloth covering was removed from her face to reveal her new home and husband.

Her official welcome into the Huang clan at Huang Cun would have occurred in Jin Shi Di, as would her eventual departure. By the nineteenth century, Huang lineage members were using the grand structure for their weddings and funerals.

Though she retained her father's family name, as all Chinese women did, the young bride, following the age-old traditions, literally married into her husband's family. Her loyalty, from then on, was to be entirely to the Huangs. Her own parents, and brothers and sisters, were no longer considered her jia (her family) or her home. In time, the Huangs would indeed pay deep honor to her, but on her wedding day, as a still-unworldly young girl, unaware of the direction her life within the family would follow, she certainly would have been intimidated by her new surroundings and responsibilities.

Cooking, washing, feeding, growing vegetables, carrying water from the well, sewing, tending to the whims of her in-laws, and worshipping the ancestors of her husband, these were all the duties of a young bride:

In the old days, mothers-in-law were tough. It was difficult to be a daughter-in-law. You had to wait on the entire family. It was very hard. You had to do everything right. . . . I cried. The bride was judged. Making shoes, making clothes, farming, cooking, if you didn't know how to do any one of those tasks, people looked down on you. It was hard to be a daughter-in-law in those days. We had to obey all kinds of rules. After you put a meal on the table, if your mother-in-law didn't eat, you wouldn't dare eat.

—Huang Cui'e, born 1904

Because the family genealogies only often offer the date of a death, and not always the year of death, it is no longer apparent who the occupants of Yin Yu Tang were when the Cheng girl first arrived. Most likely, her new husband's elder brother, Huang Huanwen, was still alive and his wife, three years the new bride's senior and also surnamed Cheng, was living in the house. Though the genealogy plaque lists no heirs for Huang Huanwen and his wife, the couple probably had at least two daughters[24] who, having married into other families, would not have been included on a list of Huang family ancestors, and a son, who perhaps died before marrying.[25] The in-laws of the new bride, who would have been in their late forties, may also have been still alive and living in the house. Huang Huanwen, like his younger brother, the Cheng girl's new husband, was probably a traveling businessman, and the two daughters-in-law would have been left alone in Huang Cun to take care of their older in-laws. Did their mother-in-law have more sympathy than the stereotypical Chinese mother-in-law, since they all shared the surname Cheng? As the newest arrival into the household, the youngest Cheng girl would have had to carry the heaviest burden.

And who was the primary man—when he was home—that the young Cheng girl would be serving morning, midday, and evening meals; preparing water for his baths; washing and mending clothes; and sharing a bed? Huang Yangxian, also known as Huang Yigu, was born in 1857, weighing a hefty eight *jin* (equivalent to 8.82 pounds). For that initial and notable event in his life, he was nicknamed Bajin, "Eight Pounds." Though just a year older than his bride, by the time they married, Eight Pounds was likely to have been far worldlier than she. As was the custom in Huizhou, he had probably left home at the age of thirteen or fourteen to work at a business in a distant city. A traveling merchant, he was following in the footsteps of his family elders and his fellow countymen.

Eight Pounds' Wife, Ba Jin Sao, as she came to be known, while still in her early twenties, gave birth first to a girl and then to two sons. A son was a celebrated arrival in a Chinese family. The male offspring ensured the continuation of the family line, a financial support for the elders in the family, and, just as important, an heir to worship the ancestors. Two sons, one following the other, was an even greater cause for joy in a household. Certainly Huang Yangxin would have been pleased. As for his wife, Madame Cheng, the birth of the boys would have been great relief, as a woman was never fully accepted into a family until she produced a son.

The celebrating had probably just begun to calm down and Madame Cheng was settling into the routine of carrying for a toddler and two young children, when disaster fell on the family. It was 1885, just two years after the birth of the second son, Huang Zizhi. The imperial Qing government in Beijing was encountering continued conflicts with European and Asian nations. The Japanese had occupied the Ryukyu Islands (also known as Okinawa) in 1874. In 1885 the French were attacking and taking control of the Penghu Islands off Taiwan, and two years later the Portuguese had completed their take over of Macao. At the same time there was an initial, but not yet strong, thrust for industrialization. Some of the Chinese students who had gone to the United States to study were beginning to return home. Among them were four Chinese women trained to be doctors. Mining companies, steamship companies, a telegraph company, and a railway were trying—though not always successfully—to make headway in China. A cotton mill, called the Foreign Cloth Factory, was about to be launched by the statesman Li Hongzhang in Shanghai.[26] Shanghai, already with French and international concessions well established, was on its way to becoming a major metropolis. And a British entrepreneur, with the assistance of a Shanghai artist, Wu Youru, had begun China's first lithographic printed serial pictorial, *Dianshizhai*. Just then, as China was on the verge of radical change, Eight Pounds of Huang Cun, away from home, perhaps even on his way to that developing boomtown of Shanghai, was killed as he was traveling toward Hangzhou on business:

My grandfather was a merchant. When he was in his thirties, he was traveling from Hangzhou to Tunxi [a small city then located in Xiuning County,] and was robbed by bandits. We were not born yet at the time, and we heard from our mom that bandits robbed him and pushed him into a river. He drowned.

—Huang Zhenxin

My grandfather was taking a boat to go from Hangzhou to Tunxi. . . . He was a merchant. He would work for three years and then come home and rest. He was on his way home. . . . When he got to a place called Seven-Mile Long, pirates killed him by pushing him into a river. . . . All the money he had earned for three years was robbed from him. . . .

—Huang Xianying

The death of Huang Yangxian caused great (and over the years, increasing) hardship for the Yin Yu Tang household. Madame Cheng had three small children to raise, possibly aging in-laws to care for, and no income. Records do not document when her husband's brother passed away, but family and village tales testify to a severe financial struggle for those living in Yin Yu Tang.

The twenty-eight-year-old illiterate widow scrambled to secure funds for the household. Though the family probably owned some land that they rented out to tenants, the profits may have been paid only in rice, or have been minimal. To survive, Madame Cheng took in sewing jobs from neighbors, making shoes and clothes, in order to feed, clothe, and educate her precious sons. She rented rooms in the large house to villagers who could not afford to build their own houses and who, after marrying and having children of their own, could no longer live in their parents' small quarters. Eight Pounds' Wife also borrowed from other members of the extended Huang clan and from her own parents' family.

My grandmother had a hard life, too. She did needle work, such as making shoes for other families. There was no source of money for the family. It was really a hard time.

—Huang Xianying

Ultimately, the financial struggles took the Yin Yu Tang household deeply into debt. Four rooms of the house had to be given up to the wealthier sixth branch of the Huang lineage, whose house was adjacent to Yin Yu Tang. The seventh branch, who occupied Yin Yu Tang, were descendants of the seventh son of an unknown patriarch from an unknown time period prior to the nineteenth century. The sixth branch would have been descendants of the sixth son. The four rooms of Yin Yu Tang, on the southeastern corner of the house, abutted the sixth branch's own large home. The date of this transfer is unknown and, like many facts, is not in the memory of any living persons, suggesting that it happened in the last years of the nineteenth century, while Madame Cheng's children were still young. Undoubtedly, the transfer of the property was painful for the widow who had been charged with the maintenance of the seventh branch, but she carried on:

Eight Pounds' Wife was the most hard up. She had to sell [part of] her house. Her husband died. The seventh branch really suffered. All her life, in marriage, too. Her husband died right after she had two sons. She was very capable. She and her sons grew coarse grains for themselves. She managed to get both of her two sons wives. She came from a poor family. Her parents were peasants, too. This woman was so good, so filial to elders, and took good care of her children. Her sons . . . were good boys. They ate little and worked hard. They had a big house, leased rooms to people who didn't have enough space in their own houses. They were kind to people. Nobody in their family, old or young, ever did anything bad.

—Huang Cui'e

When her struggles to make ends meet failed to provide enough earnings to raise her family, Madame Cheng turned, somewhat ashamedly, to the family into which she had been born. The Cheng family had had a successful candidate in a provincial examination, and therefore had some money and power:

As you know, after the death of my grandfather, life became harder and my grandmother felt like she had lost face. I never met her, but I heard from my mother that her life was very difficult, very difficult. At New Year's she wouldn't have enough money to celebrate. She would go to her younger brother's house to borrow money. Because we were poor, other people looked down on us. My mother [sic] wouldn't go into her brother's house. She would stand at the edge of the village and if she saw a villager, she would ask them to bring a verbal message to her brother to say so-and-so had come, and ask him to come out. My grandmother's younger brother would know and he would send some money out to give her for New Year's. This is what I heard from my mother.

—Huang Zhenxin

Though many details of the ebb and flow of Madame Cheng's life are long gone, letters and documents reveal her perseverance and the successful result of that perseverance: the success of her children. She managed from day to day, caring for her children and the house, possibly even working the land herself, until the boys were old enough to set off on their own. One of her sons saved letters she had written him, once he had left home to work, like his forbearers, as a merchant in a distant town. The letters—scribed by the local schoolteacher, as she, like most women of her stature, was illiterate—offer hints at how she and her children managed in the early years of the century.

With the aid of relatives, both sons eventually located jobs as clerks and accountants in shops and pawnshops. Huang Zixian, the elder boy, found a job in the large city of Hangkou, and a few years later Huang Zizhi was working in the smaller town of Raozhou, in Jiangxi Province, just a few days' journey south from Huang Cun. In the age-old tradition, they sent money home to care for their mother and the again growing household.

The letters written between the two brothers and between each of them and their mother reveal more than polite filial respect. The hardworking widow had inspired a unique degree of warmth, caring, and sincere filial devotion:

Fig. 58 While Huang Zixian was away working in Hangkou, his mother, Madame Cheng, cared for her beloved little "Nian," as Huang Zixian' son, Huang Zhenzhi, was nicknamed. Here, the elderly woman is photographed with her younger son, Huang Zizhi, and her grandson, dressed completely in blue and white dye-resist clothes. The photograph was taken in the early 1910s.

Fig. 59 & 60 **Envelopes of letters sent between Madame Cheng and her sons, Huang Zizhi and Huang Zixian, (above) and between the two brothers (below).**

I have written to our mother that from now on she should take care of herself and not engage in any labor. More important, she should rid herself of all worries. Although our family has great worries, we two brothers may encounter good fortune in the future. All our debts should be cleared in three years or so. For a long time our mother has deeply worried about our [financial] difficulties. She does not want to hire people even for work that requires heavy labor such as carrying water and vegetable gardening. Instead, she has managed to do them herself, but she has exhausted both her body and soul. . . . Thus, I asked Miss Shuang, our cousin, to come to our home to assist her.

—Letter from Huang Zixian to Huang Zizhi, circa 1910

Last winter, I asked Mr. Youjin to mail twenty dollars home, but I have not yet received a reply so far. Yesterday I mailed another letter to check. I am afraid that if the money was not received, there will be great difficulties at home in celebrating the New Year. When I think of that, I burn with worries.

—Letter from Huang Zixian to Huang Zizhi, circa 1910

By about 1907, Madame Cheng had decided it was time for her eldest son, Huang Zixian, who was almost thirty, to marry. The widow borrowed a great amount of money for the wedding and its elaborate preparations, putting the family in debt, gambling that the marriage would produce a subsequent generation to care for the elders and ancestors. The financial burden of the wedding celebrations and then the additional person in the household became a source of great anxiety for the single matriarch, but she must also have been relieved to have a younger woman in the household to assist her.

Auspiciously, the financial risk seemed to pay off. The new bride, also surnamed Cheng, soon gave birth to a son, and cele-

brations were warranted. They called the boy Huang Nian. The young child brought cheer into the long disquieted household, and the widowed grandmother became passionately attached to her first grandchild.

Tragically, however, like the birth of his uncle, the child's joyously welcomed arrival was only to be followed by a sudden death. Huang Zixian's young bride died and left the infant Nian to be cared for by his aging and increasingly ill grandmother. Though only in her fifties, the grueling aspects of her life were taking their toll on Madame Cheng. The boy's father noted his concern regarding the heavy onus on his mother of caring for the young and mischievous child in letter to his brother:

Since my wife is gone, the infant is left. He turns out to be a burden for our mother to care for. . . . Mother tells me in her letter that my son is very annoying. I am very angry with him. As soon as Miss Shuang comes back to our home, please tell her to sleep with my son. When he wants to pee at night, she could help him instead of our mother. Otherwise, our mother will be getting up, while only wearing her underwear, and that will make her cough even worse.

—Letter from Huang Zixian to Huang Zizhi, circa 1910

Despite her diminishing health and weighted down by increasing responsibilities, Madame Cheng persevered and lived to see her younger son's marriage. With the assistance of her sons, she scraped together money, made arrangements for a suitable wife, and oversaw the complex marriage process again.

The marriage of Huang Zizhi to the young Hong Zhaodi would surely have been a relief for the aging widow. Having seriously taken on the responsibilities of being the Huang matriarch, and loyalty to the Huang family, the marriage meant another opportunity for the seventh branch to continue their line. Moreover, the marriage would mean the company of another young lady and an additional hand in the house to help with the niggling grandson.

Among the letters between the sons and their mother, the discussions focus primarily on family events, finances, health, and work:

Mother's spirit is declining day by day and she is suffering from various diseases. This is because our incomes cannot meet our expenditures and she worries about that day and night. Since I got married, she has been in a worrisome mood, especially when my income was very low in the beginning and there were many members of our household. The expenditures keep increasing and the debt keep rising. Our mother cannot bear such worries. She was injured in the floods two years ago and has not yet fully recovered. . . . I heard that after taking medicines prescribed by Dr. Cheng Zemin, she was getting better. I hope that she continues to take the medicine and become

healthier. . . . How is our uncle? I heard that he failed to find a job in Shanghai. In recent years, his aunt died and the funeral expenses put him in debt. He will be forty years old next year, but he has not yet had a son.

—Letter from Huang Zixian to Huang Zizhi, circa 1910

Meanwhile, as Huang Zizhi was preparing for his wedding and worrying about his mother's health, a revolution was fermenting in China's larger cities. In 1911 the imperial rule was overthrown and a republic established. The only evidence among the letters of such radical changes are the post office cancellation marks. Before the inauguration of the Chinese Republic on January 1, 1912, the traditional Chinese cyclical calendar was the primary (both publicly and privately) manner used to record dates. With the establishment of the republic, the Gregorian calendar was adopted. The pre-1912 letters are all cancelled with postmarks comprising one of the sixty pair of characters used cyclically to denote a year. After 1912 the cancellations specify the years with, for instance, "first year" to indicate the first year of the republic, or the "second year" to indicate the second year of the republic.

Despite the lack of remarks among Huang family members on the structure of the government, some changes were visible around them. Early globalization was evident when manufacturers from Xiuning sent products all the way across the sea for the 1915 Panama-Pacific International Exposition. Huang Cui'e, now age ninety-nine, was born and raised in Huang Cun, and began school just before the change in national leadership. She distinctly remembers the world shifting around her. Girls were cutting their hair short, men and boys were cutting off the queues that the Manchu Qing government had insisted be worn by all Han Chinese men, and the flag flying over Huang Cun's primary school had a new design:

We went to school when we were eight years old. . . . In my first year [1911], there was a royal flag with a dragon on it. In the second half of the year, they changed it to a five-colored flag with red, yellow, blue, white, and black [stripes].[27] . . . Boys cut off their queues. My brother cut off his queue. My mother scolded him, but he insisted on cutting it off.

—Huang Cui'e, born 1904, speaking in 1999

Letters between the Huang brothers at this period consistently reveal fretting anxiety about their mother's health, her cough, her small feet, and her injury during a flood. The photographs of Madame Cheng indeed seem to depict what appears to be an aged woman. In fact, she was only in her fifties. In 1915 her illnesses and fragility defeated her.

Fig. 61 The unusual photographing of an altar was an act of tribute at the funeral of the much-loved and much-respected Madame Cheng. For the funeral, held in the rear section of Jin Shi Di, reserved for funerals of the Huang family, many friends and relatives presented calligraphic expressions of their grieving and their reverence for the hardworking widow and mother. The four-character banner at the top was tendered by the national government in honor of her years of chastity and devotion to her husband's family line. On either side of the central altar table are paper-and-bamboo figures, servants, who will be burned and serve her soul in the underworld.

The Funeral

Lonely sons in sorrow
Huang Zude[28]
Huang Zupei[29]
Kowtow with bloody tears.

The formal death notice for Madame Cheng, written in ritual fashion, is melodramatic, and perhaps formulaic, but may have truly expressed the emotional distress felt by those she left behind.

I was there when she died. Her sons couldn't stop crying. Her daughters-in-law were pretty filial, too. I was at school then. A lot of people in the village cried at her funeral. People sympathized with her, they said life wasn't easy on her.

—Huang Cui'e

When she died, they put her coffin in Jin Shi Di. You were allowed to put your casket there if your last name was Huang. . . . When someone died, two people would carry the corpse out, into the Hall, and then lay it into the coffin. It was the same with every family. The coffins were made ahead of time and were stored in the Hall. There are two rooms specifically for the coffins in the back. I was really scared. . . .

For the funeral, rich people hire a band. Poor people carry out the coffin, and that was it. Some people burned pumpkins, made sedan chairs or a house for use in the spirit world, and also paper figures.

—Huang Cui'e

A photograph of her funeral altar in Jin Shi Di, the grand shrine of Huang Cun, demonstrates the extreme reverence for this woman among family and fellow villagers.

The usual paper servants, one man and one woman, to care for Madame Cheng's soul in the underworld can be seen clearly on the altar table in the photograph. They would have been burned at her burial. Between them on the altar table are the five objects of garniture that typically grace any altar table: an incense burner at the center, two candlesticks, and two vases. What most distinguishes this funeral from most women's are the numerous laudatory calligraphies surrounding the altar table. Among them are many lines praising the grand matriarch:

Having endured the hardship of keeping chaste for over thirty years, [she was] fortunate to have brought up two children who, in turn, nurtured their mother after growing up [themselves.]

The root of the sugar cane is still sweet [even after the cane has been cut].

Serving the family, caring for the children, she tasted all kinds of hardships.

The graceful model will be long lasting and followed by fellow villagers.

We sadly exalt the chastity and filial piety of Grandmother Cheng, the senior lady of the Huang Clan, who will be remembered for a thousand years.

The dew on the leaf of a wild garlic pains [us.]

Most extraordinary among the calligraphies is the uppermost horizontal four-character scroll stating that "chastity and filial piety will spread like a beautiful fragrance." The scroll is signed with the following most noteworthy inscription:

Authorized by Mr. Ni, sent to Anhui [by the Central Government], who, according to the regulations of the Ministry, after reporting to the President of the Republic, confers this certificate to the wife of Huang Yigu, surnamed Cheng [illegible], to express the appreciation of her chastity and filial piety with this banner.

Respectfully raised on an auspicious day of the sixth month of the fourth year of the Republic of China.

The prominent government-issued statement refers to two prized virtues: *jie*, chastity, and *xiao*, filial piety. The veneration of such chastity reinforced the Confucian order and the all-important continuation of the family line. Women, marrying into a family, even if widowed, were urged to remain in that family, caring for the in-laws, worshipping the ancestors, and producing and raising heirs (even if it necessitated adoption), in order to carry on their husband's line of descent. At times, the devotion carried out by women went to extreme extents:

Her husband died before the wedding . . . [but] after the engagement. He died before she even saw him. They had a stone tablet made for him, so she married a stone tablet. She didn't remarry, just stayed a widow. Her husband's family was poor. She didn't go out and work. She stayed home and spent her days thinking of him. She wrote letters and burned them for him. She refused to see any men. If a man came into the house, she would walk away. She wanted to preserve her chastity.

—Huang Cui'e, recalling a woman in Huang Cun

From 1815, the nineteenth-century *Xiuning County Gazetteer*, like gazetteers produced in counties all over China, listed and memorialized exemplary women who suffered situations similar to that of Madame Cheng. Among the many from Huang Cun were:

Mrs. Jin, the Wife of Huang Honghong

Married to [Huang Honghong of] Huang Cun and widowed at the age of twenty-one. She kept her chastity since then. In the twenty-sixth year of the Emperor Qianlong (1761), people petitioned to grant her a reward banner. At that year, she was sixty-four years old.

Mrs. Cheng, the Wife of Huang Zhiqing

A native of Chakou, she was married to [Huang Zhiqing of] Huang Cun and was widowed at the age of eighteen. She kept her integrity for fifty-eight years until her death. In the twenty-seventh year of the Emperor Qianlong (1762), people petitioned to grant her a reward banner.

Mrs. Jin, the Wife of Huang Yaodou

A native of Wangxi, she was married to [Huang Yaodou of] Huang Cun and widowed at the age of twenty-two. She took care of her son(s) and kept her chastity for forty-nine years until her death. In the twenty-seventh year of the Emperor Qianlong (1762), people petitioned to grant her a reward banner.

Madame Cheng and others living in Yin Yu Tang would certainly have walked by the Huang Cun paifang, honoring a chaste widow, daily. Had she lived in an earlier time, this wife of Huang Yangxian, surnamed Cheng, might have earned a few lines in a gazetteer or even a stone archway. Instead, she received the banner from the Republican government and a photograph. Remarkably, almost ninety years after her death, her reputation and virtuous eminence have remained ingrained in the minds of her still-living descendants, none of whom ever met her but who continue to repeat her legend.

Fig. 62 **A traditionally shaped coffin.**

The Thirty-third Generation

My parents lived in the room right across from here. As the family was doing well at that time, they had a set of furniture made. The locals call the furniture "a roomful of redness." The furniture still looks very good now, more than sixty years later.

—Huang Binggen

Of the many personalities who inhabited Yin Yu Tang, one man's life best illustrates the breadth and struggles of a Huizhou merchant's life. Though Huizhou merchants appeared as common characters in Chinese fiction, typified by their peripatetic pursuit of financial deals, the documents left behind of one particularly meticulous man and the memories held of him by those still living offer an opportunity to more fully examine the day-to-day life, the struggles, and the complex interfamily relationships of a specific individual and his kin. Huang Zizhi was not a hero or a villain, not a saint or a fiend. From the perspective of almost seventy years after his death, his most significant attribute was his meticulousness and his interest in saving ephemera. He retained numerous letters written to him, as well as recording the daily expenditures in his household. From these documents and the memories of his surviving descendants, we have been able to piece together an intriguing picture of a life within a family.

The two sons raised by Madame Cheng represent the thirty-third generation of the Yin Yu Tang Huang family. Following a Chinese naming tradition, the brothers' given names shared a prefix. The prefixes of a lineage were a set sequence to be followed by every member of the community. The custom of all members of a generation sharing a prefix, or a suffix, to their given names allows members of a lineage to immediately know whether another member is of an older or younger generation and therefore who has seniority. As one Huang family member explains today:

When relatives and friends met, they would call each other according to their given names, which reflected to which generation they belonged. Children were taught this practice in their early childhood.

—Huang Qiuhua

Reviewing the YYT Genealogy, the custom is readily apparent. The members of the eleventh generation all had the prefix *Tian*, as in:

Tianwei	The eldest son of Maozong
Tianyi	The second son of Maozong
Tian'an	The third son of Maozong
Tianjuan	The fourth son of Maozong

In the thirteenth generation, the prefix *Xi* was employed for most sons:

Xizhou	The eldest son of Yi
Xiyu	The eldest son of Zhao
Xiren	The third son of Lian
Xili	The fifth son of Lian
Xihe	The eldest son of Qi
Xiluo	The second son of Qi
Xiqing	The sixth son of Lian
Xiwang	The second son of Yi
Xikai	The second son of Ju

The system was based on the importance of order and respect for hierarchy in a family and in society, as such order and respect could ensure harmony. The system continues to be used in many villages today and was used at least through the mid-twentieth century in Huang Cun. Huang Zhenxin of the thirty-fourth generation, who lived in Yin Yu Tang during the twentieth century, shared the prefix *zhen* in his name with a distant relative of the same generation, Huang Zhenduo.

Thus the two sons of Huang Yangxian were named Huang Zixian and Huang Zizhi—sharing the syllable *Zi*. The two, as they grew into men, both followed the traditional Huizhou merchant route through life, though each pursued his own personal ways and manners. Huang Zixian, the older of the two, is remembered by family members as being chubby, kind, and generous. Huang Zizhi is recalled as being thin, of ill health, serious, and excessively strict with his children.

Both boys grew up in the grand structure of Yin Yu Tang and in the temporary circumstances of their family's poverty, having lost their father at a young age.

With no income, their mother had to scrape for funds to care for her young sons and her mother-in-law. Her earnings from sewing and embroidering for neighbors, proceeds from land rentals, and loans from relatives kept them going. The anxiety over money undoubtedly had an impact on the two boys in their later lives. The situation did, however, spur them on to find good sources of income, in the family tradition of trade.

Huang Zixian

Though the date at which Huang Zixian first left home is unknown, his destination and early location of employment is clear. By 1910 Huang Zixian was working, like many of his fellow Xiuning merchants, in the large river port city of Hankou.

Fig. 63 (left) **Huang Zixian, 1910s.**

Fig. 64 (right) **Postcard of Hankou depicting a street in the Chinese section of town.**

Fig. 65 (below) **A wooden Standard Oil Eagle candle box found in Yin Yu Tang at dismantling.**

A STREET IN THE CHINESE CITY, HANKOW.

Hankou, located on the Yangzi River, approximately 435 miles (700 km) inland—or 596.5 miles (960 km) on the river—from Shanghai, by the mid-nineteenth century had become a primary center for trade, both domestic and international. The dominating trading countries of the world—Britain, France, Germany, Russia, and Japan—all had major concessions in the city and by the 1920s were finding the spot a most desirable one from which to conduct trade. Economic development attracted more businesses to the city.

Huang Zixian's letters from Hankou to his younger brother, Huang Zizhi, reveal that his time in Hankou was not a personal financial success. He worries about having enough money to send to his mother for the New Year's festivities and confesses that he cannot contribute to his younger brother's wedding. He returns home only when, after his first wife dies, he needs to marry a second wife to help care for his infant son. The impetus to ensure the continuity of the family line surpassed all financial obstacles.

Several years later, still looking for a more promising enterprise, Zixian returned to the Huizhou area when a new business opportunity became available. In the 1920s he became a manager in a kerosene shop in Tunxi, a job perhaps obtained through his second wife's brother, who also worked there. Though living and working just a day's walk from home, he, like his fellow Huizhou merchants, rarely visited his home in Huang Cun. However, he did provide for his wife, growing son, and two daughters by his second wife, and only fond memories of him have been passed down:

My mom told me that my grandfather and Binggen's grandfather were very nice people. They were virtuous merchants. They even set free eels that they had purchased. Both my grandfather and his [Binggen's] were very well educated and cultured. Their calligraphy was just superb. We can't write like that now. Their regular script in small characters is really beautiful! My grandfather had learned some medicine as well. He could diagnose minor illnesses. For example,

when my mom's feet were chapped, he made some ointment to apply on the chapped area. And it soon recovered. I still keep a little ointment of that kind. When villagers grew boils, he would make plasters and send them to people for free. From the stories told by my mom, and from his portrait, I have a very deep impression of him. . . . He befriended the poor peasants in the village. That's why all these much-told tales have passed on to our generation. Though we have never met our grandfathers, the memories seem very fresh.

—Huang Xiqi

Huang Zixian's work at the kerosene business brought not only kerosene to light Yin Yu Tang—making it the brightest house in the village—but also funds to repair the family graves and the deteriorating Yin Yu Tang home. Tin gutters replaced the old tile ones, and he was generous enough to have his son's bridal room papered with imported wallpaper from Europe:

When evenings came, many neighbors would come to our house to have fun. Though our house was not that rich, we had kerosene lamps. At that time, every family used oil lamps, and homes were very dim. So everyone came to our house because we used kerosene lamps. . . . They played mahjong. It was very lively.

—Huang Zhenxin

My grandfather had a kerosene shop in Tunxi. Gradually, the family had become more prosperous. It was at that time that my grandfather had the house repaired. For example, he changed the gutters from tiles to tin. . . . He did many other good deeds as well, such as having the ancestral graves repaired.

—Huang Xiqi

When Huang Zixian died of a sudden stroke in 1929 at the age of fifty-two, the family in Yin Yu Tang was distraught. Though he was rarely at home, his spirit as the reigning patriarch of the thirty-third generation had made an emotional impact on the household:

He died of high blood pressure one noon. The whole family was heart-broken when a messenger from the shop broke the news. He died so suddenly, while everyone in the family, young and old, still depended on him for a living. It was very sad.

—Huang Zhenxin

Though their lives were intertwined from birth to death, and they both followed in the path of their ancestors' occupations, the course of Huang Zixian's younger brother's life with his own health problems and, more important, his distinct temperament, left behind a very dissimilar trail.

Fig. 66 **Huang Zizhi**, 1920s.

Huang Zizhi

Huang Zizhi was born at twelve noon on the fourteenth day of the tenth month in the ninth year of the Guangxu emperor's reign (1875–1908),[30] that is, in 1883. Of the thirty-third generation of Huang family, he was the second son of Huang Yangxian (b. 1857) and his wife, who was surnamed Cheng (1858–1915), of Fanggan Village.

How far Zizhi went in his education and how he engaged himself in the years immediately following his schooling is not clear from either family records or his childrens' memories. We do know that he was literate and skilled in writing and accounting. He would have been schooled as a child, either by a tutor or, more likely, in the local Huang Cun Clan school.[31] According to villagers, classes were held only for children of Huang families inside an old temple located at the edge of the village. Schooling in the years before the turn of the century would have consisted of studying traditional Confucian texts. One of the basic primers for learning characters was the *Qian Zi Wen* (the Thousand Character Essay), a volume of which was found among papers in the house.

Most boys in Huizhou of merchant families, having gained a basic knowledge of writing and the Confucian classics, would have left their home villages by age fourteen, to apprentice as merchants in larger towns. No records or documents provide information regarding Huang Zizhi's activities until he was twenty-four years old. Certainly, he was trying to make money to assist his mother in making ends meet at home. Was he laboring in the fields with the peasants of his village? Was he able to secure a job in a dye shop, as a

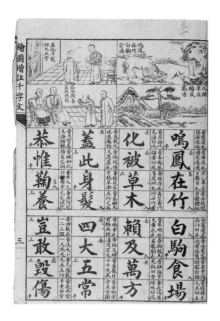

Fig. 67 (left) **This page is from the 1912 edition of a child's primer** *Hui Tu Zengzhu Qian Zi Wen* (**The Illustrated** *Qian Zi Wen* **with Supplementary Commentary), published by the Jin Zhang Shu Ju.** *Qian Zi Wen*, **Thousand Character Essay, an essay that first became popular in the Sui dynasty (581–618) was often copied for calligraphy practice because of the variety of characters it contains.**

Figs. 68 & 69 (right and below right) **A small porcelain teapot with overglaze design of bamboo and rocks, given as a present to Huang Zizhi by his cousin in 1902, when he was nineteen years old.**

younger relative once surmised? Perhaps he was working with his brother, or learning accounting. Though the details are not clear, his later career path demonstrates that he had certainly used those early years to prepare himself well for sophisticated clerical employment.

Huang Zizhi may not have been keenly aware of events in Beijing during those years. More than likely, he was primarily focused on the well-being of his own community and family and did not pay attention to the dramatic events occurring in the capital. Did news of the Boxer Rebellion of 1900, in which several hundred foreigners were killed, reach Yin Yu Tang? Such episodes had little impact on the daily life in remote Huang Cun. And the local people, many of whom still had sharp memories of the violence of Taiping Heavenly Kingdom's occupation, certainly would have preferred to turn their attention to their private affairs.

Few items or records offer any sense of Huang Zizhi's whereabouts during the first few years of the century. One object found in the house does offer a clue. it is a small, fine, white porcelain teapot with an ink overglaze painting of rocks and bamboo around the exterior. Porcelain was not inexpensive, and the personal painting made it even more out of the ordinary. An inscription reveals that the teapot was a special gift to Huang Zizhi in 1902:

Rocks have the nature of being unyielding and thus are my real friends. And bamboo which is empty inside [modest] is my teacher.

This teapot is given with respect to Mr. Zizhi, my elder brother-in-law [cousin] to appreciate and enjoy. —Written by Cheng Huan in the Fall of Renyi Year [1902].

Cheng Huan may have been a cousin related to Huang Zizhi on his mother's side of the family, as her surname was also Cheng. The occasion of and reason for the gift to the nineteen-year-old Huang Zizhi is unknown. However, the poem does give a sense of eruditeness and suggests that both the giver and the receiver had some degree of education.

In 1907 Huang Zizhi's efforts to assist his mother and brother in bringing funds into the household had landed him a job in Raozhou, a town in northern Jiangxi Province. An undated fragment of letter suggests that friends and relatives had been enlisted and great efforts expended to assist Huang Zizhi with the complex process of obtaining decent employment:

[I] met especially with Mr. Shouren and related all the details to him. Previously, I had entrusted him to go to Mr. Di, the senior gentleman, to reiterate the issue of your [employment]. [This time,] he said he had talked to Mr. Di. . . . Mr. Di had intended to hire you. At that time, hands were urgently needed at the pawnshop. Later, however, the vacancies were all filled. The previous opportunity was lost on account of me. Fortunately, the earlier discussion made by Mr. Shouren was highly appreciated by Mr. Di, and he asked me to write to you to the effect that you should wait a few months, until next year, and that he will keep you in mind. Since he had such a good intentions, I will beg Mr. Shouren to ask him again. Then you should mail a letter to Rao[zhou.] According to Mr. Di, both Zhixuan and Zongtai had spoken to him about you. Thus, he knows that you have excellent writing skills and a very honest character.[32]

Raozhou (also known as Shang Rao) is a town known historically for the natural springs, where the great eighth-century tea master Lu Yu wrote his famous *Scripture of Tea* and praised the quality of the waters as superb for tea making. By the late-nineteenth century, the main product of the region was another leaf, tobacco.

Raozhou was 99.4 miles (160 km) from Xiuning County as the crow flies over mountainous terrain. Most likely, Zizhi traveled there by boat following a longer, more circuitous but faster route. The journey from Jingdezhen, through which Zizhi may also have passed on his way to Raozhou, was described by Harry A. Franck in 1923:

The fare was one "Mex" dollar for a trip of about twenty-four hours without stop. . . . There were nearly a dozen Chinese passengers, naked to the waist, as is the all but universal and not unjustifiable male summer costume in this region, and the "berths" were smooth narrow planks covering the hold of the boat and neither quite wide nor quite long enough for a normal man. The means of transportation were rowing, sailing, wading, pushing, poling, whistling and shrieking for wind, and towing at the end of a rope along the difficult bank—except

that there was no sailing and mighty little rowing. . . . The boatmen were as tireless as donkeys, and seemed to have about the same outlook [on] life, poling, wading, or pulling by night as well as by day, with rare pauses, now and again shooting some shallow rapid. But though they poled, waded, and pulled almost all the circuit of a bright full moon, it was not until three the next afternoon that we reached Jaochow [Raozhou].

Its waterfront was endless with boats . . . and the waterfront was not without interest. Long rows of little feet in their tiny triangular shoes stuck out behind the women kneeling on the shore end of the plank wash-boards on which they scrubbed their clothes with brushes, and men supplying the town with water came incessantly with two big buckets on shoulder-poles to dip them full in the midst of the washerwomen. . . . A boat with a dozen cormorants squatting on outrigged poles far out over the water came in from a day of fishing on the lake.[33]

In this busy river town, Huang Zizhi had managed to find a job, working in neither the tea nor the tobacco realms but instead in the trade of his forefathers, at the Hu Hexing Baodian (The Hu Family Peace and Prosperous Pawnshop). There he would eventually rise to the post of chief accountant. As a filial son, he would regularly send funds home to his mother to assist in the management of the Yin Yu Tang household, and she, with the calligraphic assistance of the local schoolteacher, would write back to him, informing him of her receipt of the money, conveying any requests from friends and relatives for objects from town, and updating him on home affairs. These letters, carried by friends, by the postal system, or by private carrier, were essential papers that tied the dispersed members of the small, tight family.

On the fifteenth day of the first month of the lunar year in 1907 or 1908, Eight Pound's Wife wrote her son:

Zizhi, my son,

I hope you read this letter with good fortune.

All your letters have been received. The letter you mailed during your travels on the twenty-third of the twelfth month via Leping was sent on to us before the Yuanxiao [Lantern] Festival [fifteenth day of the first month]. The twenty dollars enclosed were also received.

I am glad to know that everything at your pawnshop is well. That makes me feel extremely happy and at peace. . . .

Aunt Sui asks you to buy a pair of bracelets for her child. Hu Chunjiu asks you to buy a summer [bed] netting for him. It should be used but not worn.

I, your mother, am taking care of your sister-in-law. And I, your mother, have no health troubles and am feeling very vigorous. Your sister-in-law is happily pregnant and is healthy. There is nothing for you to worry about. . . .

Your mother, writing in peace

A few months later, Huang Zizhi, still at his post in Raozhou, received the news, two-thirds of the way through a letter from Huang Zuyin (a relative and the teacher at the Huang Clan Primary School) that is always cause for major celebration in a Chinese family:

In regards to your family, your elder brother's wife safely gave birth to a son during the night, the day before yesterday.

Having grown up without a father, and with a limited sense of a household, Huang Zizhi must have been thrilled to see his family expanding again with this little nephew. His elder brother, the father of the boy, was not as meticulous in saving his letters, and so we have no remnants of the congratulations that Huang Zizhi sent to him. However, when Huang Zixian's wife suddenly died a short time later, Huang Zizhi recorded for posterity in his notebook a draft of the letter he sent to her spirit:

Let your soul stay here, my elder brother's wife, Madame Cheng of the Ruren title,[34]

For eight years, you labored diligently in caring for your son and serving your in-laws. Just at this critical moment when my brother was relying on you as he improved his business, you have sadly left him alone forever, and caused him sorrow for his whole life ahead.
  How can we comfort your soul?

Younger brother,
Huang
Kowtowing with tears in writing this condolence.

Letters to the deceased are a usual part of the ritual of paying respect at the time of death. But we can assume that the sentiments in Huang Zizhi's letter were at least partially heartfelt and that he himself had perhaps received nurturing from his older sister-in-law when he was still residing at home. The sudden death of a young, vibrant woman in just her late twenties no doubt left a large hole in the Yin Yu Tang household.
  While his mother was struggling at home in Huang Cun with a household and a grandson, and Huang Zixian was toiling to finance the household, Huang Zizhi was becoming increasingly dissatisfied with his own surroundings and circumstances. His mother had

already sensed his unhappiness there in 1908 and promised to try to help him, through friends or relatives, find a new position:

[I know] it is very difficult, but you must have patience and wait for an opportunity. At the same time, I will ask someone to make arrangements for you. . . . You should not be too ambitious.[35]

A year or so later the determined widow seems to have succeeded, and Huang Zizhi—certainly with some relief—was in a new town and a new place of employment:

My dear son Zizhi,

The letter as well as the five dollars you asked elder brother Xiao Hui to bring me was received.
  I am happy to know that you have moved to Leping to take up the vacancy of the accountant at the Yonghe (Forever Harmonious) Cloth Company. This was a favor done by your cousin. I feel extremely grateful to him for his assistance, recommendations, and concern. However, cloth business is something new to you and it is my hope that [you] will be attentive.[36]

The position in Leping agreed with Huang Zizhi, and he stayed on for many years. During his lifetime, Huang Zizhi repeatedly demonstrated a desire to repay the favor of job-recommending for friends and relatives. Many of these men may have been born and raised in grand houses built by their ancestors, but the economic situation of the early-twentieth century made earning money far more difficult for them. Among the numerous letters he saved are several from cousins, uncles, or relatives requesting assistance. This system of reliance on friends and family for job recruitment and job recommendations was part and parcel of the Huizhou merchant world.
  For at least one acquaintance, Zizhi went as far as being a guarantor. Among his artifacts are drafts of an official recommendation. One of them reads:

Chen Zhiliang is now being recommended to Zhu Yuanhe to be in charge of outer accounting. In case he makes any false calculations to obtain more than his proper commission, I, the guarantor, shall take full responsibility.
  On an auspicious day of the second month of the gengshen year [1920]
Guarantor: Huang Zizhi.[37]

Huang Zizhi was intent on perfecting the recommendation letter. There are four drafts of this short text, each with slightly different wording.

Fig. 70 (below) **Hong Zhaodi.**

Figs. 71, 72, & 73 (right)
**Xiazhuang, Xiuning County,
the hometown village of Hong
Zhaodi, in 2001.**

Like Raozhou, Leping is a somewhat nondescript small town, 93 miles (150 km) from Xiuning, but to the west of Raozhou and probably a bit more conveniently located. Just twenty-five miles (40 km) south of Jingdezhen, the center of imperial porcelain production, and not far from river transportation, Leping may have been an easier journey from Xiuning.

Huang Zizhi's satisfaction with Leping as a place of work can be concluded from his length of stay there. He was based on and off in this small town for more than sixteen years. However, within that time, this Huizhou merchant did not seem to find a specific place of employment that brought him content. In 1910, the year of his engagement to Hong Zhaodi, he was working at Anji Bao Lou, a shop selling fabric and imported Western objects.[38] One year later, he was at the Yonghe (Forever Harmony) Cloth Company,[39] a job he obtained on account of a cousin's recommendation. Letters do not reveal the specific complaints Zizhi had with his employers, or the complaints they may have had with him, but his children in recent years have been open in their recollections that he was a gruff and strict man.

Such qualities may not have made him an easy employee. If he had little patience for his children, he probably also had little patience with employers or customers.

At the age of twenty-seven, Zizhi was already quite old to be marrying. Possibly his family's difficult financial situation had caused his mother to wait until there was at least enough cash to find a decent wife. Weddings were lavish affairs with enormous expenses on the part of the groom's family. Matrimonial relations could offer significant financial connections, and gathering enough capital to afford a wife from a respectable family could be worth the wait. Clearly funds were tight in these years in the Huang household. Loans taken out for the first son's wedding had put the family in debt. In letters from Huang Zixian, Huang Zizhi's older brother apologizes to him for not being able to help out more with the younger man's wedding:

I heard that your marriage has been decided and the wedding will be next spring. I will do my best to help you. Please let me know the exact date by mail so that I can have time to prepare and borrow some money to mail back to you. I am quite weak financially now, and I can only present you with about 50 dollars. As the saying goes, "One is unable to do what one really desires." I feel very ashamed in writing this.

Despite the scarcity of funds, a respectable bride was found and the Huang family did come up with the finances for a wedding. The bride was seventeen-year-old Hong Zhaodi, the eldest girl of a large farming family in the nearby village of Xiazhuang. She was, like most girls of her time, illiterate and had bound feet, but as her son would say many years later, "My mother was a very good-hearted lady and was very able."

The custom in Huizhou was that the groom's family and the bride's family would negotiate the amount of money and objects, including clothes, fabric, food, and furnishings. For the engagement alone, the Hong family asked for jewelry, silk, food, plus payments to various assistants and masters of ceremonies. The official negotiated document was written up in fine calligraphy on red paper, red being the color of happiness and all matters related to marriages.

"I have received the red silk and red cotton cloth; they have already been sent to your fiancée's home," Huang Zizhi's mother had written in a letter asking her son, who was now working in a cloth shop, to purchase and send home from Leping some of the necessary goods for the marriage. With Huang Zizhi's marriage, his mother had fulfilled one of her primary responsibilities as head of the household: to ensure the continuation of the family line. Moreover, Eight Pound's Wife knew she was aging and, with her first son widowed, needed more assistance in holding together the home front and caring for her mischievous young grandson. She found her younger son a very suitable wife, ten years his junior, from a nearby peasant family with some merchant pretensions and potential connections. A bride much older than Hong Zhaodi's seventeen years would have been considered suspicious. The mother-in-law, who would spend more time with, and be more reliant on, the daughter-in-law than would her son, was relieved that the selection of the girl seemed satisfactory. "There has been no gossip concerning this marriage," she wrote.

Hong Zhaodi was the eldest of eleven children in the Hong family from the village of Xiazhuang (Rainbow Village), a mere five li (1.2 miles) from Huang Cun. Her given name, a common one for girls, reflects the age-old desire in China for male children, who instead of marrying out of the family like girls, and being only a financial drain, remain home to care for their parents and ancestors and carry on the family line. Zhaodi means, literally, "Beckoning Little Brother." Her parents would have given her the name in hopes that her birth was a portent that the next child would be a son. Surely to their dismay, the next pregnancy produced yet another daughter. They named her Zhuandi, "Next Turn Little Brother." This second girl was followed by Jiudi, "Definitely [the Next Will Be a] Younger Brother," who did indeed portend the arrival of a son. The trend of girls, and their names, however, continued. By the time she married, Hong Zhaodi had six younger sisters and four younger brothers. As a child, her feet, like those of her mother and her mother-in-law, and women for many generations

Gifts Needed for a Girl Who Will Marry into the Family

Engagement Ceremony:

Name of item	Quantity
Gold Crown	one
Jewelry of Gold	hundred liang[40]
Other Jewelry	at request
Red Satin of Tribute Quality	two chi[41]
Red Weave	pair
Violet-red Silk	one chi
Light red Weave	pair
Golden-Flower Brand Wine in Big Jug	pair
Shuangsheng Brand Cakes	two large packages
Fine Dry Fruits from Beijing	two large packages

Bride Making Up Ceremony

Name of item	Quantity
The Set of Gifts Listed on Golden Paper	Kept in Bridegroom's Home
The Set of Gifts Listed on Silver Paper	Kept in Bridegroom's Home
[Award for] the Hall Master	10 taels [of silver]
[Award for] the Chanters	4 taels [of silver]
[Award for] the Assistants	4 taels [of silver]
[Award for] the Speaker	20 taels [of silver]
[Award for] the Ritual Master	10 taels [of silver]
[Award for] the Ceremony Master	4 taels [of silver]
Golden-Flower Brand Wine in Big Jug	pair
Shuangsheng Brand Cakes	two large packages
Fine Dry Fruits from Beijing	two large packages
Five Kinds of Sacrifices	two large packages
Food for Service Persons	8 taels [of silver]

Marriage

Name of item	Quantity
Double-head Candles of Various Colors	40 packages
Oak Trees as Symbol of Rapid Grow	100
[Award for] Assistant Wedding Master	certain yuan
Small Presents	extra
Phoenix Decoration [symbol of marriage]	pair
Paint of Hundred Floral-crowned Children	complete set
Colorful Sedan for the Bride	complete set

The Second Month of Summer, 1910
Prepared by Hong Family of Xia Village (Shide Hall)

preceding them, were bound. Her daughter, who was born in modern Huang Cun in 1921 and managed to avoid the custom, recalled, "Mother had small feet. In the past they were called 'three-inch golden lotuses.' The smaller the foot, the more beautiful. At age seven, her feet were bound. Her grandmother was very severe."

Though in Chinese society women are technically no longer part of the family into which they were born once they marry, several of these brothers and sisters would later continue to have close involvement with the Huang family.

The marriage to Hong Zhaodi did, in fact, produce potentially helpful financial connections for Huang Zizhi. At least three Hong family men were merchants in Shanghai, one working in a pawnshop in the British Concession. The relationship between the two families remained tight for many years. In 1929, almost twenty years after his marriage, when Huang Zizhi returned to Huang Cun from his work in Hankou, he brought his in-laws a number of gifts, including dried fruit, dried shrimp, canned biscuits, brand-name towels, "foreign" silk handkerchiefs, and two small combs.

According to a letter from an uncle on his mother's side, Huang Zizhi's devoted mother had asked a certain Mr. Bao to select any auspicious day for the wedding. The determination of the proper date was a serious affair, and the uncle explained that as "Mr. Bao has not yet recovered from an illness, and his spirit is not yet restored, you will have to wait until the last month of this year or the first month of next year." The date was finally chosen, and with his mother having made all the arrangements, Huang Zizhi returned to Huang Cun for the ceremony. His usually supportive older brother, however, could not be present. In a lengthy letter Huang Zixian explicates that he has just begun a new job at a pawnshop in Wuchang (a section of modern-day Wuhan) and does not feel comfortable leaving. "For your marriage, I should be going home to assist. However, I now live under another's roof [working for someone else], and it is difficult for me to control my schedule. In addition, I have just accepted this significant job, and it is impossible to ask for a leave. What I can do is send you a hearty congratulation."

Fig. 74 **Just before Madame Cheng had died and soon after her son Huang Zizhi had married—about 1912—this photograph was taken in front of a backdrop depicting a European house. From right to left: Huang Zizhi; his mother, Madame Cheng; his wife, Hong Zhaodi; and in front, the endearing but mischevious boy Huang Zhenzhi, son of Huang Zizhi's brother. It is interesting to note that the newest member of the household, the bride Hong Zhaodi, is somewhat separated from the rest of the family, perhaps because she had not yet given birth to a son. The arrangement of the subjects reflects proper Chinese heirarchal placement with the ruling matriarch of the house Madame Cheng, in the most powerful position in the center. If one imagines that the group is posed in, for instance, the reception hall of a house, and they are facing south, her second son, Huang Zizhi, is in the secondary position at her east. Huang Zhenzhi, the young boy, the eldest son of her eldest son, stands in front of his grandmother, ready to take up his eventual position as family patriarch. Hong Zhaodi, the lowest in the family heirarchy, stands at the far west, the position of lowest status.**

Though we have no records or memories of the wedding, and though both his father and elder brother were absent, one can imagine that it was an elaborate affair. This was not a simple marriage whereby the wife had been brought into the family first as a servant and then elevated to wife status—as was not uncommon for girls from poor families.

Soon after the ceremonies, the young groom certainly would have returned to work at Leping, leaving his wife back in Huang Cun to care for his mother and young nephew. How often Huang Zizhi returned home from Leping in those early years of his marriage is not known. His workplace may have been just several days' travel from Huang Cun, but his boss may not have allowed him to leave often for an extended time. It was not uncommon then for men to stay away from home for four, five, or six years at a time. Huang Zizhi's children remember him returning only once every several years. The son of another merchant in Huang Cun recalls his father returning only twice in the first fourteen years of his life.

The date on the engagement document is the summer of 1910. From various letters traveling back and forth among Huang Zizhi in Leping, his brother in Wuchang, and his mother in Huang Cun, it appears that the marriage took place in the spring of 1911. Within just a few months, not only had Huang Zizhi married and the Huang lineage taken on new directions, but the power structure of the entire country had changed course. On October 10, 1911, a Republican insurrection overthrew the Qing imperial forces in the city of Wuchang, where Huang Zixian was working in the Dasheng Pawnshop. A few months later, on January 1, 1912, Sun Yatsen established the Republic of China in Nanjing—approximately 186 miles (300 km) north of Huang Cun. This new non-monarchal concept of governing had been gaining favor among many of the elite and educated members of society in China but presented a novel, less hierarchal structure than had ever been attempted for this country.

The radical change among the administrators of society did not seem to have stirred the Huang family of Yin Yu Tang. Among the many letters from this time period, there are no remarks among the family members regarding the revolutionary transformations. One line in a letter from Zixian to Zizhi may have been alluding to a sense of instability in China: "When you go back home by land," he warns, regarding the younger brother's trip home to get married, "you should be careful and heighten your vigilance." Otherwise, the family's personal welfare, expansions, and modifications took precedence in their correspondence.

In 1912 Zizhi contracted malaria and was gravely ill but did not, at least not immediately, return home. His brother and mother both sent him medicine in hopes that his health would improve and he could continue working.

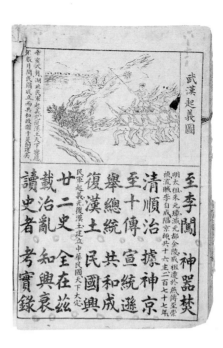

Fig. 75 *San Zi Jing,* a traditional children's primer republished circa 1912 in a lithographic edition, with an illustration of the 1911 uprising in Wuhan that led to the overthrow of the Qing government.

His brother writes from Wuchang, a year after the revolution, on October 19, 1912:

On the seventeenth of the chrysanthemum month [the ninth month], I mailed you a letter describing the present circumstances and enclosed in it a well-proven and effective prescription for curing malaria. I think it should have already reached you. Since the Autumn Moon Festival, when your malaria struck, it quieted down for a while. I don't know if you have suffered any new episodes, or have recently been able to rid yourself of the disease. This is a deep concern of mine. . . .

At noon today, the post office delivered a letter from our uncle, mailed from Wuhan. . . . He said that this spring, when he passed through Raozhou, he saw you and that you were very weak. He was deeply concerned. As soon as he arrived in Hankou, he asked Dr. Cheng Zemin to write a prescription for you. . . . If the huahe *herb is not effective you can just stop using it.*

Even when your disease has been cured, eggs soaked in infant urine should still be taken continuously. Presently, it is wintertime, and eggs are appropriate for eating [during this season]. . . . Every morning you should eat gruel. . . . Whether the yellow croaker's maw is appropriate [for your condition] or not, please consult with someone who knows medicine well and take it only after they have approved. From now on you should take special care of yourself in all aspects [of your life]. You should be cautious and careful in your sleeping, your eating and your working. If you continue to do so, it will truly benefit you physically.

Fig. 76 (above) **Vegetables drying on a bamboo drying tray in Huang Cun.**

Figs. 77 & 78 (left) **A bamboo drying tray made by a local basketmaker for Huang Zizhi in 1919. Bamboo drying trays are basic implements in a rural household. In the pickle-making process, vegetables are first dried. Drying certain vegetables, such as beans, is an excellent way of pre-serving them until they are ready for use. Cabbage, fungi, radishes, or chili peppers would be laid out in the sun on a drying tray such as this until they reached the desired level of dehydration. Many crafted implements used in common village areas, such as this tray and other baskets or buckets, are inscribed with dates and the owners' names.**

Fig. 79 (below) **Buckets for carrying water from a village well back to the home. The buckets would be slung at either end of a pole carried over the shoulder.**

The lack of heirs at this point could indicate, though does not prove, that Huang Zizhi was staying in Leping during the years just after his marriage. Whether it was to help out his mother or to be cared for himself by his new wife, Huang Zizhi must have finally returned to Huang Cun for a visit in 1913. His first son, Zhenxin, was born in 1914. Four more children were born in the next ten years, indicating that the young man certainly returned again about 1917 and, as we know from records, in 1921 for a longer stretch when an illness, presumably malaria, kept him homebound for several years.

Huang Zizhi's wife spent her days, as had her mother-in-law, maintaining the household; caring for the children; planting, harvesting, drying, and pickling vegetables; cleaning; washing clothes at the stream; and, the most labor-intensive, preparing the food. A large woven-bamboo vegetable-drying tray with the inscription "ji wei [cyclical date for 1919] made by Zizhi [of] Yin Yu Tang" certainly would have received much use in a household of Huang Cun, where every family dries cabbage, radishes, bamboo, mushrooms, and a variety of other vegetables as part of the routine food preserving process. A favorite dish of Hong Zhaodi's children was a radish noodle soup. She would knead rough flour into dough, cut it into long thin strips, and cook it with strings of radish. Known for her generosity, she always would give any leftovers to other families in the village.

Hong Zhaodi kept in contact with her own family, her father often visiting once a week,[42] and when the housework became overwhelming, one of her sisters would come to help out. The children assisted by carrying night soil out to the vegetable plot. Bound feet did not restrict the responsibilities of Hong Zhaodi's days. Each morning she would rise and rub the crippled flesh to restore the circulation in her feet. Walking with a heavy weight on her shoulders, however, was difficult, so occasionally a local peasant would be hired to carry the large buckets of water from the well to the kitchen.[43]

Like her mother-in-law, she had had no education and was illiterate, dependent on a local letter writer and reader for communicating with her distant merchant husband. The postal system and traveling-friend letter-carrying system were essential for maintaining not only communication between husband and wife but also for the household finances. As time went on, the monetary hardships at Yin Yu Tang were relieved. Huang Zizhi was making more money in Leping, each month sending five dollars back to Yin Yu Tang.

As Hong Zhaodi was quite frugal, she was able to enjoy the luxury of the extra cash and, according to her children, often spent it on commissioning carpenters to make furniture. In her spare time, after lunch, she would play mahjong with other women.

The mahjong parties did not entail cash for gambling on a daily basis. They would keep accounts in their head and pay up three times a year (on Duan Wu Jie, a holiday falling on the fifth day of the fifth month; the Autumn Moon Festival, on the fifteenth day of the eighth month; and New Year's.) According to her children, Hong Zhaodi won most of the time.[44]

One of Hong Zhaodi's primary mahjong companions was a new sister-in-law, surnamed Wu. Huang Zizhi's elder brother, widowed, married for a second time about 1915, bringing another woman into the household. The stepmother to the mischievous son of Huang Zixian would herself give birth to two more children to join the growing Yin Yu Tang household.

Over mahjong games, the women would chat. Gossip about various marriages would invariably arise, and the presence of a virtually single mother living in Yin Yu Tang would not have been ignored. While Huang Zizhi was still in Raozhao, he remained in touch with a fellow Huang Cun native, Huang Shaoqing, who already had a job in Leping. As the contents of some letters demonstrate, they would assist each other with sending money and letters to and from Huang Cun. Perhaps it was Huang Shaoqing who was instrumental in Huang Zizhi's obtaining his job in Leping. Huang Shaoqing, for a time at least, was also working at the Anji Bao Lou fabric store.

In marital matters, however, Huang Shaoqing had chosen an alternative, though, not untraditional path, and Huang Zizhi's Yin Yu Tang household stepped forth to help him out. The path would certainly have been open to Huang Zizhi as well, had he so desired. Like Huang Zizhi, Huang Shaoqing had married a woman from a village near Huang Cun, settled her in Huang Cun, and during the 1910s had had two children by her. However, he was also living during these years in Leping, working in fabric stores, and eventually found himself in Leping with what is commonly known in China as a "little wife." We must assume that Huang Shaoqing's own parents had passed away or for some reason his wife was not compelled to care for them and, therefore, was not living with them. Perhaps there were already too many older sons still living with Huang Shaoqing's parents. Huang Shaoqing therefore moved his first wife and children into two empty rooms in Yin Yu Tang that he rented from his friend Huang Zizhi. There, Huang Shaoqing virtually abandoned them. (Huang Shaoqing did seem to return for New Year's 1926, as Huang Zizhi makes note in his household account book of giving Huang Shaoqing "5.2 silver dollars to buy fish, melon seeds, candies, and cakes"). Huang Shaoqing's wife lived in Yin Yu Tang until 1968—from all reports, an understandably unhappy and sullen woman. Such was the risk of marrying a Huizhou merchant, always away from home.

Fig. 80 (top) **A game of mahjong depicted by Wu Youru, illustrator of the Shanghai lithographed pictorial** Dian Shi Zhai Huabao, **published between 1884 and 1898.**

Fig. 81 (above) **Mahjong set.**

Huang Shaoqing's first wife and children were not the only non-Huang family members to be living in Yin Yu Tang during these years. Both Hong Zhaodi and her mother-in-law, according to relatives and villagers, were generous women and, not opposed to earning a few extra coins, would rent out rooms in their spacious household to less fortunate people. One recipient of this generosity was the Shao family. The father of the family was a peasant, the second son of six boys of a peasant father. By the time he married, there was no room in his father's small brick house for him and his wife. Hong Zhaodi and her mother-in-law offered the young couple a room. Descendants of the couple would continue living in Yin Yu Tang until the mid-1960s.

Atypically for a Huizhou merchant, during the 1920s, Huang Zizhi returned home to Huang Cun for an extended period of time. His illness had become overwhelming, and he needed constant care. His son recalls that his father spent much of his time alone in his room, resting and trying to recover:

Fig. 82 **Huang Zizhi's account book from the first lunar month of the year according to the Chinese calendar, in 1922.**

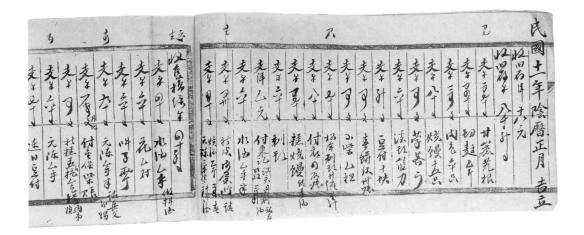

We did not see my father during the day. He would sleep until noon. During the evenings he would paint and write letters. He spoke very few words and seldom communicated with us. Even at dinner, he had dinner in his own room. He ate very slowly. It took a very long time for him to complete a dinner. My mother and we the kids had dinner in the living room. We children were all afraid of our father. We thought he was very strange. As soon as we did something wrong, we had to kneel down in front of him. Otherwise, he would beat us. Our family was very strict. When we failed to understand something, [he] would knock our heads. I was very mischievous when I was young. But I kneeled down just once that I remember. He [Huang Zhenxin] kneeled down many times. Sometimes we had to kneel down for one or even two hours. . . . If we refused to do so, we would be beaten by our father.

Huang Zizhi, however, did not spend his time just resting and disciplining his children. A serious businessman and skilled accountant, he was watching over the family's finances. From his records, we see an unprecedented meticulousness that probably had rewarded him in his work as a clerk and would continue to reward him in future years. Detailed account books kept by Huang Zizhi record the funds coming into and going out of the Huang family household. The books are a clear window into the eating, feasting, and other activities that were stirring within Yin Yu Tang.

The first pages of the account book, beginning on the seventh day of the New Year festivities, reveal great amounts of money being spent on pork, pork dumplings and pork buns, preserved eggs, tofu, and rice wine. There is also firewood for fueling the stove, a constant cost through the year, and a special item to brighten the household, potted plants.

The account book demonstrates that despite Huang Zizhi's illness, the family was eating quite well and that there was always extra cash for such luxuries as flowers and candy, and, as accounted for as the days went by, opera performances, temple visits to Ma'anshan, songbirds, a flashlight bulb, kerosene, and even repairs to the house and family tombs.

The account books also confirm the serious illness in the family. Expenses for doctors, medicines, and doctors' transportation costs are all noted in detail.

Medical treatment was both expensive and distant. The family had to pay for medicines, doctors' visits, and transportation for doctors to come from towns that were several miles away. The account book indicates with a sudden frequency of two different doctors' visits and regular purchases of medicine that Huang Zizhi's illness was worsening in the fall of 1926.

Huang Zizhi was still ill in late 1926 when defeated troops of the warlord Sun Chuanfang invaded Huang Cun, looting and pillaging. The account book clearly marks the date with an expenditure for an "ambulance," a sedan chair, that took him, followed on foot by his wife and children, into the hills to hide in a peasant's home.

By early 1927, this volume of the accounting ends and Huang Zizhi seems to have recovered. In January, just before the Chinese lunar New Year, the newly vigorous businessman began various home projects. Sharing the expenses with his brother, they performed the most filial act possible by repairing their parents' tombs, erecting a new tombstone. Moreover, both in tribute to their ancestors and in an endeavor to care for their offspring and descendants, they made additions and repairs to Yin Yu Tang. The account book tells of adding a building, repairing bricks on the main house, repairing the gate with newly purchased stone, and purchasing tung oil, perhaps to retouch the wooden walls in the main house.

Excerpts from Huang Zizhi's Account Book

Auspiciously started from the first month of the lunar calendar, the 11th year of the Republic of China.

Silver dollars inherited from previous account: 18.
Copper cents inherited from previous account: 8060.

The 7th Day (February 3, 1922):
- Expending 170 copper cents for buying 29 pieces of sugarcane.
- Expending 140 copper cents for buying one lb. of chopped noodles.
- Expending 200 copper cents for buying 60 meat stuffed steamed buns.
- Expending 80 copper cents for buying 15 steamed dumplings.
- Expending 100 copper cents for buying 500 grams of water chestnuts.
- Expending 60 copper cents for paying the labor of the basket carrier at Xitou [Source of the Stream, seems name of a place].
- Expending 50 copper cents for buying 10 pieces of tofu.
- Expending 100 copper cents for buying 30 pieces of thin pancake [spring roll pastry].
- Expending 100 copper cents for buying 100 lb. of cut firewood.

The 8th Day (February 4, 1922):
- Expending 70 copper cents for Songnian's [Zhenxin's] haircut (20 cents) and shampooing (50 cents).
- Expending 80 copper cents for buying 400 pieces of skin of tofu.
- Expending 170 copper cents for buying rice cakes and steamed dumplings for the Spring Banquet.
- Expending 60 cents for [my] haircut.
- Expending 1 silver dollar paying to Bing's [Butcher Shop] for buying about 4 lb. and 11 oz of pork and received this time 3.5 lb. for the Spring Banquet.
- Expending 60 copper cents for buying 1.5 lb. of rice wine.

The 12th Day (February 8, 1922)
- Expending 130 copper cents for buying 11 preserved duck eggs for the Spring Banquet.
- Expending 110 copper cents for buying 1 lb. of spirit and 3.5 lb. of aged rice wine for the Spring Banquet.
- Income 45 copper cents for selling cotton thread.
- Expending 40 copper cents for buying 1 lb. of rice wine (used for cooking wine).
- Expending 60 copper cents for buying a pair of [potted] flowers.
- Expending 60 copper cents for buying two pieces of "jiaozi" [literally, the first character means yelling, and the second character is a suffix meaning "small".]

The 14th Day (February 10, 1922)
- Expending 90 copper cents for buying 1.5 lb. of aged rice wine for a dinner in which [my] father-in-law and nephew were invited.
- Expending 400 copper cents for paying the firewood debt to Jinbao (price per silver dollar: 50 lb.).
- Expending 100 copper cents for buying muffins and a package of candy as gift to my brother-in-law.

The 15th Day (October 21, 1926)
- Expending 6 silver dollars for paying to Dr. Cheng Zemin as visiting fee.

- Expending 1 silver dollar for prescription fee.
- Expending 3 silver dollars for hiring a sedan for Dr. Cheng.

The 18th Day (October 24, 1926)
- Expending 1 silver dollar for paying Dr. Cheng for his revisit.

The 19th Day (October 25, 1926)
- Expending 3 silver dollars for hiring a sedan for Dr. Cheng.
- Expending 1 silver dollar for going to Tunxi for buying medicine and [illegible]. (Grandfather-in-law went there.)
- Expending 1 silver dollar for going to Longwan to buy medicine. (Change: 600 copper coins)

The 23rd Day (October 29, 1926)
- Expending 16 silver dollars for inviting Dr. Songyou to visit.
- Expending 8 silver dollars for hiring a sedan for him.

The 26th Day (November 1, 1926)
- Expending 1 silver dollar for buying medicine at Tunxi (Change: 410 copper coins).

The 28th Day (November 3, 1926)
- Expending 0.4 silver dollar for buying medicine at Longwan.

The 29th Day (November 4, 1926)
- Expending 2 silver dollars paying to Dr. Songyou as the prescription fee.
- Expending 1 silver dollar for hiring a sedan for Dr. Songyou.
- Expending 1 silver dollar for paying the assistant of Dr. Songyou.
- Expending 1 silver dollar for buying medicine at Longwan (Change: 520 copper coins).

The 1st Day of the 12th Month (January 4, 1927)
- Expending 4.5 silver dollars for the labor of Father and Mother's tomb stone made in the 3rd Month (total 9 dollars divided).
- Expending 2.02 silver dollars for paying the labor of repairing my parents' tomb in the 7th Month (total 4.04 dollars and equally divided).
- Expending 5.134 silver dollars for building the Seventh House Hall inside the Gate in the 8th Month (total 10.268 dollars and equally divided).
- Expending 1 silver dollar paying to the brick man for his eight units of labor (total 2 silver dollars and equally divided).
- Expending 0.25 silver dollar paying to the carpenter for his two units of labor (total 0.5 silver dollars and equally divided).
- Expending 0.5 silver dollar paying to the brick man for his three units of labor in repairing the big house (total 0.75 dollar and equally divided by the three families).
- Expending 0.8 silver dollar for the four units of labor of the carpenter in repairing the gate (including meals for him, total 1.6 dollars and equally divided).
- Expending 0.5 silver dollar for buying a piece of stone to repair the inner gate.
- Expending 0.4 silver dollar for the two units of labor of the mason (stone man) to repair the inner gate (including meals for him, total 0.8 dollar and equally divided by the two families).
- Expending 0.107 silver dollar for buying tung oil and iron nails (total 0.215 dollar and divided by the two families).

A Wedding Poem

Unfold the curtain! Unfold the curtain!
Decorative candles spark in the bride's chamber.
Today the new couple has come to marry,
The whole family is filled with happiness.

Unfold the curtain from up high!
The newly wedded couple will drink the wedding wine tonight,
Their brows will be laughing and their faces lit up with pleasure.

Lift the curtain at the center!
[The newly wedded couple] is a match arranged in Heaven,
    a pair of mandarin ducks.[46]
Tonight for the first time, this pair of mandarin ducks will intertwine
    their necks.
Bride and bridegroom,
Are you not rejoicing?

Unfold the curtain in the east!
Today's happiness is truly different from any other.
The bride's chamber is crowded with boisterous guests,
Who have come to congratulate her as she marries her lord.

Unfold the curtain in the west!
[The new couple] is a fine pair.
May you cherish each other, white-haired, through the final days
    of your lives.
May you enjoy a life as ever-lasting as the South Mountain,
And great fortune, as abundant as the East Sea.
Ah, bride and bridegroom,
Do you not think this fine?

Unfold the curtain in the south!
The ox herder and the weaver maiden[47] have come together
    for the first time.

Unfold the curtain in the north!
The couple will rest their heads on the same pillow
    and will tune their zithers [clear and pure].[48]
Their music is harmony,
And they will give birth to a noble son,
A noble son who will climb high, up to the laurel in the moon.[49]
Unfold the curtain on the head of the bride,
She will produce sons who'll become kings and dukes!
Unfold the curtain on the head of the bridegroom,
May wealth and nobility continue from generation to generation
    without end.

Unfold the curtain at the center!
The love of the new couple is as deep as the sea.
They will surely give birth to a future president next year!

Unfold the curtain! Unfold the curtain!
What a happy heaven! What a joyous earth!
The family is full of good fortune and longevity.
Salutations to you, the bride and the bridegroom!

The sudden repairs of the house may have been instigated by the imminent marriage of Huang Zixian's eldest child and only son, the once ever so mischievous Huang Zhenzhi. Huang Zixian, as can still be seen by the current condition of the groom's bedroom, was determined to create an impressive wedding environment for his precious son. Huang Zixian may have suggested to his younger brother that the time was appropriate to spruce up the family home.

The proud uncle of the groom, Huang Zizhi penned a poem, found among his papers, celebrating the marriage. As none of his children married while he was still alive, the poem most probably was written in elation over this first marriage of the next generation, which would in turn produce another generation of the Huang line. The poem depicts both the joyous moments of the wedding celebrations—"The bride's chamber is crowded with boisterous guests"—as well as the more intimate encounter in the wedding chamber — "Tonight for the first time, this pair of mandarin ducks will intertwine their necks. . . . The couple will rest their heads on the same pillow and will tune their zithers [clear and pure]. Their music in harmony." The poem ends with the classical desire of all Huizhou merchants: sons who will become government officials: "And they will give birth to a noble son, A noble son who will climb high, up to the laurel in the moon. . . . Unfold the curtain on the head of the bride, She will produce sons who'll become kings and dukes! . . . They will surely give birth to a future president next year!" Coincidentally, it was just about this same time that Chiang Kai-shek toppled his competitors and gained ascendancy, setting himself up in his own government in Nanjing, as the leader of Republic of China.

Having tended to and completed the expansion of the family and the significant home-improvement project, Huang Zizhi traveled to Shanghai when a work opportunity arose. Shanghai in 1927 was in full swing of its golden era. Jazz music and Art Deco architecture were infusing the city with a powerful new atmosphere. Foreign businesses based on the Bund were bringing wealth, industry, trade, and European lifestyles into China.

While many of residents of Shanghai were enjoying themselves, Chiang Kai-shek and his forces were intent on reconsolidating their hold over the country, crushing the Communist revolutionaries in Shanghai and trying to diminish the power of the warlords in the rest of China.

Huang Zizhi arrived in this multifaceted world of Shanghai by way of a relative's introduction. A worker in a pawnshop on Bingnan Road was taking his periodic home respite after working for the customary three years and needed a replacement for his regulated six-month break. Huang Zizhi, perhaps interested in continuing to pursue the occupation of his ancestors, went to take up the prospect.

Fig. 83 **A gold-plated hairpin that had slipped between the first-floor floorboards and was found during the dismantling of Yin Yu Tang.**

The bridegroom is only fifty years old. His beard has several white strands, There are two skin ulcers festering on his head. And when he talks, he has a bit of a stammer. They made a spoken agreement that [the Chen family would offer] a hundred taels of silver, and not a cent more. They picked the sixth day for presenting the engagement gift—a pair of gold hairpins.

—From *Untitled (Four Letters in Poetic Form)*, a novella by Wang Yaozhen, a matriarch of Yin Yu Tang

By the time the temporary position had come to an end, Huang Zizhi apparently was conferring with friends in regards to starting a pawnshop in the bustling metropolis of Hankou.

Huang Zizhi's brother had worked in Hankou for many years, and the family had ties there. Huang Zizhi's two new partners most certainly also hailed from Huizhou and would have had contacts there. Though Hankou, 456 miles (750 km) west of Shanghai, had existed as early as the Song dynasty (960–1279), it had not become a major trading port until the arrival of eager European traders in the second half of the nineteenth century. Since 1861, when China was defeated in the Opium Wars, foreign countries including Britain, France, Russia, and Japan were allowed to establish concessions in Hankou. Tea was the biggest commodity they were trading there:

Hankou signifies, in Chinese, the mouth of commerce. It is, indeed, a great commercial center. The river is navigable for men-of-war and the largest ocean steamers up to this point. When I stood here a huge three-funnel merchant steamer from Odessa, Russia's great port on the Black Sea, lay at anchor in midstream. Russians are the greatest tea-drinkers in Europe, and they drink Chinese teas almost exclusively. Ships from all parts of the world come here for tea; so, I think, for gigantic tea-parties Hankou holds the record. Do you see the tea being discharged from the ship on which we stand? Our steamer brought a cargo from a point down the river to this place for transshipment, or possibly to be first transformed or pressed into what is called brick-tea. Should we go ashore a little distance from this shipping front, we would see many places where tea is pressed into hard bricks, chiefly for shipment to Russia, although the best grades of tea are not put up in this manner. Though this is the most important tea center in the world, I want to tell you that the nearest point where tea is grown is one hundred miles from Hankou. This is merely a great shipping entrepot. Tea is brought here from the hill and mountain districts, where it is grown; it is brought from smaller ports up and down the river to Hankou, where it is sometimes repacked and sent to all parts of the world.[45]

Just after opening the pawnshop in Hankou in 1928, as arranged, Huang Zizhi waited in Shanghai for his eldest son, now fourteen years old—the age at which all Huizhou boys would leave their home to apprentice in a shop—and together they took the steamboat to Hankou.

The partners called their newly established pawnshop Ju He Dian, the Assembling Pawnshop, and located it in the French concession, near the Chinese neighborhood of the city. Pawnshops had large staffs, each member being in charge of his own specialty. Huang Zizhi's expertise was authenticating and appraising jewelry, an important and essential position for any pawnshop. To misappraise an object could cause great losses to the business.

Ju He Dian must have achieved a certain degree of success: by the early fall of 1929, Zizhi was already returning home to Huang Cun laden with a massive number of gifts for friends and family. Had he not been making money, he would not have been able to make the journey or purchase the gifts. He made an extensive list of the gifts and to whom they were destined. The number of objects he carried back to Huang Cun would have necessitated at least one porter.

The list reveals not only the types of objects that were desirable—such as perfume, towels, and canned foods—but also who among his friends, neighbors, and relatives were significant enough to receive gifts. He evidently felt strong obligations not only to his father's side of the immediate family but also to his mother's side, and to his in-laws. Such preference given to the maternal side of a family is unusual in China, but in Huizhou ties to women's families were not insignificant.

Brand-name objects are particularly recurrent on Huang Zizhi's list of gifts. These prepackaged foods in their pretty tin cans with colored paper labels conferred a certain status and played a decorative role in remote Huang Cun. In 1997 paper advertisements and packaging from Shanghai biscuits, fruits, and fabrics were still adhering to the walls and furniture in Yin Yu Tang pasted there to brighten rooms with the rich, printed colors.

In addition to the gifts, Huang Zizhi brought jewelry, probably from his pawnshop, back to the village. These may have been objects that were pawned and never retrieved by the original owners. A list of gold earrings—recording their specific weight, shape, and value—hints that he may have been planning to sell the jewelry while back in Xiuning. Notations are written under listings of some of the pieces—for instance, a buyer and the sale price are recorded for a pair of pure gold earrings in the shape of a heart. The sales would have brought in extra income for this relentless Huang businessman.

Huang Zizhi's gifts and jewelry were not his only bequests of urban items to his small, remote hometown. In addition to luxurious objects, his concerns for the education of the younger generation seems to have compelled him to send numerous textbooks from the city to Huang Cun for the Huang Clan Primary School that was ever hankering to be a modern school. A list of books he sent includes commercial letter-writing manuals, arithmetic texts, modern Chinese language books, and one of his favorite subjects, as apparent from his account books, household accounting. Like Huizhou merchants since the Song dynasty, he yearned to provide Huizhou merchant children with a fine education to prepare them for their life in trade or, possibly, officialdom.

Fig. 84 **A printed packaging papers depicting a Chinese legend found in Yin Yu Tang. The packaging was for cotton fabric imported by a Japanese company, Toyo Menka Kaisha, which during the 1920s bought the cotton from the United States. The packaging, which probably served as a memento of city goods and cheerful decoration for a Yin Yu Tang woman, demonstrates the increasing globalization in the early-twentieth century that brought American goods to remote villages in China.**

Items Brought Home [excerpted from Huang Zizhi's inventory]

List of the Gifts Presented to Relatives and Friends When Returning Home on the fourteenth day of the Eighth Month of the Jisi Year [1929]

To Cheng Zemin, Brother-in-Law:
- Three Friends brand large towel — Two
- Lin Wenyan brand No.11 perfume — Two bottles
- Great Harvest brand rose-flavored red fermented bean curd — Two cans
- No. 2 biscuit in prism box — Two boxes

To Father-in-Law and Mother-in-Law:
- Dried longan — One jin
- Biandong[50] dried shrimp — One jin
- Great Harvest brand biscuit in painted cylinder can — Two cans
- No. 2 towel with blue edge — Two
- Foreign silk handkerchief — Two
- Small comb of date wood — Two

To In-Laws of the Third Sister, Seventh Sister, and Mr. Jun (Wife's Brother): Each has the following set of gifts:
- Great Harvest brand biscuit in painted cylinder can — Two cans
- Great Harvest brand dried noodles — Two boxes
- Foreign silk handkerchief — One
- Small comb of date wood — One

To Sister Teng's In-laws:
- Great Harvest brand biscuit in painted cylinder can — Two cans
- Double Happiness brand towel — Two
- Profit brand handkerchief — One
- Roaster brand dried noodle — Two boxes

To Qiu Lunhai, Wife's Elder Sister's Husband, Who Lives in Yang Village:
- Great Harvest brand biscuit in painted cylinder can — Two cans
- Double Happiness brand towel — Two

In May of the Eighteenth Year of the Republic of China (1929), I returned home. Various relatives and friends came from afar to see me and below is a list of the gifts [I presented to them.]

To Qiu Jianwen, Cousin's Father:
- Chicken with black mushroom — Two cans
- Black-flower litchi — Two cans
- Green bean cake — Two boxes

To Hu Zijia, Niece's Husband:
- Black fungus — One jin
- Lotus seed — One jin
- Harmony brand tropical fruit — Two cans
- Great Harvest brand assorted biscuit, L size — Two cans

To Hongjun, Sister:
- Lotus seed   Two jin
- Ground lily bulb   Two boxes

To Mr. Zhu Lisheng:
- Ten Thousand Lucks brand rosé wine   Two bottles
- Global Shaking brand tropical fruit   Two cans

To Mr. Bao Huigeng:
- Beautiful Phoenix brand cigarette   Four cans
- Big Square biscuit   Two boxes

To Uncle Guanxiang:
- Good Health brand spirit   Two bottles
- Five Harmony brand tropical fruit   Two cans

To Mr. Xu Shenqi:
- Ten Thousand Lucks brand spirit   Two bottles
- Assorted biscuits, L size   Four cans

To Zhu Xiaota:
- Advantageous Gathering brand spirit   Four bottles
- Great Harvest biscuit in painted can   Eight cans

To Mr. Hu Pincan and Mr. Zhu Shaoyun:
- Harmony and Prosperity brand
  biscuit in painted prism can   One can
- Guansheng Garden brand orange-
  flavored preserved fruits   Two cans
- Grounded lotus root from West Lake   One box
- Butter biscuit in prism can   One can

The Eighth Month of the Traditional Calendar, the Eighteenth Year of the Republic of China (1929). Recorded on a propitious day.

A List of Gold Jewelry Brought Home

- Baocheng (Treasure Completion) brand pure gold earrings in the shape of fall leaf, one pair
  Weight:[51] 14 fen[52]
  Price: 8.70 yuan (including material and labor)
- Qingyun Fortunate Cloud brand pure gold earrings in the shape of a leaf, one pair
  Weight: 1 qian[53]
  Price: 6.00 yuan (including material and labor)
- Lao Tongzhen brand pure gold pendant earrings, one pair
  Weight: 12 fen 6 [li[54]]
  Price: 7.65 yuan (including material and labor)
- Lao Fengxiang [Old Flying Phoenix] brand pure gold earrings in the shape of heart, one pair
  Weight: 8 fen 2 [li]
  Price: 5.2 yuan (including material and labor)

On the eleventh day of the Ninth Month sold to Cuiyou, a payment of 5 yuan was received, then and an additional payment of 4,100 wen (cent) was received on the thirteenth.

- Wuhua brand pure gold earrings in the shape of heart, one pair
  Weight: 15 fen 9 [li]
  Price: 8.96 yuan (including material and labor)
- Old Xiehe brand impure gold ring, one
  Weight: 1 qian 2 fen
- Baocheng brand impure gold ring, one
  Weight: 8 fen
- Pure gold eardrops with foreign letters, one pair
  Weight: 6 fen 2 [li]
  Price: 3.98 yuan

On the second day of the Ninth Month sold to Da Lanzhi, received then a payment of 2 yuan. An additional payment of 2 yuan and 4,000 wen was received on the twelfth. Still unpaid amount: 7,100 wen. 7,100 wen was received in the second month [of following year].

- Impure gold eardrops with the character shou [longevity], one pair
  Weight: 2 fen 5 li
  Price: 1.525 yuan (Including material and labor)
- Shanghai pure gold hanging earrings in the shape of heart, one pair
  Weight: 5 fen 5 [li]
  Price: 3.05 yuan

On the second day of the Third Month received a payment of 7 yuan from Yi, received from Lian.

A List of Books Bought

1. *A Rudiment Text of Various Characters with Pictures*, one volume, 3 cents, ten copies.
2. *A Concise Text of Abacus Calculation, Newest Version with Pictures*, two volumes, 7 cents, fifty copies.
3. *A Classical Chinese Reader by Autumn Water Publishing House with Detailed Textual Research and Annotation*, two volumes, 17 cents, ten copies.
4. *Correspondence Writing for Both Academic and Commercial Purposes*, by Tang, two volumes, 11 cents, fifty copies.
5. *Records in a Jade Box, the Secret of Household Management*, expanded edition, two volumes, 10 cents, ten copies.
6. *A New Style Reader for Students, Classical Chinese with Modern Interpretation*, two volumes, 16 cents, thirty copies.
7. *A Student Dictionary of Modern Chinese Pronunciation*, one volume, 11 cents, thirty copies.
8. *New China Medium Dictionary*, one volume, 16 cents, thirty copies.
9. *A Quick Command of the Chinese Language*, new edition, one volume, 18 cents, ten copies.

In total, I have selected eight books of thirteen volumes. Please check whether the books are too many or too few when you receive them.

The return of Huang Zizhi from Hankou may not have been occasioned solely by a desire to see home and lavish his friends and family with presents. In the summer of 1929, shortly before he made the journey, death fell again on the seventh branch of the Huang family. Huang Zixian, Huang Zizhi's cherished elder brother, died suddenly of a stroke at his place of work in Tunxi. The whole family, nurtured for so many years by this kind man who watched over the entire household and who freely gave medical care to his poor village neighbors, was devastated.

Undoubtedly, Huang Zizhi was also deeply pained by the loss of his brother. He left no written expression of his loneliness or hurt, but among his documents there is an extensive list of people to whom Huang Zizhi sent notices of his brother's death. The list demonstrates the wide expanse of acquaintances that this Huizhou merchant maintained. Many local Huizhou merchants, as well as some living as far away as Dalian far north of Beijing and Shanghai, received news of the unexpected passing of Huang Zixian. His death would have serious ramifications for the family he left behind—his wife; two young daughters, ages seven and nine; and his just married but fiscally irresponsible son.

As much as he could, Huang Zizhi cared for his brother's family. But with children of his own, there was not much left over for the others in the household. Huang Zizhi returned to Hankou and carried on with his work at the pawnshop.

There is no indication that Huang Zizhi returned again to Huang Cun in the following five years. The deaths of two of his children from measles (one, in 1932 at the age of ten; the other, in 1933 at the age of fifteen) did not send him running back to his hometown. The low standing of girls and young unmarried boys in a family did not merit full fatherly devotion.

Huang Zizhi did travel from Hankou to Shanghai at the end of 1932 for over five months. He may have agreed to work in a pawnshop there while a friend or relative went on home leave. Perhaps he used the opportunity to investigate the possibility of opening a pawnshop in Shanghai.

The worldwide depression of the 1930s eventually caught up with the international treaty port of Hankou. By 1934 floods, civil war between the Nationalists and the Communists, and the general decrease in trade brought understandable anxiety to the merchants. The Yangzi River flooded in 1931, bringing devastation to the port city and beginning a financial downward spiral. Newspapers reported the collapse of many businesses and the subsequent economic consequences for the people of Hankou:

Bad Times for Trade

Many bankruptcies are already reported from the native city, and the outlook for many others is not very bright. Losses have been made in practically every line of business, including export commodities, of which only wood-oil can be said to have made money. Distress also is very prevalent, and it is estimated that at least 70 per cent of the inhabitants are on the verge of starvation, through lack of business and consequent unemployment. How long these conditions are allowed to continue is no doubt in the hands of the Government, and the only feasible solution is to get trade going, which can be accomplished by reduction of the taxes and heavy duties, which, combined will permit a resumption of export of the many commodities which at present are unsaleable.

—*North-China Herald*, February 13, 1934

It was in this state of affairs that Huang Zizhi and his two partners at the Ju He Dian pawnshop decided to close down their shop. Together, they split the profits and property, each receiving one-third of proceeds, and then going his own way to try his luck elsewhere.

Huang Zizhi determined that his future lay back in Shanghai. With his son to accompany him, he planned the return steamship journey to that great Paris of the East. Before he left Hankou, Huang Zizhi took his son on a sight-seeing trip across the river. On the Lantern Festival, the fifteenth and last day of the New Year festival, February 28, 1934, they visited the statuesque Huang He Lou, the Yellow Crane Tower, on the banks of the Yangzi River in Wuchang. The five-story, fifty-meter high building was a replica of a multistoried pavilion built in the third century, where luminaries and poets gathered to write poetry. Over the centuries, more than three hundred poems have been composed in reverie for the building that had been destroyed and rebuilt numerous times. In 1884 it completely burned to the ground, but by the time Huang Zizhi and young Huang Zhenxin visited, the entire edifice had been reconstructed. The two purchased a photograph of the beautiful historic building and then paid for a professional photograph to be taken of the two of them, father and son, before a painted backdrop of the pavilion. Pots of plum blossoms, which bloom at Chinese New Year, were placed at their feet. Huang Zizhi inscribed the photograph, noting in his characteristic calligraphy the circumstances of the event and that it would be a souvenir of the visit with his son. The photograph would become a reminder of their last sanguine days together before the ill-fated journey to Shanghai.

The most dramatic moment of Huang Zizhi's life was probably the one that led to his death. Standing on wharf, having just closed his pawnshop and divided the profits and valuables with his partners, he was set to board a boat up the river to Shanghai where he would start anew. Laden down with suitcases and trunks filled with his treasures, he sent his twenty-year-old son off to purchase a bit of *fenjiu*, a strong grain liquor. While Huang Zhenxin, his eldest son whom he had been training in the pawnshop for six years, was on his pursuit of the liquor, Huang Zizhi was approached by an aggressive porter. The porter, typical of most on the Yangzi River piers, grabbed the suitcases from Huang Zizhi's hands. The merchant was determined not to let go of his hard-earned possessions. He pulled back. The porter, angered, rammed a fist into Huang Zizhi's face.

When the young Huang Zhenxin returned with the purchased spirits, he found his father seriously wounded. "They battered him and hit his chest so hard that he spit blood," Huang Zhenxin recalls. With difficulty, he managed to get his father on the boat to Shanghai and, once there, to the Ping-an Hotel. "A doctor was called to visit him. The doctor wrote a prescription and I had to go to a pharmacy to get the medicine. Since I had just arrived in Shanghai, and it was my first visit [here], I did not know where I could find a pharmacy," Huang Zhenxin remembers. Despite much administering by doctors and his son's fervent care, Huang Zizhi, at the age of fifty-two, never recovered from the infections and passed away a month later, still in the small Shanghai hotel. Like his own father, he had suffered and died from the hazards of being a Huizhou merchant, on the road and away from home.

My father was too stingy. He did not want to spend any extra money. Had he given them [the porters] some money, he would not have been beaten to death.

—Huang Zhenxin

Thus, the thirty-third generation of the seventh branch of the Huang Cun Huang family came to a close, leaving only the wives and children of these men. Neither man lived to see his grandchildren, but both had sons who in turn also produced sons, and the Huang family line carried on.

Fig. 85 (above) Huang Zizhi and his son Huang Zhenxin, February 28, 1934, visiting the Yellow Crane Tower in Wuchang, had their photo taken in front of a cloth backdrop of the building, just weeks before Huang Zizhi was fatally assaulted at the pier on their way to Shanghai.

Fig. 86 (left) The Butterfield and Swire pier at Hankou circa the end of the nineteenth or the beginning of the twentieth century.

Fig. 87 (right) **Huang Zizhi (center) and two of his children, Huang Ciuhong (left) and Huang Zhenxin (right), circa 1918.**

Fig. 88 (top) **Huang Zhenzhi**

Fig. 89 (above) **Wang Yaozhen**

The Thirty-Fourth Generation

The thirty-fourth generation of the Huang lineage exemplified a new direction for the family. Among the males, there were two that survived to adulthood to carry on the line. Like their fathers these two men, Huang Zhenzhi and Huang Zhenxin, went into business. In fact, they went into business together for a time. Their new attitudes and actions, however, influenced their children and allowed their wives and the next generation to go beyond the traditional expectations and down new pathways.

Huang Zhenzhi

Huang Zhenzhi, the eldest son of Huang Zixian (himself an eldest son) at first was raised primarily by his grandmother. His father was away in Wuhan working in a pawnshop, and his mother died when he was an infant. A mischievous boy much cherished by his grandmother, he exhausted the older woman. His father soon married again so that a younger woman could assist in the household. By this second wife, Madame Wu, Huang Zixian had two daughters.

Huang Zhenzhi studied at the Huang Clan Primary School and later graduated from the Anhui Province Second Normal School. Normal schools were vocational high schools that trained students to become teachers, and Huang Zhenzhi, unlike his forefathers, seemed headed for an occupation in education. For a time, he taught at the Huang Clan Primary School in Huang Cun.

As the years passed, restless Huang Zhenzhi became impatient with his teaching career. Teachers at the school were paid in rice rather than in cash, so Huang Zhenzhi was unable to earn much of a living. When an opportunity arose to participate in a business venture with his cousin, Huang Zhenxin, he immediately jumped at the prospect and moved to the big city, Shanghai.

Wang Yaozhen—the Literate Daughter-in-Law

Several years before the move to Shanghai, having arrived at the marriageable age, Huang Zhenzhi was engaged to a young woman. The child of a middle-class merchant family in the village of Hongni, just a few miles away, Wang Yaozhen was not a stranger to the Huang family. She was the granddaughter of a Huang Cun woman.

Huang Xianying, Huang Zhenzhi's cousin, recalls how they played together as children: "Originally, she was a relative. I called her 'older sister.' After she married into our family, I called her *sao sao*, 'sister-in-law.' Her grandmother was surnamed Huang. We went to visit them every year at New Year's. Sometimes we would stay there a few days, play for a few days, and then come home. Our relationship before was nice, and after she married here, it was even more intimate. . . . She was twelve years older than me. She would have been ninety-two this year."

Owning lands that were rented out to peasants, the family had a comfortable lifestyle. They were traditional and bound their daughter's feet, but were open and cultivated enough to educate her. She had a private tutor who taught her the *San Zi Jing* and *Bai Jia Xing*, the classic, traditional Confucian primers—texts that spoke primarily to boys, not girls:

Great great grandfather, great grandfather, grandfather,
Father and self,
Self and son,
Son and grandson.
From son and grandson
Onto great grandson and great, great grandson.
These are the nine agnates.
Constituting the kinships of man. . . .
Learn while young,
And when you grow up, apply what you have learned;
Influencing the sovereign above;
Benefiting the people below.
Make a name for yourselves,
And glorify you father and mother,
Shed luster on your ancestors,
Enrich your posterity.[55]

Influenced by modern times, her parents then sent their young daughter off to the county seat of Xiuning, where she attended the Longfu Girls Middle School. After a year of study there, for an unknown reason she returned home. While at home as a teenager, Wang Yaozhen assisted her parents in the household. According to her son, she would "write in her journal, read books, embroider, and sometimes go up in the mountains to cut kindling. Those were the carefree days." She also took up smoking tobacco under the influence of an elderly female neighbor.

As she approached the age of twenty, in 1927, Wang Yaozhen's parents and Huang Zhenzhi's parents, related by marriage, decided that the two should become husband and wife. As the son of a prospering manager of a kerosene shop in Tunxi, the descendant of presumably many prosperous merchants, and a graduate of the Normal School trained to be a teacher, Huang Zhenzhi seemed like an excellent match for Wang Yaozhen. And she, a literate and industrious girl from a well-to-do merchant family, seemed a superb new daughter-in-law for the Huang household.

Huang Qiuhua, Wang Yaozhen's granddaughter, who was raised by her, writes: "Zixian was thrilled about Zhenzhi marrying. Drums thundered, and Chinese trumpets blared. There were deafening fireworks; the room was filled with people; a hundred banquet tables were laid out. This was the last high point of Yin Yu Tang. After the two married, she [Wang Yaozhen] felt very lucky."

When the couple married, a second-floor room was assigned to them. Huang Zixian was at the height of his prosperity, and as was proper for all weddings, he had spent an extravagant amount of money on the wedding. The wedding chamber was completely redecorated for the occasion. The outside facade of the room was painted pink and purple with black outlining, and the interior walls and ceilings were covered with imported flowered wallpaper. This commodity must been quite unusual and expensive, having been imported from England or Germany to Shanghai and then carried inland, perhaps by a member of the family.

Living in the home, in addition to her husband, were Wang Yaozhen's in-laws—Huang Zixian, Madame Wu, and their two daughters. Huang Aizhu would have been about nine, and Huang Ailan, five. Huang Zixian, working in the town of Tunxi, rarely came home. Madame Wu and her children lived in a room on the first floor, and Wang Yaozhen would have shared a kitchen with them. No doubt, as in a traditional Chinese home, she—the new daughter-in-law—was expected to do much of the cooking. In addition to the direct family relatives, there were many others living around her within Yin Yu Tang. In the rooms just below the wedding chamber were Huang Zizhi, Huang Zhenzhi's uncle, and his wife and their children. Elsewhere on the first floor were Huang Shaoqing's wife and children and the Shao family; and nonfamily members who, for one reason or another, did not have their own homes and rented rooms in Yin Yu Tang. The large home that Wang Yaozhen had entered was a busy and bustling household. With Huang Zixian's kerosene shop in Tunxi and Huang Zizhi's pawnshop in Hankou, each sending funds home once a month, there was never a sense of want.

Though Yaozhen eventually found warm relations with some women in the house—including her husband's female cousin Huang Xianying—she did not (as was typical in many Chinese households) get along with her mother-in-law. "The two of them argued," recalls Huang Xiqi, Wang Yaozhen's son, "about nothing in particular. It was just 'chicken feathers and garlic skins' [nothing important]. These situations were very rough on my mother. She was very busy, right and left, but she always had to be careful not to anger her mother-in-law. . . . If she did or said something and crossed the will of her mother-in-law, the latter would refuse to talk to her for several days. When that happened, she would have to bring her tea, kneel down, and apologize."

Within a year of Yaozhen's marriage, the atmosphere in Yin Yu Tang began a slip for the worse. Huang Zixian, at the age of fifty-two, suddenly died of a stroke in 1929.

The income that his family had come to depend on was now gone. Fortunately, Huang Zhenzhi could still bring in some cash, and the family property that was rented out provided a bit more. Still, the reduced income was immediately felt in the household. In addition to his stepmother and her two children, soon Huang Zhenzhi and his wife were overseeing a growing family. Their first child, named Xilin, born in 1931, had fulfilled the traditional desire for male offspring. A daughter then followed the boy.

By this time, Huang Zhenzhi was following the age-old pattern of Huizhou men and leaving the village to find work in the business world. His wife's father had recommended him for a job at the Yangshu Pu in Shanghai, a silk store, where he was in charge of maintenance. The flash and excitement of Shanghai appealed greatly to the man who, as a child, had been described by his father as "annoying," "stupid," and unwilling to obey his elders.

In 1934, when Huang Zhenzhi's uncle, Huang Zizhi, suddenly died, leaving his son Huang Zhenxin a moderate provision of cash, Huang Zhenzhi persuaded his cousin to become his partner in a coal business in Shanghai. As was the custom, Wang Yaozhen stayed home, raising her children, caring for her aging mother-in-law, smoking with her sisters-in-law, perhaps singing verses with the other women of the household, and tending to worshipping the Huang family ancestors and household deities. Though neighborhood women often gathered in the reception hall of Yin Yu Tang to play mahjong and pass the time, Huang Xiqi has adamantly declared, "My mother never played mahjong."

With her husband away, Wang Yaozhen seems to have spent time, most likely in her second-floor wallpapered room, composing a short lyric novella. This way of occupying time would have been quite unusual among the women of Huang Cun. But Wang Yaozhen had been educated both in Confucian classics and in a high school. She was literate and perhaps had read contemporary literature. Certainly she was familiar with letter writing, as Huizhou merchants and their families, separated for years at a time, were assiduous letter writers.

Wang Yaozhen wrote her tale in epistolary form, as a series of letters between a woman in a small Huizhou village and her husband, a clerk in a pawnshop in a distant city. The wife describes details of a variety of occurrences within the household: an ill child, two servants discovered having a tryst in the grain warehouse, a cousin's wedding, a mother-in-law losing too much money at mahjong, and, most distressing, a younger sister about to be married off to an older, rather wretched, husband.

As the story progresses, various descriptions echo specific aspects and details of Wang Yaozhen's own life within Yin Yu Tang. Among those details is a wife warning her husband about prostitutes in the city:

In the outside world, there are many luxurious places,
Do not go to the brothels!
Your temperament is not restrained enough.
Moreover, you are quite young.
If you become infatuated with a prostitute,
You will spend a lot of money.
And you will certainly not think of me then.
I would rather die than bear such things.
You would be luxuriating in the warmth while I was
    suffering in the bitter cold.
If you ever did such a thing, I would certainly drive her out.
We could have a third-party judge, but I would surely bring
    disaster on that cheap [expletive].
It would either be a sharp murderer's knife [for her],
    or a hemp rope [for me].

Wang Yaozhen's life changed dramatically in numerous ways during the late 1930s. First she had the painful experience of losing two daughters. One died in infancy, and another, whom she always recalled loved to sing and dance, died from pneumonia at about the age of six. Then her husband, unlike most young men of the village, returned to reside in Huang Cun. He found jobs teaching in nearby schools, at Gulin Elementary school in Wucheng and at the Xintang Elementary school not far from Tunxi.

The late thirties were troublesome years in China. Japan was occupying an appreciable portion of China's landmass in the northeast and the east, and was threatening to devour more of the country. Transportation between Japanese-occupied cities, such as Shanghai, and Huang Cun made travel difficult. However, it was not the political situation that sent Huang Zhenzhi back home.

The reasons offered by later generations for Huang Zhenzhi's eventual return differ. According to her son, Wang Yaozhen asked him to come back home: "She was afraid that he would go to brothels if he was away from home for too long, so she forced him to come back.... Actually, my father was a man of good conduct. The real reason was that my mother felt alone at home and didn't have anyone to talk to . . . so he returned home and worked as an elementary-school teacher."

Huang Zhenxin, the cousin with whom Huang Zhenzhi opened the coal shop, explains the situation differently: "When my father died, he [Huang Zhenzhi] invited me to come to Shanghai [to open a business] because he knew that my father had left me some money. Our business was poor, and then other businessmen cheated us and we lost money."

Back in the Huizhou area, Huang Zhenzhi could be at home more often, a situation that hopefully pleased his wife. Drawings he did in his spare time of horses, fish, and boats—evidence of his presence—were pasted onto cabinets in Wang Yaozhen's bedroom. While in Huang Zhenzhi's eyes, Wang Yaozhen perhaps could not compare with the women of Shanghai, he did maintain his marital relationship with her. By 1940, she was pregnant again.

As Yaozhen's pregnancy progressed, Huang Zhenzhi's health disintegrated. In 1941 Yaozhen gave birth to her second son. The name Xiqi was given to the new infant, ten years his brother's junior. The boy may have been a momentary comfort for Wang Yaozhen after losing her two daughters. The character *xi* of his name was assigned to all male members of his generation, while the *qi* is a mythical animal meant to deliver sons who will become high government officials. Wang Yaozhen had great hopes for this child.

Within two weeks of the arrival of Xiqi, and the great happiness that accompanies the birth of a son, Wang Yaozhen's husband was dead. According to Huang Xiqi, his father died of a very high fever. And, as is said in Chinese, *tian fan, di fu*, "the sky flipped upside down and the earth overturned." The family—Wang Yaozhen, her two sons, her mother-in-law, and her two sisters-in-law—was now completely without any income and any adult male on whom they could depend.

Huang Qiuhua, Wang Yaozhen's granddaughter, describes the situation: "Even though he [her husband] did not have much of a salary as a primary school teacher, she had still lost a primary ridge column [a critical supporting element]. All she had left was

Fig. 90 **Charcoal sketch of a horse by Huang Zhenzhi, c. 1930s.**

just-born Huang Xiqi, and ten-year-old Huang Xilin. And a grand-mother—a heavy financial burden and a heavy mental pressure. All day her face was washed with tears and she had nothing happy to speak of."

Huang Ailan, one of Wang Yaozhen sisters-in-law, recalls the difficulty of those years: "[We were so poor that] Huang Zizhi's wife sometimes would buy us mushrooms. We only ate chicken at New Year's." Meals consisted primarily of rice and vegetables. Even eggs and doufu could not be eaten every day.

One of the household's first decisions was to completely unburden the family of a girl. Huang Zixian's youngest daughter, Huang Ailan, had been engaged since she was nine. Relatives of a woman who had married into Huang Cun had noticed fatherless Huang Ailan when she was still a child and decided they wanted her as a daughter-in-law. Once engaged, she moved to her fiancé's home and began working as a servant there, waiting for her husband, who was a year younger, to mature. With the death of her half brother and the financial tension in the house, a proper betrothal could not be held. There was little money for a suitable wedding.

"I never had a real wedding," she recalls, now almost sixty years later, her eyes filling with tears.

For many girls of low-income families, a wedding, like the one celebrated by Huang Zhenxin, was an unknown and painful absence in their lives. Many poor families could not afford to feed their daughters, whom, in essence, they were raising only to be part of someone else's family. Financial circumstances forced them to make the decision to sell their daughters as servants to families with young boys. The girl would become the nurse/nanny for the boy infant. When the boy was old enough to consummate the marriage, a modest ceremony would be held. The situation was often an uncomfortable marriage, as the bride and groom often regarded their spouse as a sibling.

Soon after Ailan married, her older sister, Aizhu, was also married off to further relieve Wang Yaozhen of financial responsibilities. Still Wang Yaozhen had her own two boys and her mother-in-law to feed. With no other viable moneymaking avenue open to her, the filial daughter-in-law and caring mother did what few women in Yin Yu Tang had done before her: she found jobs herself.

Liberated feet—women's feet that had been bound at child-hood but were then unbound and released to spring back for a more comfortable walking pattern—were becoming more popular in the forties and fifties. The more liberal parents of young girls were deciding not to bind their daughters' feet, and middle-aged women were unwrapping the cotton ties around their feet and allowing their heels to touch the inner soles of their shoes. It may have been about this time that Wang Yaozhen liberated her feet, allowing her to do more physical work.

The young mother first went to Yuetan, a nearby town, to help out doing housework and childcare in the home of her mother's sister's husband's family. A few years later she found a job as cook in the Huang Cun Primary School:

Her work burden was very heavy. Every day there were two or three tables of people who were eating. Every day she would [make] the long walk to the well, three or four times a day, to carry buckets of water. She was a good cook and also very clean and hygenic, and was praised by the teachers. In the winter, they ate primarily vegetables, radish, doufu, salted vegetables. Sometimes they had salted vegetables with pork. And she made eggs for the teachers.

—Huang Qiuhua

About this time, a member of the household left home—meaning one less person to feed—and a new national government was marching into place. In March 1949, the Communist Party had begun functioning in Xiuning County. On April 28, 1949, Xiuning County was officially liberated by the Communists. Wang Yaozhen's older son, Huang Xilin, already eighteen years of age, like many boys his age at the time, was moved by the fervor of the Communist movement. He, without delay, joined the People's Liberation Army and traveled east with the troops to liberate Shanghai.

Changes in the national leadership, with the 1949 Communist revolution, altered the makeup of the Yin Yu Tang residents in a number of ways. In addition to the absence of Huang Xilin, the family members were joined by a number of new non-Huang residents. The Sixth Branch, to whom Wang Yaozhen's grandmother-in-law had given four rooms of Yin Yu Tang to relieve her of a debt, still had possession of those rooms. Land reform, which was completed in Xiuning in November 1951, altered the situation. During this reform, a total of 101,493 mu (24 sq miles) in Xiuning County was confiscated from wealthy landowners, landlords as they were labeled, and redistributed among 19,046 poor peasant households.[56] Moreover, houses and property of these same landowners were confiscated and redistributed among the local, poorer populace. Huang Zhengang of the Sixth Branch was labeled a landlord. The village cadres confiscated his large mansion as well as two of his rooms in Yin Yu Tang. He and his wife, with nowhere else to go, moved into their two remaining rooms on the second floor of Yin Yu Tang. Two poor peasant families moved into the two rooms that had been confiscated and "redistributed" on the first floor. The Huang family accepted the course of events within their home, and were thankful that they had not received a critical label. Just after the liberation in 1949, most probably both for monetary gain as well as for political propriety, Wang Yaozhen sold a parcel of land remaining in the family's name.

Huang Xilin's army salary was of some assistance to Huang Xiqi, his mother, and their grandmother. In Yin Yu Tang the reduced family raised their own chickens and ducks to supplement their diet. Wang Yaozhen planted vegetables and corn on the hillside and made salted vegetables to eat in the winter months. The clothes she and her son wore were all made of rough home-woven cotton that had been handed down from other family members.

Huang Xiqi, who has endless admiration for his mother's hard work in those difficult times, recalls their life together: "All the shoes I wore were made by my mother. The bottoms of the shoes were made with white cloth and there was a belt for each shoe so it would not fall off. She planted cotton and puffed the harvested cotton by herself to make quilts. Her whole life was frugal and hard. . . . We also grew ramie. When it was harvested, we put the ramie in water to get rid of the green outer skin and to make rope which was very durable. . . . We placed the peeled-off ramie on our laps and twisted it into thread on roof tiles." One of the few objects Huang Xiqi saved from his mother's personal belongings was the decorated roof tile she used for making hemp rope.

The hardships of Wang Yaozhen's life as a single mother were multiplied during two years that proved disastrous for the whole country, 1959–60. The collectivization of land in China began in 1958. Villages were organized into communes that farmed the land together and distributed the proceeds among all. The villagers even all ate together—the 185,000 farmers in Xiuning ate communally in 1,219 dining halls. (The Huang Cun communal dining hall was located just east of Jin Shi Di.) As a result of the collectivization of the land, a series of unfortunate weather conditions, and a sequence of horrifying bureaucratic missteps, China suffered a massive famine in 1960.[57] In June and July of 1958, the rainy months in the Huizhou region on which the crops depend, there was a drought. No rain fell for an extended period of time. The water in rivers stopped flowing and ponds dried out.[58] According to some sources, the communes, feeling forced to prove their successes, falsely amplified their actual 1958 harvest records. They were then forced to pay higher grain taxes, leaving them without enough to eat. Though no proper accounting was ever done (in an attempt to keep the disaster from becoming internationally known), most estimates claim that over 30 million people died during the period. Population records for Xiuning County reveal that while the population had been growing by four to five thousand people annually in the early 1950s, in 1959 the county population decreased by 1,601. In 1960 the decrease was 13,470. Altogether, the population dropped by 15,000 during the years between 1959 and 1961, indicating that almost 10 percent of the people in the county were lost to famine.[59] After 1961 the numbers start to increase again.[60] The famine took its toll not only in deaths but in

births as well. Few women were healthy enough to become pregnant. In 1961 there were only 1,333 births, compared with 9,183 births in 1962.

As the sixties progressed, the citizens of the new nation, now over a decade old, began to be accustomed to the new idealogies and routines. However, in 1966, worried that old habits and manners were creeping back into daily life, the government unleashed the Cultural Revolution. Every landlord, intellectual, and bureaucrat was re-investigated for possible unrevolutionary thoughts or actions. The inhabitants of Huang Cun were not left unconsidered.

Huang Xiqi, who had followed in the footsteps of the father he never knew and become a schoolteacher, was transferred from a nearby village school back to Huang Cun to teach at the Huang Cun Primary School. It was the early years of the Cultural Revolution, and intellectuals and cadres were being sent back to their hometown villages.

In 1968 there were new developments within the family as well. Wang Yaozhen's mother-in-law—with whom she had not always lived harmoniously, though whom she had always served filially—passed away. The death meant not only was there one less mouth to feed, but also that there was now an available room in the house. As was appropriate to proper room allocation, Wang Yaozhen moved from the second-floor room into the first-floor room where her in-laws had lived.

Huang Xiqi had just married the sister of a student of his. Together, the new couple moved into the very same wallpapered bedroom in which his parents had spent their early married years. Life had changed drastically since 1927, when Yaozhen had first moved in. The fortunes of the family had long ago slipped away, numerous strangers had joined their household, and the daily struggles of living had become a familiar routine.

Fig. 91 **Wang Yaozhen (1908–1994) used this unusual tile decorated with impressed designs for creating hemp string. The hemp would be stripped of its outer bark using the scraper. The resultant strands would then be twirled together into a functional string by rubbing them together across the tile. The concave tile would fit neatly on the homemaker's knee. This is how Huang Xiqi remembers his mother making string with which to sew together the soles of the cotton shoes she made for the family members.**

After the Cultural Revolution, many of the nonfamily members built their own homes or went to live with their children who had moved away. By 1981 Huang Xiqi, his wife and children, and Wang Yaozhen were the only occupants living in Yin Yu Tang.

For Huang Cun, the year 1981 marked a radical change in lifestyle. Electric lines were brought into the village, and Huang Xiqi had two lightbulbs installed in Yin Yu Tang. One proudly hung at the entrance hallway and one was filially installed in Wang Yaozhen's room. Huang Xiqi himself continued to use kerosene in the rooms he, his wife, and children shared.

Despite the modern accoutrement, Wang Yaozhen's elder son, Xilin, decided it would be better for his aging mother to live with him in the outskirts of Shanghai. As a filial son, he felt obligated to care for his long widowed mother who had suffered inher own youth, toiling for her children. Shortly after her lightbulb was installed, Wang Yaozhen left Yin Yu Tang for the last time. She died in 1994 in Shanghai, at the age of eighty-six.

Wang Yaozhen lived through a turbulent century. In her early years she was able to benefit from modernizing efforts in China. She had been able to receive an education. She had also been fortunate enough to be born into a moderately well-to-do family and married into a family of similar standing. Circumstances of hard luck forced her onto a path of hardship.

In the story that Wang Yaozhen wrote as a young married woman—and kept tucked among her papers until discovered by her son after her death—the narrator writes to her husband, with profound sympathy, about the arranged marriage between the husband's cultured and well-educated sister and an older, unsophisticated farmer:

Your younger sister is only sixteen,
But she already has a mature appearance.
A previous arrangement for her marriage fell through.
Last month, however, an engagement was suddenly settled.
She will marry into the Chen family of the North Village,
A family that relies entirely on farm work.

Your sister is not pleased with the arrangement.
She sits in her room weeping.
Father-in-law and mother-in-law asked me to comfort her.
I spoke with her, trying to cheer her up, until the stroke
  of the third watch.

Had she lived in an earlier time Wang Yaozhen might have earned a few lines in a gazetteer or even a stone archway. Instead, having received an education, she penned a novella that became a memorial both to herself and to the many thwarted women of her era.

Untitled (Four Letters in Poetic Form)
a novella by Wang Yaozhen, a matriarch of Yin Yu Tang

Bowing and chanting thousands of blessings to you, I, Liu Yue'e, greet you,
  Qiguan, my husband.
Since we separated in the eighth month, my heart has not been at peace,
  neither day nor night.
Above, in the hall,[61] my father-in-law and mother-in-law are all in good
  health,
Below, on the mats,[62] both our son and daughter are safe and sound.
Your brother's wife[63] and your younger sister are very well,
My own father and mother are also safe and sound.
As for my husband, surely everything in your pawnbroking business is
  proceeding according to your desires....
The son of your third uncle[64] got married on the eleventh day of the
  tenth month.
They invited me to be a wedding assistant.[65]
[I wanted to go but I feared] I didn't have the proper jewelry or clothes.
Your cousin's family is prosperous, and they have all and every kind of
  garment.
My father-in-law did not want to lose face, so he instructed me to go by
  sedan chair to borrow clothes from them.
I borrowed some gold bracelets with pearl-decorated edges and a pair
  of earrings as well.
They were all very fashionable and each pearl was large and well formed.
I also borrowed a sky-blue coat with fringes of snow weasel fur,
And a dark brown skirt with fringe of squirrel fur.
Your cousin's wife was really stingy.
She hemmed and hawed and was not really willing to lend me anything.
Fortunately, her mother-in-law is a nice woman.
She forced her daughter-in-law to loan me the items....
On the tenth day of the month, I got up in the middle of the night and
  began carefully making myself up.
Had I not paid attention to my appearance,
My husband would have lost face.
I tied up high my disheveled hair,
And set in it a very long hairpin.
I made up my face with black wax lines.
And powdered it with a fragrant powder.
My eyebrows were painted in the shape of the Chinese character
  for "eight."
I could have won a beauty contest with Guanyin.[66]
The embroidered bright red shoes I wore were only three cun[67] in length,
Their pot-shaped soles were made of white silk with decorated edges.
My yellow silk trousers were embroidered with small golden lotuses.
The ebony tobacco pipe had an ivory holder.
And my purse was in the latest fashion....
The arrival of the bride at the gate was quite exciting.
Surrounded by candles, she was led to the bridal chamber.
When the scarf covering her head and face was removed,
I was so surprised that I jumped out of the room.
Then the people around took a close look at her.
They burst into laughter, laughing so hard their bellies hurt.
Her face resembled the Kitchen God,
And her hair looked like that of an eighty-year-old man.
When she extended her hands to comb her hair,

They were both completely red with boils.
And when she opened her mouth to answer a question,
She sprayed spit in every direction....
Third uncle's wife said that I looked stunning,
And that my speech was refined and stylish when talking to guests.
Thus, she had asked me to take care of the bride in the bridal chamber.
The male guests were disorderly and unrestrained.
Although in name they had come to see the bride,
Their eyes, in fact, all fell on me.
I could not find a place to hide,
Nor could I be too strict with them....
When we got home there were no lamps lit.
In the dark, as I sat in the living room,
My father-in-law came to pester me.
Thinking that I was my mother-in-law,
He grabbed ahold of me, and engaged in improper behavior.
When I clarified that it was me,
He grasped me even harder.
I panicked, and screamed aloud.
My mother-in-law heard me and came running in.
She grabbed him immediately,
Slapped his face, and whacked him again and again.
After she finished beating him, she came over to comfort me.
She said I shouldn't think it strange, that my father-in-law was becoming
     muddle-headed,
And he must have been possessed by a fox spirit.
I was furious and quickly turned to run to my room.
But in my hurry, I bumped against the oil lamp.
It fell and the oil spilled on my clothes.

Huang Zhenxin and Huang Xianying

All of us have big feet. My mother's generation had to wear their hair in a special way, but our generation didn't. We didn't need to bind our feet either. We all had big feet. We were equal to men. It was very invigorating, refreshing.

—Huang Xianying

At age fourteen, Huang Zhenxin set out from his hometown, like his fellow sons of merchants, for a big city. Though he was going to meet his father in Shanghai, he cried as he walked down the paths and roads leading away from Huang Cun and toward the waterway that would take him farther. It was a whole day's journey just to the river in Tunxi—a hired hand carrying his extra clothes and goods on either ends of a shoulder pole—and then several more days on a boat. Comforting Huang Zhenxin as the distance grew longer was the conviction he always held in his heart that he would go home again. This life's journey took him to Shanghai, Hankou, and back to Shanghai. Almost seventy years later, in 1996, still living in Shanghai, he was still determined to retire to Yin Yu Tang. "Leaves fall toward their roots," Huang Zhenxin often says, quot-

ing the Chinese saying that describes the custom of older people returning to their hometown.

In many ways, Huang Zhenxin's life pursued a pattern set by his father and grandfather and many generations before them. The life of a merchant entailed leaving home at age fourteen, and Huang Zhenxin, biting his lip, abided by that fate. But in other manners, the streams of history, personal preference, and the coincidences of random events, tragic and lucky, presented him and his descendants with new and unexpected opportunities.

It is worthwhile to return first with Huang Zhenxin to his childhood in Yin Yu Tang. Called Songyan as an infant and toddler by his family, the boy was the eldest son of Huang Zizhi and Hong Zhaodi. His birth as the first child and first son was most certainly celebrated. Though he has no memory of her, his aging grandmother was still living during the first year of his life. As a toddler, he would have played with the other children of the house, including his grandmother's treasured first grandchild, his cousin Huang Zhenzhi, several years his elder.

Life in Yin Yu Tang, as Huang Zhenxin and his younger sister Huang Xianying recall it today, was quite different from the Shanghai apartment where he now resides. Twenty to thirty people lived together in Yin Yu Yang, mostly women and children. Practical, daily matters in the house, such as lighting, washing, obtaining food and water, entailed a great deal of physical labor, and Huang Xianying clearly remembers those daily routines:

[Clothes washing was done] at the small brook. Sometimes, [hired] people were called to carry water to our home for washing the clothes. The water was brought up from wells. My mother's feet had been bound and she could not walk long distances, so she had to ask others for help.

We did not have electric lights, but we had kerosene lights. One kind of [kerosene] lamp was placed on tables. Another kind had hooks and could be hung up on walls.

We raised some hens and roosters, but no more than five or six. They were for us to eat. They went out in the day and returned home at night.

If we needed pork or fish to eat, we would buy it. As for vegetables, they were gardened by my mother. That is to say, we grew our own vegetables. We also helped our mother to do that. After school, we would carry the human manure to the garden. We were very busy.

It was very cold in winter, especially when it was snowing. In winter, we always ate inside, and used foot warmers, which were fueled by charcoal. Everyone had a foot warmer. Winters were really tough. You couldn't open the windows. Instead of glass, the windows were paper. Hardly any light could get through. There were also huotong, fire buckets. Underneath was a foot warmer that a kid could stand

Fig. 92 (right) **Huang Zhenzhi and his younger sister Huang Xianying in Shanghai, 1999.**

Fig. 93 (below) **Wooden child minder, called a *huo tong* (fire bucket) in Chinese. A child would stand on an interior slatted shelf. Below, on the ground, a brazier full of charcoal would keep the child warm during winter months. (In figure 167 a child is seen in a child minder.)**

on. Every family had one. It's about this high [about one meter], with a board in the middle that a kid could stand on. When adults were busy, say with cooking, they could leave kids in there.

When it was really cold, and when our hands and feet were frozen, we'd stand in the buckets to have our meals before we went to school.

—Huang Xianying

And of course, there was school. Like his Huang family predecessors, Huang Zhenxin and his brothers and sisters were privileged to be able to study at the Huang Clan Primary School in the village. Each morning and afternoon, with a break in the middle to return home for lunch, the boys and girls studied mathematics, Chinese, sports, arts and crafts, music, gardening, and even English. Though intent on giving the children a sound education, the school in this remote village also sported a playground for a well-rounded edification, with wooden horses and swings for the children:

[As a child I liked] sports and singing. Reading and studying was very tense. In the morning, I went to school and there were four classes. At twelve we would return home to eat lunch and at one o'clock we would have more classes and wouldn't return home until 4:30 in the afternoon. . . . We studied mathematics, physics, and chemistry. It was called a foreign-style school. We studied English, too. . . . I would go with Mother to the vegetable plot to water the vegetables and spread the fertilizer. Sometimes I'd catch insects, then we'd eat dinner and do homework. . . . We played hide-and-seek, the old eagle catches the little chicken, and we would sing. There weren't any toys.

—Huang Xianying

The days in Yin Yu Tang, as in most houses in Huang Cun, revolved primarily around the mothers and children. Even when Huang Zhenxin's father was home, during his illness or on a break from work, there was little interaction with him. Avoiding him, the children discovered, was their best strategy.

Only annual festivals and special family events such as births, weddings, and funerals broke the daily routine of school and housework. These exciting occasions left deep impressions on Huang Zhenxin and his sister, Huang Xianying:

During the New Year's celebration, the ancestral portraits would be hung up. They were long scrolls. The people are sitting on chairs. One portrait had five persons and another had two persons. There are both gentlemen and ladies. There was also one that had only one person. They were hung up only during the New Year's celebration, starting on the twenty-fourth day of the last month and ending on the eighteenth of the first month of the New Year.

—Huang Zhenxin

When offering sacrifices to ancestors, the ceremony was held on the first floor. The statue of the Bodhisattva Guanyin was placed on the second floor. [The shrine] was like a small room. The statue of Bodhisattva was inside it. The statue was made of porcelain. It was a sitting figure. She was the Goddess of Mercy with thousands of hands. We worshipped her in the evenings. Each morning, the adults also worshipped her, but we children had to go to school.

—Huang Xianying

Beyond ancestral and family occasions, the most powerful and frightening memory of that time for Huang Zhenxin was an incursion into Huang Cun and an attack on their home, Yin Yu Tang. The episode caused a complete upheaval of the otherwise seemingly serene village life of a child. It was not an event, however, for which the family was unprepared. Aspects of the house, and those of its neighbors—such as the doors that lock over the stairwells—had been specifically designed by Huang ancestors for such incidents. Most certainly, the invasion of 1926 was a repetition of events the ancestors had experienced themselves:

When we were young, we liked a small room in the old house of Huang Village. You could go up the stairs, open the door, and hide in there. At that time, there were many battles between warlords. And deserters who had lost battles would escape to our village, where they would attempt robberies. We'd close our front entrance, and they'd try breaking it open with bricks. When they couldn't get the door open, they went down the lane to try another house in the back.

—Huang Zhenxin

Neither newspaper accounts nor historical documents offer the actual facts of this invasion. What is clear is that a group of looting bandits, possibly deserting soldiers or enlisted soldiers, invaded Huang Cun and began raiding the residents' homes for food, clothes, and anything else they could grab:

When I was about ten, deserting Nationalist soldiers arrived. Wherever they went, they looted and plundered. Our main gate was secure, and couldn't be pried open. The people [living in the house] behind us were broken into. They demanded everything; they even wanted the bamboo stalks. My nephew was wearing a hat, and they even grabbed that.

We knew that the deserting soldiers were coming and that it was dangerous. As soon as my parents and I became aware of them, we went to hide in the gong tower. At that time my father was sick. There was nothing else we could do. We waited until the deserting soldiers had left until we came down. The head of the village came out and called neighbors to help carry my father into the mountains to hide. If they had been caught, their lives would have been finished. We hid in the mountains for a long time.

—Huang Zhenxin

The *Xiuning Gazeteer* makes note of the event and offers more historical context than a young boy may have been aware of: 40,000 defeated soldiers under the command of the warlord Sun Chuanfang had retreated to Xiuning County. Even English-language newspapers published in Beijing reported the events:

The countryside is infested with bandits and the country people have been fleeing to the city and elsewhere to escape them. Homes have been devastated and women and children carried off. Letters at hand constantly refer to such depredations.

Ningkuofu[Ningguo], a neighbouring city, has had its ups and downs with the military, then all suddenly left and peace reigned for a week or two. Suddenly 10,000 soldiers arrived from no one knew where and quartered themselves on the citizens. Their arrival caused apprehensive fears, which a few days later were justified. Suddenly, one day, shooting was heard, looting began and a great part of the city suffered before they took their leave by the East Gate. Three large market towns, ten, thirty, and seventy li distant were similarly treated. This came upon the city like a bolt from the blue and took place within the last three weeks.

From this it will be gathered that normal conditions have not yet been restored, and the people still sigh in vain for "the good old times."[68]

In the middle of the night, the Huang family was guided to the small village of Gewu, approximately 4 li west of Huang Cun.

Today it is a half-hour walk, uphill, through rice paddies and along uncultivated hillsides. Eventually, the path reaches a narrow passage, planted with rice, between two high hills, with a few houses on the side of one hill. Much less accessible than Huang Cun, and even today with houses more modest than those in Huang Cun, the cluster of simple homes was an intelligent place to seclude a vulnerable family from bandits.

As documented in Huang Zizhi's account books, the amount of funds that he was able to spend toward this escape demonstrates the healthy financial situation of the family at that time, and the large amount they were clearly worried about losing:

The 16th Day (November 20, 1926)
- *Expending 8 silver dollars for escaping from military riot to Gewu. (4 dollars were paid to the luggage carriers and 4 dollars were paid to my ambulance carriers.)*

The 16th Day (December 20, 1926)
- *Expending 6 silver dollars. (When escaping from the military riot, [we] went to the family of Chen Laowu. This money is paid to him as for his service as well as food and firewood.)*

Huang Zizhi's account book ends several months after the escape to Gewu, and it is likely that he had recovered sufficiently by New Year's of 1927 that he could return to work in Leping.

Since Huang Zhenxin's birth, his mother had given birth to another four children. The youngest, a boy, was just three years old. When Huang Zizhi returned to work, he left Huang Zhenxin, the other four children, and their mother to continue their daily schooling and life in Huang Cun, hoping that another major invasion did not occur.

But by mid-1927, Huang Zhenxin had finished primary school. The next inevitable step for a boy of his age was to leave the village to apprentice in a business. Huang Zhenxin, however, had different desires. He wrote to his father in Leping, explaining that he was preparing to go to Xiuning County High School. His father, according to the son, wrote back saying that "we did not have the financial conditions, that the family was in difficult straits, and that I would have to abandon my ideas of going to school. There was, he said, an opportunity for me." Huang Zizhi was just establishing a pawnshop with two other partners in the large, international town of Hankou. The son would be able to serve as an apprentice in the pawnshop.

Huang Zhenxin traveled to Shanghai to meet his father, walking a day's journey to the larger town of Tunxi and then taking a four day boat journey to Hangzhou, the attractive city designed around a lake that had once been the capital of the Southern Song

dynasty almost a thousand years before, and where many Huizhou merchants had once made their fortunes.

I had always been only in Huang Cun. I had never been anywhere else. Because I didn't have much money, I had to sit at the back of the boat. I missed my mother and cried. I was also seasick. The old wife of the boat captain gave me a little to eat, and I felt a little better . . . [but] I was terribly homesick.

—Huang Zhenxin

Once in Shanghai with his father, there was little time or available sympathy to pine for home. Together, the son and the strict father traveled by steamboat down the Yangzi River to the major port of Hankou.

The number of people, the density, and size of the buildings in both these large cities made a distinct impression on young Zhenxin, but before he could focus for long on the sights of the cities, he was quickly caught up in the daily and strict routine of pawnshop life. Items as diverse as clothes, gold and silver jewelry, and copper teakettles arrived in the shop on a daily basis. The attendants were responsible for writing receipts, authenticating the objects, cataloguing them, wrapping them, storing them and dispensing the cash to the clients. The young man and his father slept on the second floor of the pawnshop, doubling as nighttime guards for the valuables.

Sometimes, even a copper pot [would come in] if its owner was in urgent need of money. The pawnshop's [service] was like providing a small loan. If someone had nothing to eat for today's dinner, he could send such things to our shop to get some money to buy rice.

—Huang Zhenxin

While hard at work learning the many meticulous processes of working in a pawnshop, Huang Zhenxin occasionally took time to study the world around him and to venture into the urban life with fellow pawnshop workers from Huizhou. Huang Yusheng, a "nephew" several times removed, who was just a year younger and had grown up with Huang Zhenxin in Yin Yu Tang, worked at a separate Hankou pawnshop. The two young apprentices splurged one day—perhaps after having proudly saved a small sum of money—on a studio photograph of themselves at the Hua Xin Photo Studio in the French Concession. They stand, both in cotton robes, in front of a painted backdrop of trees, their arms resting on the fundamental element of a Chinese scholar's garden, a large, twisted rock, trying to project an air of sophistication.

Huang Zhenxin, like his father, kept a notebook for taking down significant items. Into his book he hand copied letters he wrote and articles that caught his interest. He inscribed, for instance, a section of a detective story translated from a foreign language into Chinese. On January 1, 1931, he took the time to carefully write out the complete text of a newspaper article about the Japanese invading the Yu Gorge. This ominous moment, which seems to have disturbed young Huang Zhenxin, would lead to Japan's occupation of China's northeast provinces with their coal mines and excellent ports. For the moment, though, Huang Zhenxin still felt safe in Hankou.

Though he was working in Hankou, Huang Zhenxin's mother and the warmth of home was never far from his mind. In an appropriately polite but passionately sincere letter, he sends her birthday greetings on the heralded occasion of her fiftieth birthday. Despite the formal framework of the letter, the sixteen-year-old cannot restrain himself from childhood desires to be nurtured. He adds a postscript to the letter, asking his dear mother to please make him more shoes:

The twenty-first year of the Republic of China [1932], December 21
An auspicious day

Great Mother,

[I send this letter from] beneath your knees,[69] respectful recipient of my appeal.[70]

Yesterday, I received a letter from my honorable father[71] and was very pleased to know that the blessed person is in a state of peace and good health, and that my younger brothers and sisters are all well. I cannot help but celebrate this.

I accompany Father in Hankou. We eat and sleep well; everything else is fine as well. Please do not worry about us from afar.

The most auspicious day of the fall this year honorably falls on your fiftieth birthday, my honorable mother. And the most auspicious day of this month happens to occur on the grand celebration of Father's fiftieth birthday.[72] I wish you pair of mandarin ducks prosperity, wealth, and longevity, like that of the mountains and the rivers.

Because I, your son, am [currently] a traveler dwelling in a distant land, I could not express my wishes in person with the others. But from afar, I will gaze up, on my tiptoes, at the Star of Longevity above, and bow to the mountains [for you]. The height of the Tianmu peak has inspired me to say a prayer of blessing for you, and I will carefully write it on sheets of red paper, wishing you lives of a thousand years, wishing you prosperity and peace, and congratulating you as well for bringing this great happiness to the entire family.

Your son,
Zhenxin, bowing and kowtowing thrice

Fig. 94 **Huang Zhenxin and his younger relative, Huang Yusheng, also from Huang Cun, posed for a photograph in a studio in Hankou, circa 1930.**

I want to beseech you again to assist me in making two pairs of double-layered shoes made of black cloth. The style is the same as the ones you mailed me last year, but two fen shorter. The soles in front should be less thick and more pointed; and the shoe openings can be made larger so that they are more comfortable to wear. Please have them made immediately, and inform me when they are finished so that I can tell you where to mail them. As for the cotton-padded shoes that you sent me last year, they are still fine for wearing, You don't need to make more for me this year.

Shortly after sending off this letter, Zhenxin, still in Hankou, received another missive from his mother. One of his younger sisters had died. A few months later, came another letter. His younger brother had died: "When I received that letter, I was in Hankou, working in the pawnshop. I cried."

In 1934, with the Hankou economy teetering and conflicts brewing between the three pawnshop partners, Huang Zhenxin's father made the decision to close the business. Huang Zhenxin's desire at that time, he now recalls, was to return home again to Huang Cun, but his ever aspiring father wanted to go to Shanghai to set up another pawnshop. At the age of twenty, barely out of his teens and just at the age his apprenticeship might be developing into a job, he could not refuse his father's wishes. They packed their funds and their portion of the pawnshop properties.

Though Huang Zhenxin had seen, or at least heard, the violence of the invasion into Huang Cun, and surely sensed the absolute fear that incursion had prompted in his family, he had escaped and no one in the family had personally suffered. At the pier in Hankou, where his father was fatally assaulted, the situation was different.

The emotional strain of dealing with his father's death and the burden of caring for the details could not have been easy for young Huang Zhenxin. After dealing with the steamship ride to Shanghai with his injured father, the rather inexperienced young man had to make arrangements with hotels and doctors in Shanghai, and finally the funeral arrangements.

Before Huang Zhenxin could even contemplate his future, he needed to tend to extensive funerary rituals. The day after his father's death, he arranged for the purchase in Shanghai of a lacquered coffin, made of wood from Jiangxi Province, with an outer gold-colored surface and interior of vermilion, which he purchased for the price of 126 yuan.[73] He also had to pay for clothes for the deceased, known in Chinese as longevity garments (*shou yi*), Taoist priests, and transporters of the coffin.

While still in Shanghai, Huang Zhenxin had quickly turned to the group of people who regularly assisted with these matters—the Huizhou Brotherhood Association. Such regional associations were established as clubs and service centers for merchants working or traveling through large urban areas distant from their hometown. Huang Zhenxin may not have been able to afford to pay for the body to be shipped back to Huang Cun immediately. The receipts reveal that he owed the association—which accepted and stored Huang Zhenxin's father's corpse—seventy-six yuan when he himself hurried home to be with his grieving family:

I went home to worship and make offerings to my father. Friends and relatives sent presents. I placed my father's ancestral tablet [in the ancestral hall]. At that time, the rituals were very grand and solemn. [The funeral] went on for more than a week during which we invited monks to read sutras.

—Huang Zhenxin

The journey to establish a new pawnshop in Shanghai with his experienced father had not gone as expected, and Huang Zhenxin was now faced with an unknown prospects. Back in Huang Cun, recovering from the shock of his father's death, he put his future in the hands of his elders.

Hong Zhaodi, Huang Zhenxin's mother, was now even more alone in the world. Her in-laws had long passed away, her husband had died, as had her husband's brother several years earlier. She certainly must have been sensing the vulnerability of life. Two of her younger children, Cuihong and Henian, a boy and a girl, had died of measles in the previous two years. There was barely a man in the household to support her and the remaining children, and she would have been anxious about her duty to ensure the continuation of the family line.

Local custom held that a young man in mourning for his father had to either marry within three months of the funeral or wait for another three years. Hong Zhaodi decided, as her mothers-in-law had before her, the time of her son's marriage. She would have her son marry sooner, rather than later. Possibly she was thinking that a marriage would financially tie her and her family to another well-to-do household, or perhaps she was looking forward to a daughter-in-law to help in the household. She contacted her sister, married to a man in the village of Yang Cun, who found a young girl there, Chou Lijuan:

My marriage was of the "feudal" style. My mother made the arrangement. The matchmakers were my aunt and my sisters. The procedure, such as bowing to each other, was quite complicated ritually.

The bride came carried in a painted sedan chair that had been hired to go to Xindu to get the bride. When she arrived in the village, firecrackers were set off. Then they came along the side of the village and when they arrived at Jin Shi Di, the painted sedan chair was put down and I personally went to the sedan chair to greet her. I did not know her [the bride's] appearance until I lifted the red cloth head cover during the wedding.

After the wedding ceremony, we drank wine and ate, and then we went over the hemp bags. . . . Those carrying the bride called out "one generation is transmitted to another generation" [a pun on the sound dai, *which means both "bag" and "generation"] and "the husband sings and the wife follows."*

In the past, in the old society, the woman had to listen to the husband. There was also a saying [that they would call out], "sons and grandsons filling the hall."

—Huang Zhenxin

Huang Zhenxin's younger sister, Huang Xianying, was just a teenager at the time of his wedding, but she still distinctly remembers the grand event: "He was twenty-one years old, I was fourteen. He married in Jin Shi Di. . . . It was the liveliest wedding I have ever seen. There were 100 banquet tables. As they were carrying the bride [into the village] they had to recite auspicious words, and threw cakes for everyone to eat. . . ."

After the festivities of the wedding—following on the grim heels of the patriarch's death—and the entrance of the new bride into the home, the question of the future of Huang Zhenxin once again loomed. Though the situation was not urgent, as he had inherited a sizable amount of money from his father's share of the pawnshop, a decision still had to be made about how to best invest the money.

Huang Zhenxin's mother's father, his only living male elder, though not of the Huang family, still retained an advisory role to the young man. He strongly recommended using the money to purchase land. Land, he said, could not burn.

My maternal grandfather advised us. He knew I had a sum of money. He told us to buy land. He said land cannot be stolen by robbers, it cannot be burned. Buying land was worth the money. I thought if I bought land, I could only live in the countryside. Then I considered the situation again. In business, making money is fast. If I bought land, I wouldn't be able to do business, and earning money would be slow. It would be better to do business.

—Huang Zhenxin

Figs. 95 & 96　**A chest, one of a pair, given to Chou Lijuan to bring to her new home when she married Huang Zhenxin in 1935.**

Fig. 97 **Hong Zhaodi, seated, poses with her son Huang Zhenxin and daughter-in-law, Chou Lijuan, and their two children, Huang Binggen and Huang Yanjun, in Shanghai about 1950.**

Huang Zhenxin's cousin Huang Zhenzhi urged him to follow in his father's footsteps and return to Shanghai and open a business.

After a few months at home with his new bride—and, of course, his cousin, who also lived in Yin Yu Tang—Huang Zhenxin made his decision. He and Huang Zhenzhi, who was eager to leave Huang Cun, would go to Shanghai to try their hand at a business. Using the money Huang Zhenxin had inherited from his father, the two young men became partners in a coal-trading business. Meanwhile, Huang Zhenxin's sister Huang Xianying graduated from primary school and, unlike her brother, was allowed to go on to high school and study teaching.

In Shanghai, the two Huang cousins rented a room. They started off trading in coal tokens, but after being swindled several times out of large amounts of money, they came to the conclusion that opening their own shop would be a better strategy. The shop, The Zhonghua [China] Charcoal Ball Company, was located in central Shanghai, at no. 13, Alley 122 of Changle Road. As Huang Zhenxin tells the story, the enterprise would have been more successful had his older cousin been more business-minded. Instead, much of the money was drained off by visits to Shanghai entertainments.

In a desperate move, Huang Zhenxin wrote a letter to his mother, the only one in the Yin Yu Tang household with the authority of seniority, begging her to come to Shanghai and assist with an uncomfortable situation. The letter was found in Yin Yu Tang, ripped into many pieces. Not all of it is legible, but even the pieces that exist give some sense of the anxiety young Huang Zhenxin was feeling:

Dear Mother,

This letter is sent from under your knees and is written with great respect to you. . . . I am very glad to know that you, the blessed, are healthy and that our home is filled with good fortunes. . . . Since I was joined by my old[er] brother [cousin] in Shanghai to carry on a business two years ago, there has not been a single day without worry. . . . We were cheated by men from other regions in the first steps of our business. Later, I made an acquaintance with a certain Xu, from Nanli, and was swindled by him as well. . . . We formally started our business in the fourth month of the Chinese calendar. . . . He does not get up until noon every day. After lunch he will go out. And after dinner, they go out to play. He does not get back to our store until one or two A.M. He acts this way every day and does not take care of the business. On the contrary, he has spent all of the money the store once had. . . . Several times, his wife has written him to ask him to go back home. But how can he leave such a colorful Shanghai? In her letters, his wife mentions that there are some rumors about him at home. My older brother is still staying at the store. He often takes three, five, eight, or even ten dollars from the business. How can I manage such a business? I cannot even meet the needs of our family at home and have no money to mail back. All the money has been wasted by him. My suggestion is that you come here with Yanian [the youngest son] immediately. . . . All the money is under your direct control. In this way, the store will have a sliver of hope. . . . Please do not tell the others the contents of this letter as his wife and mother should not know of it. . . . Come here immediately As for the travel expense, please borrow money and I will mail it back as soon as you arrive in Shanghai. My financial situation is now very difficult. Wishing you golden safety.

Your son, Zhenxin,
Twenty-ninth day of the third month [c. 1936]

Having received the frantic letter from her son, Hong Zhaodi did indeed walk to Tunxi and find a bus—transportation had improved since Huang Zhenxin first left home—to Shanghai to assist her son. She stayed in Shanghai and was—in some fashion, as the elder—able to resolve matters. Her nephew Huang Zhenzhi soon returned to his wife in Huang Cun.

While the Huang family was experiencing their own inner turmoil, around them the city of Shanghai was soon itself spinning from devastating attacks from abroad. In 1937 Japan continued in its quest to conquer all of China, raining unexpected bombs on the country and cities. Huang Zhenxin's son, Huang Binggen heard many stories from his father about this time as he was growing up:

When the Japanese attacked in 1937, many fellow villagers tried to persuade my parents to go back [to Anhui]. My father [Huang Zhenxin] decided that it was not easy to get to Shanghai and there would be better conditions for us [in Shanghai]. He insisted on staying here. At that time, they lived in the area that was managed by France, so it was comparatively safe. But they still heard the bombs and guns shooting.

—Huang Binggen

Politics had a minimal, but not completely absent, impact on the young Huang businessman. Traveling between Shanghai and home had become more difficult, and sending letters was less reliable. Huang Zhenxin remembers his wife coming home one day with a quickly diminishing sack of grain that had been punctured by a nasty Japanese soldier's gun. However, while a great deal of China's population (the wealthy businessmen, the politicians, and the armies) was mobilizing in response to the Japanese invasion, the Huangs were not distracted from family matters.

In the early 1940s, a first son was born to Huang Zhenxin and his wife. The child died as an infant, but soon another son arrived. The timing was appropriate, as in the same year the previous generation—Huang Zizhi—was finally going home to be buried.

By the end of the decade China was sensing a change of wind. The victory of the Communists over the Nationalists seemed near. The Huizhou Brotherhood Association in Shanghai intuited that its mission could soon be curtailed and decided that the time had come for the corpses of its brothers who had died in Shanghai to be sent back to their hometowns to be buried. Among those bodies was Huang Zizhi, Huang Zhenxin's father:

According to the philosophy of our hometown, when people get old, they have to return to their hometown. There's a saying, "A tree may grow as high as 1,000 zhang, but when the leaves fall, they return towards their roots." So, according to custom, we were obligated to send Father home. . . . I knew that it would cost a great deal of money to send him home, but it was also an indescribable happiness.

—Huang Zhenxin

Only now that the body had returned home the proper funeral rites be performed. The importance of a person being buried in their hometown cannot be underestimated. Souls not buried in their hometowns, with their ancestors and their descendants to care for them, are considered to be restless and unhappy. Huang Zhenxin returned to Huang Cun to participate in his father's funeral and provide a proper and definitive burial.

My father's grave was arranged by mother. In the countryside, when you arrange a grave, you must first invite a man to analyze the fengshui. If the grave is done well, the sons and grandsons of the family will prosper, so you have to invite someone to consider the fengshui, see if the location is good or bad. If its good fengshui, looking across [from the grave], there will be a dragon.

—Huang Zhenxin

Announcements of Huang Zizhi's death were sent out to relatives and friends of the deceased and, in proper Confucian tradition, faulted the son, Huang Zhenxin, for insufficient filial piety. One announcement was never posted and remained among the family papers. (Though the document notes that Huang Zhenxin brought the coffin back on the day of his death, he and others all remember distinctly that the coffin did not return until just before the Communist liberation. The document definitely dates from a later time period as Huang Xiqi, a nephew of the deceased, born in 1941, seven years after Huang Zizhi's death, is listed as one of the mourners.)

To Mr. Hu Hairong[74]
Greatest Favors and Honest Words
Issued by Dasheng Fuel Oil Company at Tunxi
Obituary Notice

The Deceased was a native of Huang Village, in the southern Region of Xiuning County.

His son Zhenxin and others who failed to practice filial piety did not serve [their father] well, which led to a disaster falling onto our excellent father. It is a great sorrow that he passed away when traveling to Shanghai at approximately 10 P.M. on thirtieth of March of the twenty-third year of the Republic of China (i.e., the sixteenth day of the second month of the obsolete calendar).

He was born at twelve noon on the fourteenth day of the tenth month of the ninth year of Guangxu period (1883). He died at the age of fifty-two.

His son Zhenxin, who failed to practice filial piety, accompanied him when he was dying and watched all the procedures of donning the garments and placing him into the coffin. On the same day of his death, [his son] carried the coffin back home to bury him.

We announce his death in great grief to his relatives and related clan members.

We cautiously choose May second to hold the funeral at home.

His lonely sons:
Zhenxin and Zhenying
Kowtow with bloody tears.

His Grandsons of Direct Line
Xiying and Xijun
Kowtow with bloody tears.

His nephew
Zhenzhi
Kowtow with running tears.

Zhenzhi's sons
Xilin and Xiqi
Kowtow with tears.

His cousin
Dafu
Kowtow.

In 1949 Shanghai was rocked once more with the victory of the Communists over the Nationalist government and the socialization of the economy. Because he was not a capitalist or major land owner, Huang Zhenxin did not suffer the confiscation of property and loss of dignity borne by wealthier and more successful Shanghai businessmen. Instead, he carried on in his modest way for the next decades, selling coal and later, when he retired from the coal shop, selling milk at a corner store. Keeping a low profile, he and his family endured during the years of turmoil. He laughs now, remembering his maternal grandfather's advice to buy land, and is thankful, knowing how landlords fared after 1949, that he did not follow the elder's earnest recommendation.

On the fifth day of the fifth month in 1970, the Duan Wu holiday in the Chinese calendar when traditionally children would wear embroidered images to ward off evil forces, Huang Zhenxin's wife stood over the stove making noodles for the family's breakfast. As she cooked them, an odd smell arose from the pot. The food had become rotten. The family sensed the occurrence was an omen. Within a few hours, Hong Zhaodi, Huang Zhenxin's mother, had passed away. Her eighteen-year-old granddaughter, Huang Wenjun, was, like most young Shanghai women during the Cultural Revolution, living in a village in the distant countryside, learning from the peasants. She open the letter from home, saw it contained a black armband, a symbol of mourning to be worn by the family of the deceased, and burst into tears. Just as she did so, a thermos on the ground beside her exploded. The death of this stalwart Huizhou widow, who had traveled so far from her home village to help her son in his big-city business, was a powerful upset to the Huang family in their temporary metropolitan surround.

Throughout his years in Shanghai, and despite his comfort in the urban world, Huang Zhenxin always yearned for his hometown. There was no doubt in his mind that upon retirement, he would return to Yin Yu Tang and Huang Cun. When he reached his seventies, he purchased kitchen appliances—pots and spatulas—to reestablish his household in Yin Yu Tang. For years, his son discouraged him from moving back to the village. In 1996, when Huang Zhenxin was eighty-two years old, his son Huang Binggen finally agreed to bring him back to visit the home, to view the circumstances, and let him decide for himself. It had been almost fifty years since he had been in Huang Cun last, to bury his father:

Why did I bring my father back here for him to take a look? Because when he retired at sixty, he had [the] idea . . . to move back here to stay. We told him that all of us children [were] working now, and it would be inconvenient to take care of him if he was alone here. We couldn't set our hearts at rest, especially in terms of the medical serv-

ices and so on. But he insisted that from his childhood memory, he remembered that the air here was very fresh, and that it's close to mountains and rivers. He also asked us not to worry about him. . . . When my father was walking around in the village [when we returned in 1996], he met many friends from his childhood. Everyone was very excited. There were even some people with whom he had apprenticed outside the village, but they came back to the village and became farmers.

—Huang Binggen

I'm eighty-four years old now. I went back to the village in 1996, planning to stay there. As the saying goes, falling leaves settle on their roots. But our old house is not livable anymore. The house is huge, but no one lives there. . . . I was bitterly disappointed. My wife and I could not survive in the countryside. We couldn't buy anything with money; we'd have to work in the fields, but we don't have any land anymore; people have taken our land away. So we had no choice but to return to Shanghai.

—Huang Zhenxin

After he made his decision to remain in Shanghai and relinquish the ancestral home, Huang Zhenxin sat down to compose a document to assist his descendants in managing their lives. If the house were no longer to be there in Huang Cun to come home to, at least these words could guide the descendants into their future. The advice is primarily quite practical and ethical: take off your clothes if you feel too hot; when ill, seek a doctor; work hard; don't cavort with women; be loyal, sincere, and honest; don't cheat others; and respect the social and familial hierarchy. The words are sensible and sincere. And in the manner of an elder sharing wisdom with his juniors, it is very much in keeping with the ways of his own ancestors.

Throughout the centuries, many older Chinese men have written texts to pass on their knowledge about managing a home for younger generations. Huang Zhenxin wrote the following in 1997 at the age of eighty-three for his children and their children.

Aphorisms for Managing a Home
By Huang Zhenxin
Translated by Pauline Lin

1. The outlook on life
The principles of being
[Is to] learn to be a good person
[All] generations should understand this.

2. The sun and the moon pass on
Human beings move with the sun
To live, to sustain
To compose essays, and to inquire into facts.

Fig. 98 (top) **Huang Zhenxin and his wife, Chou Lijuan, after a banquet in a Shanghai restaurant, 2000.**

Fig. 99 (above) **Huang Zhenxin in Yin Yu Tang during his 1996 return home to Huang Cun and Yin Yu Tang.**

3. Health is of utmost importance
Live life sturdily
Culture is important
Morality should accompany it.

4. Three nights in equal balance
Sleep comfortably
When hot, take away [clothing]; when cold, add on
Do not ever be negligent [about it].

5. When sick with illness
Seek a doctor for cure
Should the demon of ill health not pass
Fight it with patience.

6. In living one's daily life
Plan out the key focus
To be high-minded or rash
Are all not the best stratagem.

7. When opportunity descends
Strive vigorously, seek out results
Gather securely [that which] you already have
Vigilantly prevent it from shrinking.

8. Work conscientiously
Practicality is of utmost importance
[As for] those poisonous and harmful pleasures
Be sure to shun them.

9. Stay warm and fed, and be wary of
Cavorting with women, and gambling
[They] corrupt your body, wealth, and name
And [are] not beneficial to the self.

10. Your manner [should be]
Gentle and affable
Honor and respect each other
Assist one another
Understand one another.

11. Be clear about public and private [properties]
Be clear about [who is] superior and [who's subordinate]
Be clear about who's [in charge of] domestic and external [affairs]
Be clear about truth and falsehood.

12. Be clear about the time/era
Be clear about weighty [versus] light [matters].
Exert your fullest effort
Never do anything stupid.

13. Be honest, proper, and straight-forward; and abide by the rules
[For] to harm others [is to] harm yourself
To swindle others is to swindle yourself
To deceive others is to deceive yourself

14. [And] to manipulate others is to manipulate oneself
Goodness will have good rewards
Evil will have grave rewards
Loyalty and sincerity are best.

15. Be earnest in work
[Let there be] a beginning and an end [in undertaking a task].
Be prudent in dealing with people:
Be wary of those secret arrows [that may come your way.]

16. Adapt quickly to changing circumstances
Combine [it] with objectivity
Thoughts and ideas [should be] stable
[These are the] important ways of life.

17. [To be] fully contented
[With regards to] both parties' emotions
[One has to] accommodate whenever one can.
[For] rendering help to others is [true] happiness.

18. When you encounter hardship
Attack it wholeheartedly
Endure and bear resentment
Be skilled in resolving [problems].

19. Look at the large picture
Past events need to be recorded
[And] work hard toward the future
Be at peace and in unity [with one another].

20. The words expounded above
When appropriate, follow them
When not fitting, then be done with them!
Use reality to testify [the aphorisms].

21. Inside the family
Mutually educate one another
Mutually elevate one another
Never pass it on to outside the family.

22. If there are errors
One can alter it
In places that are lacking
One can add to it, supplement it.

May 15, 1997
Leaving these words , Zhenxin

The 35th Generation

The two sons of the thirty-fourth generation of the seventh branch of the Huang Cun Huang clan, Huang Zhenzhi and his cousin Huang Zhenxin, produced between them four sons—the thirty-fifth generation. In accordance with the family's list of given name prefixes, the thirty-fifth generation was assigned the character *xi* as the first character of their given names. The men of this thirty-fifth generation, living most of their adult lives after the 1949 revolution, followed different paths from that of their merchant fathers and grandfathers. Unlike their ancestors, the falling leaves rarely dropped in the direction of the roots, but were instead blown along other routes.

Huang Zhenzhi had, in total, four children. The two girls both died young, one in infancy and one at about the age of six. The two boys, Huang Xiqi and Huang Xilin, both lived to adulthood.

Huang Zhenxin had two sons and a daughter. The first son died at a very young age. At the birth of his second son, in the summer of 1947, Huang Zhenxin and his wife, anxious to maintain the health of his second son, went to a fortune-teller, who noted that the young boy's physical makeup needed more fire, one of the five elements (the *wu xing*: fire, wood, water, earth, and metal) that comprise all objects in the universe. He recommended that one of the characters for the child's name contain the character fragment, known as a "radical," for fire. Therefore, the parents, veering from tradition and the family name cycle, gave this boy the name Binggen. *Bing*, meaning "bright and luminous," contains the character for fire, and *gen*, meaning "root," was intended to secure him to the world of the living. His parents also insisted that their precious son wear a braid for the first ten years of his life, as the word for wearing a braid, *liu*, in Chinese also means "to remain." This measure was again to ensure the son's continued existence.

Huang Binggen is still very much thriving in Shanghai, where he has lived all his life. Having originally trained in the army, he became a civil engineer for the city of Shanghai, working on many important skyscrapers in the metropolis where his father had once opened a small coal shop. Huang Binggen returned to Yin Yu Tang only three times in his life. He went to resolve financial transactions of the ancestral home—representing his father, the eldest male of the family and therefore the nominal owner of the house—in 1976, and twice, in later years, to pay homage to his ancestors and their graves. Though Huang Binggen still considers Huang Cun his hometown, his generation and his daughter's generation

Fig. 100 (right) *Good Boys Become Soldiers*. Published in March 1951, this children's book updates traditional rhymes and gives them a revolutionary twist. A traditional saying declared that "good boys don't become soldiers," but this book reverses the sentence to read "good boys become soldiers." The text continues to say: "What kind of soldiers? Liberation Army soldiers. New China is better than a big factory. It is a government, an economy, a military, a culture, and all kinds of machinery, booming day and night. The Communist Party is the engine, and the switch is always held by Chairman Mao."

Fig. 101 (far right) **Huang Xilin (1931–2001), the elder brother of Huang Xiqi who left Huang Cun in 1949 to join the People's Liberation Army.**

have carried the family line far from Anhui. He has effectively begun a new Shanghai branch of the family, just as Huang Keyuan did eight hundred years ago:

So my father came back here in 1934. Then he came back again in 1947. After that, he didn't come back for fifty years. On October 1 of last year [1997], I took my parents, my elder sister, my wife, my younger brother, and his wife back to the countryside again. There were seven of us, and it so happened that I was away for twenty years; my father was away for fifty years; my elder sister was also away for fifty years, since my mom took her back when she was seven; and my younger brother was away for more than twenty years, since he brought my grandma's cinerary casket for burial in 1972.

—Huang Binggen

In Huang Cun, the eldest member of the thirty-fifth generation was Huang Xilin, born in 1931 to Wang Yaozhen and Huang Zhenzhi. He attended the Huang Clan Primary School and was among the top students of his class. His mother could not afford to send him to middle school, but Cheng Xianghou, a well-to-do gentleman in the village of Fanggan (the hometown of Huang Xilin's great-grandmother) who often offered financial assistance to students of poor families, came to his aid. Huang Xilin was able to attend Xiuning County High School and was an excellent student.

In June of the historic year of 1949, as the country was on the brink of complete conquest by the Communists, Huang Xilin, like many people of his age from Huang Cun, joined the People's Liberation Army, and with them entered and liberated Shanghai. From then on, his family was essentially the army, and his work in an army factory. Though he maintained relations with his mother and brother, he divorced himself considerably from Yin Yu Tang and the concept of it as his home. He passed away on December 28, 2001, at the age of seventy-one.

Huang Xiqi, Huang Xilin's younger brother, proudly considers himself the living family member who resided in Yin Yu Tang the longest. Born in a first-floor room in the northwestern corner of the house, in 1941, he resided there—with a few gaps spent in other towns to teach—until 1982. Having lived most of his life after the 1949 revolution, Huang Xiqi's course through life brings to light radical alterations in the ways of Huizhou merchant descendants. The traditional Huizhou merchant lifestyle was no longer a possible occupation after the Communist liberation. Commercialism and private enterprise were not a part of the socialist system. With the handicap of growing up without a father, without money, and flapping in the winds of the many political campaigns, Huang Xiqi found his own path.

Huang Xiqi

In 1996 Huang Xiqi was a schoolteacher in the fourth grade in the Longwan Primary School, a twenty-minute bus ride from Huang Cun. He lived, like many teachers, in a single dormitory room at his work unit, the school. The room was within the school courtyard, just across from the classroom of small desks and chairs where he taught. His living quarters were cramped with a bed, a desk, a few chairs, and cardboard boxes full of a lifetime of miscellany.

He had been transferred to teach at Longwan in 1982 from the Huang Cun Primary School. In a sense, the transfer was a promotion. Longwan is a much bigger town than Huang Cun, with shops and marketplaces, and is located on a main road. The wider availability of goods, transportation, and communications was a great improvement over rural Huang Cun.

When Huang Xiqi was born in Huang Cun in 1941, wars were raging around the world. In Europe, France, Germany, England, and Italy were engaged in a war; and in Asia, the Japanese were occupying much of China, Burma, and Korea. In 1939 thirty-seven people were killed when the town of Tunxi, not far from Huang Cun, was bombed by the Japanese. And in October of 1940, the war had gotten as close as nine miles (15 km) from remote Huang Cun, when planes from the Japanese army bombed Huizhou High School (today called Xiuning High School) in the town of Wan'an killing one student and injuring three.[75]

Within the walls of Yin Yu Tang, the atmosphere was equally destabilized. The excitement of the birth of another baby boy, and the hope for his survival, was countered by the acute illness of his father, Huang Zhenzhi. Just two weeks after little Huang Xiqi was born, his father died from a raging fever.

Huang Xiqi grew up either staying with his maternal grandmother in her village or following his mother in her quest to bring income into the household. He followed her to live in schools, where she did maintenance work; to private homes, where she was a maid; and back to Huang Cun, where she cooked for the local primary school. It was a transient and, compared with the lifestyle of his wealthy forefathers, meager life.

From the early years of his life, before the 1949 revolution, Huang Xiqi has strong memories of the traditional customs and ceremonies of Huang Cun. He can recall the elaborate weddings and funerals, the ancestral worship, and the annual rituals. The Confucian devotion to family and filial piety instilled in him by his mother, made a strong impression on Huang Xiqi, and he has always maintained those values. Propriety meant that "when a guest came to visit, he would be seated in the most primary seat. Tea and tobacco would be served. When the guest left, the host would accompany him or her outside. . . ."

I remember that when I was a teenager, we still worshipped ancestors at the first month of the year (Zheng Yue). Portraits of all ancestors would be hung in the reception hall on the first floor. Before dinnertime in the evening, candles would be lit, and the ancestor worshipping began. I did it, too. I still have the memory of liquors and dishes laid out on the table for the ancestors. It was done to express our cherished memories of our ancestors. We were taught to respect the elder generations, so I have very deep impressions of ancestor worshipping.

When I worshipped the pictures, I was very sincere, kowtowing and lighting the candles. I was in great reverence.

Celebrating Chinese New Year's was very important. The eighth day of the last month of the Chinese calendar was called the laba *holiday. On that day people would clean their house and ate a specially made gruel with eight grains and dried fruits. We would make stuffed rice cakes, glutinous rice cakes, and rice dumplings wrapped in bamboo leafs.*

Sacrifices were offered in front of the pictures of the ancestors, and people would kowtow to them. In the evening all the members of the family ate their New Year's Eve dinner together. There were so many dishes that the leftovers would not be gone until the third day of the first month of the new year. This food was called the "crossing the year extras," and it symbolized that there had been a surplus in the past year and would be more in the new year. After the New Year's Eve dinner, children would greet the seniors and receive from them money believed to safeguard their lives in the coming year. People would not sleep until midnight, and firecrackers then ushered in the new year.

The first day of the new year was the beginning of the Spring Festival. In the morning of that day, both adults and children would wear new clothes and worship ancestors in front of their pictures. The worshippers would be arranged from the eldest to the youngest. Then they would drink "good business tea" and eat "long life noodles" and "gold ingots" (boiled eggs with tea flavor and salt), along with cakes and red bean soup. The male members of the family would go out to worship in the Huang Ancestral Hall. On that day, when people met one another, they would offer best wishes. Using knives, scissors, and needles was not allowed. They would also not cook stir-fried foods, because in the Chinese language, the pronunciation of "stir-fry" is the same as that of "quarrel." They would not touch brooms, so as to avoid sweeping away good luck. They would pay great attention to their utterances to avoid any unlucky word or words with similar pronunciations.

Living on the cusp of change, Huang Xiqi retained these memories, and his reverence for his ancestors:

The other thing was to hang money at the graves. Our ancestral graves were exquisitely built. I still have the impression of how they looked in the fifties and sixties. They were all made of stone—the base, the railings, and the dome. There was a hole in the middle for hanging money. But in 1968, there was a craze for digging up graves. At that time, some of my ancestors' coffins were not rotten yet, and there were some clothes in them; though the bodies were rotten, there were still some bones. I still have the memory of piles of graves with stone tablets.

The destruction of the ancestral tablets during the 1950s, when the ancestral halls were destroyed in the Great Leap Forward, and when "people made use of the tablets for firewood or for the soles of sandals" deeply affected Huang Xiqi.

The world of education, so ingrained in the Huizhou merchant culture, also made a strong impression on the young man. He studied, like his father before him, at the Huang Primary School, where his mother was working as a cook.

In the early forties, the school building, located within an old temple dedicated to the deity Guan Di, seemed near collapse, and the lineage decided to invest in a new building, to be positioned just across the path from the old school. When the new school opened in 1948, just as young Huang Xiqi was old enough to start school and just as the Communist liberation was arriving in China, it was converted from a lineage school into a public school, open to all and supported in part by the government. The new building included classrooms, an auditorium, teachers' dorms, restrooms, and a kitchen. The handsome grounds dedicated to education included a playground, a garden, and a fish pond. Students of first to sixth grades studied Chinese, math, science, history, geography, singing, sports, handicrafts, and painting. As Huang Xiqi recalls, he and his classmates all wore school uniforms: gray- or blue-colored clothes with upright collars and cloth buttons, trousers with loose waist and cloth belts, knee-high cotton socks, and cotton shoes with "shoe-belts."

In that sparkling new village school, Huang Xiqi enjoyed Chinese, calligraphy, and painting most. In recalling those days, he notes that he hated math class, and perhaps even more intolerable were the weekly school assemblies, primarily held to discipline students. The boys to be disciplined had to take down their trousers and were beaten by the teachers with copper rulers.

Huang Xiqi quickly put his education to use to better society. When he was a third-grader, adult schools were set up in many villages to reduce illiteracy. Huang Xiqi and his classmates participated in the movement and went to nearby villages to teach reading and writing to elderly people characters. the project lit Huang Xiqi's passion for teaching.

During school vacations, Huang Xiqi would go to his aunt's home in the large town of Tunxi, where her husband worked in a cigarette factory. This aunt was Huang Aizhu, the elder daughter of Huang Zixian and his second wife, Madame Wu, and she opened

Fig. 102 **Class picture of Huang Xiqi and his classmates at the Tunxi Normal School, 1962. Huang Xiqi is third from the left on the top row.**

new world's up to her nephew. A fan of all kinds of operas: Beijing opera, Yue opera, and the local Huizhou regional Huangmei opera, she would buy tickets for herself and young Huang Xiqi. The two had a special relationship, and because she had no sons of her own, Huang Aizhu had wanted for many years to adopt Huang Xiqi.

Having graduated from the Huang Cun Primary School, Huang Xiqi, unlike many of his classmates, had the grades and intellectual abilities to go on to be a boarding student at Xiuning High School, the top school in the county. And in 1959, ten years after the liberation of China, Huang Xiqi was able to enter the Tunxi Normal School, where students learned to be educators. For the son of a merchant family, this was a glorious leap into the world

of education and scholarship. At that time, normal schools in China were vocational schools at the upper high-school level that taught young people to become teachers. Traditionally, becoming a teacher was a major leap in social status, as it implied scholarliness. When the merchants in Huizhou first began to increase their wealth in the Ming dynasty, they immediately began to build academies. The hope was to educate their sons to rise from the merchant ranks and into the erudite ranks of scholars and officials. At the normal school, Huang Xiqi joined the student association and was in charge of the student newspaper. His graduation certificates, his awards, and his class photographs decorated the walls of his proud mother's bedroom for many years.

While Huang Xiqi was at the Normal School in Tunxi, radical changes were happening back in Huang Cun. In 1958 the two ancestral halls—no longer in use—were taken down so that the bricks and wood could be contributed to a county reservoir project. As in villages all over the country, the land and residents were being organized into communes. No land was being privately farmed. Instead of eating at home, all villagers were eating in communal cafeterias.

The massive famine of 1960 also left its mark on the residents of Yin Yu Tang. Huang Jixian of Huang Cun recalls.

When I was in my second year of high school, I had seen corpses of people who had died from starvation on the side of the street. It made a deep impression on me. . . . When I was studying at school sometimes, there would be a week when no grains were supplied. We only ate soybeans. After a week you couldn't eat any more. Our stomachs had a difficult time. . . .

Huang Ailan, one of Huang Xiqi's two aunts who had been married off as a young girl, was living at the time in the hometown of her husband, a small village deep in the mountains of western Xiuning County. Even today, the village is accessible only by foot, an hour's walk from any road along a narrow path. By 1960 she had already given birth to six children. All but one of them died in the famine of 1960. A few years later, after she herself had regained her strength and emotional stamina, she had another son.[76]

In Yin Yu Tang, the famine was also taking its toll. Huang Zhengang, who had already suffered severely at the time of liberation, had no goodly soul that dared care for him. Strict political parameters meant that most people had to stay away from Huang Zhengang. When he died of starvation in 1960, the village had to pay for his funerary expenses because there was no family member who would step forward to acknowledge any relationship to a former landlord.

In 1962, just as the country was recovering and returning to a more normal rate of food consumption, Huang Xiqi graduated. Like all graduating students at that time, the government assigned him a job. This first work assignment was teaching in a primary school in the town of Wu Cheng, 8.7 miles (14 km) south of Huang Cun. After the 1949 revolution, clan buildings, such as ancestral halls, were often converted into public or Party property. In Huang Cun, Jin Shi Di had been converted into a hall for public meetings, and in Wu Cheng, the grand eighteenth-century Huang Clan Ancestral Hall, was transformed into the Wu Cheng Primary School. There Huang Xiqi taught and with his earned income was able to support his mother and his now widowed aunt in Tunxi.

Fig. 103 (top) **Official marriage photograph of Huang Xiqi and Tong Xihao.**

Fig. 104 (above) **Huang Ailan, Huang Xiqi's aunt.**

Five years later Huang Xiqi made the fundamental step in his culture of getting married. He married the young Tong Xihao, who was twenty years old and whom he had known as the daughter of one of his students. Unlike his father and his grandfather, and the other men preceding him in his family line, his wedding was not an elaborate affair. The year was 1967 and the Cultural Revolution had begun. Lavish spending on a wedding was considered feudal and decadent:

When I got married, it was the Period of Difficulty. We just registered. My aunt in Tunxi sent me a quilt and a quilt cover. I got two cotton bed pads myself. . . . There was no inviting people to wine and dine. At that time the new ways were being advocated.

—Huang Xiqi

Not only were the newly prescribed marriage ceremonies completely different from earlier weddings, but the basic underlying principles, according to the government regulations, were also different. Tong Xihao and Huang Xiqi's marriage certificate expresses, and on the back explicitly delineates, the intended parameters for

Fig. 105 (above) **A painted wooden cosmetic case given to Tong Xihao on her wedding.**

Fig. 106 (right) **Huang Xiqi and Tong Xihao's marriage certificate, dated February 27, 1967.**

结 婚 证

字第　号

自願结婚，经审查合於中华人民共和国

婚姻法关於结婚的规定，发给此証。

公元一九六七年　二月二十七日

matrimony under the new marriage laws—laws that would provide women with equal standing and equal rights in the newly visualized China. The front of the certificate displays four red flags of the People's Republic of China, two on either side of a medallion enclosing a five-pointed star. The medallion has the toothed edge of an industrial gear along the top and sheaves of wheat, representing agriculture, on the bottom. To the left of the flags are high-tension electric towers, and to the right are smoking factory chimneys to demonstrate the future industrial power of China. Large characters through the center of the certificate indicate the route to that accomplishment: "Unity and Mutual Assistance." At the base of the florid frame, eight characters grace the opposing pages of a book, declaring "Diligent Study, Collective Improvement." The smaller central characters explain that Huang Xiqi and Tong Xihao married, of their own free will, on February 27, 1967, in accordance with the Marriage Laws of the People's Republic of China.

Half of the reverse side of this colorful certificate provides several lines of Article Three of the Marriage Laws, "Rights and Obligations between Husband and Wife":

The seventh clause: In the partnership of shared life, husband and wife have equal standing in the family.

The eighth clause: Husband and wife both have obligations for mutual love, mutual respect, mutual assistance, mutual support, harmonious unity, labor and production, bringing up children, the family's good fortune, the construction of the new society and shared struggle.

The ninth clause: Both husband and wife are allowed to have the freedom of selecting an occupation, of participation in work and participation in the activities of society.

The tenth clause: Husband and wife have equal rights to, and rights in resolving, family property.

The eleventh clause: Husband and wife have rights to use their own given name and surnames.

The twelfth clause: Husband and wife have equal rights of inheritance.

The other half of the reverse side of the marriage certificate launches, without any timidity, into the intimate issue of birth control.

Soon after his marriage, with the rising momentum of the Cultural Revolution, Huang Xiqi was required to return home to his own village. He went back to live in Yin Yu Tang. Huang Xiqi's widowed mother, Wang Yaozhen had moved downstairs at this point,

Fig. 107 **Family portrait of Huang Xiqi, Tong Xihao, and their two children, Huang Zhaofeng and Huang Qiuhua, in the mid-1970s.**

to occupy the room previously inhabited by her mother-in-law, who had passed away. Huang Xiqi and his wife were therefore able to move into a second-floor bedroom—as was appropriate for a young married couple. They moved into the same wall-papered room in which his parents had begun their marriage almost forty years earlier. For this marriage, however, there were no new renovations and no new wallpaper. They lived in the room as it stood.

In Huang Cun, Huang Xiqi taught at the primary school during the day and assisted his mother with farming in the evening. His new wife, who had graduated from Tunxi Normal School in 1966 but had not been assigned a teaching job, also moved to the village to farm with the village commune. The members of the seventh branch of the Huang clan, who for so many generations had relied on purchasing rice and meat—growing only their own vegetables—were now, like their fellow villagers, farmers. Each morning Tong Xihao went to the communal fields. And each year the family raised and slaughtered a pig.

Huang Xiqi and his wife were not the only people moving into Yin Yu Tang in 1968. A massive exodus of people from urban areas to the countryside was imposed by the government, which wanted its intellectuals, bureaucrats, and ex-capitalists to further comprehend the toil of working the land. An elderly woman, the sister-in-law of one of the Yin Yu Tang daughters-in-law, a lonesome widow of an ex-capitalist with nowhere else to go, came from Shanghai to stay at Yin Yu Tang for several years. Too old to work in the fields, she helped take care of Huang Xiqi's children.

Fig. 108 **Chalk marks on the wall outside a second-floor bedroom in Yin Yu Tang: "Fanggan, 16 women."**

The Yin Yu Tang household was also joined periodically by locals from other villages who had come to Huang Cun for military training. With a plethora of spare second-floor rooms, the family was asked to provide housing during brigade-wide military practice periods. Remnants of these visits can still be seen on the second floor in the form of chalk markings: "Comrades, Be Quiet!" and "Fanggan [a nearby village] 16 women." indicating that sixteen women were assigned to sleep in one small bedroom on the second floor.

Other chalk marks on the walls of the house are distinct reminders of the atmosphere of the town. Scribbled in chalk on the outer wall of one second-floor bedroom are the words "Down with the counterrevolutionary element Wu Xueqin." Wu was a village schoolteacher. The characters were most likely written by a child, but they reflect the often random and always harsh victimization of individuals during the Cultural Revolution.

Another document found among papers in the house is the draft of an application letter to join the Communist Youth League. Such membership would certainly advance one's future career potential. The letter illustrates the urgent desire, present among most young people at that time, to be accepted by the Communist momentum around them, and also demonstrates the age-old bond between a person and his or her family. In this adolescent's case, his father had been a major in the Nationalist Army and, therefore, an enemy of the "people." This stain of his family background would have been a basic demerit in any pursuit. In his application, the boy tries to emphasize his father's desire to reform himself and stresses his uncles' role in the Communist liberation. Lastly, he tries to dispense with the feudal notion of tying one's reputation to that of one's family members and insisting on his aspirations to "work for the people." The letter communicates the resolute spirit of the time to follow the "revolutionary road":

I firmly choose the proletarian road and will advance unceasingly on this revolutionary road. Below is a report of my family status:

Father: Before liberation he worked as teacher and headmaster of an elementary school, teacher of an informal teacher-training school, [and was a] captain-ranked secretary and major of the army of the Nationalist Party (Kuomintang). He also acted as a branch head of the Nationalist Party.

After liberation, he returned [to his] hometown and became a peasant in 1949. He was arrested in October 1954 and pressed to confess problems of the past (to confess problems of both his own and others). He was released home in September of the next year and engaged again in agricultural production. During one year's imprisonment, he was not put into reform through labor. Instead, the main things he did then were to confess problems of the past and to read newspapers.

He became sick in 1960 and was hospitalized in the commune hospital. At that time, each member of the commune got a quota of 250 gram[s of] grain per day. He, along with other patients, enjoyed subsidies from the commune and got a quota of 500 grams of grain per day and special provisions of soy bean, sugar, etc. He died at home in 1961.

Uncle (Mother's Brother): A student before liberation, he joined the [Communist] army in 1949 and has been in the People's Liberation Army since then. Now he is a captain-ranked military surgeon on the Fujian front line.

Elder Sister and Her Husband: Both are teachers at Xiuning High School.

Uncle (Mother's Sister's Husband): Formerly a [Communist] guerrilla, he worked as a political instructor of the People's Liberation Navy and then the vice president of the intermediate court of Wuhu (Anhui Province). Now he works in the supervisory committee of Huizhou district, and is one of the six members of the district committee of Chinese Communist Party.

One's history is written by oneself, and cannot be done by anyone else. I would like to work for the people diligently for my whole life, and thereby write a red history.

I hope the Communist Youth League can provide me with supervision, stimulus, and help.

Huang Qitai
Date: March 1, 1965

In 1968, at the height of the Cultural Revolution, the Huang family expanded to encompass a new generation. Tong Xihao—at an age far younger than the twenty-five years advocated by her marriage certificate—gave birth to a daughter, Huang Qiuhua. And two years later—again, not following the four- to five-year break suggested by her marriage certificate—she gave birth to a son, Huang Zhaofeng. Both children were born in Yin Yu Tang and were cared for by their mother, and even more so by their grandmother, Wang Yaozhen. Though the Cultural Revolution had dispensed with many traditional customs and rituals, when Qiuhua was a month old, Tong Xihao put a small black hat on her head. Silver items, such as scissors and rulers, decorated the traditional hat to symbolize her future abundance. She donned a bib in the shape of a lotus, and in the winter, when the weather turned cold, she was fitted with a traditional hat with a tiger's face to ward off evil forces.

The years of the Cultural Revolution affected the family and its centuries-old routines and rituals. Images of ancestors were replaced by images of Mao. The ancestors were no longer to be worshipped. The multi-armed bodhisattva Guanyin on the second floor could no longer receive her offerings. Ancestors' graves were dug up. As many have commented, the world had turned upside down.

In 1976 the zealousness of the Cultural Revolution had begun to calm down and a new energy was seeping into Huang Cun. With the arrest of the Gang of Four, the Cultural Revolution, though never officially denounced, was over. By 1979 new economic reforms and the formal decollectivization of the land began.

Wang Yaozhen, meanwhile, was aging. In 1981 Huang Xilin, her eldest son, had beckoned her to come join him in Shanghai. A year had barely passed before Huang Xiqi received a new assignment, to teach in the primary school of the larger village of Yuetan. Huang Xiqi was the last family member to reside in Yin Yu Tang. When he left in 1982, he asked his neighbor Wang Youjin to watch over the house. Huang Xiqi himself would return from month to month to check the condition of the house, make minor repairs, and, on specific family anniversaries and Qing Ming, pay his respects at the family graves.

In 1998 Huang Xiqi began construction on a new home for himself in the town of Xiuning, the county seat of Xiuning County. The three-story concrete structure with glazed exterior tiles does not resemble the home in which he grew up. However, the spirit with which he built the house is in keeping with the intentions of his ancestors who built Yin Yu Tang. "After the matters of the house our ancestors gave us were settled, I began building a new house for my descendants. I plan to hang up portraits of the past generations of our family in the highest place in the house, and at New Year's and holidays make offerings to them."

Fig. 109 (far left) **Huang Xiqi's new home in the county seat of Xiuning, 2002.**

Fig. 110 (left) **Huang Xiqi's bedroom in his new house, 2002. he sleeps on the bed given to his parents for their wedding.**

Next page: Fig. 111 **The skywell of Yin Yu Tang from the second floor.**

Architecture embodies and expresses the temperament and structure of a society as thoroughly as works of literature or fine art. Unlike the creations of writers and artists, however, buildings are collaborative efforts strongly influenced by a host of pragmatic considerations— function, cost, strength of materials, and site, among others.

—Robert Thorpe "The Architectural Heritage of the Bronze Age"

The forms and spaces of Yin Yu Tang acquired their shapes and decor by being at the confluence of a certain temporal evolution of architectural design and a specific geographical place. In the hands of specific carpenters, masons, stone carvers, and wood engravers—who were in turn guided by both their own masters as well as the Huang family patriarch—the building took on its individual construct and appearance. Once completed, the Huang family members living within those special spaces continued to mold and impact the atmosphere they inhabited, merging, as home dwellers do, their lives and the home that cradled them.

The size and variety of geography of China, a nation that covers over nine million square kilometers, have meant that the country's regional residential architecture has developed over the years in many different directions.

In the northwest, many people still live in the traditional cave houses (*yaodong*) carved out of the loess hillsides. In southeast China, in the Fujian provinces, the Hakka minority group as well as some Han Chinese often inhabit large circular, rammed-earth multi-unit, two- and three-story dwellings. And in Beijing, though some people have recently moved into high-rise concrete apartment buildings, traditional, gray brick one story *siheyuan*, courtyard houses, still dominate some parts of the capital city.

These diverse types of houses evolved from the very different regional geographies, climates, available materials, resources, and social situations. In the northwest, the dry climate allowed for cave and underground dwellings, which were warm within the earth's surface in the winter and cool in the summer. The massive, multi-unit Hakka houses probably developed as fortresses to protect the

minority, nonindigenous group living in Fujian. And, side by side with these regional residential architectures that were designed for comfort, familial relations, and social adhesion, an imperial architecture also developed in the capital cities.

Despite the broad range of houses in China, people of most regions adhered to a number of specific characteristics, creating a basic generally accepted Chinese architectural foundation. Those characteristics, which were tweaked and modified in accordance with climates, customs, times, and unexpected circumstances, include a central courtyard onto which all rooms face; a preference for significant spaces to face south; laterally symmetric buildings with an odd number of bays; a timber-frame column-and-beam wooden structure supporting the roof; and orientation and construction of a building determined in accordance with *fengshui* (geomantic) principles.

Fig 112 **Round, tamped-earth house seen from above in the mountains of western Fujian Province.**

Courtyards

The ubiquitous courtyards of China—in underground cave dwellings in Ningxia, round houses in Fujian, and siheyuan in Beijing—speak to a millennia-long architectural framework. The courtyard offers advantages to inhabitants. The unpunctured surrounding walls of the house provide privacy as well as safety for the people within. And the central courtyard confers ventilation, sunlight, and an interior, nonpublic gathering or work space for family members. The convenience of this configuration seems to have overruled any interest in large, outward-looking windows until very recently.

A drawing reconstructing a building in Fengchu, Qishan, Shaanxi, from the late second millennium B.C.E. makes clear that the courtyard layout was already a developing format, at least among the aristocracy, more than three thousand years ago. There are at least two other remains of buildings in Erlitou, Yanshi, in Henan Province—one a palace—with clearly identifiable courtyard arrangements, from the early second millennium B.C.E. Robert L. Thorpe describes the advantages of courtyard arrangements at that time: "They segregated the activities of those within from the remainder of society; they controlled the movement and position of persons entering through the disposition of gates, steps, courts and halls; they provided gathering places with a well-designed 'stage' overseeing the open courtyard; they expressed social and ceremonial status through a hierarchy of levels and interior spaces."[1]

Courtyards continue to be evident in later dynasties. Among the ceramic funerary objects found in Han dynasty tombs are model houses representing a place for the deceased soul to inhabit. Many of these houses have courtyards.

Song dynasty paintings of urban streets and streetlife also clearly display houses with lively inner courtyards. Later paintings, such as the eighteenth-century depiction of the Qianlong emperor's *Journey to the South*, which illustrates both southern and northern lifestyles, also demonstrate that the courtyard was a fundamental residential ingredient for those who could afford it.

Master carpenter Zhu Jiming, of Shexian, Huizhou, who assisted in the preservation work of Yin Yu Tang, remarked that "where we live, if a house does not have a courtyard, it is not called a house."

Southern Orientation

Each direction in Chinese cosmology has a color, an animal, an element, and a respective characteristic associated with it. Of the five directions—east, south, west, north (as they are ordered in China) and center—south and east are the most potent. These two direc-

Fig. 113 **Exterior of a round, tamped-earth house in the interior mountains of western Fujian Province.**

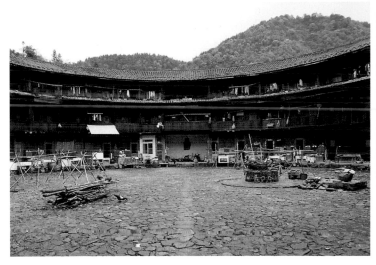

tions are endowed with an abundance of yang. Therefore, orienting a house to the south not only climactically provides an abundance of sunlight and warmth but also offers copious amounts of yang forces.

A foundation of a Shang dynasty palace dating back to about the twelfth century B.C.E. was discovered by archaeologists at Xiaotun, Anyang, Henan Province. The buildings are all arranged on a north-south axis.[2] And at least one gravesite there shows a definitively primary entrance facing south.[3] A compound at Erlitou, in Yanshi, Henan Province, from the first half of the second millennium B.C.E. also had its primary gate on the southern face of the outer wall, and the primary building was located on the northern end of the interior courtyard, facing south.[4] (In Chinese this arrangement is called *zuo bei, chao nan*, "sitting at the north, facing south," and is considered the most auspicious siting.)

Fig. 114 (top left) **Northern China residential compound with courtyard (*siheyuan*). Wu Tai Shan, Shanxi Province.**

Fig. 115 (top right) **Cave (*yaodong*) dwellings, carved out of loess. Shanxi Province.**

Fig. 116 (bottom left) **Round, tamped earth house in the interior mountains of western Fujian Province as seen from the center courtyard.**

Fig. 117 (bottom right) **Underground cave (*tianjing yaodong*) dwelling. Ningxia Province**

Fig. 118 (above) **Columns embedded in masonry wall of shrine. Shexian County.**

Fig. 119 (below) **First floor plan of Yin Yu Tang with reception hall marked in red.**

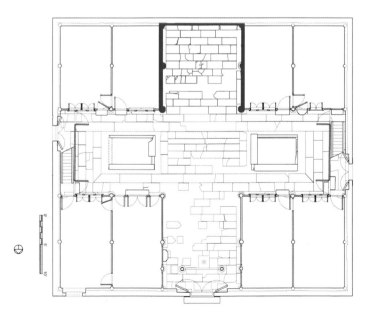

Horizontal Symmetry

Chinese convention maintains that a central location in most structures be allocated to a most revered person or spirit. In a Chinese family, the most revered spirits would be the ancestors, and symmetrical construction around an axial room in a home allows for a central location for the ancestors, or a respected guest, just as the symmetrical layout in a temple allows for a centrally located supreme deity, often with subdeities on either side. In the Chinese tradition, odd numbers are considered yang, and even numbers yin. A house, according to building customs, is far more disposed to good fortune if it comprises an odd number of bays. Moreover, an odd number of bays across the width of a structure by definition creates a central bay that is available for worship.

The interest in horizontal symmetry can be seen in China at least as early as the Shang dynasty. The elaborate relief designs on bronze vessels from the Shang (c. 1600–1050 B.C.E.) and Zhou (c. 1050–256 B.C.E.) almost always display a predilection to strict lateral symmetry. Drawn reconstructions of Shang and Zhou buildings also reveal laterally symmetrical layouts. A drawing of a courtyard from the late second millennium B.C.E. at Fengchu, in Qishan of Shaanxi Province, shows a two-courtyard building with central entrances into each section.[5]

However, the symmetry of Chinese houses is rarely complete or strict. The house may be symmetrical from east to west, but not north to south. Decorations may balance each other on east and west, but are not mirror images. This twist to symmetry can add an unexpected dynamism to a space.

Column-and-Beam Construction and Wooden Joinery

The wooden structure of columns and beams in a timber-frame building supports the roof. The outer masonry walls are curtain walls, standing alongside and surrounding the wooden structure but not bearing the weight of the heavy roof. The wooden components of a Chinese column-and-beam (or timber-frame) structure are joined together with complex mortise and tenon joinery.

Wooden joinery, being more flexible than nails, allows custom-fitted joinery and more elasticity in case of an earthquake. Since the material for metal nails and the process to transform the raw metal into nails are both expensive, wooden joinery and pegs were also a more cost-effective means of construction. Metal nails can easily rust, and the rust could in turn damage surrounding wood. In some cases of persistent humidity, metal can rust away before the wood decays and thereby weaken the structure.

In Chinese column-and-beam construction, the vertical columns are almost always round and the horizontal beams are primarily rectangular. The result is an elegant combination of shapes, but joining them takes a great deal of precise workmanship.

Inside the house, in the rooms and courtyard, the massive round and rectangular wooden members and the techniques that join them are readily visible to the eye. Round columns jut out from walls, beams run across ceilings, brackets support overhanging eaves, and wooden pegs protrude from the intersections of beams and columns. The exposed timber frame, the bones of the house, is usually so predominant that it becomes a major component of the space's aesthetic.

Mortise and tenon joinery was used in Chinese house construction as early Neolithic times. An archaeological dig of a Neolithic site in Hemudu, in Zhejiang Province, revealed clear evidence of mortise and tenon joinery.

In Shang dynasty (c. 1600–1050 B.C.E.) sites in Henan Province, the presence of postholes around and within the building perimeter indicates that columns were already a distinctive building element.[6]

The direct placement of the upright columns of Shang building in the postholes of the pounded-earth floor would eventually cause the wooden columns to decay from moisture. Over time, columns were placed on stone bases (also known as stone drums, because of their shapes) to keep wood from direct contact with the moist earth.[7]

During the Shang period, the roof's weight was still partially supported by the solid outer walls. As building sizes expanded, the timber frame of columns and beams were developed to become more resistant to compression. The tie beams became more tightly joined to the columns, and additional beams were joined to the columns to help them resist buckling under a heavy load. With this added strength, the timber frame could eventually support the entire weight of the roof.[8]

Fengshui

Fengshui, literally meaning "wind and water," is a method by which the most auspicious orientation and location of a house, or grave, is selected. The selection process is guided by principles that assign forces to various landscape features, such as mountains and waterways, which bring or block auspicious energies to the house, or tomb, and its inhabitants. A particularly auspicious location is one that is surrounded at its back by a mountain and looks out on an open plain. As early as the Tang dynasty (618–907), fengshui masters were writing manuals to disseminate knowledge on this "science." By the Song era, these methods of determining the best orientation for homes and gravesites had become more common. In the village of Wan An, in Xiuning County—the same county where Yin Yu Tang was located—a fengshui compass, known in Chinese as a *luopan*, was invented for determining locations with good fengshui. This Xiuning invention eventually became extremely popular all over China during the Ming and Qing dynasties. The luopan has a magnetic needle in the center and is surrounded by concentric circles filled with cyclical characters that the fengshui master is able to coordinate with his client's birth dates and other dignificant information. Today, as in earlier times, many people building homes or graves will first consult a fengshui master to assist in determining the best location and orientation for a new yin or yang residence, that is, for a grave or for a home.

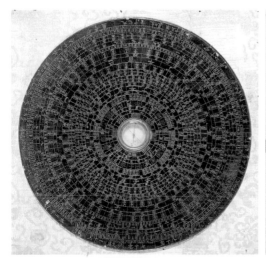
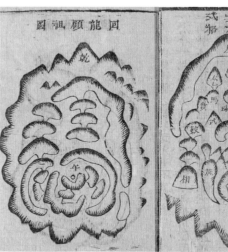
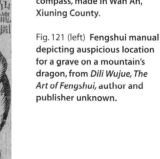

Fig. 120 (far left) **Fengshui compass, made in Wan An, Xiuning County.**

Fig. 121 (left) **Fengshui manual depicting auspicious location for a grave on a mountain's dragon, from** *Dili Wujue, The Art of Fengshui,* **author and publisher unknown.**

Fig. 122 (right) **Gable end of house with horse-head walls. Huang Cun, Xiuning County.**

Fig. 123 (below, top) **Painted decor above an entranceway, imitating the more luxurious carved-brick ornamentation of older houses. Shexian County.**

Fig. 124 (below, middle) **Hand-painted lines on house. Shexian County.**

Fig. 125 (below, bottom) **Painted decoration above an entranceway depicting a landscape and two boys, one gathering kindling and the other riding a water buffalo. Shexian County.**

Huizhou Architecture

After the merchants achieved their fortunes, they returned home to build ancestral halls, construct gardens and mansions, and erect buildings of immense elegance.

—*Shexian County Gazeteer* [9]

The high, stark white walls, with their black outlines and black roofs, create a handsome sight as they appear clustered among the bright green hills and mountains of Huizhou. The intention of the men commissioning these houses and the grand ancestral halls was not only to comfort but also, in fact, to impress.

A distinctive feature of Huizhou homes is an austere, often two-story, fortresslike exterior of high lime white walls that are enhanced with small, detailed ornamentation—carved tiles, ink designs, and paintings—and topped with the characteristic Huizhou *matou qiang*, staggered horse-head walls.

Within these high white walls is the courtyard, known in Huizhou as the *tianjing*, "the skywell," that draws the bright sunlight and its warmth into the home's interior. The walls and wooden elements surrounding the skywell are often—in contrast to the exterior—lavishly decorated. Bedrooms, facing into the skywell, have elaborate lattice window coverings that together create inticing patterns to bedazzle the eye. Large beams above may also embellish the home. At ground level, decorative carvings enhance the functional column bases and other stone elements.

As everywhere, there has been within Huizhou itself a range of house styles. The diverse types each developed with the fashions of the time as well as with personal preferences and affordability of various materials. Ming dynasty houses, for instance, tended to have wider columns. Qing houses were often inclined to have more carved wooden decoration and more representations of human figures, reflecting the general styles of mid- to late-Qing decorative arts. Post–1949 revolution houses often have large windows on the first floor on the front exterior facade of the house. These differences in houses from different time periods—which often sit side by side in one village—are complemented by equally distinct houses inhabited by people of varying incomes. Those who cannot afford fired bricks for exterior walls often used rammed earth to surround the timber-frame structure of their homes. And for many years, those who could not afford fired ceramic roof tiles made do with straw roofs.

The architecture of Huizhou today, as in the past, is influenced by information and fashions from far beyond its borders. Many young people feel that the timber-frame houses are old-fashioned. The complaint that it is difficult for a man to find a wife if he and his parents live in an old-style home is heard often. Other griev-ances against these houses include the difficulty of putting a sofa up against a wall with a round column protruding from it, and that they are cold in the wintertime. As a result of the 1990s economic reforms, a subsequent growing amount of prosperity, and a short-age of wood, families are tearing down their older houses and erecting multiple-story concrete homes with colored exterior tiles.

A schoolteacher of Huang Cun who was not willing to comply with his unmarried son's wishes to tear down their seventeenth century home came up with an innovative solution to lure a wife with a modern house. Not wanting to be an obstacle to the con-tinuation of the family line, he allowed his son to completely ren-ovate his own room with modern interiors, as long as all work was reversible and the house could revert, if they so desired, back to its earlier appearance. The son, a carpenter, installed walls, cabinets, mirrors, newly shaped doorways, and fluorescent lights to re-create a fashionable interior. Within a year he had found a wife, and a year later they had had a son, fulfilling his fundamental obli-gation to the family line.

Fig. 126 (above left) **Rammed-earth house. Huang Cun, Xiuning County.**

Fig. 127 (left) **Qing dynasty house. Guan Lu, Yixian County.**

Fig. 128 (above) **Renovated bedroom in an early Qing dynasty house. Huang Cun, Xiuning County.**

Building Yin Yu Tang

In an undetermined year during the late-eighteenth century, a man surnamed Huang, the seventh son of a man whose name is no longer known, decided to begin the construction of a home. The home would be built in his hometown of Huang Cun, where his ancestors had lived for at least twenty-seven generations. It would house his immediate family and, he hoped, the many future generations of his descendants.

Like many of his kin in the county of Xiuning, he probably earned a good living as a traveling merchant and, most likely, as a pawnbroker.

The late-eighteenth century was a particularly prosperous time for the men of the surrounding area of Huizhou and for the country in general. Under the Qianlong emperor, Gao Zong, who reigned for almost sixty years, from 1736 to 1795, the country expanded to new outermost limits—enveloping Tibet and the Tarim Basin within its borders—and flourished. Under this emperor, an emphatic patron of the arts and a great collector of paintings and calligraphy who was never hesitant about incorporating newly encountered European aesthetics, the culture of China bloomed in unforeseen directions. Though his grandfather, the Kangxi emperor, had had numerous interchanges with Europeans, the Qianlong emperor became even more immersed in "foreign" realms. Luxury objects from foreign governments, such as magnificent clocks, flowed into his palace known as the Purple Forbidden City. Qianlong engaged in written communication with European monarchs and approved a trade agreement with the new nation of the United States in 1784. The reign of this unusual non-Chinese Manchu monarch proved to be, in many ways, a boon for China.

The golden years of the Qianlong emperor also had an impact on Xiuning County, 682 miles (1,100 km) south of the capital in Beijing. More and more merchants were investing their capital in pawnshops (as was the imperial government) and were reaping high profits. Their prosperity in turn allowed sponsorship and successes of local scholars, bringing further glory to the county.

The three primary wishes in Chinese traditions are for *fu*, *lu*, and *shou*—good fortune, becoming a high official, and longevity. In addition to becoming wealthy, many young men in Xiuning County were also becoming officials. In the thirty-first year of Qianlong's reign, seven scholars from Xiuning passed the highest level of civil examinations in Beijing. And between the fortieth and forty-fifth years of Qianlong's reign, three men from Xiuning became *zhuang yuan*, winners of the highest grade in the highest level of civil examinations, a rank of extremely high honor.

While many of the merchant and scholar households of Xiu-

ning were thriving, a few disasters rumbling through the region during the Qianlong era. On the twenty-sixth day of the twelfth month of the twenty-second year of Qianlong's reign (1758), just four days before the great celebration of the New Year festival, an earthquake shook the county, and small quakes continued for several days. In the fifty-third year of Qianlong's reign (1789) a major flood swept through the district. More than 3,100 houses were carried away and 4,400 mu of fields were destroyed.

It was during this relatively blossoming time period for China that the seventh son decided to build his new home. Despite the contact between Qianlong emperor and foreign states, and despite the fact that a seventeenth-century Huizhou ink manufacturer Cheng Dayue had borrowed images of Jesus crossing the water from a Jesuit missionary friend—Matteo Ricci, one of the early Jesuit missionaries to reach China—and reprinted them in a Huizhou-printed ink manual, *Cheng Shi Moyuan*,[10] the seventh son probably had little idea of the major international events—such as the American Revolution—occuring on the other side of the earth. Instead, his personal focus and concern were most likely on the all-important task of creating a solid and fine dwelling to shelter his many generations of descendants. The exploration below of that process, the result of the process, and the evolution of the result is an attempt to bring to light one example of the life of an architecture.

Pre-construction

When a rich man wants to build a house, he must first estimate the resources at his disposal and then determine the size of the house to be built. He will go and consult one of the best master carpenters. He will tell him the number of houses he wants to build and ask in what amount materials and labors are needed, how long it will take, and where to get the materials such as earth, stone, bamboo and reeds. The carpenter will then tell him where to get all the materials required and how much is the cost and labor involved. By following his advice, the man is able to complete the construction of the house on schedule. It is due to the fact that everything has been carefully planned ahead that the new house is found all in order.

—Su Dongpo's (1036–1101) in *Some Thoughts on Good Governing*.[11]

In reconstructing the original construction process of Yin Yu Tang, it is necessary first to step back and consider what might have initiated building such a house. When and why does a man or family decide to build a new home?

There are several main reasons for house building. The first, of course, is to create a roof over one's head. Why would a son (and more than likely, it would be a man, not a woman) build a house, when custom usually decreed that a son live with his parents and care for them in their old age?

If there were too many sons, the parents' home might not be able to contain all their sons, daughters-in-law, and grandchildren. Such was the case, for instance, of the father of Huang Cun resident Shao Zhiyu's father in the early part of the twentieth century. Shao Zhiyu's father was the fourth son of a poor peasant family who lived in a small brick house at the center of Huang Cun. When this fourth son married, his father told him that he and his wife would have to find other accommodations, as the father's home was too small for all his sons and their families. The first son would have been expected to stay with his parents, but the youngest son would have last priority on accommodations in the family home. Luckily, the young couple was able to rent a room in Yin Yu Tang. Most likely, the seventh son who first built Yin Yu Tang was also tossed out of his father's overpopulated house.

Yin Yu Tang is known among the local residents of Huang Cun as *Qi Fang*. *Qi* means "seven" and *fang* can mean "house," "room," or "branch," as in a branch of a family. The application of an architectural term to a family structure is not insignificant. When a new "branch" is created with a marriage and resultant children, a new "room" or "house" is likewise constructed. The appellation Qi Fang indicates that the building was built by a seventh son for the Seventh Branch.

Eventually after many generations, the six other branches of the family all died out, and only the seventh remained in Huang Cun, inheriting the responsibilities to all of their ancestors and property.

The second important motive for building a new home was new wealth. One member of the family, Huang Xiqi, explained a family legend that indicates a sudden acquisition of riches enabled the seventh branch to construct their capacious new home:

It is said that my family ran a doufu shop. And they didn't have any money at all. So they went to a Buddhist temple and picked two bricks to build a stove. But they found the two bricks were so heavy, and only later did they realize that they were two gold bricks. And that's how the family became prosperous. This is only what I heard. I don't know whether it's true or false. I'm only telling you what I have heard. It's around the twenty-somethingth generation that we began to build this house.

Other members have cast doubt on the legend. A more reasonable explanation is that during the late Qianlong period, many natives of Xiuning County were prospering in the pawnshop business. In fact, the economy of much of the country was flush at the time, and the merchants of Huizhou had become particularly adept in the pawnbroking business. Pawnshops were the banks—the moneylenders—of their time and flourished during this period.

As was common in Huizhou, the seventh son may have gone off at the age of thirteen or fourteen to apprentice and returned home to marry. By the time he returned from his next work cycle or the one after that, he may have earned enough money to begin construction of a home for his wife and children.

Where this first occupant of Yin Yu Tang went as an apprentice or as possibly a pawnshop owner cannot yet be determined. It is possible that he went as far as the city of Hankou, located on the Yangzi River, about 248 miles (400 km) west of Huang Cun. The Huizhou merchants were so numerous and prosperous in Hankou in the eighteenth century that they had built a lavish *huiguan* (an association hall) for themselves, with a temple, lecture hall, and dormitory. The investments of Huizhou merchants in property in Hankou at that time had provoked an economic boom for the city, and when the White Lotus rebellion rose up in the 1790s in Hankou, the Huizhou salt merchants grouped together "to finance" a military defense of the city.[12]

But Huang Cun, not the town of his business, was where the seventh son intended to maintain his home and family. Among the many layers of poetic implications expressed by the words Yin Yu Tang, the name that the first occupants chose for their home in Huang Cun, is the desire that the house would shelter members of this family branch for many generations. Children did indeed propagate in the home, and the building remained continuously in the hands of the direct descendants of the patriarch of the Seventh Branch, as hoped.

After Yin Yu Tang was moved to America, Huang Xiqi, one of those descendants who was born and lived in the ancestral home for much of his life, immediately began construction of a new home for himself, his ancestors, and, most important, his descendants. The new house, like the old one, symbolizes a shelter for, hopefully, innumerable generations of descendants.

The Construction

What might have been this seventh son's first step in creating the new branch, the new house? According to local tradition, the first contact would be with a master carpenter, who would manage the overall project as well as propose the general design. The owner would delineate the desired number of stories, the number of bays, and perhaps the style of the house's layout, and the carpenter would tell him the amount of necessary materials:

Usually it's like this. The owner wants to build a house. What type of house does he want to build? He'll tell you. First you have to look at

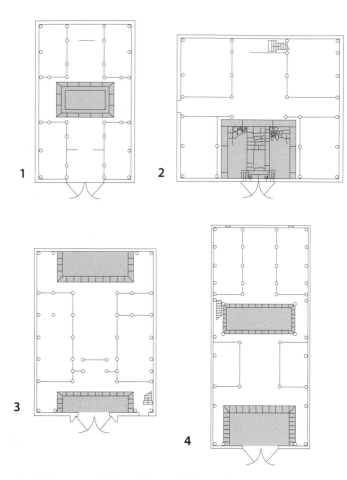

Fig. 129 **Four types of Ming and Qing period house plans:**
1. *kou*-shaped; 2. U-shaped; 3. H-shaped; 4. *sun*-shaped.

the land. Then the carpenter will make him a design. Is it a three-story or a two-story? They are all different. And the carpenter has to make a list, to give to him [the owner] to prepare the materials.

—Zhu Jiming, master carpenter

In Huizhou there are several basic house layouts. They are referred to by Zhang Zhongyi, the first architectural historian to do a full analysis of Huizhou domestic architecture[13] as the *ao*-character type (similar in shape to a U); the *kou*-character type (kou is "mouth" in Chinese, and the character for it is a square shape with an empty center); H-shaped type, and the sun-character type (shaped like a square with a line through the center). The *ao*-character type home consists of a central building, with a reception hall in the center, flanked by bedrooms. At either end, the house and roof extend perpendicularly forward. The remaining void between the two extensions becomes the tianjing, the courtyard. A wall crosses the tianjing, parallel to the main house, connecting the two

extensions, to offer privacy. The *kou*-character type building is essentially two physical structures with a courtyard in between with covered staircases at either end. The H-type house is essentially two *ao*-character houses back to back.

The shape of the house and number of bays would depend on the owner's personal preference, economic capability, and the size and shape of the purchased property.

The seventh son, rather than the carpenter, probably was the one who decided on a two-story building with five bays, in the *kou*-character type design. This design was a major decision, as it provided more rooms than the more common *ao*-character or H-type houses. Having five bays, rather than the more usual three, was also a significant decision, adding an additional eight bedrooms to the house, four on each floor. The seventh son may have been expecting to have many sons, and such a house could contain the most rooms in a restricted amount of space. Perhaps he did not want to put any sons into the uncomfortable position of having to move out of their father's home. Unfortunately, no further generations in this branch ever produced as many sons as his own father had.

The *kou*-character design is known in Huizhou as *paomalou*, or "a building for running horses." The term was coined, as an elderly Huizhou man explained, because a horse could run, or at least walk, completely around in a circle (or rectangle) on the second-floor galleries, as on a race track.[14]

The paomalou can be considered two almost identical, parallel structures, facing each other across the courtyard, attached by staircases and second floor galleries. Both structures are two stories high. The rear structure, facing the entrance of the house, is the more important and is called, locally, "the upper hall." The front structure is called the "lower hall," and its roof is slightly lower.

Once the general shape and size were determined, the seventh son possibly signed a contract with the chosen master carpenter. This specific contract no longer exists, but some from that time period are still extant. In his thorough study of the *Lu Ban Jing*, a carpenter's manual first complied in the fifteenth century but based on earlier texts, Klaas Ruitenbeek describes two types of contracts that were definitely in use during the past two centuries: the *baogong* and the *jigong*.[15]

In the baogong contract, the owner would pay a fixed price for the whole project, to be completed within a prescribed amount of time. In the jigong contract, the owner would pay by the workday. One man's day of labor is known in Chinese as a *gong* (meaning "work"), and contracts were often written in terms of gong.

In both types of contracts, a provision was made determining who—the owner or the carpenter—would be responsible for obtaining the materials. In most situations in Huizhou, the carpenter wrote the owner a list of the needed materials—how many columns, how many beams—and the owner hired a separate individual to cut the timber.

The owner also hired a mason, who, directed by the carpenter's plans, determined the amount of stone and brick necessary for the construction, which the owner also had to obtain.

Formally executed plans were not part of the contract procedure for most residential structures in regional Huizhou. A quick sketch by a carpenter might have been made for the owner, but such plans would have been quickly discarded after the building of the house. In imperial buildings, models of papier-mâché were sometimes created, some of which still exist in Beijing. But for a commoner's home, such as Yin Yu Tang, this would have been a never-considered extravagance.

Once a proposal had been agreed upon and the contract signed, the owner might have hired a fengshui master, in Huizhou often called a *dili xiansheng*, a "location master," to determine the best orientation for the house and the most auspicious day to commence work. Meanwhile, the master carpenter would have gone about planning the construction and his negotiations with other hired hands.

The Record of a Xiuning Construction

A Xiuning County manuscript from the seventeenth century regarding the reconstruction of an ancestral hall in Wan An Jie (Wan An Street), a village just east of the Xiuning county seat—the same village where centuries before the fengshui compass had been invented—offers clues regarding the many types of laborers that would have been involved in a building project.[16] The manuscript itself is full of fascinating, rarely available material. It records both the construction and labor costs as well as the process of the campaign for funding the project.

Before examining the manuscript—a handwritten record now located in the Harvard Yenching Library—identifying the differences between this construction project and Yin Yu Tang is important. First, the ancestral hall project took place probably at least one hundred years before Yin Yu Tang was built. This may be a minor difference, as construction practices probably did not change drastically during the first half of the Qing dynasty. However, the ancestral hall project was a major endeavor that took ten years to complete (1693–1703) and required raising massive amounts of money from lineage members. More than likely, as ancestral halls were grand affairs, the resulting building was far more extravagant and ornate than Yin Yu Tang and, therefore, a much larger undertaking. Nevertheless, in the absence of any documents regarding the construction of a residence, the manuscript offers a great deal of information.

Within the detailed manuscript are lists of workers, the different kinds of workers and the expenses involved in their labor. Among the specialized laborers listed are coopers (makers of buckets and other round wooden objects), tile artisans, sawyers, carpenters, carvers, metal artisans, lacquer artisans, bamboo artisans, miscellaneous laborers, cooks, and several other artisans whose role is not yet understood, but who may have had ceremonial duties. In addition, there were costs for fengshui masters to determine the auspicious days on which to begin construction and on which to raise into place the ridge beam.

The document includes the amount of labor needed and the salary paid to workers. The labor is measured in gong, just as it is by local workmen in Xiuning today. The document does not detail the number of laborers; just as a carpenter or mason working today would not. Ten gong could entail five men working for two days, or two men working for five days, or four men working for two and half days.

In some instances, the document details exactly what work the artisans would be doing. For instance, the manuscript reads: "The coopers will make large jars, buckets and basins, for six days of labor and [providing their own] food, for which they will receive 5.1 qian."

By comparing the man-hours of the various expertises, the relative status of the artisans can be determined. The sawyers, according to the document, would, for twenty-two days of labor and food, earn 1 liang, 5.7 qian—or .85 qian per day.

The carpenters would devote probably more time than any of the other artisans, with an estimated eight hundred labor days, making 32 liang, 4.4 qian, giving them less than half a day's pay of that of a cooper or sawyer. On the other hand, they were being promised a much longer job contract plus food. Labor costs for the project's cooks (159 liang, 9.8 fen) were also included in the contract.

The ancestral hall must have been elaborately ornamented. The carvers, according to the manuscript, were to work for an extraordinary length of time. Their labor entailed 437.5 days of labor, for which they were to be paid 19 liang, 6.1 qian. Their rate was slightly higher rate than that of the general carpenters, perhaps because they were working for a shorter amount of time, or because their work entailed an even finer skill.

One of the interesting aspects of this document is that we see a differentiation between the carpenters and the carvers. Today, many of the carpenters do wood carving as well as carpentry, but in the construction of a dignified structure, the labor seems to have been made quite distinct.

The lacquerers provided 89.5 days of labor, for which they were paid 3 liang, 5.1 qian. The information regarding the lacquerers is most interesting not only for their time and payment but also for the materials they were using. Under "materials," there does not appear to be any cost for lacquer per se, but there are expenses for tung oil, and it was most likely this material that the lacquerers were spreading on the wood.

As essential as those providing the physical labor were those who supplied more cerebral work. These were the men (presumably they were men) who selected the auspicious days on which to initiate construction and on which to raise the ridge beam. Budget notations are included for such matters as "selecting a time period" and "selecting a day for construction of the stone bridge."

The document also makes notes on material costs, which include wood (primarily fir, the same material from which much of Yin Yu Tang was constructed), 240 jin of tung oil, and iron nails (150 jin, 9 liang 5.1 qian).[17] Though the cost of vegetables and food for the work was not recorded, 1 liang, 22.2.qian was recorded as being spent on a goat for sacrificing at the ridge-beam-raising ceremony.

Siting the House

Before breaking ground, the first step in building Yin Yu Tang, would undoubtedly have been for a geomancer to determine the most auspicious orientation for the house on the site and the most auspicious date on which to begin construction. As is apparent in the Xiuning ancestral hall construction records discussed above and from conversations with carpenters today, this was an important and essential part of the construction process and budget:

It all depends on the geographical location. That spot [in Huang Cun] is quite good. A mountain and two streams. "Two dragons playing with a pearl." According to masters of the previous generation, the orientation all has to do with the geographical location. On the first day of building a house you have to find a geomancy master to look at the fengshui; only then can you break ground for making the foundation. It is [determined] in accordance with your surname, how old you are, when you were born, what your zodiac sign is, and whether or not there is any conflict [between those aspects] with setting the foundation. If the fengshui is good, the house will be prosperous.

—Carpenter Zhu Yunfeng

The usual and auspicious traditional orientation for houses in China is facing south with a mountain behind the house. In Huang Cun the older (pre–1949 revolution) houses all face north.

Several rationales have been given for the unexpected orientation of the Huang Cun houses. The first, as noted in several books on Huizhou culture,[18] relates to the five cosmological elements, known as *wu xing*. According to Chinese tradition, the universe consists of five basic elements (metal, wood, water, dirt, fire), and all objects, occupations, time periods, and any other matters of the world are designated under one of the element types. The five directions (north, south, east, west, and center) are each assigned elements as well. Merchants are, logically, assigned the metal element because of their association with metal coinage. The direction south is assigned the fire element. According to this theory, if merchants' houses face south, the fire element of the south would overcome and melt the metal element of the merchants, and their wealth would be depleted. This explanation could not account for the north-facing orientation of Jin Shi Di, the 1531 shrine built in honor of a Huang Cun native who passed the highest level of civil exams. Clearly, if he had passed these exams, he was an official and not a merchant.

The second rationale relates to Jin Shi Di. In surveying the village as part of the Yin Yu Tang project, students from the architecture department of Dongnan University in Nanjing noted that Jin Shi Di is oriented directly toward Beijing—north—and therefore, they surmised, the houses face north in hope that their sons will become officials.

The third explanation for the house's orientation is the most plausible. Fengshui principles call for mountains to be behind the houses. In the Huizhou region, the geomantic principles also stress the importance of water flow and the entrance of water flowing into a village. This point of entry, the *shuikou*, the "water mouth," is considered the entrance to the village. Since water represents prosperity in local symbolic vocabulary, it was important in Huizhou villages that the houses face the shuikou so that prosperity would flow into the households.[19] The shuikou in Huang Cun is in the northeast corner of the village, and the houses therefore need to face north.

The mountains were green and the water was clear. Our house is facing the north. I guess that is because there is a very tall mountain to the south of the house. If the house faces south, then we would have felt pressured or blocked. If it faced north, then the mountain is behind and there is open land in front of it. I guess that's why the house is facing northward.

Directly opposite our house is a mountain with a big boulder on the top. The mountain is called "White Tiger Mountain." To protect us from evil, we had a stone statue of a Buddha built on the roof the house. The Buddha holds a sword [pointed] at the mountain. That's probably why our house faces the north. The mountain behind the house is really high. You can see Tunxi from the top of the mountain.

—Huang Xiqi

Once the actual direction of the house was determined, the carpenters and occupants treated the house as if it faced south:

If a person stands at the position of the main entrance [facing away from the house], east is on the left and west is on the right (zuodong youxi). It is all according to the definition created by the main entrance.

—Zhu Jiming

In fact, most of the beams and columns from the actual west side of the building are labeled east, and the eastern beams and columns are labeled as west.

Conceptually reorienting space is not uncommon in Chinese daily life. For instance, when eating at a banquet in a restaurant, the most important person is seated facing the entrance, which becomes conceptual south. This location is both the most auspicious (receiving the most yang) and the safest, as the person will be aware of intruders first. The second most important person sits to the conceptual east of the most important person, which is on his left.

As the story of building and occupying the house unfolds and develops, the importance of direction and orientation to that direction by the carpenters and the occupants continues to be apparent. The text refers to both the conceptual direction—that is the direction according to the carpenters' and occupants' point of view—and the actual compass direction. In most cases, the conceptual direction—which, as demonstrated in the case of Yin Yu Tang, can be completely the opposite of the actual direction—takes precedence.

Gathering the Materials

The first step in building a house is often gathering the materials—the wood, the bricks, and, of course, the funds to pay for the wages and meals of the carpenters and masons. Depending on the contract, the obtaining of materials might have been the responsibility of either the carpenter or the owner.

Yin Yu Tang is constructed of four primary materials: stone for the paving, the foundation (above and below the earth), the column bases, the stretchers beneath the first-floor bedrooms, the door jambs, and the balustrades around the water ponds; bricks for the outer curtain walls and some interior walls; wood, for the frame, floors, partitions, and other finish work; and tiles, for the roof, gutter, and exterior decoration.

A hallmark of regional residential architecture is the use of locally available materials. The stone used in Yin Yu Tang is primarily a red sandstone easily procurable in Huizhou and similar to the brownstone of many New York City houses. The stone was possibly quarried in the hills right around Huang Cun. Even today, Huang Cun housebuilders quarry stone for their foundations in the hills at the perimeter of the village.

The bricks and tiles for Yin Yu Tang were, likewise, probably made from the high-clay-content earth around Huang Cun. Today, tiles and bricks are still made at a tile-and-brick-making production site on the path between Huang Cun and the nearest neighboring village to the east, Dongzhou. Water buffalo help mix the clay, while an age-old ingenious technique is used for making roof tiles. Rudolf P. Hommel, in his remarkable book on Chinese tools and techniques, *China at Work*, describes a roof-tile-making method

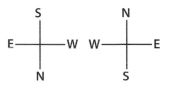

Fig. 130 (far left) **Roof-tile production, Huang Cun, Xiuning County.**

Fig. 131 (left) **Quarrying and shaping stone for a house's foundation in Huang Cun, Xiuning County.**

Fig. 132 (right) **In Yin Yu Tang, the conceptual directions are opposite from the actual compass directions. The compass on the left shows the actual directions, while the one on the right shows the conception directions for Yin Yu Tang.**

that he documented in the 1920s in Zhejiang Province and that is identical to the process in many regions of southern China, including Huizhou:

The raw material, river mud . . . or clay, is taken to the pottery and deposited upon the ground in the open. It is sprinkled with water and thoroughly worked over by the workmen who tramp it with their bare feet. [In Huang Cun, a water buffalo now does this work.] . . . The potter for his daily needs cuts big chunks from the heaps outdoors and carries them into his hut where he thoroughly kneads them into the proper consistency for working. . . . The tile maker forms from the chunks he has brought into his hut a big rectangular batch of clay, about 4 feet long. . . . A slice of clay, about 3/8 of an inch thick, is cut from the top surface of the batch. . . . The tub-like roofing tile maker's mold is made up of wooden staves like a flexible window shutter or roll up top of a desk which are hinged upon three separate strips of stout fabric which pass through the slender cross mortises penetrating the staves. The end staves are longer than the others and serve as handles for the mold. The mold, consisting thus of strips hinged together, forms a many-jointed, flexible cylinder, and when stood up on end a hoopless tub is formed. The mold is stiffened by slipping a tightly fitting moist cloth cover over it to hold the whole thing together. Four vertical bamboo strips equidistant from each other, and parallel to the joints of the staves, are fastened with wooden pegs, or with wire, on the outside of the staves. The object of these strips is to indent the inside of the clay cylinder to be formed upon the mold, so as to form guide-lines along which the clay cylinder when dry will easily break up into roofing tiles.

When the tile-maker proceeds to make clay cylinders, he places the mold upon the top of his wheel. . . . Then he cuts a slice from the batch of clay, takes it up with both hands and lays it around the mold. Next he gets his shaping tool, and turning the wheel slowly, smooths the surface. . . . Next the mold is ingeniously collapsed by turning the two projecting end staves towards the center of the mold, whereupon the mold is rolled up inside the cylinder and easily withdrawn. When finally the cloth is pulled out, the cylinder is finished and is left to dry in the sun. . . . After a day, the cylinders are hard enough to be piled on top of each other. . . . Before being put in the kiln the cylinders are broken into four tiles. The workman takes the cylinder between his hands, each palm over one of the impressed lines and pushes the cylinder inward with the result that it collapses, breaking into four concave segments, exactly along the guide lines.[20]

On the opposite side of the path from Huang Cun's local brick-and-tile-making shed, a kiln bakes the bricks and tiles. The color of the bricks and the tiles is gray. This has been the color of bricks and tiles in China for many dynasties. Han dynasty tiles, collected

Fig. 133 **Bricks from Yin Yu Tang with the maker's mark in relief.**

for their beautifully impressed calligraphic and pictorial designs, are a definitive gray. The color is achieved by pouring water through the top of the kiln toward the end of the firing procedure. According to local brick makers, the water steaming against the baking bricks produces a more durable building material.

Not all the bricks that make up Yin Yu Tang's walls were necessarily from the same kiln. There is a wide variety of sizes. Moreover, mixed among the many bricks are several with makers' names imprinted in relief on the bricks. These may have been old bricks gathered from a dilapidated building site, then recycled in the construction of Yin Yu Tang, or they may have been purchased from a separate kiln site.

In gathering the wooden materials for the house's frame, the owner would have asked his master carpenter to make a list of how much wood—how many beams, how many columns—he would need. The owner then would have hired a woodcutter to harvest the wood from the forest. The wood gathered for erecting Yin Yu Tang was primarily of three species: *Cryptomeria* (*shanmu*, in Chinese), which translates as "fir," but is a separate species found only in temperate parts of East Asia; yellow pine (*songmu*), which is very similar to American yellow pine; and Chinese chestnut (or *chinkapin*), a rot-resistant hardwood used for the first-floor columns around the courtyard and some small crescent beams and struts. The shanmu, which grows extremely straight and has only small knots, makes up approximately 60 percent of the house's frame, the songmu about 30 percent and the chinkapin about 9 percent. There is one column that is made of a tree known in China as *xiangchun* (*Toon sinensis*), which, according to the carpenters dismantling the house, promises longevity for the house's occupants. The tree's name sounds like *chun*, meaning "spring," and therefore ensures that the occupants constantly stay in the spring of their life. The wood, like camphor, also repels insects.

Once the wood, stone, and tiles were acquired, and the funds for the workers available, the actual construction could be considered. This process for building Yin Yu Tang may have taken several years, or even longer.[21]

Preparing the Materials

Before the house components were brought to the site, the masons and carpenters first refined the materials and prepared them. The masons first shaped and carved their stones, and the carpenters formed the beams, columns, and the intricate joints that hold them together. This work was often done in a public common space in the village. An ancestral temple—or in Huang Cun, Jin Shi Di—would have been an ideal space for carpenters to spread out their extensive wood supplies and work. The carpenters and masons may not have all been natives of Huang Cun, and if they lived more than an hour or so away, the seventh son would have been obliged to house them. He would have either put them up in his own home or, if he could not accommodate them, have found friends in the village who were willing to take in the artisans for months at a time.

Breaking Ground

The stonemason's job is more labor-intensive [than that of a carpenter]. People say that a stonemason consumes thirty liters of grain per month whereas a carpenter [consumes] three liters. A stonemason uses a great deal of energy. A carpenter works delicately. The saying "a carpenter uses threads while a stonemason uses bundles of threads" implies that carpenter work is more delicate.

—Ling Qizheng, a master stone mason involved in the preservation of Yin Yu Tang

Though the master carpenter has top seniority in planning the overall structure of the house, the masons are also significant. Their initial, and necessarily precise, work—as described by Ling Qizheng, a traditionally trained stone mason—establishes the foundation on which the rest of the house is built.

When I am hammering on the stones, I focus on how to make them good. I can only have one mind, not two. I can't think about anything else.

—Ling Qizheng

Once the masons had cut and dressed the necessary stone pieces—the foundation blocks, plinths, and column bases—the first stones could be placed and the "breaking of the ground" could begin. All the artisans, carpenters, and masons would have been present, on site, at this occasion.

An auspicious date for the occasion would have been chosen with the assistance of a person trained in reading the Chinese calendar, which notes auspicious (or inauspicious) dates for beginning such projects, starting out on journeys, and undertaking other significant ventures. Klaas Ruitenbeek has noted that the Chinese calendar has more references to auspicious dates for housebuilding

events than almost any other category, including marriage, burial and exam-taking. There are more dates only for farming than for housebuilding.[22] The masons and carpenters would have conducted a brief groundbreaking ceremony in respect of the deity of the earth, burning incense and paper money and notifying the deity that earth was about to be moved.

With the on-site "breaking of the ground" (two expressions are used in China, *potu*, "breaking the ground," or *dongtu*, "shifting the ground"), the carpenter would designate the locations for the column bases, the points that would receive the most weight of the structure. At these significant load-bearing spots, including the column bases and the bases of the perimeter stone and brick walls, the mason might have first tamped the ground down and then placed roughly dressed underground foundation stones to prevent the column bases and perimeter stones from sinking into the ground over time, thus giving additional support and stabilization to the structure.

Physically and psychologically, the column bases carried an important burden. It is on them that the weight of the entire wooden structure—the columns, the beams, and the roof—rested. The column bases, being of a larger diameter than the columns, were able to distribute that weight to a wider area. They were, more so than the stones below the outer curtain wall, the foundation of the house. They protected against moisture moving up to and deteriorating the bottom of the columns. They also formed an excellent barrier to prevent termites in the ground from reaching the wooden components of the house. To draw attention to their importance, and to add a lower-level visual ornamentation to the courtyard space, those bases visible in the courtyard were each carved in a unique design.

Fig. 134 **Ling Qizheng dressing an exterior foundation stone.**

The Wooden Structure

While the stone masons laid their stones, the carpenters would have begun making the house's wooden components. Huizhou carpenters involved in the re-erection of Yin Yu Tang estimate that there were at least eight carpenters working on this stage of the house and that it would have taken them eight hundred gong (or one hundred days of eight men working) to complete the preparation of the beams and columns.

As with laying the first stone, the owner, with advice from a fengshui master, had to select an auspicious day to begin this work. On the first day, the carpenters' only task would have been to build themselves a pair of sawhorses. The owner's obligation for this day was to prepare the carpenters a banquet of auspicious food, such as noodles (for longevity), eggs and watermelon seeds (for fecundity), and candy.

The many wooden components of a structure—the columns, beams, and pegs—were entirely cut, carved, and fitted with tenons and mortises before the structure was erected on site. During the days following the ceremonial first day, the carpenters began to shape the wood that had been delivered to them. As they were substantially and conceptually more important, the columns were shaped first, then the beams.

The initial step for the carpenters would be to look over the wood and select which pieces would be used for which components. For the columns of the reception hall and the central room on the first floor of the upper hall, the bigger and better pieces of wood would be chosen. Once all the columns had been shaped, they were placed together on a large frame off the ground. Then the beams were shaped, with their widths and the profile of their shoulders determined according to the dimenions and shape of the columns.

With the columns and beams shaped, the carpenters could delve into the more complex process of fabricating the intricate joinery that would hold the components together. Tenons needed to be formed at the end of the beams, and the mortises needed to be incised into the columns. The three-dimensional conceptualization to design the joinery and the techniques to create it were remarkably intricate and complex. Examples of some of the joinery are shown in figure 142. There were at least fifteen discrete joints created and employed to construct Yin Yu Tang, including the basic mortise and tenon, dovetail, bridle, half laps, cogs, slots, and variations on each.

To shape and create the many wooden components of Yin Yu Tang, the carpenters employed an array of tools. Many of the primary tools would be familiar to the carpenters' colleagues around the world. Frame saws and planes of various sizes were used to shape the parts and smooth the surface of the wood. But the carpenters utilized axes and adzes just as often. Mortises in columns were usually chopped out with a chisel, driven by the back of an axe head, while a small backsaw was used for cutting out the smaller mortises in the dovetail joints.

To determine the exact placement of these mortises and tenons, and to ensure that they would fit, the carpenter had to first produce a series of straight lines on the shaped columns and beams. These straight lines represented the conceptual division of space in the house more accurately than would the timber components.

Unique to Chinese carpentry are the methods of planning and delineating the sizes and forms of columns and beams, as well as the intricate mortises and tenons to bind them together, and the tools to make those determinations. The two most important tools in this process are the ink line, the *modou*, essential to all carpenters in China, and the *zhujiazi*, a tool common in Huizhou but not necessarily in use in all areas of China.

Fig. 135 (right) **Two single-tenon beams that will meet within a column. The square holes in the tenons will accept the wooden pegs that penetrate the column and the beams' tenons to secure the joint.**

Fig. 136 (middle) **Two multiple-tenoned composite beams that will meet within a column.**

Fig. 137 (far right) **Four beams on the upper sections of first-floor bedrooms, entering a column. The long mortise at the front of the column will accept a long tenon of yet another beam. The multiple mortises weaken the strength of the column.**

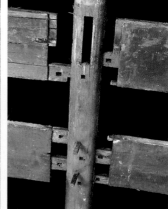

The modou is used for permanently marking straight lines on a column or beam. The modou—made of wood or bamboo, ink, and string—is most basically a small pot with a cotton wad to hold ink (to which water was occasionally added to liquefy it), a string, and a reel on which the string was wound. Because of the important function that this tool played in constructing a house (or furniture) the carpenter, who would have made all his own tools, often supplemented this tool with a decorated exterior. Some modou are even carved into the shape of shoes or dragons. The string, wound up on a spool, goes through the ink pot, where it is covered in ink, and exits the ink pot through a small hole. The string usually has a nail or small deer antler at the end that both keeps the string from returning completely onto the spool and can be hitched onto the wood to allow the carpenter to engage the tool without a helper to hold the string end.

With the ink-line system, every member of the frame had ink center lines struck on its surface, or in the case of columns, on four faces. These lines, more than the columns and the beams, were a three-dimensional grid, which became the basis on which the house was constructed. All joinery was centered on these ink lines. The ink lines made by carpenters over two hundred years ago in the construction of Yin Yu Tang are still visible today. They were indispensable in the creation of the original Yin Yu Tang, and they are still indispensable today in the re-erection of the house.

Once the columns had been formed into their tall, round lengths and the beams formed into their widths, the carpenter immediately fetched his modou and began to consider the wood. He would work on the components of the house, starting with those from the east and working toward the west. A column might have had some twists and turns, and not have been perfectly straight, but the carpenter, with his modou, easily mitigated any imbalances that those irregularities might be expected to cause.

The most essential spot for the carpenter to first locate on his length of column was the place where the most mortises might be needed, the place where the tenons of two or more beams might enter the column. The more mortises necessary in one spot, the weaker the column would be. This spot in Yin Yu Tang—and in many buildings—is about twelve feet from the bottom of the column, at the top of the first floor and just below the floor level of the second floor.

According to propriety, before striking the lines, the master carpenter would have had to ask the owner the desired height of the first-floor ceiling. It is there that beams and joists enter the columns to carry the weight of the second-story floor and tie together the columns. To precisely accept so many penetrating

Fig. 138 (above) **An array of carpenter's tools.**

Fig. 139 (left) **Modou, or ink line, used for marking straight lines on wood or stone. A bamboo stylus sits in the inkwell. The antler, on the side, is attached to one end of the reel of string. It hooks onto the end of a piece of wood to create tension and allow the carpenter to pluck the string and mark the wood. A modou with string extended. Wang Xi Village, Xiuning County.**

The Stone Mason's Training

To be trained in a traditional craft, carpentry or masonry, the apprentice must participate in a prescribed formal relationship with a master. Here Huizhou stone mason Ling Qizheng describes this relationship:

When I was about fifteen or sixteen years old, I asked friends to find me an experienced master. I entertained him at a dinner party to formally acknowledge him as my master. Then the master took me to his place and taught me for three years.... I didn't pay any tuition. The master didn't pay me a wage either. Usually the master is someone you have a connection with, a relative or a friend. You don't learn from strangers. The masters make their apprentices pay deposits because they are afraid that the apprentices may run away.... After the apprenticeship had finished, I arranged another dinner party in honor of my master to express my gratitude.

Then the master asked me whether I wanted to learn more. Because only basics were taught in the first three years. I still didn't feel confident enough to work somewhere else completely on my own. However, the master paid me a half-wage this time. After a year or two, he gradually increased my pay. Slowly, I became more independent and eventually worked alone.

During my apprenticeship, I was obligated to present my master with four gifts for each of the three major annual festivals, that is, mid-autumn festival, dragon boat festival, and spring festival (Chinese New Year's). I gave him cigarettes, wine, fish, and meat. The master gave me a red envelope with money in it.

Fig. 140 **One of many inscriptions on the columns and beams of Yin Yu Tang, written by the original carpenters to denote the specific location of each wooden component.**

Fig. 141 **The *zhu jiazi*, "column clamp," used to measure widths of columns and mortise placement.**

Fig. 142 **(below) Axonometric drawing of the joinery of Yin Yu Tang.**

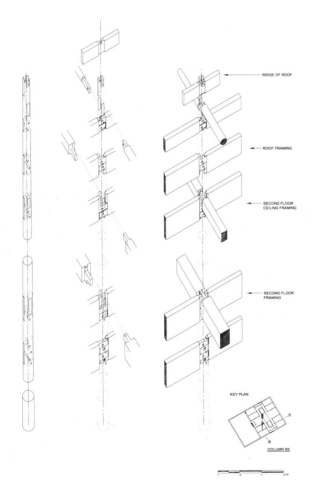

RIDGE OF ROOF

ROOF FRAMING

SECOND FLOOR CEILING FRAMING

SECOND FLOOR FRAMING

KEY PLAN

COLUMN B5

tenons, the mortises here must have very even spacing, and it is here, not at the bottom or top of the column, that the carpenter would have divided his column into four even quadrants. Once he had done so, the carpenter would have used his modou to snap four parallel lines down the length of the column, and across the top and bottom. At the tops and bottoms, the snapped lines rarely divided the surfaces into even quadrants. However, such evenness is necessary only at the point where the multiple tenons enter the column. The two ink lines crossing at the bottom of the column will eventually line up with the crossing ink lines on column bases, thereby "centering" the columns on the bases. Inscribing the lines on the columns and beams might have taken the carpenters several days.

Stonemasons also learn from [master and guardian deity] Lu Ban. He was both a carpenter and a stonemason. [There is a legend] about a modou. When the modou was filled up and plugged, the great master Lu Ban pulled an ink-soaked thread out of the pot along the surface of the stone, and the stone automatically split. However, once there was a time when the ink pot of the modou had dried up. Lu Ban told his apprentice to refill it with water. The apprentice was unwilling to walk far for the water, so instead he filled the ink pot with his own urine. When he came back, the modou could be used only to make ink marks on the stones. It would not split stones anymore. Now we have to split stones by hammering the blocks after marking them with threads. Originally stonemasons only had to mark stones with inked threads and the stones would split by themselves. Lu Ban's apprentice ruined the ink pot.

—Ling Qizheng

Once the column's ink lines were snapped, the carpenter could begin to chisel out his mortises. The first hole to be cut was the peghole that would eventually accept the square wooden peg that would lock together the column and beam joints. This peghole was always cut tangential to the ink line. With that peghole fully formed, the carpenter could begin to cut out the large mortises that would accept the tenons of the beams.

The mortises on a round columns would be created first; then the rectangular horizontal members, the beams, and their tenons and coped shoulders were cut to match. Matching this complicated joinery was a complex task, again made easier by the ink lines and the help of a specialized tool called the *zhujiazi*, the "column clamp," a three-piece wooden clamplike implement.

The two legs of the zhujiazi were fixed to a pair of column center lines on either side of a column's mortise, while its third member acted as an artificial horizon above the mortise and the column. Marks made on bamboo sticks placed between this horizon and the column surface at salient points around the mortise were then

Fig. 143 (below) **Section of Yin Yu Tang, within courtyard looking south.**
Fig. 144 (right) **North facade and entry of Yin Yu Tang.**

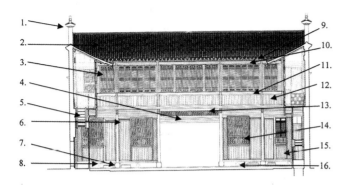

1. 馬頭墻 *matouqiang* -- horsehead wall (parapet)
2. 屋面 *wumian*-- ceramic tile roof
3. 活动的格子窗 *huodong de gezi chuang*--movable lattice window screen
4. 直枋 *zhifang*— connector beam
5. 楼梯 *louti*--stairs
6. 房门 *fangmen*—room door
7. 石柱鼓 *shi zhugu*--stone column base
8. 地府 *difu*—stone stretcher
9. 滴水瓦 *dishuiwa*—drip tiles
10. 上引 *shangyin*—lintel
11. 窗框 *chuangkuang*—window sill
12. 挡风板 *dangfengban*—balcony paneling
13. 满天星 *mantianxing* – 'sky full of stars' lattice screen
14. 固定的格子窗 *guding de gezi chuang*--fixed lattice window screen
15. 板壁 *banbi* -- wooden partition, wood panel
16. 通气眼 *tongqiyan*—carved vent

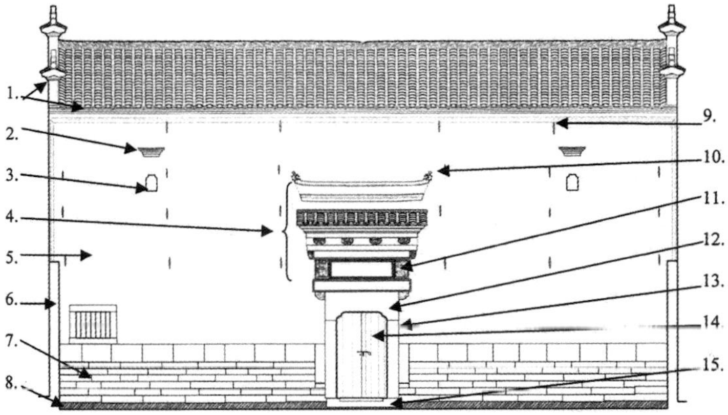

1. 三線 *sanxian* -- brick corbelling
2. 窗沿 *chuangyan* -- window hood
3. 窗户 *chuanghu* -- window
4. 門楼 *menlou* -- door hood
5. 外砖墙 *waizhuanqiang* -- exterior brick masonry wall
6. 拐石 *guaishi* -- cornerstone
7. 外石墙 *waishiqiang* -- exterior sandstone masonry wall
8. 白石 *baishi* -- stone sacrificial course
9. 鐵箭 *tiejian* -- metal anchor
10. 泥塑捏 *nisunie* --molded brick ornament
11. 转调 *zhuandiao*-- carved brick
12. 門沿頭 *menyantou* -- stone lintel
13. 石柱子 *shizhuzi* -- stone column
14. 大門 *damen*—front door
15. 石門檻 *shimenkan*—stone threshold

transposed along and around the center line of the horizontal girt (beam) designed to join with it. This system produced a scribed fit between the most irregular members without ever bringing the pieces into physical proximity until final assembly. It had the further advantage of great accuracy without the use of numbers, except for determining overall lengths. Understanding this method and the tools employed was essential in comprehending the original erection and enabling the eventual re-erection of Yin Yu Tang.

As each major beam and column in Yin Yu Tang was being made, the master carpenter inscribed on it with brush and ink its intended location in the house. The markings are often long calligraphic inscriptions describing the exact location of the component. For instance, one component may say "upper hall, upper story, eastern second beam front beam toward the ridge beam." The inscriptions were always located in spots on the wood that would rarely be noticed by the occupants or visitors to the house. They were high up in the rafters, often facing the ceiling or hidden by connecting parts of construction. The structure was, in a sense, a kit of premade parts, ready to be assembled on site.

Dismantling the house and the subsequent discovery of these inscriptions has had several benefits for researchers. First, the wording of the inscriptions offers a vocabulary of components and spaces that were in use when the house was built. Interestingly, the same vocabulary is still in use among regional carpenters in Huizhou today. These terms and their English equivalents are given above.

The inscriptions on the columns also reinforce the original perception of the house's orientation, that is still-maintained today. The original carpenters built the components of the house as if it would face south, and the occupants lived in the house as if it faced south. The inscriptions all maintain the conceptual orientation of the house as facing south. The carpenters marked the components that were intended for the conceptual east, as "east," and those intended for the conceptual west were marked "west." These directions were irrelevant to the actual compass directions. Beams labeled as being on the east side, for instance, were inserted on the compass west side.

With the lines snapped, the master carpenter could estimate how long it would take him to complete the joinery work on the columns and beams. At this stage in the project, the owner would come to the master carpenter to ask for that estimate and then go to the fengshui master to determine the most auspicious date for raising the frame.

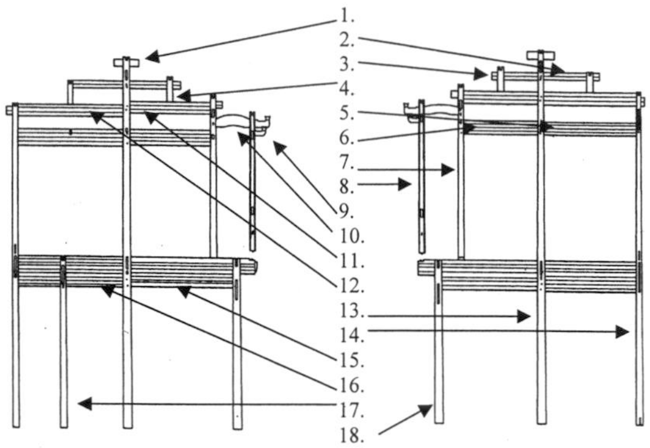

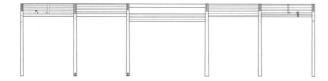

1. 脊頭枋 *jitou fang* -- ridge column clamp
2. 後步子架枋 *houbu zijia fang* -- rear purlin strut beam
3. 前步子架枋 *qianbu zijia fang* -- front purlin strut beam
4. 前步子架柱 *qianbu zijia zhu* -- front purlin strut
5. 後步下列枋 *houbu xia lie fang* – rear outer bottom beam
6. 前步下列枋 *qianbu xia lie fang* -- front outer bottom beam
7. 各上前今柱 *geshang qianjin zhu* -- upper front inner column
8. 各上前步柱 *geshang qianbu zhu* -- upper front outer column
9. 斗拱 *dougong* -- a system of brackets inserted between the top of a column and a crossbeam
10. 各上駝背枋 *geshang tuobei fang* -- upper crescent beam
11. 前步枯頭枋 *qianbu kutou fang* -- front outer top beam
12. 後步枯頭枋 *houbu kutou fang* -- rear outer top beam
13. 脊柱 *jizhu* -- ridge column
14. 後步柱 *houbu zhu* -- rear column
15. 前步列枋 *qianbu lie fang* -- front outer lower beam
16. 後步列枋 *houbu lie fang* -- rear outer lower beam
17. 後今柱 *houjin zhu* -- rear inner column
18. 前步柱 *qianbu zhu* -- front outer column

Fig. 145 (above) **Elevation of upper hall (on right) and lower hall (on left), looking west, columns and beams.**

Fig. 146 (below) **Elevation of first floor columns and beams at courtyard edge, looking south.**

Creating the Wooden Components

The principal components of the timber-frame structure of the house are the columns and the beams, the vertical members and the horizontal members. They constitute the framework of the house, and its completion is a moment of celebration in the construction of any house. But before considering the members as they are joined together, it is appropriate to first inspect them as individual pieces, as each was created separately and uniquely.

In the frame of the main house, there are 1074 wooden components, of which there are 64 columns and 256 beams.

Columns

Of the sixty-four columns in Yin Yu Tang, twenty-four reach from the ground to the heights of the roof. Twelve measure 27 feet 5 inches, reaching to the central ridge in the upper and lower halls, and twelve measure 23 feet 10 inches, reaching to the eaves of the exterior north and south walls.

The remaining columns are all between 12 and 13 feet high. These columns reach only between the first-story ground and the second-story floor, or between the second-story floor and the roof.

In Huizhou architecture, the carpenters also identify the columns according to their location within the structure. The columns reaching up to the central ridge on the roof are called the *jizhu*, "ridge columns." The outermost columns of a bent (a row of columns)—for instance, in Yin Yu Tang those that are either on the outside perimeter of the building or on the courtyard perimeter—are the *bu* (meaning "step") columns. These are further differentiated. Those on the courtyard perimeter are called *qian bu zhu*, front bu columns; those on the outside are called *hou bu zhu*, rear bu columns. The columns between the ridge column and the bu columns are referred to as the *jin* ("now") columns, and are also differentiated as the front and rear jin columns. In the disparate regions of China, these components may have different names or characters associated with them.

The thinness of Yin Yu Tang's columns (with base diameter ranging between 6.5 and 8 inches—as compared with those of the ceremonial shrine of Jin Shi Di, with diameters of almost 20 inches, or even the 9-inch diameters of typical Ming homes) is palpable. There are several possible reasons for this thinness. The first may have been stylistic fashion. For instance, illustrated woodblock-print books and paintings from the Ming dynasty display full, rounded human figures. Woodblock prints and paintings from the mid-Qing period present tall and slender figures. The scarcity of wood by the mid-Qing period is also a known circumstance and certainly could have contributed to the decision to use younger, thinner trees.

The columns taper as they rise toward the roof. The diameters of the column tops average only about 4 1/4 inches in diameter, a small width in which to often fit crossing beams.

Beams

Like the columns, the beams (or girts) in the house are of various types and sizes. Chinese carpenters differentiate them as being in two primary categories: the *liefang* and *zhifang*. The liefang are the north-south (front-back) beams of the house that define the individual bays (the voids within which are the rooms) of the house. A row of columns, connected by the liefang, is called a *lie*, known in English as a bent. The zhifang are the beams connecting the columns in an east-west direction and are known in English as connecting girts or connectors. In total, there are 256 beams, of which 98 are zhifang and 158 are liefang.

The many beams of the Yin Yu Tang take on a wide variety of shapes and heights, depending on their location and function. Most of the beams are straight and rectangular in cross-section.

The four major exceptions to these straight, rectangular components are the four arched beams, all zhifang, that annunciate two of the most important and celebrated spaces in the house. These beams are known as *tuobei*, "hunchback," beams. The two rooms with tuobei beams are the central rooms of the house on the second floors of the upper and lower halls. Two tuobei beams cross the center of both of the rooms: one connects the ridge columns and the other, in front of the first, connects the jin columns. The tuobei beams all arched in shape and have rounded ends and arc-shaped incisions at either end. Local carpenters refer to these arc incisions as "eyebrows." There is no definitive explanation for why this form was used, but it is the shape of the most important beams in most fine buildings in Huizhou. The importance of these beams, one of which is the all-important ridge beam, is further expressed by their weight. These beams are made of yellow pine and weigh up to four hundred pounds each.

The small thin connector beams in the bedrooms that lie just below the ridge of the house are also arched and not straight, but their modest size and finish does not approach the grandeur of the four in the central rooms.

The rectangular beams vary greatly in makeup. Some are solid and almost square—such as the central zhifang beam in the entry area at the center of the lower hall. Others, the composite beams, are very tall, thin, and fabricated of a multitude of thin pieces of wood laminated together, such as the liefang and zhifang along the walls of the bedrooms.

The two grandest of the rectangular beams are both in the central rooms of the upper and lower halls, on the first floor. Like the tuobei beams above them on the second floor, they stretch between the central ridge columns. Both of these beams, being located in significant locations, are larger in height and depth and have fine applied carvings adorning them. The carvings are pierced work depicting flowers and animals with a faux-gold painted-paper backing.

To create the composite beams, thin horizontal pieces of wood were laid on top of one another, each curved to accept the next. Tapering tenons were then driven through chiseled-out mortises, through the complete group, to tightly bond them together into a single mass. No adhesives or nails were used. This laminating technique appears in both Ming and Qing dynasty houses in Huizhou and was probably *not* developed because of a shortage of wood. Composite beams, constructed from many small trees, are less likely to warp, and maintain the flat surface necessary between two columns. In Yin Yu Tang the composite beams are most common in the more important rooms, where even small (7-inch) members are composed of two or more lamina.

Toward the top of the columns, just below the slanting peak of the roof, small vertical struts supported by beams offer support for the purlins. Each piece of the structure has its own particular name. The small vertical struts are called *zijia duizi* and the horizontal member is called a *zhong zi*, because it resembles the character zhong, meaning "center." Assembling these many and varied columns and beams, in their correct and intended locations, created the sound timber-frame structure that became Yin Yu Tang.

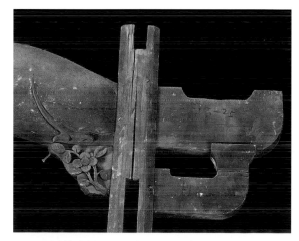

Fig. 147 **Small *tuobei*, "arched beam," one of many spanning the second-story corridor, with joined beam and bracket.**

Erecting the Wooden Structure

Arranging of the columns and beams into the structure of the house is as intricate as the mortise and tenons that hold them together. There are two major types of column-beam structural systems in China, the *tailiang* and the *chuandou*. The chuandou is described by Ruitenbeek as "'through jointed' i.e., the cross-beams are mortised into the columns, and the purlins rest on the ends of the columns." This system was more common in southern China. In the tailiang system, Ruitenbeek notes, "the cross-beams are not mortised into the columns, but rest on top of them." This configuration was more frequently employed in northern Chinese construction.

The column-and-beam arrangement of Yin Yu Tang is of the chuandou variety. Thus, the construction necessitated intricate joinery wherever a zhifang beam meets a column.

Fitting the many components together on the seventh son's property would have entailed hiring dozens of people. As many as sixty carpenters and miscellaneous laborers would have been gath-ered for the four to five days it probably took to erect the columns and beams that the carpenters had been working on for months.

On the ground, a group of columns and beams would have been fitted together the previous day, into *lie*, or "bent." A bent, a transverse cross-section unit of framing, consists of the series of columns in a north-south axis of the house, and the north-south beams (the liefang) that hold them together. The components of a house were traditionally erected in bents beginning with the first lie on the conceptual east side of the house and moving toward the conceptual west gable end of the house.[23] In Yin Yu Tang's case, the erection of the components, therefore, as well as the placement of the column bases, would have begun at the compass west side of the house, in the upper hall:[24]

These beams would all be arranged on the ground, and all the joints would be inserted together, and then it would be raised up. After the two sides are standing the zhifang are inserted on ... You have to start from the east. It's a traditional concept. The east is bigger. You can't start from the west.

—Zhu Yunfeng

Fig. 148 (top) **Columns and beams joined and secured with wooden pegs.**

Fig. 149 (below) **Wooden peg from original construction of Yin Yu Tang.**

Grasping long bamboo poles tied with ropes to an assembled unit of columns and beams, the gathered crowd would lift each lie into place. The master carpenter would stand on the ground, directing the many participants. The most difficult move with each lie would be lifting the entire assemblage onto its column bases. Since the wood was still quite green, it was more moist and heavier than dried wood would be. After the second lie was brought up, the carpenters, standing on ladders inserted the east-west beams that would reach between the two lie and lock them together into a solid framework. The intricately designed and sculpted mortises and tenons would allow a tight and solid joint to hold the beams and columns together. In contrast, there were no joints, adhesives, and bonds to hold the columns to the column bases. The columns were lifted onto the stone bases, and the force of gravity held them in place.

Seven hundred eight wooden pegs, fitted into precreated peg holes, fastened the columns and beams together into a tight and permanent fit. These pegs are called *guanjian* in Chinese, a word that also means "the critical point" and underscores their significance.

The carpenters conserving Yin Yu Tang estimate that it may easily have taken four days to completely fit together the frame of this two hall, five bay house. The framework of a smaller, three bay, one hall house, can be fit together in one day, though carpenters and laborers may rise from their beds at two in the morning to insure that they can complete the project on the auspicious day selected for the ridge beam ceremony.

Ridge Beam

The culminating beam in the frame's structure is the ridge beam, in Chinese called the *zheng liang*. This beam is primarily a ceremonial beam rather than an important structural beam, but it is considered the beam that stabilizes the entire structure, tying together all the many components. According to custom, it represents the spirit of the house.

The ridge beam lies east to west just below the central-ridge purlin, tenoning into the two central columns on either side of the upstairs reception hall. The carpenters fit this beam into the structure only after all the other columns and beams of the building had been raised and inserted in their proper place. It was necessary to spread the two central ridge columns in order to fit in this last significant beam.

According to custom, the raising the ridge beam must occur on an auspicious day. An obligatory ceremony and feast, paid for by the owner, would also have been held for the family and all the carpenters and masons.

The ridge beam ceremony of Huizhou has five basic stages:

Stealing the beam. According to custom, the ridge beam must not come from the land of the house's owner, but must be taken from another person's land just prior to the ceremony.

Receiving the beam. At the ceremony the beam is properly welcomed into the house, and incense is burned.

Praising the beam. After the beam is welcomed, the master carpenter praises the superb quality of the beam.

Sacrifice and offerings. Offerings of wine are made to the heavens and the earth, and meat, fruits, and doufu are laid out on an offering table. Blood from a rooster's comb is dabbed on the ends of the beam to ward off evil spirits.

Raising the beam. After the beam is fit into place, the carpenters, using large ceremonial hammers, ram pegs into the tenons to secure the beam. Having completed the insertion of the beam, the carpenters set off firecrackers and toss candy, the five grains, and pairs of small red hammers to the people below. The small red hammers, made especially for the event, called *zisun chui,* "son and grandson hammers," promise a multitude of male heirs for all who grab them.

It is on the ridge beam that traditionally auspicious objects are hung—red bags of the five grains and banners of five colors—and auspicious words are written. In Huizhou the master carpenter often writes "Civil on the East" and "Martial on the West" on the conceptual east and west ends of the beam. These words imply that the family will produce sons who will become both civil and military officials.

Often the date and year of the ridge-beam ceremony is also inscribed on the beam. A close inspection has revealed that unfortunately there are no such inscriptions on the Yin Yu Tang ridge beam. Either none was written—perhaps because the owner was away and the carpenters were eager to cut another corner—or layers of lacquer, soot, dirt, and grime have eliminated the writing. Had the writing existed or lasted, the exact date of the house's erection would be clear.

And you have to say special words . . . like he [the geomancy expert] takes a chicken and says, "In my hand I hold the owner's rooster. The head grows tall, the tail grows down." He talks like that, then he cuts open the rooster's comb, and blood comes out, and then they start to put up the ridgepole and he says, "The rooster's blood falls to the east, every generation will have sons and grandsons." And they say other special words. I can't remember them all. Every column has to have chicken's blood dabbed on it. It keeps away evil spirits.

—Zhu Jiming

Fig. 150 (left) **Red hammers made for use in the ridge-beam-raising ceremony to hammer in the pegs securing the ridge beam.**

Fig. 151 (below) **North elevation of upper hall beams and columns. The curved beam in red at the top is the ridge beam**

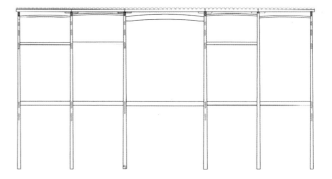

Though no inscriptions or remnants of auspicious color cloths appeared in Yin Yu Tang, the dismantling of the house did reveal a number of objects placed within the framework of the house to ensure good fortune for the family. Between the top of the central ridge columns and the ridge purlin, on both the east and west sides of the upper reception hall, coins and pairs of chopsticks were inserted. The chopsticks, *kuaizi*, indicate a hope for many male descendants, as the word kuaizi sounds like the words for "quickly sons." Many carpenters and masons also included a piece of old wood and a piece of old stone to demonstrate the longevity of the house and that it will continue to stand for many generations.

After, or during, the erection of the columns and beams, the owner or carpenters (or both) also placed coins on a number of the column bases underneath the columns. The coins promised prosperity for the many generations that would live under Yin Yu Tang's roof.

A number of coins from different time periods were found under the columns. The earliest coins found slipped into various notches in the house date from the Han dynasty, and the latest dates from the Qianlong period (1736–95) of the Qing dynasty. In Huizhou, the custom of placing coins beneath the columns is called cai jin qian, "stepping on the money," implying that, like a lizard, "stepping" on it will prevent the money from running away.

Bronze coins in China, a basic form of currency since at least the Zhou dynasty (1050–256 B.C.E.), have long been used among the populace as amulets as well as monetary exchange. Ancient coins are considered particularly auspicious, and many people have collected them for good luck. The *wu zhu* coin from the Han dynasty is among the most potent, and the seventh son placed one of them under the columns of the house.

The placement of the coins followed a long tradition of builders' placing objects within the house to ensure good fortune for the house's occupants—or in the case of an angry or vengeful carpenter, bad luck. The *Lu Ban Jing* (The Sutra of Lu Ban) a carpenters' manual named for the guardian deity of carpenters, makes note of a large variety of objects and amulets that, placed in the proper location in a house, could alter the occupants' fortunes.

Ling Qizheng, the older mason from Huizhou, heard from his master various devious ways a carpenter or mason could cause discomfort for a despised house owner:

[If the carpenters are angry at the owner,] they can put a miniature "night pitcher" [urinal] between pieces of wood in the house. This will cause the children of the house, every night, to call out that they need to urinate just as the owner is falling asleep. The carpenters can also dab a bit of blood from their middle finger onto a beam and it will cause the owner to feel a heaviness on his chest as he sleeps.

In disassembling Yin Yu Tang, no direct evidence of mischief on the part of the carpenters and masons was uncovered. However, the carpenters who participated in the dismantling and conserving of the building noted many times that they felt that the original carpenters who made the structural components were sloppy. The twenty-first century carpenters all felt that workmanship apparent in any visible components—such as the window lattices, the stairs, and the exposed decorative brackets—was superb. But they insisted that the interior work, which the owner would not have seen if he was away while the house was being built, did not meet their own standards. The original carpenters, they maintained, were lazy and took advantage of the absence of the owner, cheating him out of fine work. The possibility that the owner was away while the work was being done is logical if this Huang patriarch, like his descendants and many of his Xiuning compatriots, was a pawnbroker in a distant city.

It seems, the way we see it, that this house was built as a contracted (chengbao) project, as the seventh branch was doing business away from home. The workmanship is well done in the places that are well done, but only fair in the places that are fair. Like that wall is fair, the beam is small, they were skimping on materials, skimping on labor. From this, you can see that it was done on contract. Things on the outside the owner would notice, but many of the places on the inside are just done fair. In the places where there should be double tenons, they only made a single tenon. With a building that's so tall, there should be double tenons. So from this, it's possible to see this was a contracted job. . . . If you didn't dismantle the building, you would never know that it was one tenon. From the outside, you can't tell.

—Zhu Yunfeng

Roof

Once the primary structure of the timber frame had been raised and secured, the artisans would hurry to build the roof, to protect the wood. The tiles would immediately shield the newly erected structure from rain falling directly into the grain of the vertical elements and shed the water away from the entire framework. Moreover, the heavy tiles would weigh down the structure, further stabilizing it and allowing the columns and beams to settle into their permanent locations.

Rafters (chuanzi)

The first step in creating the roof would be to attach the rafters to the purlins. There are two different lengths of the long, thin rectangular rafters on Yin Yu Tang. On the outer sections of the roof, individual rafters stretch from the ridge to the eave, measuring between 8 and 8 1/2 feet long. On the inner sections of the roof, facing into the courtyard, there are two rafters: a short one between the ridge and the first purlin, and a longer one stretching from the first purlin to the eave. The rafters lie on the purlins and are nailed into place. This is one of the few places—other than flooring—in Yin Yu Tang where nails were used. The purlins create a roof angle varying between 22 and 26 degrees. In addition to lying on the purlins, the rafters slip into a slotted comblike strip of wood sitting atop the purlins. These comblike strips, which we have called "combs," are not common to all houses in the Huizhou area. Many simpler houses suffice without such extra stabilizers. The advantage of the combs is that they offer a rectangular space for the rafters to slip into and add an extra degree of friction to the rafters to keep them from sliding off the purlins and thereby help the roof plane resist distortion.

The inclusion of these combs in the construction of Yin Yu Tang is evidence that the house was a more luxurious undertaking than a commoner's residence. The combs also exist on Jin Shi Di.

The rafters on Yin Yu Tang, as is typical of many houses in China, do not create an entirely straight-angled roof. Long, thin triangular wooden boards, called *fei chuan*, "flying rafters," or "kick rafters" in English, sit atop the bottom 38 inches of each rafter, attached by nails, to give an upswing to the roof ends. The kick rafters on Yin Yu Tang, cantilevering from the eaves, have a 5-degree taper within themselves that further lowers the pitch locally to around 19–20 degrees.

The reason for the upturn on the ends of Chinese roof, more exaggerated in southern China, has long been a subject of debate.[25] Some scholars have reasoned that the upturn reflects a reminder of tent living, where the corner poles make an extra flare at the edges of the tent. Others argue that the upturn keeps the roof tiles from slipping down the rafters. And several have proposed that the upturn assists in shedding the water from the roof more quickly and shoots it farther away from the walls of the house.[26] The desire to shed water as quickly as possible and prevent it from having an opportunity to leak into or onto the wooden walls and floors of the house was great. This theory would argue that the more southern the region, the more rain, and therefore the greater the upturned angles on the eaves. This is indeed the situation in China.

The lack of much deterioration of the wood on Yin Yu Tang's rafters, which have probably been protecting the house from rain for more than two centuries, demonstrates the success of the tile system.

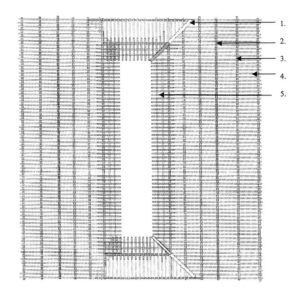

1. 斜沟 *xiegou* -- valley board
2. 桁条 *hengtiao* -- ridge purlin
3. 屋桁 *wuheng* -- purlin
4. 屋椽子 *wu chuanzi* -- rafter
5. 翘投椽 *qiaotouchuan* -- kick rafter

Fig. 152 (top) **Yin Yu Tang roof rafter plan.**

Fig. 153 (above) **Two of the iron nails used in the original construction of Yin Yu Tang to attach the rafters to the purlins.**

Fig. 154 (left) **A Huizhou-published woodblock-printed book illustration depicting the construction under Emperor Sui Yangdi (reign 605–617), from *Xin Juan Xiuxiang Tongsu Yanyi Sui Tangdi Jueshi*, published in 1631 by Ren Rui Tang, reprinted in *Huipai Banhua Yishu* (*The Art of Hui-style Woodblock Prints*), Zhang Guoji, editor, Hefei, Anhui Meishu Chubanshe, 1995.**

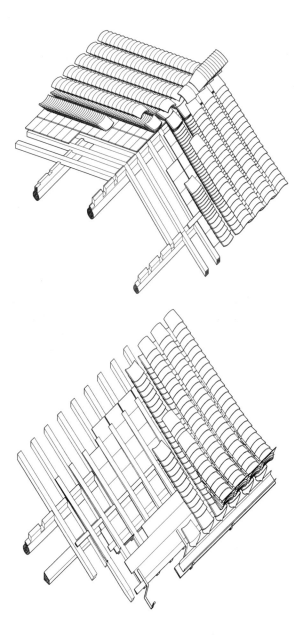

Roof Tiles

Once the rafters had been put in place, the *wajiang*, the tile artisans (and perhaps as many as twenty laborers) could begin the essential task of "putting a roof over the heads" of the occupants and their descendants.

The three primary types of tiles that cover the roof are concave tiles, convex tiles, and flat tiles, this last group referred to as bricks by Chinese artisans. (The concave and convex tiles are the same type, just placed in different orientations.) None of these tiles were attached to the wooden structure of the roof with any adhesive, clay, or nails. Only gravity, their specific arrangement, and their locations held them to the roof. (In northern China, where insulation is more important and winter weather more damaging, a layer of mud is used to assist in the adhesion of the tiles to the roof.)

Yin Yu Tang has a layer of flat tiles laid directly on the rafters. These vary in size from 7 7/8 x 7 1/8 inches to 8 1/2 x 6 1/2 inches. This layer was a luxury item and was not (and still is not) used in most dwellings. It was an extra layer of protection from the rain and an aesthetic embellishment.

On top of the flat tiles, the semicircular roof tiles were laid down in a particular order. First the tile layer covered the surface with rows of tiles, their convex side down. Atop these, he then laid rows of tiles with their concave side down, overlapping the convex-side-down tiles on either side. Repeating this pattern created a pattern of undulating tile across the breadth of the roof and, more important, a series of funnels for the rainwater to run down. The rainwater would slip sideways off the concave-down tiles and then vertically down the funnel created by the convex-down tiles.

At the bottom edge of the concave-down tiles' row was a specialty concave-down tile with a crown edge (see figure 156). This edge forced any water that might still be on the concave tiles off to the side, into the convex-tile funnels. At the end of each such funnel was a specialty convex drip tile with a decorated triangular ending

Fig. 155 (top) **Concave and convex roof tiles over a layer of flat tiles.**

Fig. 156 (above) **Roof tiles with crown-edged and triangular drip tiles.**

Fig. 157 (right) **Tile-covered roof constructed so rainwater drains into the home's central courtyard. Sanxicun, Xiuning County.**

hanging over the eave. This triangular shape directed the water to drip from the point of the triangle down, thereby controlling the flow of the water off the roof and keeping it from splashing indiscriminately over the interior of the house. When Yin Yu Tang was first built, the water flowed from the triangular tiles into a rectangular tile gutter that hung from iron brackets. The horizontal gutter carried the water to a vertical shoot that sent it down below the ground floor.

A glance at the interior of Yin Yu Tang quickly demonstrates that the roofs around the courtyard all slant in, sending the water into the courtyard, rather than away from the house. This arrangement is typical of most houses in Huizhou, locally called *si shui dao tang*, "the four waters pour into the hall." The explanation for this design is that water represents prosperity—as is also expressed in Huang Cun houses' orientation toward the village's shuikou, water entry—and the house owner therefore did not want it to slip away from him.

The moment when the timber frame was up and the roof covered with protective tiles was an important juncture. Marking the completion of the first major stage of the house, the occasion demanded a celebration. The owner of the home would hold another banquet for the workers, his friends, and relatives. Some owners who could not afford to continue building might have stopped the process at this point and waited months or even years before completing the house.

Red couplets would be pasted up on the structure's main columns. Friends and relatives would present the owner with red silk blankets that would also be hung up, and strings of firecrackers would be set off. At the banquet, tables would be set up with the guests sitting in proper hierarchal arrangement. The head carpenter would sit in the most honored position, at a square table on the conceptual east side of the reception room, facing south. The owner's mother's brother, a respected relation in Huizhou families, would sit at the western table, also facing south. The owner himself would not sit, but walk among the tables, toasting his guests.

The day after the tiles were up the carpenter, mason, and tile mason would have to make sure that all the columns were correctly aligned, readjusting the column bases if necessary. The diagonal lines between the columns in the house had to be ascertained to be straight to ensure that the structure would be stable.

The Curtain Walls

With the tiles weighing down the roof, the columns settled into their permanent positions. Only then could the outer stone and brick walls be raised. Had the stone and brick masons put up the outer walls before laying down the tiles, the subsequent additional weight of the tiles could have caused the columns to shift their positions. In shifting, they might have leaned against the outer wall, which was not built to support the weight of the house—it was the timber-frame structure that held up the massively heavy roof. The curtain wall merely assisted in sheltering the occupants from rain and the intrusive eyes of inquisitive neighbors.

The Yin Yu Tang curtain wall is primarily brick, but has a significant base of sandstone blocks reaching in some places as high as seven feet. Above the stone is another 20–26 feet of laid brick. The stone close to the ground would have received splashing water from rain as well as moisture from the ground. Because stone does not deteriorate from moisture as fast as brick, it was preferable to use stone at the base of a wall.

Stone Walls

In constructing the curtain wall of Yin Yu Tang, the masons and the owner needed to decide what percentage of the wall would be stone and what percentage would be the less-expensive brick.

With the exception of the oddly constructed conceptual west wall, the wall with the highest stone section is the front facade. It reaches almost 5 1/2 feet and is distinguished by a taller course of capstones at the top of the stone coursing. Since stone was more expensive than brick, the seventh son must have made an economic decision to show off more stone at the front of the house, where his guests would enter, than on the sides. The back wall of the house has a height of 5 feet, and the conceptual east (actual west) side of the house has a 4 1/2-foot-tall wall.

Fig. 158 **Stone coursing of Yin Yu Tang for the north, west, south, and east exterior walls.**

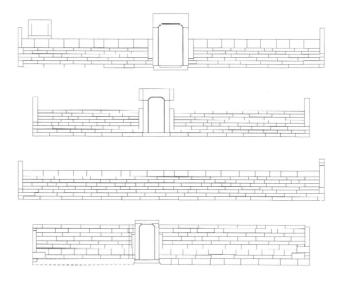

The conceptual west (actual east) wall of the house is an anomaly. Unlike the beautifully squared rectangular blocks of the front, back, and conceptual east wall, the west wall seems to be made of reused stone from a previous construction. And instead of the wall being one stone thick, it has at places the thickness of three thin stones, each laid vertically in a sandwich fashion. The reason for the disparity among the wall heights and quality can be explained by several circumstances. The primary circumstance to be considered is the orientation of the house and the direction of the wall. The conceptually west side is the least important side. It is on this least significant west wall that houses traditionally had abutting buildings or structures. Kitchens, for instance, would be on the conceptual west wall. The west wall of Yin Yu Tang shared a wall not only with the kitchen structure but also with a home built by the fifth branch, presumably an elder brother of the seventh son. The irregular stone wall on the conceptual west was not extremely visible to the outside world, tucked between buildings, and as the carpenters noted regarding the wooden interior nonvisible structure of the house, those rarely visible areas were where the builders cut corners.

The stone sections of the walls were eventually stabilized by the weight of the brick. But before the brick was laid, simple joints holding one stone to the next provided stabilizing support. On the top edge of each stone, at either end, the masons made a triangular notch. Wood or iron butterfly-shaped cramps placed in the notches would have held one stone to its neighbor. This cramping system, used also in medieval cathedrals in Europe, made stone walls more stable structures and kept them in line as the walls were being erected.

Before leaving these stone walls, it is worth noting that the number of stones along each band is always odd, as even numbers were considered unlucky

Brick Walls

Bricklayers in China used many bricklaying patterns. For Yin Yu Tang, the bricklayers varied their bonding pattern, using both a box bond and a running bond. The bricks were held together with a mortar made entirely of a lime and sand plaster.

Once the bricks were laid atop the stone, the entire wall was covered with a lime plaster mix, inside and out. Though lime was considered a hygienic element, it was also practical in directing the heat and light of the sun. This outer lime coating, typical of Huizhou houses, was a bright white and reflected the sun's heat away from the house, keeping it cooler in the summer months. Inside, particularly in the bedrooms, the bright white lime walls made bedrooms brighter than they would have been with only dark wood paneling.

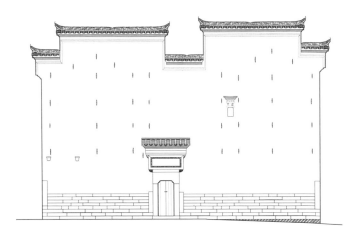

Fig. 159 (above) **One layer of stone coursing on the south wall.**

Fig. 160 (below) **West exterior elevation with horsehead walls.**

Horse-head Walls

The distinctive top of Yin Yu Tang's curtain walls echo a style commonly preferred in Huizhou since at least the Ming dynasty. On both ends of the house, the east and west ends, the walls are much higher than at the front and back. But their tops are not straight across. Instead, these gable walls are stepped in a manner locally called "horse-head walls."

The walls on Yin Yu Tang actually step up and down, then up and down again. This high outer brick wall was a way to prevent fires from skipping from one house to another, or from the kitchen into the main section of the house.

Huizhou villages are primarily located in small valleys, and often for security reasons, the houses are clustered together, frequently abutting one another as in a dense urban area. For this reason, the horse-head wall became a common and convenient method of keeping fires from spreading from house to house. The steps relate to the changing height of the roof. The highest steps of the horse-head walls are over the two ridge peaks of the upper and lower halls' roofs, and the lowest areas are above the courtyard span.

Masons would further elaborate the elegance of the horse-head wall, with upturned roof tiles at the ends, and paintings of auspicious images at the top corners of the walls. With these decorative and fortune-inspiring designs, a striking style of black and white houses developed.

The mason for Yin Yu Tang selected auspicious calligraphic designs for the horse-head walls. Sayings calling for good fortune decorate these high edges and reflect both the Chinese interchangeability of auspicious words and images and perhaps a certain literary leaning of the occupant.

Horse-head walls were already being constructed by the Ming dynasty. There is evidence of a horse-head wall on a long woodblock-print handscroll of a wealthy Huizhou publisher's garden home, the Huan Cui Tang Yuan Jing Tu. This home, built at the beginning of the seventeenth century, was located in Xiuning County but unfortunately is no longer standing.[27] Most of the buildings in the capacious garden mansion do not abut one another and are open to the views on all four sides, so there was little reason for such a wall, but one building (in fact, the main hall called Huan Cui Tang) does sport a horse-head wall.[28]

After the horse-head wall was erected, its top edge was covered with roof tiles standing vertically on end, along the horizontal length of the wall. The dark line of the tiles on the white wall accentuates the handsome outline of the building form.

The Entranceway

The front facade that greeted guests and inhabitants faced an auspicious direction, allowing both humans and good forces to flow into the house and preventing evil forces from entering. The grand ornamentation around the front door to Yin Yu Tang announces its crucial function.

Above the doorway is a projecting hood with a tile roof, in imitation of larger rain-protecting hoods on grander edifices. Below the hood are a series of four affixed carved-brick ornaments depicting pairs of magpies, phoenixes, mandarin ducks, and swallows—all symbols of harmonious matrimonial union. Below these accessories, on the right side of the door, hangs a representation of a fish, a symbol of abundance of both riches and sons. On the left side of the door hangs a representation of a rabbit, likewise symbolizing fecundity. Two larger rectangular tiles, one on each side of the central rectangular panel, portrayed scenes from opera stories. Figures in opera garb stood under traditional roofs and lean against decorative balustrades. Just below each of these opera tiles were smaller images, also of carved tile, of lions to protect the house from evil spirits. Like the door hood, they were smaller versions of the large stone lions that guarded ancestral halls and official buildings.

Fig. 161 (top) **The south (rear) wall of Yin Yu Tang.**

Fig. 162 (above) **Horse-head walls on a house in Huang Cun, Xiuning County.**

Fig. 163 (right) **Carved tile of phoenix located above the front entrance doorway.**

Fig. 164 **Front facade and entryway of Yin Yu Tang while still located in Huang Cun.**

The front facade is intentionally austere. In fact, the houses of Huizhou have often been compared to fortresses. Originally the only windows that looked out from this wall were two tiny lookouts from the second floor, each measuring 12 x 18 inches. Like most houses in the region, Yin Yu Tang was built to withstand attacks by marauding bandits or soldiers. The high outer walls and high, small windows functioned as deterrents.

The windows, though petite, were not left undecorated. Small hoods, miniature versions of the one over the front door, shielded rain, and fresco ink paintings on the lime surface beneath the hood gave the opening visual interest.

The masons of Yin Yu Tang further enhanced the building's facade with ink paintings at the upper right and left corners of the house. The paintings, put on like frescoes just after the last coat of lime plaster was applied to the brick, had all but faded from two hundred years of dirt, sun, and rain. Faint images of a *qilin*, mythical creatures that deliver sons who will become high officials, can be made out in photographs taken of the house in 1996. In the tradition of many artisans, masons in Huizhou (even today) often work with design manuals that they have either created themselves or inherited from their masters. In this way, designs are passed down through generations.

Inside

Once the column-and-beam structure was erected, the tile roof constructed, and the curtain wall wrapped around the frame, Yin Yu Tang was enclosed from and protected from the outdoors. Only doorways, small windows, and the courtyard could allow in humans, air, precipitation, and sunshine. Having created the basic envelope, the masons and carpenters could begin work on the interior: that is, the partitions to separate the rooms, the doors to provide entrances, the interior lattice windows to offer sun and ventilation, and floors to walk on.

Floors

For the ground floor of Yin Yu Tang, masons cut a multitude of paving stones (from the same red sandstone used on the building's exterior) to cover the interior courtyard, front entryhall, and reception hall. Stone flooring is found in many houses, but certainly not all. Some houses of similar age, even in Huang Cun, have raised wooden floorboards in the reception hall, and some homes of less well-to-do families have only dirt floors.

Wooden floorboards in Yin Yu Tang are found only on the second floor and the first-floor bedrooms. These floorboards consisted of two types, often found in the same room: those made of composite strips (similar to some of the beams) and single flat, wide boards.

The seventh son, who most likely was proud of this handsome entrance to his home, certainly would never have foreseen the intentional destruction of its elements. During the Cultural Revolution, a campaign to "destroy the four olds" (old ideas, old culture, old manners, and old customs) erupted in an effort to create a new culture for China. To demonstrate loyalty to the Party line, and in fear of accusations of being counterrevolutionaries, many people destroyed their personal collections of art, literature, and anything that reflected a decadent and "feudal" lifestyle. Huang Xiqi therefore took it upon himself to break the beautifully carved opera scenes and protective lions on his doorway. Huang Xiqi's actions also probably helped save much of the rest of the house from destruction by Red Guards:

The carved tiles at the entrance were smashed by me at the time of the Cultural Revolution. The primary reason was to destroy the four olds. All the "gifted scholars and beautiful women" [characters in traditional Chinese romances] had to be destroyed. . . . I couldn't think of anything else to do [about it.] I burned a lot of classic short stories. I did not harm anything else. I did it voluntarily. But it wasn't only my home. Other people also did the same in their homes. . . . I was loyal to Mao Zedong thought and loyal to Chairman Mao. . . . Now, of course, I realize that those [carved tiles] were cultural inheritances.

—Huang Xiqi

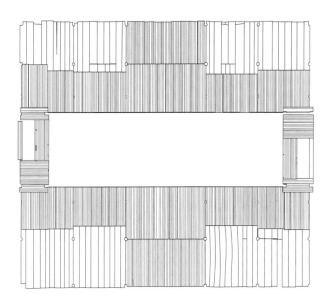

Fig. 165 **Floorboards of the second floor of Yin Yu Tang. Wider boards are at the back ends of bedrooms.**

Master carpenter Zhu Jiming explained the situation this way: "If you are living in a bedroom on the second floor, and your baby has diarrhea, it might leak down to the first floor if you have wide floorboards with warping and openings between them."[29]

The floorboards lie on joists. In some places they were held down by the weight of the partitions, but elsewhere the rare nail was employed. On the first floor, the joists were further supported by bricks placed directly on the ground below. Unlike most wooden components of the house, the floorboards were often attached to the joists of the building with large (3- to 5-inch-long) metal nails.

The first-floor floorboards sat on supports approximately 14 inches above the bare ground. This space of 14 inches allowed air to circulate below the bedrooms and impeded deterioration of the wood from moisture in the ground. Stone stretchers with decorative ventilation holes below the sills hid the empty area below the bedrooms, allowing ventilation into that area, while also preventing animals from living under the floorboards.

In spite of the provision for ventilation, the floorboards of Yin Yu Tang, particularly those on the first floor, must have deteriorated easily and were replaced when necessary. The deterioration is clearly noticeable in photographs and videos taken of the house just before it was dismantled.

The front section of the room usually consists of two-inch-thick boards, each made up of approximately six to seven thin (1 1/2 to 2 1/2 inches thick) strips of wood laminated together. In Yin Yu Tang, all these laminated boards are made of *shanmu*, Chinese fir. None of the strips that make up these boards is straight. The carpenters used available lumber and economically let the shape of the strips follow the natural form of the individual piece of wood. The strips were held together in two manners. First, the side edge of each strip was curved either convexly or concavely to fit into the adjoining strip. Second, several long, tapering tenons were slipped through a series of mortises in the strips to connect and fasten the strips together into a complete board of ranging in width from 15 to 22 inches. The tenons were then spread with wedges at each end to bind the lamina together.

The back section of most of the Yin Yu Tang bedrooms was covered with simpler floorboards, flat boards of widths ranging from 7 1/2 to 12 1/2 inches wide. All of these boards are yellow pine. The bed at the back of the bedroom covered a large section of the boards, so they were not visible.

According to the local carpenters today, the composite boards are greatly preferred to the single wide boards because they lie more flat and are less likely to warp, shrink, or crack. They also entailed more work and therefore showed off to visitors that the owner of the home could afford to pay for such labor intensive work.

Partitions

Once the house was protected from rain and blustering wet winds and covered with floorboards to allow carpenters better access to all areas, the inner partitions of the house could be placed between the columns. The open space could be divided into rooms for the many and varied individuals who would come to inhabit them.

These partitions in Yin Yu Tang are of several different types. There are wooden partitions, and, unusually, there are also masonry partitions. The wooden partitions are between the central public rooms of the house (the reception hall, entryway, second-floor reception room, and second-floor storage room) and the bedrooms abutting them. Between those more central bedrooms and the outside corner bedrooms, the walls are made of thin masonry bricks coated with a lime plaster. The masonry walls may have added some extra load-bearing support for the extra-wide, five-bay house. Inner masonry walls were also used in the same positions in Jin Shi Di, which was also five bays wide.

There are usually two or three wooden partition panels between any two columns. Therefore, for instance, in bedroom number six, there are, separating the bedroom and the reception hall, three partition components between the front and middle columns, and another two between the middle and back columns. Between each partition section and the column is a separate component (termed here a "column liner"), which is scribed and coped to meet the round column. The column liner serves as an intermediary between the round column and the flat surface of the partition's edge.

These complex partitions served not to support the roof but to divide the spaces of the houses into common areas and private areas, to separate areas for one specific function from areas for other functions.

Lattice Windows

After the wooden frame, curtain walls, floorboards, and partitions had all been constructed and installed, the elegant lattice windows that endow Yin Yu Tang with their unique character would have been mounted in place. While the simple inner shutters and frames of the large lattices would have been made by the house carpenters, the owner most likely hired expert carvers to fashion the grand, finely worked lattice panels of the first floor. With these decorative yet functional elements in place, the main house of Yin Yu Tang would have been finished. With the completion of the kitchen and the stove—which could be built only after the primary building was finished—Yin Yu Tang would have been ready to welcome the generations of Huang family members and their honored guests.

Heating, Cooling, and Plumbing

Two integral parts of architecture's function is protection from outdoor temperature changes and governance of the flow of water into and out of the house. The inhabitants of Yin Yu Tang and other Huizhou houses resolved these needs in a variety of ways.

The intense heat of Huizhou's summers is greatly regulated by the bright white lime covering on the exteriors of the houses. The white deflects the sun's strong rays. The narrow east-west courtyard likewise prevents sunlight from directly entering the interior of the house during the daytime. The masonry walls hold the cool air from the evening. The result is a refreshingly cool atmosphere in these houses during the summer months. Winter, however, was not as comfortable.

It was very cold in winter, especially when it was snowing. In winter, we always ate inside, and used foot warmers, which were fueled by charcoal. Everyone had a foot warmer. Winters were really tough. You couldn't open the windows. Instead of glass, the windows were pasted by paper. Hardly any light could get through.

—Huang Zhenxin

These are no built-in provisions for heating Huizhou houses during the winter, when temperatures often drop to below freezing and snow falls (though it melts quickly). To shield themselves from the cold, Huizhou inhabitants wear multiple layers of clothing,

including cotton-padded jackets and pants. Additional warmth is provided by a variety of mobile charcoal braziers. Charcoal was a refined by-product of wood cooking fuel in the kitchen and was also produced as a side trade by local villagers. Hand braziers, baskets with metal interior trays, held the heat-radiating charcoal as did braziers on stands placed under a table where all could rest their feet. Parents often stood their small children on raised shelves within tall, cone-shaped buckets. At the bottom of the bucket, below the shelf, charcoal glowed in a metal basin, warming the child while the bucket prevented him or her from running about the room and getting into trouble:

[We had] "child buckets." Every family had one. It's about this high [one meter], with a board in the middle, so a kid could stand on it. When adults were busy—say, with cooking—they could leave kids in there.

—Huang Zhenxin

When it was really cold, and when our hands and feet were frozen, we'd stand in the buckets to have our meals before we went to school.

—Huang Xianying

Communal wells for drinking water were a convenient and more economical method of water retrieval than each household's having its own individual dug well. Huang Cun had at least five wells for drinking water. (No water was drunk directly from the wells. All water is boiled before being consumed.) Each day, members of the household went with a pair of buckets, slung at either end of a pole, to fetch water from the well and carry it home. The water is heavy, and in the 1910s, Huang Zixian noted in a letter to his brother that a young local boy was being paid to help their aging mother, with her small, bound feet, to carry the full buckets back into the house.

Fig. 166 **Woven-bamboo hand brazier fit with a metal tray for the charcoal, and a grill on top to keep the person carrying it from being burned. Small metal tongs hang on the sides of these braziers to arrange the charcoals.**

Fig. 167 (left) **Child standing in child minder, watching his family prepare New Year's meal. Huang Cun, Xiuning County.**

Fig. 168 (right, top) **Washing clothes in stream. Yixian County.**

Fig. 169 (right, below) **Well. Huang Cun, Xiuning County.**

To wash clothes, dishes, and vegetables, women of Huang Cun, and Yin Yu Tang, would carry their bundles to one of several streams that flow around the village. As in most villages, there are set spots along the stream for washing different objects. For hygienic reasons, food is always washed at the spot farthest upstream.

Human and animal waste products are, in the Chinese agricultural sphere, an important element in crop cultivation. Therefore, instead of discarding the waste, family members assiduously collect it and distribute it in their vegetable fields as fertilizer:

At dusk every day, when my sister and I came back from school, we would work with our mom to scoop up the manure from the buckets and carry them to the garden. We were still young at the time and couldn't lift the buckets, so we just pulled them to the garden and spread them out.

—Huang Zhenxin

Inside the house, wooden chamber pots and urinals were kept in the bedrooms, usually conveniently located next to or under the bed.

The technologies and techniques for heating, cooling, and water conveyance made Yin Yu Tang not only a structure, but a habitation that could be enjoyed in all seasons and for centuries of seasons.

Fig. 170 (left, top) **A fine porcelain urinal, from the nineteenth century, from Yin Yu Tang. This porcelain piece, with its underglaze blue design, would have been a far more luxurious object than the less expensive stoneware urinal.**

Fig 171 (left, below) **A stoneware urinal with green glaze from YinYu Tang.**

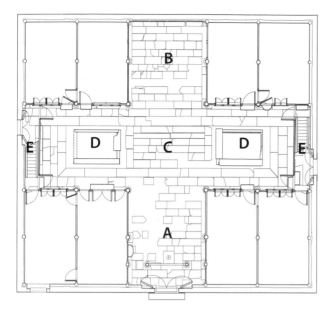

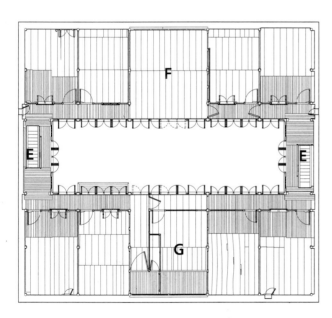

Fig. 172 **Plans of the first (top) and second (above) floors of Yin Yu Tang.**

A: Entryway
B: Reception Hall
C: Courtyard
D: Fishpools
E: Stairways
F: Upstairs Reception Hall
G: Storage

Spaces

With the columns, beams, and partitions, a number of spaces were created within the walls of Yin Yu Tang. Each space would take on its own function, its own furniture arrangement, and, in time, its own events and memories. The partitions created, within the main framework of the house, several types of rooms: reception halls, bedrooms, the courtyard, and staircases. And beyond the main rectangular frame of the house, the kitchens were erected on the conceptual west (compass east) side of the house, and a forecourt, enclosed by a high masonry wall, was located at the front of the house.

The house consists of two "halls," an upper and a lower one, separated by a central skywell. The upper hall, which is physically slightly higher than the lower hall and is more important because it faces the more significant conceptual southern direction, is located on the far side of the skywell from the entrance. The lower hall, in whose central bay one stands immediately upon entering the house, faces conceptual north and therefore carried less status.

Whereas most residences of the non-elite are three bays wide, Yin Yu Tang is composed of an unusually wide five bays. The central rooms of each "hall" are common spaces: reception halls, entryways, or, as in the case of the second floor of the lower hall, storage space. The rooms to either side of these central rooms were private bedrooms, allocated to various members of the family.

The Common Rooms

The Entryway

The first common room that a guest or occupant would enter in Yin Yu Tang would have been the entryway of the house. Upon crossing the threshold of the house, one would immediately encounter a spirit wall, 3 feet 6 inches inside the door. This *zhongmen*, central door, consisting of four removable vertical partitions sitting on a frame between two column bases, was intended to deflect evil forces from entering the house, as such forces were believed to travel only in straight lines and could not, therefore, manage the turns around the wall. An additional function of the spirit wall was to ensure greater privacy within the house and skywell common area while still allowing air to flow through the building. Entering the house would necessitate walking around, either to the left or the right, the zhongmen and then through the entryway.

Though this space primarily functioned as a thoroughfare into the building, it was celebrated with several finely carved wood components. The first celebratory wood fittings to be encountered would be two tuobei, arched beams on either side of the zhongmen. Anyone entering the house would walk under one of these beams. The beam served to stabilize the structure and the zhong-men, but it also visually marked the welcoming path into the house. Though the large majority of the beams in this house are rectangular, certain key areas are decorated with tuobei beams. This custom is typical in Huizhou houses and halls. Shaping wood to form the arch undoubtedly required additional labor and displayed an extra visual verve in a space. The tuobei beams here in the entryway are, interestingly, flat on either side.

The central east-west beam called the *zheng zha*, directly below the ridge of the lower hall, is a large square piece of solid wood. Laminated to the bottom of the beam at either end, and therefore apparent to any visitor looking up, were beautiful thin, wooden panels, with pierced carvings in the shape of a *ruyi*. The ruyi is a symbol, and a pun on the words "may you have all you wish." These ruyi are further elaborated with carvings. Flash photography of them has revealed that the original builders had placed a sheet of gilt paper between the laminated wood carving and the beam. When the house was brand-new, the shimmering gilt from behind the animal carvings—reflecting light from a hanging lantern—must have made a mesmerizing impression on visitors.

Visitors would also have been struck by a lattice hanging just below the edge of the courtyard, across the width of the entryway. The horizontal lattice, constructed of many strips of wood joined together, not only creates a fancifully designed frame for the view of the courtyard but also forms auspicious characters to rain fortune on the occupants. The character *shou*, for longevity, is placed directly in the center of the lattice grille. To either side are two more *shou* characters.

Huang Xiqi recalls that when he was younger there were still pivoting vertical panels below this lattice grille, sitting on a wooden threshold. The doors were solid below, with a *shou* character incised on the board, and open lattice above. They, along with the threshold, were removed in the 1950s.

The center design on the upper beam here is the character for "longevity." There's a legend that the house was a gift to our ancestor for himself on one of his birthdays. That's how the saying goes, but in terms of what has actually happened, there is no detailed information available. That's only what we infer.

—Huang Binggen

The entryway originally had no purpose other than a welcoming place for visitors, a pause before a more formal event. Over time, the function of the space evolved. By the early-twentieth century, when a vague division of the house between two brothers had come to pass, one brother and his descendants took many of their meals in the entryway.

Fig. 173 (above) **The lattice screening above the entryway displays the decorative form of the character *shou*, "longevity."**

Fig. 174 (above right) **Carved wooden decoration, one of a pair, laminated onto the central overhead beam in the entryway of Yin Yu Tang.**

Fig. 175 (below) **A view of the entryway and the lattice screening from the second floor.**

The Reception Hall

Across the courtyard from the entryway was the most important room in the house, the reception hall, known in Huizhou as the *zhengtang* (the proper room) or the *ketang* (the guest room). This room, entirely visible from the entryway, is completely open to the courtyard on its front side. Because of the overhang from the second-floor corridor above, rainwater does not enter the space.

Yin Yu Tang's reception hall may have once had a series of wooden-lattice screen doors, set on stone sleepers, separating the space from the courtyard. The stone paving on the ground of the reception hall suggests that there was never a wood floor in the room, as can be seen in other houses, but slits on the sides of the column bases on either side of the room suggest that a sleeper crossed the length of the room and that lattice doors would have sat atop it. Such an arrangement would have been appropriate and proper in a home such as Yin Yu Tang.

The location of the reception hall, facing conceptual south and in the center of the structure, made it the most auspiciously located room. Whether a structure is a temple or a home, whether located in northern China or in southern China, this auspiciously located space—facing conceptual south and centrally located—is always the most esteemed place in a building.

In Yin Yu Tang, the reception hall is celebrated not only by its position but also by several architectural details that set it apart.

Figs. 176 & 177 (above) **Reception halls with altar table, square table, and television. Xu Cun, Shexian County.**

Fig. 178 (right) **Reception hall with altar table and layers of celebratory decorations. Xiuning County.**

Fig. 179 (far right) **Altar table in reception hall of family celebrating a wedding. Xiuning County.**

Like the front entryway, the central east-west beam of the reception hall, directly below the ridge beam, is a large, solid 10 1/2-inch square piece of wood stretching 14 feet across the hall, decorated with two finely carved, laminated slats of wood with ruyi shaped ends. Under this distinguishing framework of beams, the family would gather at appointed times to worship their ancestors, reassert their family bonds together at festive meals, and properly entertain guests.

The furniture arrangement in this room, typical of proper reception halls in all Huizhou, would be symmetrical and standardized. A long altar table would run east to west along the back wall of the room. In front of the altar table and abutting it would be placed a square table and two chairs, facing conceptual south on either side of the square table. Other chairs and tables would be lined up against the east and west walls of the room.

In Huizhou it was typical to place a vase on one side of the altar table and a mirror on the other. This setup is referred to as *dong ping, xi jing*, "east vase and west mirror." Since the word for vase (*ping*) sounds like the word for *peace*, and the word for mirror (*jing*) sounds like word for *calm*, the table display indicates the hope for peace and harmony within the household. Yin Yu Tang family members, in recalling the reception hall, often include this detail.

Because the room was used for daily, informal occasions as well, the furniture, except for the altar table, was often moved about. For instance, if four people were dining together or playing mahjong, the square table would be temporarily moved away from the altar table, and four chairs would be slipped into position at the table's four sides. Benches, to seat two or three people, could also be brought in to accommodate more diners.

Over time, the role of the reception hall altered subtly. After the 1949 revolution, ancestor worship was slowly discouraged and the Mao cult promoted. By the late 1950s, few families were hanging up ancestral portraits at New Year's. Instead, Mao's portrait would hang in the exact same location of respect, above the altar, facing the entryway. Mao had figuratively replaced the ancestors as the fatherhead of the family of China. In Yin Yu Tang, printed quotations by Mao also decorated the sidewalls of Yin Yu Tang, where, in the past more literary calligraphy may have originally hung. A printed pair of vertical lines of poetry were also pasted on the side columns of the hall, where calligraphy would have traditionally been hung on celebratory occasions.

This couplet, printed and distributed by the Xinhua Publishing Company in 1968, is a Mao poem:

The five continents are being shaken by wind and thunder,
The four seas are being tossed by the angry winds and the clouds.

The Skywell

The courtyard, or skywell (*tianjing,* as it is known in Chinese) was the central void created by the partitions forming the surrounding rooms. This fundamental common space in Yin Yu Tang was the essential core of all proper Huizhou houses. "If a house doesn't have a courtyard, it cannot be called a house," noted Zhu Jiming, a traditionally trained carpenter who assisted in the preservation of Yin Yu Tang. Since the windows on the outer facade are minimal, the courtyard becomes an essential means of ventilating and lighting the house. It would also function in a more ethereal sense to bind together the family members whose personal spaces, the bedrooms, line the 14 foot 8 inches by 44 foot 6 inches courtyard.

The whole family enjoyed the light and air of the courtyard. It was a place for women to sit and sew and for children to play. The space was decorated not only by the lattice of the rooms around it but also by flowers and fish pools:

There were flower pots in the skywell by the fish pools. There were two, one was an evergreen, which was very big. The red blooms looked beautiful.

—Huang Xianying

There were flower pots by each fish pool in the skywell. There was also a pot of orchids in the spring. And chrysanthemum was the flower during autumn.

—Huang Zhenxin

The two fish pools, as the family called them, punctuated the courtyard at either end. Though such pools were not common in Huizhou, they were not unknown and were a desirable element. Yin Yu Tang, unlike most houses, was fortunate to have been built above an underground stream. The fish pools were connected to the stream, which filled them with water. The most practical reason for the pools was fire prevention. Should the house catch on fire, water would be immediately available for extinguishing the flames. A secondary purpose for the pools was decorative. The family could keep ornamental fish in the pools for visual entertainment. The domestication and cultivation of goldfish as live house ornaments has a history in China of at least a thousand years. Huang Zhenxin has confirmed that the fish kept in the pools were primarily for decoration and not for eating. Only on special occasions would live fish be kept in the pools as a form of refrigeration, until they were ready to be cooked.

They [the pools] were something very precious left by our ancestors. [There were] goldfish in them. There were black and red fish, and

Fig. 180 **Yin Yu Tang's *tianjing*, "sky well," courtyard with fish pools.**

even turtles. The water was fresh, so you could raise a lot of things in it. If the water was bad, you couldn't raise anything.

—Huang Zhenxin

The courtyard contains various elements and decorations, from decoratively carved column bases to decoratively molded roof-tile ends, from the first-floor bedroom lattices to the second-floor corridor lattices, intended to delight the eye. Together these elements made the courtyard into the most dynamic and striking space of the entire building.

Fig. 181 **Pickle jar with longevity character, *shou*, design from Yin Yu Tang. Stoneware jars are a common sight in all households in rural Huizhou even today. Pickling vegetables is an important way of preserving extra foodstuffs to be eaten during the winter seasons. Despite the utilitarian function of this jar, there was still an interest in decorating it.**

The Kitchens

One had to leave the courtyard—and, in fact, leave the basic rectangular footprint of the house, exiting through the conceptual west doorway—to enter the kitchens. The location of the kitchens, outside the high masonry walls of Yin Yu Tang, was typical of many houses in southern China. The placement beyond the high walls, as with the fish pools, was a fire precaution. Should the kitchen catch fire, the high horse-head masonry walls would prevent the fire from spreading into the more important wooden structure of the main house.

The location of the kitchens on the conceptual west side of the house was a specific, fengshui-oriented decision. Since the conceptual west was less important than the conceptual east, abutting buildings would be attached only on that side of the house.

Until 1976, there were at least three kitchens that belonged to Yin Yu Tang. Multiple kitchens were needed, as there were multiple daughters-in-law at any one time—the house was certainly built to accommodate multiple daughters-in-law—and each would need her own kitchen. Two of the kitchens were small, but a third larger kitchen was used for preparing the pig and making special rice cakes at New Year and cooking for other major festive occasions.

The primary object in the kitchen was, without a doubt, the stove. If, as in France, houses and furniture are divided up into movables (the furniture) and immovables (the house), the primary stove of a Huizhou kitchen is an immovable. Brick masons who built the walls of the house also constructed these massive brick and mortar stoves, often measuring over 6 1/2 feet long and 3 1/2 feet wide. Like the outer walls of the house, the mason would cover the stove's exterior with a bright, white lime plaster, often decorating it with painted ink designs. The stoves, usually kidney-shaped, were built of bricks with a hollow center. An opening on the back side allowed the cook to feed kindling and firewood into the stove, and fan the fire with a bellows. Usually the mason also included a chimney to draw the heat through the stove. Round cooking pots, with rounded bottoms, fit into round holes on the upper surface of the stove and were thereby completely surrounded below by fire. The cooking action—stirring, steaming, and frying—took place on the side of the stove opposite from the fire opening. Clay models of this type of stove, found in Han dynasty tombs, demonstrate that the design was in use as early as two thousand years ago.

Discussions with family members about the kitchens conjured up myriad memories, of festival meals, of the kitchen god as well as the daily routine meals.

Fig. 182 (far left) **Kitchen stove, Shoucun, Xiuning County.**

Fig. 183 (left) **Kitchen. Chengkan, Huizhou District.**

It was like this. There was a small room in the middle [between the house and the kitchen], which was kind of dark. It was used specially for storing firewood. You know we used firewood [as fuel] in the countryside. The kitchen next to it . . . was our own kitchen, which was used by my whole family. Still next to our kitchen was the kitchen of Huang Xiqi's grandfather. His kitchen was twice as large as ours. There were two huge stoves with big pots in them. When winter came and it was time for the New Year, we would use pots this big to cook zongzi [leaf-wrapped stuffed rice]. And we would use their big stoves to steam the New Year rice cake. The big pots were for everyone to use.

—Huang Zhenxin

In the kitchen there was a statue of the kitchen god above the stove. On his left was a phrase: "safe and peaceful during all the seasons"; on his right was a phrase: "great peace for all under heaven". . . . There used to be statues of a little deity on every stove in those kitchens. On the Chinese New Year's Eve, incense would be burned in front of all statues in all kitchens. Women were the busiest on that evening. They had to cook the sweet soup, Eight-Treasure Soup, served on the first day of the New Year, as well as worship the [kitchen] deity. They would busy themselves until after midnight. It's the busiest time of the year.

—Huang Xiqi

Fig. 184 **Making *zongzi*, rice and meat wrapped in leaves and then steamed for eating on New Year's. Huang Cun, Xiuning County, 1999.**

In the feudal society, you were not supposed to put things too heavily onto the stove, nor could you say bad words or scold children by stoves, though the kitchen god was deaf. But that was all nonsense. It's not true at all. We don't know why. I can't tell where and when they [these legends] are from. In terms of the kitchen god, some say he will bless

Recipes of Foods Commonly Cooked by Wang Yaozhen

Huang Xiqi, in recalling life with his mother in Yin Yu Tang, noted down some of her recipes:

Salted Vegetables
Cut fresh vegetables and sun-dry them until they are half-dried. Cut them into small pieces. Add the proper quantity of salt and place them into a big jar. Press with cleaned round stone. They will be done in one to two months.

Red Bean Soup
Clean dried red beans. Put 250g of beans into water to boil. Turn to slow heat after they are boiled. Add glutinous rice. If it is for New Year's celebration, add sugar-preserved dates and sweet osmanthus.

Tea-Flavored Egg
Boil eggs in water. Break the shell and place the eggs in water again. Add salt, soy source, tea leaves, a little bit of anise, black mushroom stems, skins of bamboo shoots, dried orange skins. Boil on a low heat for several hours.

Stuffed Cornbread
Pour hot water onto corn flour to make dough. Stuff with salted lard and salted vegetables or minced turnip with chili sauce. Make them into the shape of moon cakes. Bake till both sides turn golden brown.

Dumplings Wrapped in Bamboo Leaves (Pork)
Put dry bamboo leaves in water for three or four days. Then wash them with boiling water. Rinse glutinous rice with water. Cut fresh pork into small cubes and marinate them in soy source. Wrap the rice and pork with cleaned bamboo leaves and tighten them with ropes made from palm leaves.

Dumplings Wrapped in Bamboo Leaves (Red Bean Paste)
Similar to above but replace pork with red bean paste, vegetable oil, and sugar.

Dumplings Wrapped in Bamboo Leaves (Ash Water)
Burn straws into ash. Place ash in a bag and put it in boiling water. Use the water colored by the ash to rinse the rice. The color of the rice will turn yellow. Making dumplings wrapped in bamboo leaves this way will make the glutinous rice more glutinous and will preserve the dumplings for a longer time.

Salted Duck Eggs
Mix clay with salt and water and then cover duck eggs with the mud. Place the covered eggs in a jar. Ready to eat after forty days. You can also make them by placing the eggs in salt solutions.

Fig. 185 & 186 **Candles in front of the kitchen god's shrine on New Year's Eve, Yuetan, Xiuning County, 1999.**

you, some say he will not. When he goes to heaven, he reports on your behavior to the Jade Emperor. [If you have not behaved well,] your children and grandchildren won't achieve much, nor will they become officials. That's how it goes.

—Wang Youjin

But the kitchen was also the place of everyday cooking. For breakfast, lunch, and dinner, women lit the firewood they had gathered from the hills in the large masonry stove, fried chopped vegetables and pickles, and steamed rice.

Pig fat we would have once a week. Usually it was primarily the vegetables we had grown ourselves, cabbage or whatnot. On hot days we would eat bamboo shoots. The doufu was brought to the door by a person from the doufu shop. Sometimes he would just put it on the account. It [doufu] was made in our own village.

—Huang Zhenxin

When we were young, we had to light up stoves with firewood every morning before breakfast could be made. Mostly our breakfast was stirred rice with oil, so we wouldn't get hungry easily. The conditions at that time were very limited.

—Huang Xianying

For food, we mainly ate rice. Rice gruel for breakfast, steamed rice for both lunch and supper. Except for holidays, we seldom ate meat and fish. Instead, we lived on vegetables produced in [our] own garden: Shanghai cabbage, Chinese cabbage, and turnip for winter, hot pepper, green beans, eggplant, amaranth, pumpkin, and white gourd in the summer.

—Huang Xiqi

Before leaving a discussion of the kitchen, it is worthwhile to peek just beyond the kitchen. This outside space, shared with the village, with the well, manure composting vats, and vegetable patch, had an integral role in the kitchen and the daily life of all members of the family.

The wooden kitchens in Huizhou were rarely as finely built or as important as the main part of house. Thinner wood was used for columns, and often the wood was not finished. The kitchen, after all, was primarily a functional space, not a place where guests would be invited. It was not a space that needed to be either well constructed or decorated. Moreover, the kitchens received more abuse than other parts of the house. Smoke continually permeated the structure. Water and steam often filled the air, and rodents most likely frequently scampered about in search of food. As a result of this lack of regard for kitchen construction and kitchen upkeep, kitchens easily deteriorated.

The kitchens collapsed just a few years ago. We couldn't keep them.

—Huang Xiqi

It was in 1976 that the kitchen walls of Yin Yu Tang could no longer support themselves. Few family members were living in the house at that point, and no one saw a need—nor did they have the financial resources—to rebuild the kitchens. A small shed was built in the forecourt of Yin Yu Tang, one long wall of which abutted the front facade of the house, to serve as the kitchen for the next six years.

The Staircases

The staircases of Yin Yu Tang, though not highly visible to visitors, were a common space used by members of the household. There were two staircases in Yin Yu Tang, an unusual circumstance. In Huizhou, most homes have only one. The extraordinary width, and numerous rooms, of Yin Yu Tang may have been the motivation for installing two staircases.

The stairs of Yin Yu Tang, like those of most Huizhou homes, were narrow and (in order to occupy a minimum of space) quite steep. They are at a 45-degree angle. Each riser is 8 inches high, and each tread is 11 inches deep. To afford the foot more space on the tread, the riser is slanted inward at the bottom, allowing one to ascend the stairs more easily; however, descending is still difficult on these narrow steps.

Located at either end of the courtyard, on the east and the west, the stairs were slipped behind walls and were not apparent to visitors. Hiding the staircase behind a wall, rather than revealing and proudly displaying it, was typical in Huizhou. In some houses, the staircases are located behind the conceptually south-facing wall of the reception hall, and in other homes they are located behind a wall at the east or west end of the courtyard. As two-story houses are unusual in China—in the north and south, one-story houses are far more common—the placement of the staircases cannot be compared with other regions. However, the concealment of the staircase could reasonably be attributed, like many other aspects (such as the lack of outward looking windows) to security issues. Women and children living alone in the house might want to barricade themselves from bandits by running to the second floor. Keeping the staircase out of plain view may have provided the women with a few more minutes to flee to safety. Once upstairs, they could slam down a door over the staircase and lock it. These locking doors over staircases can be seen in many Huizhou houses. Having locked the door, the women and children could also further flee to a neighbor's house, as the houses in Huang Cun were, for just such safety reasons, at one time, all connected to one another by second-story doors and corridors:

When our ancestors were building the house, they had already considered issues like security and preventing robberies. For example, there is a big wooden board on the staircase. When it's necessary, you can flip that down, and there is a wood bolt on it, so once you bolt it up, people from downstairs can't come up anymore. You have blocked the passage. So people upstairs can at least have some more time to hide. . . . The small crevice between the floor here and the ceiling on the second floor [could] also be used to prevent robberies when it was needed. Also the small window could be used as a lookout. You know this house doesn't have any windows opening outward except this kind of window. So they depended on this window to find out what was going on outside the house. Otherwise, what could they do? Our ancestors did a lot in building a safe residence for their descendants.

—Huang Binggen

Fig. 187 **Exterior east (conceptual west) wall of Yin Yu Tang with horse-head walls towering above the interior roofs and the small lookout window toward the back of the building. The now-brick-filled second-story doorway led to an abutting, no longer extant house. To the left of the door, the roofline of the abutting kitchens is apparent.**

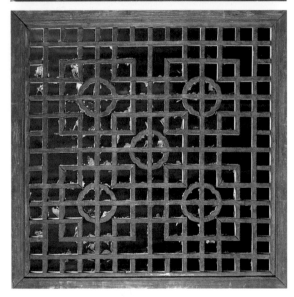

The Gallery

On the second floor, like downstairs, there were a number of commonly used spaces. A common 2 feet 6 inch-wide gallery rings the entire second floor, and the bedrooms are all accessible from off this corridor. On the courtyard side of the corridor, a 3 foot 2 inch-high solid railing keeps children from falling down into the courtyard, and above the railing rests a series of shutters, again ringing the entire circumference of the gallery.

The lattice on most of the shutters around the gallery is of simple, right-angle-crossing wooden strips. The only added flourish is cloud-shaped carving at the bottom of each shutter. Four large lattice panels, two on the east end and two on the west end, are the only four with the intention of capturing the eye with more distinctive and decorative features. Each of these panels is designed with a large circle filled with carved large C, or abstracted ruyi,

Fig. 188 (top) **One of four lattice screens on the east and west ends of the second-floor gallery encircling the skywell.**

Fig. 189 (above) **Detail of the lattice screens of the second-floor storage room.**

Fig. 190 (right) **View from gallery on second floor looking across the skywell.**

Fig. 191 **Elevation of the columns and beams of the third bent on the west side of Yin Yu Tang.**

shapes. These same shapes appear on the first bedroom lattices as well, as they may all have been carved by the same hand, or at least under the same master. These four lattices would have been highly visible from the courtyard and, along with the various decorative elements of the house, would have contributed to an overall elegant view.

In addition to the lattices and shutters framing the gallery, this narrow space was celebrated by placing a series of short arched beams running north to south at regular intervals along the lengths of the north and south galleries. Each of these beams is supported by a carved triangular bracket. The brackets appear to function as extra support for the beams, but they are also an excuse for an extra bit of decoration. Like the second-floor round lattices at the end of the courtyard, they draw the eye up for a bit of visual interest.

Following down the second-floor gallery of the upper hall, the central room, just above the reception hall, is the space called by the family the second-floor reception hall. This space—also most auspiciously located as it faced conceptual south—was dedicated to worshipping deities other than ancestors. Like the downstairs reception hall, this room had a set furniture arrangement with an altar table against the back wall.

Members of the family remember that in the 1920s, 1930s, and 1940s, a many-armed statue of the Bodhisattva Guanyin sat on the altar table. The upstairs altar table differed from the long, narrow table downstairs. A smaller rectangular table with drawers and a tiled top sat against the back wall. Since daily offerings of incense were made to Guanyin, the tiled top of this altar table helped prevent fires.

Storage Room

Opposite the upstairs reception hall, in the center of the lower hall, was another shared space. Here was the storage space.

There were many big wardrobes in this room. When my mom was around, she would put all cotton wadding and quilts in the wardrobes. When guests came, she'd take out quilts from the wardrobe for the guests.
—Huang Xiqi

This room, unlike the other common spaces, did not open to the courtyard. A wall with lattice windows filled the upper half and a door closed off the front. Within are large built-in cabinets, confirming family members' memories that this was a storage room.

The storage space seems to be one of the most altered spaces of the house, though the alterations may have taken place over a century ago. A wall splits the space into two separate spaces, each with its own entrance. One space fills two-thirds of the facade of the space. The other is a thin L-shaped space with a door to the gallery, stretching back and then around the rear of the first room. A wall with a door in it stretches across the gallery. The wall separates several bedrooms and one storage space from other bedrooms and the larger storage space. Such formal divisions occur when two sons inherited a house from their father and decided to split into two distinct financial entities. Symbolic walls are often built in a house to mark the event and property lines.

A formal division of a family is called *fenjia*, literally "dividing the family." Legal documents, *fenjiashu*,[30] are usually drawn up to specify and record the proceedings. Though there are no such legal documents extant recording a Huang family division, the decor of the space hints of one.

The latticework on the front of the storage room is quite different from that in the rest of the house: the design is different, the method of attaching it to the window frame is different (instead of turning on pivots, the lattice panels are just slipped into place with small tenons), and the carving technique is less refined. All these differences point to the storage-room walls being installed after the house was originally built.

But how much later? The style of the storage cabinets and the lattice on the front of the facade are reminiscent of nineteenth-century workmanship. This would explain the lack of recollection among living family members of any family division. The division may have occurred after the death of Huang Yangxian in 1885, or it may have been even earlier, when the family was still prosperous. Wallpaper, now somewhat deteriorated, and a New Year poster, both pasted on the interior wall of the larger storage space, appear to be from the mid-nineteenth century.

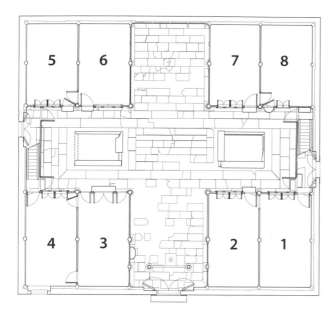

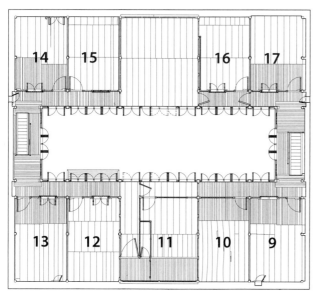

Fig. 192 **First-floor (top) and second-floor (above) bedrooms of Yin Yu Tang.**

The Bedrooms

The bedrooms can be divided generally into four types: the bedrooms of the first-floor lower hall, those of the first-floor upper hall, those of the second-floor lower hall, and those of the second-floor upper hall. Although the bedrooms are all essentially the same, with a door and window facing into the skywell, each is also unique in its own way.

It should first be noted that the first-floor, upper-hall bedrooms, which would, of course, be of higher status, as they faced conceptual south, had slightly higher floor levels. Their height is attained by a step in the courtyard, 3 feet and 7 inches in front of the upper-hall front columns. The extra height of the upper hall is carried all the way to the roofline (by increasing the height of the second-floor bedrooms), which, when viewed from a distance, can also be seen to be higher than the lower hall. (The ceilings of the first-floor bedrooms of the upper and lower halls, as well as the floors of the second-story bedrooms, are all the same height. As a result, the upper-hall downstairs bedrooms have slightly lower ceilings than the lower-hall downstairs bedrooms.) This extra height offers a configuration that is compatible with fengshui principles that call for a mountain behind a house and higher rooflines for the rear (or conceptual north) structure of a group of structures.

The downstairs bedrooms would be reserved for the more respected elderly personages of the home, because they are more convenient. Of the downstairs upper-hall bedrooms, the most important would be the one located to the conceptual east of the reception hall. This room would traditionally be designated for the eldest and most senior member of the family, and his spouse. Various circumstances may cause the situation to be otherwise (as happened in Yin Yu Tang in the twentieth century) but traditionally this was the standard.

(A system for numbering the rooms was created by the carpenters and engineers dismantling the building in 1997. To maintain consistency with other documents that discuss the house, these arbitrary numbers will also be used here.)

Room 7, located in the upper hall and on the conceptual east side of the building, would have been the room of greatest status. The bedroom measures 8 feet 9 inches wide by 14 feet 2 inches long.

The floor of the bedroom, like all the bedrooms on the first floor and as is common in most traditionally constructed wood-frame homes of the region, is raised off the ground. Raising the bedroom from the ground level was intended to keep the easily deteriorated wood away from the moist ground. Despite this prophylactic action, the floorboards on the first floor still deteriorated over time and were replaced periodically. As discussed above, the

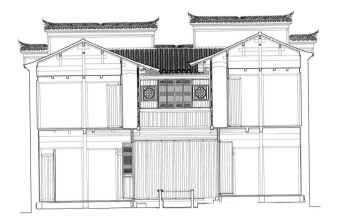

Fig. 193 (left) **Section plan of Yin Yu Tang looking east.**

Fig. 194 (right) **The stone steps (and stone column base) leading to rooms 7 and 8.**

Fig. 195 (below) **Outer lattice screen of room 6.**

floorboards sat on joists and stone stretchers with ventilation holes. In the spirit of ornamenting significant locations of the house, the ventilation holes were each decorated with designs.

Because of the raised bedroom floor, a step is necessary to enter the bedroom. Each bedroom has a unique stone step placed before its door. In front of the door to room 7 is a stone carved in a decorative shape.

Each bedroom on the first floor, except room 3, has two layers of lattice: an outer lattice covering the entire window opening and four inner shutters. Under normal circumstances, the outer lattice would not be covered by paper, but the inner shutters were covered completely with paper pasted onto their inner surfaces. The two layers allowed for varying degrees of privacy, light, warmth, and ventilation. With the shutters open, air could still flow through the outer lattice, but some privacy would still be maintained inside the room. The lattice on the four inner shutters, which rotate on wooden pivots, was a straightforward grid of right-angled intersecting strips of wood on which paper could be pasted. The larger outer lattice had a more elaborate visual expression.

Like all but one of the first-floor bedrooms, room 7 is distinguished on its exterior by an extravagant outer lattice. The entire lattice screen, measuring 6 feet 8 inches by 4 feet 11 inches is a framework within which is set five variously sized rectangular panels. Each panel is carved from a single piece of wood and is not made up of individually joined together small wooden pieces. The central panel can be lifted up to allow more air to enter the room. A wooden locking mechanism on the inside of this central panel ensured relative security. The lack of a flat surface on the back of the entire lattice indicates that paper was not intended to be pasted on. While these lattice screens successfully fulfilled their primary function of providing privacy when the shutters were open for ventilation, they also more than effectively served to enhance the beauty of the skywell space.

The two side vertical panels of the screen both depict vases on a background of a multitude of *wan* characters. *Wan* is the Chinese character for "10,000," which expresses the aspiration for longevity. The interior void of the vases is filled with a multitude of abstracted ruyi fungus shapes that signify that one should obtain all one desires. A vase symbolizes peace, as the word for *vase* (*ping*) is a homophone for the word for *peace* (*ping*). The upper central panel repeats the *wanzi* motif. The central, movable, panel displays two facing, scrolling dragons within a four-lobed begonia shape. Around the begonia shape are more dragons depicted in a rectangular, archaic style, harking back to dragons on ancient bronzes. In

Fig. 196 (right) **Found beneath the floor boards of a first-floor bedroom, this bamboo blind gives a sense of what luxurious items might have decorated Yin Yu Tang in its early years. The blind is made from speckled bamboo and was adorned with a fine silk still-life design, created by winding silk threads around the narrow bamboo slats.**

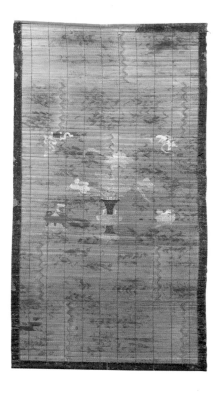

Fig. 197 (below) **Lacquered, wooden bed from Yin Yu Tang, 19th century. This red lacquered bed would have been made for a son's marriage, one of the few times in a person's life when expenses would not be restricted. (The other significant moment would be the funeral.) The bed would be the most expensive and elaborate piece of furniture for the new couple's room and was the significant surrounding for producing the next male generation in the family line.**

the lowest horizontal panel another two dragons, very much resembling a late Ming style, face each other within an elongated hexagram. The space on either side of the hexagram is filled with the abstracted ruyi forms in clustered patterns. The overall effect of these defined shapes—the dynamic dragons and the varied but strongly patterned plane—is of a stable but animated facade. The balance of the stability and the dynamism produce an elegant air.

Beyond the screen, over the threshold, and through the door of the bedroom is a rather small living space. The compass west-side wall, the wall shared with the reception hall, is made up of four framed partitions, two on either side of a central column. The back wall of the bedroom is the lime-covered inside of the exterior masonry curtain wall. The compass east-side wall, between rooms 7 and 8, is also a masonry wall, with a central column. Unlike the outer masonry wall, this wall is made of thin bricks. The reason for masonry walls between the bedrooms may have been multifold. The white of the lime would have reflected more light into the room from the door and window and made it a brighter space. The masonry of the wall might have also offered more soundproofing between the rooms. Moreover, it would have added extra stability to the house and allowed more of the roof weight to be distributed among the house's frame. This type of construction, with an interior masonry wall, is also used in Jin Shi Di.

The ceiling height of room 7, as with all the bedrooms of the first-floor upper hall, is 11 feet 11 inches, a surprisingly high ceiling for such a small room. The advantages of such a height is that not only is it visually commanding but also, in a warm climate, it allows for hot air to rise and keep the lower part of the room cooler. The height of the bedrooms of the upper hall are in total 5 inches shorter than those of the first-floor lower hall, because of the higher base floor in the upper hall.

Looking up at the ceiling in this room, five round medallions that were pasted on the ceilings many years ago can be discerned. The central roundel depicts two phoenixes. These medallions may

Fig. 198 **Central paper medallion pasted on the ceiling of room 7 depicting two cranes.**

Figs. 199 & 200 **A typical bedroom in a traditional Huizhou style home (above left). Shexian County. The bedroom in a traditional home of a newly married couple (above right) with a fashionable new-style bed.**

have been pasted up for the first-honored occupant of the room to ensure marital bliss, as *fenghuang*, phoenixes, symbols of the empress of China, also represent familial harmony between a wife and husband. While in some regions, such as in Yixian, the county just to the north of Xiuning County, painted ceilings are a common occurrence, bedroom 7 is the only room in Yin Yu Tang to have such decorations.

Within this space, often shared by a couple and their children, were a bed, cabinets, at least one chair, a desk, a commode or chamber pot, a washbasin, and most of the family's clothes and other personal belongings. With all these objects, there would have been little space for several people to move around comfortably. The crowdedness, combined with the lack of much light, meant that most people spent little time, other than when they were sleeping, in the bedrooms.

The average bed from Yin Yu Tang measures 85 inches in length and 53 inches in depth (and 90 inches in height) and would have filled almost a third of the room. The beds commonly used in Huizhou region were tester beds, with four or six posts reaching up to an upper wooden canopy. The canopy would keep dust from falling onto the sleepers, and the poles and crosspieces additionally served as bars from which to hang mosquito nets.

Room 7 is connected to room 8 through a door at the front of the masonry wall. Such interior doors connect all but one pair of bedrooms on the first floor. In the 1920s and 1930s, rooms 7 and 8 were occupied by Huang Zizhi and his wife and children. When home, he slept with his wife in room 7 and the children slept in room 8. When Huang Zizhi was gone, the daughters could sleep with his wife in room 7 and the boys in room 8.

Bedroom 8 is the exact same size as room 7, but with a few variations that would have made it a less preferable room, and therefore more appropriate for the children. Most significant was the lighting. Situated in a corner of the house, the room received less light than the more centrally located bedrooms. Because the room abuts the staircase and has a door, leading directly into the stairwell, the space on the facade available for a window is smaller. Instead of a large, extravagant full-covering outer lattice, this room has only a small, 1 foot 5 inches by 2 feet 8 inches, outer lattice to provide a measure of privacy when the shutters are open. The purely geometric lattice depicts two groupings of four ruyi shapes to form a circular flowerlike form on a background of more regular fretwork. This lattice appears to have been made by in a very different manner than the large lattice screens around the first floor. Instead of being carved from one panel of wood, it is constructed of small wooden parts, joined together with double miters (known as "frogs' mouths" in Chinese) at each junction. Moreover, the components are convex, rounded on the outside, whereas the fretwork in the large lattice screens has rectangular grooves. The more modest exterior statement of room 8 bespeaks the relative lower status of the outer, corner bedrooms.

Crossing the courtyard from room 7 and 8 to rooms 1 and 2, an almost mirror image is encountered. Because room 1 has only one exterior door leading to the space under the stairwell—unlike its counterpart, room 8, which has two exterior doors—there is more room available for a large exterior window lattice. The first occupants of the house were clearly intent on finding as many places as possible on the first floor to place these remarkable lattice carvings.

Though the multiple large multipaneled lattice screens on the first floor are intended to give a sense of classic regularity, there are slight differences among the designs. There are still five panels in each screen and they are framed in the same manner, but the design of each diverges. The two side vertical panels on the room 1 screen both mirror the screen in room 7, with ruyi filled vases on a *wanzi* character background. And the central upper panel likewise follows the pattern in room 7, of a wanzi-filled square. The central movable panel displays a round medallion, completely filled with the abstract ruyi shapes. Surrounding the circle are archaic-style dragons. The lower horizontal panel has medallions. On either side dragons circle in on themselves, biting their tails, within circular shapes. Between these two, a multicusped medallion is filled with a pattern of ruyi shapes. Archaic rectangular dragons fill the remaining space in this lower panel. The large screen of room 2 is nearly identical to that of room 7, directly across the courtyard, except that the central, movable panel depicts two swirling dragons within a large circle and a coin design—in place of a pearl—between them. Around the circle are the archaic-style rectangular dragons. The variation in the large screen-lattice designs extends among all the large exterior lattices on the first floor. Patterns of wanzi and ruyi predominate, with vases and dragons appearing and reappearing. This lack of absolute uniformity with repeating features is common in Chinese design and architecture, and adds a certain dynamism to Yin Yu Tang's inner courtyard.

In recalling the functions of the various rooms in Yin Yu Tang, Huang Xiqi noted that his mother used room 1, when it was no longer housing people in later years, for storing her pickles and pickle jars:

In winter we would use them [the large jars] to pickle vegetables. After the cabbage is harvested, it is washed clean in the stream water. Then it is spread out to dry and then salted in the jars. After half a month it is ready to be eaten. In a whole month it's still okay, after two or three months it's not so great. The small jars are for making pickles also. After you wash clean and dry off the vegetables in the sun, they are chopped up, put on a tray, and salt sprinkled on them. Then you use your hands to squeeze out the juice. They are put in the jars and a stone is used to press it down tightly. After two months you can eat [them]. They smell wonderful. . . . My mother made them. . . . the women of our village, they all knew how. . . . We also pickled radishes, red hot peppers. . . . The flavor is both spicy and sour. Delicious.

—Huang Xiqi

Inside room 2, the type of furnishings and their arrangement would have been quite similar to room 7. The major differences between the rooms are the actual size and the orientation. Room 2 and all the bedrooms on the first-floor lower hall are the same

Fig. 201 **Section of Yin Yu Tang from the courtyard looking north.**

Fig. 202 **The small, outer lattice screen of room 8.**

width as the bedrooms of the upper hall (8 feet 9 inches), but are actually deeper (15 feet 8 inches as opposed to the shorter 14 feet 2 inches). While the deeper space may have afforded more space, it was darker, and therefore less advantageous. Because the lower hall was also physically lower than the upper hall, the space reaching between the floor and the ceiling was also 5 inches higher than the bedrooms of the upper hall.

In the conceptual southwest (compass northeast) corner of the house were another two attached rooms. The room closest to the entryway, room 3, differs most radically from the rest of the bedrooms in the house. In place of a facade consisting of a single door with a large lattice window to its side and a solid panel below the opening, the front of this room is four full-length pivoting doors that are solid for the bottom 51 1/2 inches and are lattices above. The doors seem to suggest that the original function of this room was distinct from the others. Questions abound. How may this room have been used? And was the setup original to the house's initial construction?

One possible function of this room may have been a work or study room for the family patriarch, where he could continue his business or accounting work when he was home. The room faced compass south, and the multiple doors could have allowed more light into the room for daytime work. Though the different lattice may have thrown off the symmetry of the house and the courtyard, the presence of a study would also have been considered an enhancement, displaying the intellectual prowess of the occupants.

The popularity of such studies beginning in the late Ming dynasty in the homes of the elite (and later, the less elite) is sharply pointed out by a late Ming commentator, and recently noted by the historian Wang Shixiang:

The particularly strange thing is that even officials' lectors and runners who had a house would set up a place for relaxation, with wooden paneling, goldfish and various pots of flowers in the courtyard, with a hardwood table and a flywhisk, and call it a "study."[31]

The lattice on the doors of room 3, like the small lattice on room 8, seem to have been carved by different hands than those that detailed the large lattices on the other first floor bedrooms, and may have been installed in the mid-nineteenth century. Like the lattice on room 8, that in room 3 is composed of many convex wooden strips joined together rather than being carved out of one panel. As we pointed out earlier, it may not have been the only alteration to the house.

By the twentieth century, rooms 3 and 4 were being used as living spaces. On the conceptual west side of the house, and therefore the least preferable, the rooms were given over to nonfamily members in the first years of the century. A review of the occupants of the two rooms demonstrates an ever-changing cultural environment.

1910–1950

In the early part of the twentieth century, these two rooms were occupied by a nonfamily member. When Huang Zizhi was working in Leping during the 1910s, he was friends with a fellow Huang Cun native who was not an immediate relative, Huang Shaoqing. Huang Shaoqing had married in Huang Cun, but working and living in Leping, he met a local girl and took her as a "little wife." Perhaps his parents had died or he had little incentive to return to Huang Cun. Or perhaps he was not the eldest son and was not given a share of space in his parents' home. In any case, we know that Huang Shaoqing paid the Seventh Branch of the Huang family to house his wife, son, and daughter in Yin Yu Tang. The daughter was married off to an older businessman in Yuetan. As may have been expected, the wife was thought of by the children who lived in the house as a nasty woman who always had a frown and never smiled. Her son, Qijin, died at an early age, but his filial widow stayed and cared for her mother-in-law until she died. During Land Reform in 1950, the daughter-in-law was given part of a landlord's house in the village and moved out of Yin Yu Tang.

The fate of Huang Lanxian, Huang Shaoqing's daughter, was not unusual but was also not an easy one. As she was a girl from a basically fatherless family with little income, a good marriage was not easily arranged:

Being married off to a landlord was a desperate move she was forced into. One reason was [that] she was old and no one wanted her. . . . At that time, if a girl was twenty and she hadn't married, no one wanted her. After twenty, it was difficult to marry. . . . The other reason was that they didn't have any income. All they could do was marry her off to a landlord. She had two children. In three years [during the 1960s], they died of starvation. Because he was a landlord, no one helped them. She had to go bury them herself. It was really difficult, but there was nothing to do.

—Huang Zhenxin

Fig. 203 **Cousins Huang Zhenzhi and Huang Zhenxin with a non-family Yin Yu Tang housemate, Huang Qijin.**

1950–1968

After the daughter-in-law of Huang Shaoqing moved out during Land Reform, another nonfamily member who had longed resided in Yin Yu Tang moved into these rooms. In the first years of the twentieth century, a local couple surnamed Shao, like the wife of Huang Shaoqing, had nowhere to live. The husband had come from a poor family of many children, and at his marriage, there was no room in his father's home for him and his bride. The generous Huang family of Yin Yu Tang felt sorry for him and allowed the couple to live in the side room of the large front pavilion:

Our house had many rooms, it was empty. They [Shao family] didn't have a house to live in, so we gave them a room to live in. The rent was cheap. It was just two yuan a year. If they didn't pay it, it didn't matter. I don't know when they first came. . . . They were there [living with us] very early on. When my mother gave birth to me [in

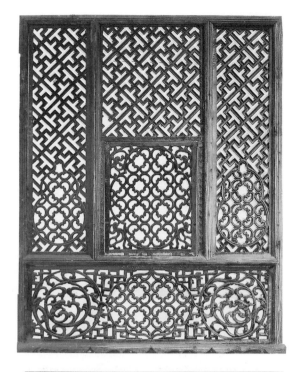

Fig. 204 (top) **Outer lattice screen of room 5.**

Fig. 205 (above) **Outer lattice screen of room 4.**

1921], it was only after seven months [of pregnancy] and she had no milk for me to drink. So I just drank Shao Zhiyu's mother's milk. . . . I grew up drinking Shao Zhiyu's mother's milk. At New Year's, we would ask them to go to Tunxi to buy us things. They had to go thirty li. Round trip was sixty li. The Shao family had many children. Their little son became a teacher, and there were three daughters.

—Huang Xianying

After liberation, when Huang Shaoqing's daughter-in-law moved out, Shao Zhiyu, the son of the couple who had moved in decades earlier, was allowed to move from the second floor into these more convenient first-floor rooms. In 1968 Shao Zhiyu, the only remaining Shao family member in Yin Yu Tang, noticed that the rooms in the house were filling up again with Huang family members, returning to their village during the Cultural Revolution. He built himself a house next to Jin Shi Di, and after almost a century of being occupied by nonfamily members, this room reverted to a Seventh Branch son.

1968–1982

Huang Xiqi, son of Huang Zhenzhi and Wang Yaozhen, the thirty-fifth generation of the seventh branch of the Huang family, just married and with a young child, moved down from the second-floor room 16 into these two rooms. Soon another child, Zhaofeng, was born here.

The convenience of being on the first floor for a young mother and infant was undeniable. The darkness of the corner room, like room 8 hidden next to the stairwell and with a smaller out lattice window, was a problem for the schoolteacher. More concerned with convenience than tradition and aesthetics, Huang Xiqi broke through the front masonry wall of the house and installed a window to bring more light into his dim corner bedroom.

Across the courtyard from these rooms was another pair of two bedrooms, rooms 5 and 6. Like the two bedrooms in the diagonal corner, they feature large lattice windows.

These two rooms, and the two above them, underwent a series of unexpected inhabitants over the past century. At the turn of the century, the family's financial situation was in such dire straits that they became indebted to their neighbors abutting the compass south side of Yin Yu Tang. These neighbors were in fact the sixth Branch of the Huang family, descendants of an elder brother of a Yin Yu Tang patriarch. In exchange for the debt, they gave over four Yin Yu Tang bedrooms—these two first-floor rooms and the two above them. For many years, the Sixth Branch did not make use of these rooms. After the 1949 revolution and the subsequent land reforms, the Sixth Branch family was labeled with the status of "landlord," and these two lower rooms were confiscated.

There was Land Reform after Liberation [Communist revolution, 1949]. . . . Those with more land were [categorized as] landlords. Those with less were [labeled as] Small Land Renters, Rich Peasants, and many other categories. It all depended on land, on how much land [a household owned] per capita.... Land, fields, mountains, and tools were all confiscated from landlords' homes and allotted to peasants. Everything was divided, including houses. Some businessmen were also quite rich, but they didn't get [their properties] divided up.

—Jiang Xiuqing, resident of Huang Cun, bamboo craftsman

The ownership of the two rooms was conferred upon two peasant families who had previously lived in an even less accommodating space. Neither of the families was surnamed Huang. Each family, including parents and children, had one of these two rooms. Within fifteen to twenty years, the children of these families had grown up and the parents moved out of Yin Yu Tang. One family moved to the village in which their child had married. Another family built themselves their own home on the land in Huang Cun upon which the ancestral halls had once stood. Both of the families, in turn, sold their rights to these rooms to Wang Youjin, a neighbor on the actual west side of Yin Yu Tang, a former poor peasant himself, with five sons. Like the members of the Sixth Branch, none of Wang's family ever lived in these rooms but used them occasionally for storage.

The Second Floor

As one ascends the stairs at the conceptual west end of the courtyard, the second-floor bedrooms come into view. Just as on the first floor, there are eight bedrooms, two in each corner. Because the first-floor bedrooms are more convenient for older people, the second-floor bedrooms were reserved for newlyweds or young women of the family who had not yet married.

The second-floor bedrooms were smaller (8 feet 9 inches by 12 feet 6 inches in the upper hall, and 8 feet 9 inches by 14 feet 3 inches in the lower hall) than the first-floor bedrooms, were not elevated, had no step before the threshold, and had a slightly different facade type. The gallery that encircles the courtyard on the second floor overhangs the rooms on the first floor—preventing rain from splashing into them but also shortening the length of the second-floor bedrooms. In many of the second-floor bedrooms, dropped ceilings were inserted, making the height of these rooms only 9 feet 2 inches in the lower hall, and 10 feet 2 inches in the upper hall, much lower than those on the first floor.

Instead of the large, visually imposing outer lattices, the second-floor bedrooms had abbreviated lattices measuring 2 feet by 3 feet, covering only the lower part of the shutters. The shorter, lower lattices are sufficient to achieve the desired privacy when the inner shutters are open. There was no need to have an extremely showy facade for the upstairs windows. Guests would rarely ascend to the second floor, and the bedroom facades, back beyond the corridor and its shutters, were not visible from the first-floor courtyard.

Rooms 14 and 15—which like rooms 5 and 6, had been given over at the turn of the century to the Sixth Branch family—experienced slightly different histories than the two rooms directly below. A son of the Sixth Branch, most likely a youngest son, Huang Zhengang, moved into these rooms, probably when he married in the first half of the twentieth century. A door on the actual south wall, the outer wall, of room 14 led directly into the Sixth Branch's family home, so the newly married son had easy access to the rest of his own family and did not have to interact much with the occupants of the Seventh Branch in Yin Yu Tang. Second-floor doors attaching buildings were common in Huang Cun. Like the doors over the stairwells, they provided extra safety features for the women and children inhabiting the house and allowed them to run to neighboring houses. For Huang Zhengang, the door allowed him to stay linked with his family's compound.

In decorating their new abode, the couple posted red *duilian,* calligraphic couplets expressing their marital devotion to each other, on the outside of one room's shutters. In a radical change, the lattice on the window of the second room was taken out and, in an attempt to let in more light and at the same time discourage summer insects, was replaced with European-style screening. Inside their rooms, the couple papered the walls with English teaching magazines from 1937.

Among the papers on the wall are pages from the March 20, 1937, issue of the magazine *Chung Hwa English Weekly,* an extremely popular periodical of the time. The magazine published short excerpts of non-Chinese language publications as a means of teaching English. The most notable excerpt is from an Isaac Babel short story. Here, pasted on a second-floor bedroom of a house in a remote mountain village, was a short story by a Russian Jewish writer, printed in English, translated from the Russian, and then for the Chinese reader studying English, into Chinese.

While the choice of printed pages pasted on the wall may have been only random, there are hints that the selection of English language text may have been a fashion statement. In his book on Chinese labor and tools, Rudolf P. Hommel writes: "Of late the Chinese have developed a taste for papering their rooms with foreign newspapers." Coincidentally, Hommel was writing in 1937.[32]

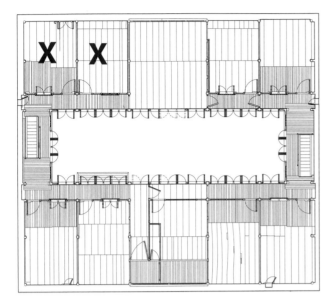

Fig. 206 **Plan of the second floor or Yin Yu Tang with Huang Zhengang's two rooms marked.**

When the revolution and then Land Reform arrived in Huang Cun in 1949, Huang Zhengang was categorized as a landlord. According to Huang Zhenxin, the label was incorrect: "Actually he did not have any land. In a [political] movement he was wrongly categorized as a landlord. He inherited some farmlands but it is unclear where they were." Like Babel, whether the label was correct or incorrect, Huang Zhengang suffered from revolutionary campaigns. All of his properties, except these two rooms on the second floor of Yin Yu Tang, were confiscated. He died during the 1960 famine, like many others in the village, from starvation. Because of his lowly status as a landlord, his relatives, afraid to be tainted, refused to participate in his funeral.

[Being labeled a landlord] was determined according to [the amount of] your land. . . . When I was small, four or five years old and not very aware, they put all the landlords' things together and then divided them among everyone. According to my grandma, they even took our cloth for binding feet. Most of the things were given to people with outside [non-Huang] surnames.

—Huang Jixian (a resident of Huang Cun)

Further along the gallery on the second floor is the room located just to the conceptual east of the reception hall, which, directly above bedroom 7, would have been the most auspiciously located

second-floor bedroom, room 16. Theoretically, this room would have been given to the eldest son of the eldest son when he married, and in the past century it did go to the eldest son of the eldest son in at least two instances.

On the occasion of the marriage of Huang Zhenzhi in 1926–27, the room was radically redecorated, and many of those alterations are now still readily apparent. The exterior of the room was painted red with purple and black outlines, and the interior walls and ceiling were papered with imported European relief-printed wallpaper. The technique for pasting the wallpaper to the walls was improvised to fit the architecture of the room. On the partition between the bedroom and the reception hall, an extra, thin partition was added on to which the paper was pasted. On the opposite masonry wall, the paper was pasted directly to the masonry and around the round columns. On the back masonry wall, the wallpaper only partially covered the wall, as it was expected that the room would conform to traditional Huizhou bedroom furniture arrangements, with the bed along the back wall, leaving little of the wall exposed. On the front wall, with the windows and shutters, the wallpaper was pasted to conform to the uneven surfaces of various frames, sills, and partition braces. In the manner of the traditional ceiling-medallion decorations, the wallpaper was also pasted across the whole ceiling, again conforming to all the joists and beams. Though the modifications to the wall surfaces were only cosmetic, and not architectural in any strict sense, they gave a wholly new and distinct appearance to the room.

The corner room next to room 16, being a corner room with less light, three cold masonry walls, and located directly next to the stairs, was less desirable and was not inhabited for much of the past century. During the Cultural Revolution, when groups of people from neighboring villages would come to Huang Cun for days or a week of military training, they would, on occasion, spend nights in Yin Yu Tang because of its vast amount of space. Room 17 was one of the empty rooms and sixteen women from the village of Fang Gan slept here in its 109 square feet.

Across the courtyard from the wallpapered room, room 10, on the conceptual east side of the house, like the wallpapered room, was redecorated in the first half of the twentieth century. On the occasion of Huang Zhenxin's marriage in 1935, this room was allocated to him, the eldest son of the *second* son—a status that may explain his assignment to the lower hall, rather than the upper hall. Though his father had just passed away, Huang Zhenxin's mother still spent extravagant amounts of money, as was proper, to adorn her eldest son's marriage room. The room was completely repainted in a glossy yellow paint, and the old style lattice windows and shutters were replaced with, for the first time in Yin Yu Tang, expensive glass windows:

We moved into a room upstairs. It was an old room before. To get prepared for the wedding, we had it painted. The floor was waxed. It was shiny clean. The bed was new, so was the woven palm for the bed board. The bride's family prepared all the items in the room. . . . The bride's family had sent over dowry gifts that included everything from tables, stools, chairs, wardrobes, dressing table, and so on. The styles were quite different from those of today. . . .When I got engaged, it cost me four hundred silver dollars. You had to pay four hundred silver dollars to the bride's family before you could get married, that was if the bride agreed to marry you. Four hundred silver dollars was quite a lot of money.

—Huang Zhenxin

Fig. 207 **Huang Zhenxin and Chou Lijuan sitting on their marriage bed in 1996, when they returned to Yin Yu Tang, sixty-one years after their wedding.**

When Huang Zhenzhi and his wife returned to Yin Yu Tang in 1996, just before they decided to sell the house, they posed for a sentimental photograph on their wedding bed in their wedding room.

The two bedrooms in the conceptual west of the lower hall are, according to tradition, the rooms of the least status in the house. In the memories of the still-living occupants, there is no recollection of people living in those rooms. Room 12 was certainly occupied at one time, as it has printed wallpaper pasted on the walls. No doubt it was decorated, like the other rooms, for a wedding. At a later time, an inhabitant pasted traditional Chinese medicine recipes on the wall, among them cures for a child ill after experiencing extreme fright and preventive medications for smallpox.

Fig. 208 (far left) **Imported European wallpaper pasted on the walls and ceiling of bedroom 16 on the occasion of Huang Zhenzhi and Wang Yaozhen's marriage circa 1926.**

Fig. 209 (left) **A commode, to hold a chamberpot, brought with other furnishings by Chou Lijuan as part of her trousseau when she married Huang Zhenxin in 1935. For those who could afford it, a commode contained the not-always-sightly appearance of the chamberpot bucket. This one also had a drawer for storing paper. Though today many people in the countryside use newspaper or other miscellaneous packaging to save money, Chinese did have toilet paper as early as the very early Ming dynasty (1368-1644).**

The far corner room has little evidence of being occupied. A tall, coarsely made shelving unit was in the room. It may have been used to store agricultural products. The room abutted not only the outside masonry but also the abutting house, with a second-floor door and passageway to the neighbors. Without a doubt, the dark corner room would not have been pleasant living quarters and was avoided by all who could.

Thus, though the bedrooms of Yin Yu Tang at first glance appear to be all of the same basic size and location, there were definite distinctions among them, and the set Confucian hierarchy of family members usually determined which rooms were allocated to whom. Once those allocations were made, each subsequent occupant formed or reformed the space to update it and customize it to fit their personal tastes as well as to define a space, if only temporarily, as their own.

A Lost Space: The Pavilion

On the right was open land for trees. There was a pine tree at the time. It was very big. You could also plant flowers and trees on that land, too. There were also fences, behind which we raised chickens. Five to six chickens could produce three to four eggs each day for the family. Firewood was also piled and aired there. At the time, all the newly bought firewood was wet, and you had to air it for several months before you could use it. After you opened the front door, you could see a pavilion, where two stone stools one and a half meters long and a half meter wide were put. They were there for anyone to relax in a cool place during hot days.

—Huang Zhenxin

A discussion of Yin Yu Tang cannot be complete without mention of a part of the compound that no longer stands, the pavilion, or *ting*, as the family members call it. The ting stood in what is now the forecourt of the house and functioned primarily as an entertaining area. An examination of the remaining house and traces left on the facade show that the ting was a luxurious addition erected years, or perhaps even decades, after the main house had been completed. According to Huang Zhenxin, wedding celebrations or funeral festivities were held in the ting: "That pavilion was for funerals and weddings, for banquets. Hangings and calligraphy were hung. It was a banquet pavilion."

From discussions with family members, an old photograph, and marks on the facade of the main building, a visual concept of the ting has emerged. The ting stretched almost across the entire forecourt, from east to west. Most of the ting was one story, except a small part at the conceptual east end that was two stories high. There was a central entrance with stone drums on either side.

Inside was an open room with columns. There may have been a spirit wall inside the entryway, as among the stone pieces that were gathered from the site at the 1997 dismantling was a finely carved stone base for a spirit wall.

At the compass west end of the ting was a two-story section, which is visible in the turn-of-the-century photograph of Huang Cun, just peaking above the forecourt wall. In the memories of all living members of the family, this second-floor room was occupied by the otherwise homeless Shao family for many years before they moved into the main living section of the compound.

According to Huang Xiqi, who was the principal family member living in the house in the late 1970s, the ting was dismantled in 1976 because the structure was dangerously deteriorating and its collapse seemed imminent. Huang Xiqi has also expressed his opinion that the dismantling of the ting helped to preserve the rest of the main building:

That pavilion, I personally resolved it in 1976. The wood of the pavilion was all about to collapse. If we didn't tear it down, an accident would have happened. I wrote a letter to Shanghai, telling Huang Binggen's side of the family that we had to resolve the pavilion. Huang Binggen came to Huang Cun and, together, we sold it. Tearing down the pavilion also benefited the preserving of the large house behind it. [It allowed for] the the air to flow through the big house and at the same time it could get more sun. It extended the lifetime of the big house.

Originally, we were going to sell it to people outside the village. The brigade [i.e., the village government, which during the Cultural Revolution was named in military terms] said that we could not sell it outside the village and we had to sell it to the local village. . . . The wood was sawed into boards to build houses.

—Huang Xiqi

If one wanders about Huang Cun, the recycling of the ancient pavilion becomes apparent. A small house sits by the stream on the path leading to where the ancestral halls once stood. It is a traditional-style timber-frame home with masonry walls and paintings above the windows that announce a 1970s construction date. The house sports magnificent, thick wooden doors at its front and side entrances, and the owner proudly notes that the doors came from Qi Fang, the Seventh Branch's Yin Yu Tang.

1996

As for residents, in our heyday, both the upstairs and downstairs were full of people. More stayed downstairs. The downstairs was always full. There were a lot of people, mostly housewives left at home when their husbands went away on business. For example, my grandmother,

mother and aunt. . . . There were mostly women. All the men were doing business outside.

—Huang Xiqi

By 1996, the heyday of Yin Yu Tang—when the house was alive with weddings and funerals, residents tending to their daily affairs, and friends and relatives visiting—had passed. The house had sat empty for over a decade; those who had been born there were all living in other cities and towns. The Huangs came to the decision to allow the house to travel to an American museum as a way to preserve the house. The project provided a challenging but singular experience of dismantling, then, literally, dissecting, and finally re-erecting this two-hundred-year-old house to understand its

inner structural workings and the lives that permeated the structure over so many years.

This arrangement is the best solution to preserve the house. It's actually a big favor for us descendents. We can preserve the house forever and it will help us to remember that our ancestors had glorious achievements and inspired us to keep forging ahead and make progress in our own careers.

—Huang Binqqen

We were destined to meet, and our realization of this matter was fated.

—Huang Xiqi

Fig. 210 **The front gate of Yin Yu Tang, looking into the forecourt where the pavilion once stood.**

Epilogue:
Preserving Yin Yu Tang
for Generations

From the beginning, the Yin Yu Tang project was to be a preservation project of a scale and magnitude never before attempted in the United States. A two-hundred-year-old Chinese vernacular house was to be disassembled, transported to the United States, recorded in infinite detail, conserved, and re-erected. In the process the house would be transformed from a multifamily residence in daily use to a museum setting where it would be visited by thousands of people on an annual basis. Yet, throughout the project every attempt was to be made to retain the character of the house, a character that reflected two hundred years of use.

A scholarly approach was adopted for the preservation of Yin Yu Tang. The project was developed to disseminate Chinese culture in the Western world, and the goal was to accurately interpret all aspects of the Huang family's house and tenure. The *Yin Yu Tang Re-erection and Preservation Guidelines* were prepared to guide the materials-conservation, restoration, and re-erection processes of the house. This document was developed by the Yin Yu Tang project team, a multidisciplined committee of museum curators, preservation architects, and philanthropic foundation representatives. The project team drafted a mission statement to identify the threefold purpose of the project: to re-erect and preserve the house, its contents, documents, and history in the United States; through that re-erection and preservation effort to present the house as an example of Chinese vernacular architecture and the related traditions of decorative arts and artisanship; and to function for diverse audiences as a window to the broader context of Chinese culture. Within the guidelines, procedures were established for documentation, for proposed conservation treatment and intervention, for the introduction of new building systems, for archiving documents and architectural fragments, and for scheduled maintenance. Subsequently, the re-erection and preservation guidelines were submitted to a panel of internationally recognized preservationists for peer review and endorsement. This project has been subjected to a level of professional scrutiny exceeded by relatively few American buildings. Ironically, however, Yin Yu Tang does

not qualify for recognition as a historic structure in the United States because it does not relate directly to a person or event in American history or represent a form of American architecture.

After a Cultural Exchange Agreement with the Huangshan Municipality was signed that would incorporate the presentation of Yin Yu Tang in the United States, Chinese craftsmen disassembled the house and crated it for shipment to the United States in nineteen 40-foot-long shipping containers. The wood and stone components of the house arrived in Boston in late 1997. In the spring of 1998, John G. Waite Associates, Architects, began a three-year process of identifying, inventorying, and documenting the individual pieces. This work was carried out in a warehouse in Melrose, Massachusetts. Gradually, subassemblies of the building were fitted together, and detailed drawings of the assemblies were prepared. Eventually, the project grew to occupy 100,000 square feet of warehouse space. As the construction was better understood, and the condition of the materials was more precisely defined, a comprehensive program of conservation was developed to clean, repair, and replace missing pieces.

As conservation progressed, the architectural planning turned to the needs of the new house site at the Peabody Essex Museum in Salem, Massachusetts. As a principal port in the China export trade, Salem was an ideal site for the re-erection of Yin Yu Tang. This synergy is accentuated by the Peabody Essex Museum's ownership of contemporary American houses, offering the ability to compare and contrast culture at both ends of the eighteenth-century China trade.

With the erection of Yin Yu Tang in the new courtyard of the museum's expansion project, issues of context had to be addressed. Although space within the courtyard was limited, an effort was made to site the house so that the urban density of Huang Cun, the village from which the house came, was re-created.

With the re-erection of the house, new building systems foreign to the original construction had to be inserted. These systems included electrical wiring and lighting for highlighting exhibits, for providing safe passage for visitors, and for enabling the museum staff to provide an appropriate level of maintenance. A new radiant and forced air heating and ventilation system was required for the comfort and safety of visitors, and for the conservation of the building. Plumbing was installed for stormwater drainage and to service the two fish ponds in the interior of the house. A fire-detection and protection system, utilizing a comprehensive sprinkler layout, was introduced to satisfy safety concerns, and to protect the building from fire damage. The structure of the timber frame, masonry walls, and roof construction was reinforced to meet the seismic criteria of the modern building code.

The original construction of the house was not forgiving or flexible when it came to inserting new building systems. The floorboards at the second-floor level were also the ceiling boards of the first-floor level. The interior wall partitions were constructed of either solid wood paneling or thin bricks, laid on edge as shiners. There was little or no room for electrical conduit, mechanical ductwork, and piping. An innovative solution was adopted. The exterior stone and brick walls required seismic reinforcement, so the decision was made to employ structural grade stainless steel for conduit, ductwork, and piping; thereby having the building system distribution network serve two purposes.

With the change in building use and relocation, other modifications were necessary to adapt the house to its new location. Yin Yu Tang was moved from an internal, southern province of China to a northern, coastal site in the United States. This has created challenges for the conservation of the building materials and for the experience of the visitors. One of the museum's primary goals was to re-erect the house in an exterior environment where the house could be experienced in a setting that reflected the natural character of the original design. However, with the relocation of the house to a New England climate, some compensation had to made for the open skywell at the center of the building. This led to the development of a panelized skylight system that could be removed in the spring and re-installed in the fall.

Of a similar complexity were the issues associated with accessibility for disabled visitors. In a house where fengshui dictates indirect and difficult passage to retain good spirits and ward off evil ones, it was a challenge to provide open access for the visitor while retaining the historic character of the house. Accessibility needs were met by transforming raised stone thresholds into automated, self-leveling thresholds; wood-paneled wall partitions were modified into free-swinging, invisibly hinged access doors.

At the east end of the house a historic shell was re-created to house an elevator/stair tower. The form and exterior finish were designed to replicate historic Huizhou architecture; the volume was developed by utilizing ghost patterns of a previous building appended to the east elevation of Yin Yu Tang. The stair/elevator tower was needed to provide a building-code-compliant means of egress from the second floor of the house. The two original ladder stairs within the house do not comply with modern requirements for egress.

Despite the modifications required for its new use, and despite its journey halfway around the globe, the re-erection and preservation of Yin Yu Tang should be considered a significant preservation success. Not only has the project resulted in the relocation of the house across cultures, but the process of disassembly, evaluation, and re-assembly has added significantly to the understanding of Chinese vernacular architecture. Traditional construction knowledge that would have remained clouded in obscurity was brought to light by the mechanism of re-erection.

—Clay Palazzo

Notes

Chronology

1. *Xiuning Xianzhi* (Xiuning County Gazeteer), Editorial Associaton, Anhui Provincial Gazeteer Series (1990), p. 19.
2. *Ibid.*, p. 20.
3. *Ibid.*, p. 21.
4. *Ibid.*, p. 408.
5. *Ibid.*, p. 23.
6. *Ibid.*
7. *Ibid.*, p. 25.
8. *Ibid.*, p. 26.
9. *Ibid.*, p. 27.
10. *Ibid.*, p. 29.
11. *Ibid.*, p. 108.
12. *Ibid.*, p. 30.
13. As calculated from statistics given for Xiuning population, *ibid.*, 95.
14. *Ibid.*, p. 31.
15. *Ibid.*, p. 35.
16. *Ibid.*
17. *Ibid.*, p. 108.

Part 1
Huizhou: Mountains and Merchants

1. Xiuning Xianzhi (Xiuning County Gazetteer), 1815 edition. He Yingsong, compiler. Preface to the section on geography.
2. Robert Fortune, Two Visits to the Tea Countries of China. (London: John Murray, 1853), p. 54.
3. A popular Huizhou adage.
4. A common Chinese saying, quoted in Jean-Baptiste Du Halde, Description geographique, historique, chronologique, politique, et physique de l'Empire Chine et de la Tartarie Chinoise. (Paris: P. G. Lemercier, 1735).
5. According to Xiuning County government statistics, Xiuning is a total of 2,135 square kilometers, or 3,200,000 mu (One mu, a Chinese hectare, equals 7,174 square feet, or 0.1647 acre). Mountains and hills make up 76.7 percent of the land, while valleys and plains make up 23.3 percent. Forests fill 1,719,000 mu (more than half of the land). Tea is cultivated on 175,100 mu. Cultivated lands are 213,600 mu (roughly 7 percent) of the land, and rice cultivation fills 192,100 mu, about 6 percent of the total land.
6. Xiuning Xianzhi (Xiuning County Gazetteer), 1815 edition. Preface to section on food and products.
7. Xiuning Xianzhi (Xiuning County Gazetteer), Wanli reign period (1573–1620) edition. Preface on local customs in the geography section.
8. Unidentified author, Dianye Xuzhi (Essential Information for Pawnshop Operation), probably published in Huizhou, circa 1900. This booklet is in the collections of the Harvard Yenching Library and was first noticed there by Professor Yang Liansheng. He published the text, with an introduction, in Shih-huo Monthly, vol. I, no. 4, July 1971, pp. 231–43. I am grateful to Pauline Lin for the translation of this text.
9. Ibid.
10. A Huizhou folksong recorded in Li Jiahong, Huangshan Luyou Wenhua Dacidian (The Huangshan Traveler's Cultural Dictionary). (Hefei: Zhongguo Kexue Jishu Daxue Chubanshe, 1994), p. 591.
11. Xin'an Zhi (Xin'an Gazetteer), 1175, as quoted in Harriet T. Zurndorfer, Change and Continuity in Local Chinese History. (Leiden: Brill, 1989), p. 85.
12. Xiuning Xianzhi (Xiuning County Gazetteer), 1815 edition, section on local products.
13. Zhang Haipeng and Wang Yanyuan, editors, Huishang Yanjiu (Research on Huizhou Merchants). (Hefei: Anhui Renmin Chubanshe, 1995), p. 252.
14. www.imperialtours.net/huizhou_history_frame.htm.
15. Qimen Xian Xinxiu Changmenxiji (Qimen County Newly Edited Records of Changmen Brook), as quoted in Zurndorfer, Change and Continuity, p. 25.
16. Xiuning Xianzhi (Xiuning County Gazetteer), 1815 edition, p. 479.
17. Fortune, Two Visits, p. 66.
18. Ibid., p. 63.
19. Walter Henry Medhurst, A Glance at the Interior of China Obtained During a Journey through the Silk and Green Tea Districts [Taken in 1845]. (Shanghai?: Mission Press, 1849), p. 135.
20. Zurndorfer, Change and Continuity , p. 49.
21. Ibid., p. 50.
22. Gu Yenwu, Tianxia junguo liping shu, as quoted in Zurndorfer, Change and Continuity, p. 53.
23. Ibid., p. 95.
24. Zhang Haipeng and Wang Yanyuan, editors, Huishang Yanjiu (Research on Huizhou Merchants). (Hefei: Anhui Renmin Chubanshe, 1995), p. 149.
25. T. S. Whelan, The Pawnshop in China (Ann Arbor: Center for Chinese Studies, 1979).
26. Among the many who noted this fact was the Englishman Edward Parker, in his article "A Journey in Chekiang," published in the Journal of the China Branch of the Royal Asiatic Society, 1884, n.s. V19, pp. 27–53. He wrote: "The pawn shope and banks at Lan-ch'i [Lanxi] are chiefly in the hands of the An-hwei [Anhui] men."
27. Dainye Xuzhi (Essential Information for Pawnshop Operation).
28. http://www.huangshanguide.com/around12.htm.
29. Published by Professor Yang Liansheng, Shih-hou Monthly 1 no. 4 (July 1971), pp. 231–43. The English translation presented here is by Pauline Lin.
30. Our Correspondent in Hsuchowfu, "In a Shansi Pawnshop," North China Herald, July 4, 1914.
31. Cheng Fujin, editor. Huizhou Fengsu (Huizhou Customs). (Hefei: Huang Shan Shushe, 1996), p. 83.
32. Ibid., p. 83.
33. Zurndorfer, Change and Continuity, pp. 37–41.
34. Ibid., p. 55.
35. For further information, see Richard Lufrano, Honorable Merchants, Commerce and Self-Cultivation in Late Imperial China. (Honolulu: University of Hawaii Press, 1996).
36. Xiuning Xianzhi (Xiuning County Gazetteer), 1815 edition, vol. 13, section on personages.
37. As quoted in Craig Clunas, Superfluous Things: Material Culture and Social Status in Early Modern China. (Urbana: University of Illinois Press, 1991), p. 163.
38. Sandi Chin and Ginger Hsu, "Anhui Merchant Culture and Patronage," in James Cahill, ed., Shadows of Mt. Huang: Chinese Painting and Printing of the Anhui School. (Berkeley: University of California Press, 1981), p. 22.
39. Written in the mid-spring month of the twenty-first year of Chenghua reign period [1485] by Cheng Bian, a Confucian scholar and candidate for the national examination, at the age of eighty-four, in the village of Taitang.
40. I am grateful to Zhu Jiajin of the Palace Museum in Beijing and Professor Angela Zito of New York University for confirming this for me.
41. Fortune, Two Visits, p. 58.
42. Recorded in Gao Shouxian, Huizhou Wenhua (Huizhou Culture). (Shengyang: Liaoning Jiaoyu Chubanshe, 1998), p. 101.
43. Xiuning Xianzhi (Xiuning County Gazetteer). (Hefei: Anhui Jiaoyu Chubanshe, 1990), p. 583.
44. Medhurst, Glance at the Interior of China, p. 147.
45. Wang Yaozhen, Untitled (Four Letters in Poetic Form), an unpublished manuscript, probably written in the 1930s.
47. Huizhou Fengsu (Huizhou Customs), p. 113.
48. Song of the Immortals, translated by Xu Yuanzhong. (Beijing: New World Press, 1994), p. 65.
49. Translation from Cyril Birch, Stories from a Ming Collection, translations of Chinese short stories published in the seventeenth century. (London: Bodley Head, 1958).
50. Medhurst, Glance at the Interior of China, p. 131.

51. Mark Elvin, "Blood and Statistic," in Harriet T. Zurndorfer, editor, *Chinese Women in the Imperial Past.* (Leiden: Brill, 1999), pp. 135–222.

52. *Xiuning Xianzhi* (Xiuning County Gazeteer), 1815 edition. Section on "Women of Integrity."

Part 2
Jia: Hometown and Family

1. From the preface to the *Huang Chuan Huang Zhi Zupu* by Cheng Bian.

2. The odes were transcribed by Yu Yun in 1486 in the *Huang Chuan Huang Shi Zu Pu*. He indicates that Huang Sisheng lived at an earlier time period.

3. It is interesting to note that Huang Zizhi calls the building a water deity temple. Most of the older people in the village today refer to it as the Guan Di Temple.

4. *Xiuning Xianzhi* (Xiuning County Gazeteer), 1990 edition, p. 20.

5. Explained by Huang Cun resident Huang Jixian, in a 1999 discussion.

6. Repeated by teachers and residents of Huang Cun in conversations with the author in 1997, 1998, 1999, 2000.

7. *Xiuning Xianzhi* (Xiuning County Gazeteer), 1990 edition, p. 196.

8. From the preface to the *Huang Chuan Huang Zhi Zupu*, by Cheng Bian.

9. Huang Zhenduo wrote:
Our Huang family started to write our clan history at the time of Ancestor Yueqi who lived in the end of Yuan dynasty and the beginning of the Ming dynasty [estimably 1400 C.E.]. Additions and re-editions were done several times respectively by Ancestors Sicong and Yihui in the Tianshun and Chenghua years [about 1500]; by Ancestor Fangshan in the Jiaqing years [about 1540]; by Ancestors Yibai (Literary-name Zhiyu), Tuan'an (Pen-name Renbao), Fangdan (Pen-name Mengxu), and Kuixuan (Pen-name Shaoji) in the end of the Ming dynasty and the beginning of the Qing dynasty [about 1660]; and by Ancestor Yiting (Zhaohong) in the Kangxi and Qianlong years [about 1710].
From then through the beginning of the Republic of China [1912], two hundred years had passed [and no re-editing was done.] When the Taiping Army was besieged in Huizhou, the sufferings [of the clan] were great and the old clan histories and documents were either partially destroyed or totally lost. My clan brother Diyuan (Kaixiang) searched the remaining documents and collecting clan-wide the lists of memorial days of all families as reference. In this way, he continued the job of addition and re-editing of the clan history.

10. I am grateful to Shen Jing for taking the time to examine the work and make this assessment.

11. The shape, location, and direction of the tomb was considered to be able to influence the comfort of the deceased and fate of their offspring.

12. Today, Qing Ming is usually celebrated according to the solar calendar, on April 5.

13. The histories of many surnames in Huizhou are recounted in the 1316 *Xin'an Dazu Zhi* (The Record of Xin'an's Great Lineages) as discussed by Zurndorfer in *Change and Continuity*, p. 15. Many Huizhou family lineages interestingly trace their histories back to this town of Huang Dun, which would have been an important center in earlier times. An early presence of Huangs in Huang Dun is evidenced by a splendid Huang ancestral hall that stood there until in the 1980s, when it was torn down, according to professor of architecture Zhu Xijie, who saw the wooden components of the structure piled up just after it had been dismantled. Many well-known members of the Huang clan in Huizhou trace their roots back to Huang Dun, including the renowned twentieth-century artist Huang Binhong and the celebrated Ming period Huang family of woodblock carvers, one of whom, Huang Yingzu, carved the blocks for an exquisite Xiuning garden landscape print (see figure 5).

14. Huang Zhenduo Genealogy.

15. Generally, the eldest son was deemed the successor of his father, and the line of the eldest sons constitutes the main stem of the family tree. However, the line of Zongqi eventually failed to produce male descendants. As a result, the line of Zongren, the second son, was deemed the main line instead.

16. As quoted in Caleb Carr, *The Devil Soldier: The American Soldier of Fortune Who Became a God in China.* (New York: Random House, 1992), p. 56.

17. His son.

18. Tuh-shih-tseun's report published in the Gazette of April, 1856, was quoted in Commander Lindesay Brine, *The Taeping Rebellion.* (London: John Murray, 1862), p. 214.

19. *Xiuning Xianzhi* (Xiuning County Gazeteer), 1990 edition, p. 19.

20. *Ibid.*, p. 19.

21. *Ibid.*

22. Jacques Gernet, *A History of Chinese Civilization.* (Cambridge University Press, 1972), p. 597.

23. For instance, the genealogy describes Huang Xizhou of the thirteenth generation and his descendants: "The eldest son of Yi. His literary name was Shangwen and his literary title was Yin lu. He had two sons. He was buried at Tingzishan (Pavilion Hill) and his tomb is the shape of a tiger. His daughter Shougui was married to the Cheng family of Xibian."

24. In the photograph of Ms. Cheng's funeral, a scroll can be seen signed by Da Zhi Nu, the eldest niece, who would have been the daughter of her husband's brother. The inclusion of the "eldest" implies that there was at least one other niece.

25. A direct nephew, Huang Zuze, is mentioned on the memorial document for the wife of Huang Yangxian, but had he produced heirs, his name would have appeared on the Yin Yu Tang ancestral death anniversary plaque.

26. F. L. Hawks, *A Short History of Shanghai.* (Shanghai: Kelly and Walsh, 1928), p. 132.

27. This flag for the Republic of China was in use from 1912–29.

28. The family's name for Huang Zixian.

29. The family's name for Huang Zizhi.

30. As was noted in his funeral notice.

31. The Huang Clan Primary School was officially established as a modern primary school in 1910. However, there most likely was a more traditional family school in the village previous to the 1910 introduction of a modern educational system.

32. Letter from an unidentified relative to Huang Zizhi.

33. Harry A. Franck, *Roving Through Southern China.* (New York: The Century Company, 1923), pp. 120–21.

34. The Ruren title for women was originally reserved for wives of nobility or officials above a specific rank. In later years, the term was used to respectfully address a woman.

35. Letter from Madame Cheng to Huang Zizhi.

36. Letter from Madame Cheng to Huang Zizhi.

37. A notation found among Huang Zizhi's notebooks.

38. An envelope, dated 1907, containing a letter to Huang Zizhi from fellow Huang Cun native Huang Shaoqing, reveals that Huang Shaoqing was working at the Anji Baolou in Leping.

39. Envelopes addressed to him there are dated the first year of the Republican era, 1912; his brother Huang Zixian was at this point in Wuchang, Hubei Province.

40. One *liang* is approx. thirty grams (1.06 oz.).

41. One *chi* is approx. one-third of a meter (1.08 ft.).

42. Huang Zizhi also kept in contact with the businessmen in Hong Zhaodi's family, and had noted their Shanghai addresses in a 1929 notebook as they could assist when he went to the large city.

43. Noted by Huang Zhenxin and Huang Xianying, 1999, in conversation with author.

44. *Ibid.*

45. James Ricalton, *China through the Stereoscope: A Journey through the Dragon Empire at the Time of the Boxer Uprising*, ed. Jim Zwick. (New York: Underwood & Underwood, 1901; revised and enlarged BoondocksNet Edition, 2000). See: www.boondocksnet.com/china/.

46. The mandarin duck is a symbol of a devoted relationship between a husband and wife.

47. This is an old and very popular tale. A celestial weaving maiden leaves heaven and goes down to earth, where she marries a herdsman. They lead a very happy life together and give birth to a son and a daughter. But the Heavenly Emperor insists the weaving maiden return to heaven to continue her duties there. The weaving maiden was subsequently only allowed to visit her husband once a year, on the seventh day of the seventh month.

48. A literary expression for sex.

49. A literary expression of a first-place ranking.

50. It is not clear whether Biandong is a name of a place or a brand name.

51. In this document, weight and price are recorded in "Suzhou code," a special form of a numbering system used by accountants in the first half of the twentieth century.

52. 1 *fen* is approximately .12 gram (0.004 oz.).

53. 1 *qian* is approximately 2 grams (0.07 oz.).

54. 1 *li* equals 1/16 fen.

55. From *San Tzu Ching* (San Zi Jing), translated and annotated by Herbert A. Giles. (Beijing: Kelly and Walsh, 1940). Originally published, Shanghai, 1900.

56. *Xiuning Xianzhi* (Xiuning County Gazetteer), 1990 editon, p. 30.

57. For a fuller account, read Jasper Becker, *Hungry Ghosts: Mao's Secret Famine.* (New York: Henry Holt and Company, 1996).

58. *Xiuning Xianzhi* (Xiuning County Gazetteer), 1990 editon, p.30.

59. *Ibid.*, p. 95.

60. *Ibid.*

61. The word "above" refers to generational ranking.

62. The word "below" refers again to generational ranking. Lower-ranking people in ancient China sat on mats.

63. The Chinese original is *bomu,* generally meaning "uncle's wife." In his poem, however, it seems to denote "elder brother's wife."

64. The Chinese language differentiates between maternal and paternal relatives. The "uncle" here refers to the father's younger brother.

65. Literally "to twist the oil lamp."

66. The Buddhist goddess of mercy.

67. *Cun* is a Chinese inch, and three cun is the coveted length for bound feet.

68. From the *North China Herald,* December 28, 1926.

69. An expression of respect spoken by a child to a parent.

70. An expression of respect used in letters.

71. Huang Zhenxin possibly mistakenly wrote "father," intending instead to have said that he had received a letter from his mother. He was living with his father at the time.

72. Huang Zhenxin made a mistake here. It was actually his father's sixtieth birthday.

73. The price is noted on the still extant receipt from the coffin shop.

74. For an unknown reason, this notice was never sent.

75. *Xiuning Xianzhi* (Xiuning County Gazetteer), 1990 editon, p. 25

76. Described by Huang Ailan during a conversation with author in 2001 in Tunxi.

Part 3
The Architecture of Yin Yu Tang

1. Robert Thorpe, "The Architectural Heritage of the Bronze Age," in *Chinese Traditional Architecture,* edited by Nancy Shatzman Steinhardt. (New York: China Institute Gallery, 1984), p. 62.

2. Chang Kwang-chih, *The Archeology of Ancient China.* (New Haven: Yale University Press, 1968), p. 215.

3. *Ibid.,* p. 219.

4. Thorpe, "Architectural Heritage," p. 63.

5. *Ibid.,* p. 61.

6. Chang Kwang-chih, *Archeology of Ancient China,* p. 215.

7. Thorpe, "Architectural Heritage," p. 65.

8. In Europe, the problem of rotting end grain of columns led to columns on stone bases and then to a horizontal wooden sill under columns, above the stones. I am grateful to Jan Lewandoski for pointing out this comparison. This final step of adding the horizontal wooden sill was not made in China. Many Huizhou Ming-period buildings have wooden blocks, with wood grain parallel to the ground, sandwiched between wooden columns and stone bases. These boards prevent moisture from traveling upward to rot the lower end of the column.

9. As quoted in Zhang Zhongyi, Cao Jianbing, and Zhuan Gaojie, *Huizhou Mingdai Zhuzhai* (Ming Perod Huizhou Residences). (Beijing: Jianzhu Gongcheng Chubanshe, 1957), p. 11. I am most grateful to J. M. Simonet, who generously presented this rare book to me as a gift after I mentioned to him that I had been unable to locate it.

10. These prints are discussed in many books, including Jonathan D. Spence, *The Memory Palace of Matteo Ricci* (London: Faber, 1985) and Soren Edgren, *Chinese Rare Books in American Collections* (New York: China House Gallery, China Institute in America, 1984).

11. As quoted in *History and Development of Ancient Chinese Architecture,* compiled by Institute of the History of Natural Sciences and Chinese Academy of Sciences (Beijing: Science Press, 1986), p. 471.

12. Susan Naquin and Evelyn Rawski, *Chinese Society in the Eighteenth Century* (New Haven: Yale University Press, 1987), p. 49.

13. Zhang Zongyi, *Huizhou Mingdai Zhuzhai,* p. 14.

14. Described by Zhu Yanjue, during a conversation with author in Yuetan, Xiuning, Huang-

shan, Anhui Province in November 2001.

15. Klaas Ruitenbeek, *Carpentry and Building in Late Imperial China* (Leiden: Brill, 1993), p. 22.

16. Much of this analysis is derived from an article on the manuscript by Fang Hao, "A Document on the Reconstruction of an Ancestral Temple in the Kangxi Period (1662–1722)," *Shih-huo Monthly* vol. 1 no. 11 (February 1972), pp. 565–69. I am grateful to Pauline Lin for her assistance in the translation of this document.

17. One pound equals .38 *qian.*

18. Li Jiahong, *Huangshan Luyou Wenhua Dacidian,* p. 509.

19. *Ibid.,* 523.

20. Rudolf P. Hommel, *China at Work* (Cambridge: MIT Press, 1969), pp. 270–72. Originally published by the John Day Company in 1937.

21. According to the masons and carpenters who assisted in the dismantling and conservation of Yin Yu Tang.

22. Ruitenbeek, *Carpentry and Building,* p. 40.

23. This traditional method was documented by the Yin Yu Tang project during the re-erection of a Ming house in an open-air museum at Qiankou, Huizhou District, Huangshan Municipality, in Anhui.

24. The traditional master carpenters from Huizhou who worked on dismantling and re-erecting Yin Yu Tang in Salem, Zhu Jiming and Zhu Yun-feng, were quite insistent that the buildings must be constructed from east progressing toward the west and that the re-erection had to happen in the same direction.

25. An indepth discussion on roof profiles can be found in Ronald Knapp, *China's Traditional Rural Architecture.* (Honolulu: University of Hawaii Press, 1986), pp. 74–77.

26. Others have proposed that the upturn at the edge of the roof provides extra weight to the rows of tiles and keeps them from slipping down off the roof.

27. See article by Nancy Berliner "Wang Tingna and Illustrated Book Publishing in Huizhou," *Orientations Magazine,* January 1994.

28. Zhang Yuhuan in *History and Development of Ancient Chinese Architecture,* p. 306, remarks that horse-head walls, which he calls "fire protecting walls," appeared during the Ming dynasty "at the latest."

29. Explained in a discussion with the author during the summer of 2001.

30. For a further discussion, see Margery Wolf, *House of Lim: A Study of a Chinese Farm Family* (Englewood Cliffs, N.J.: Prentice-Hall, 1968).

31. Wang Shixiang, *Classic Chinese Furniture.* (Hong Kong: Joint Publishing Company, 1986), p. 15, and Craig Clunas, p. 156. Clunas's book is an extended discussion on this theme.

32. Hommel, *China at Work,* p. 280.

Bibliography

Babel, Isaac. *Collected Stories*. Translated by David McDuff from an annotated edition by Efraim Sicher. London: Penguin Books, 1994.

Chang Kwang-chih. *The Archeology of Ancient China*. New Haven: Yale University Press, 1968.

Clunas, Craig. *Superfluous Things*. Chicago: University of Illinois Press, 1991.

Fairbank, John King. *The United States and China*. Cambridge: Harvard University Press, 1971.

Fao Hao, Maurus Fang Hao. "A Document on the Reconstruction of Ancestral Temple in the K'ang-hsi Period (1662–1722)." *Shih-hou Monthly* 1, no. 11 (February 1972).

Gernet, Jacques. *A History of Chinese Civilization*. Cambridge: Cambridge University Press, 1972.

History and Development of Ancient Chinese Architecture. Compiled by Institute of the History of Natural Sciences and Chinese Academy of Sciences. Beijing: Science Press, 1986.

Hommel, Rudolf P. *China at Work*. Cambridge: MIT Press, 1969. Originally published by the John Day Company in 1937.

Li Jiahong. *Huangshan Luyou Wenhua Dacidian*. Hefei: Zhongguo Kexue Jishu Daxue Chubanshe, 1994.

Naquin, Susan, and Evelyn Rawski. *Chinese Society in the 18th Century*. New Haven: Yale University Press, 1987.

Rultenbeek, Klaas. *Carpentry and Building In Late Imperial China*. Leiden: Brill, 1993.

Shatzman Steinhardt, Nancy, editor. *Chinese Traditional Architecture*. New York: China Institute Gallery, 1984.

Spence, Jonathan D. *The Search for Modern China*. New York: W. W. Norton & Company, 1999.

Thorpe, Robert. "The Architectural Heritage of the Bronze Age," in *Chinese Traditional Architecture*. Edited by Nancy Shatzman Steinhardt. New York: China Institute Gallery, 1984.

Wolf, Margery. House of Lim: A Study of a Chinese Farm Family. Englewood Cliffs, N.J.: Prentice-Hall, 1968.

Zhang Yuhuan in *History and Development of Ancient Chinese Architecture*. Compiled by Institute of the History of Natural Sciences and Chinese Academy of Sciences. Beijing: Science Press, 1986.

Zhang Zhongyi, Cao Jianbing, and Zhuan Gaojie. *Huizhou Mingdai Zhuzhai* (Ming Huizhou Residences). Beijing: Jianzhu Gongcheng Chubanshe, 1957.

Index

Acknowledgments

The past six years have been a gloriously enriching experience of diving and delving, deeper and deeper, into the many vast realms of Yin Yu Tang. Many essential, and wonderful, people have traveled on the path of this exploration—without them Yin Yu Tang would be an empty shell of wood and bricks.

Every journey begins with a single step. Thus, on a warm Chinese National Day, October 1st, 1996, a group of people gathered in the central courtyard of a home called Yin Yu Tang, in the rural village of Huang Cun. Some were reminiscing about their earlier lives in the house, while others were marveling at its architectural structure and history. None of us were fully aware at that moment that we would be embarking together on a six-and-half year long interchange across an oceanic divide. But, each of the people in the space that day became significant contributors to the effort that resulted in Yin Yu Tang standing proudly today at the Peabody Essex Museum, in Salem, Massachusetts, and the publication of this book. Among those I wish to acknowledge, I am extraordinarily indebted to everyone who met that day: Huang family members Huang Xiqi, Huang Binggen, and Chou Lijuan and Huang Xianying, who were willing to sit for endless interviews, share all of their personal histories, and, as importantly, offer their warm personal encouragement; Yin Yu Tang neighbors Huang Qirui and Wang Youjin, who patiently provided in-depth recountings of Huang Cun traditions and family history; my colleague Tara Cederholm, whose steadfast dedication to excellence guided this project and whose deep interest in the aesthetic and philosophical nitty-gritty bore fruit in the high quality of the ultimate product; and Ned Johnson, whose enthusiastic support, discerning eye, thoughtful inquisitiveness and astute insight into so many cultural and practical areas, and personal involvement, have been an inspiration for all of us.

As events unfolded, several months later, an encounter with the ever-astonishing Wang Shukai, followed by members of the Huangshan Municipal Cultural Relics Department and the Xiuning County Cultural Bureau, introduced another layer of major contributors. Wang Shukai's prodigious bounty of energy, persistence, and management skills, as well as his warm devotion to this project, has been a consistent mainstay and, as is said in Chinese, "a ridge pole column" supporting the edifice. My appreciation is extended to the tireless efforts of Li Tai, Lin Jianmin, Wang Xiang, Wang Tao, Yao Shunlai, and Hu Xiaoyan in Xiuning and Huangshan, for plodding on innumerable trips down muddy dirt roads to look at houses, villages, and pagodas, and patiently assisting with bureaucratic procedures.

Once in America, this house called Yin Yu Tang was embraced by many more willing hands, eager to assist in the fruition of its goal: Dan Monroe, Executive Director of the Peabody Essex Museum, keenly welcomed Yin Yu Tang into the already ambitious museum expansion plans; the highly professional and competent architectural preservationists John G. Waite, Clay Palazzo, Bill Brandow, and Arik Mathison and all the fine staff of John G. Waite, Architects, Associates, with the expert and congenial assistance of preservation timber-framer Jan Lewandoski, analyzed and computer-graphically sketched every component, large and minute, of the building, and this core team expertly oversaw the re-erection process; Paul Kuenstner patiently and wisely managed the ever-surprising and ever-enlarging project; Anne-Marie Soulliere who gracefully contributed her oversight and advice; Libby Caterino zealously and affectionately took on the conservation of the objects from within the house (from grand beds to cookie molds); while Melvin Wesly offered sensible and supportive counsel; and Barbara Levy, Rick Guttenberg, Susan Bean, Kimberly Alexander, Rob Saarnio Paula Noyes and Vas Prabhu provided vital interpretive observations and contributions.

A comprehension of how Yin Yu Tang was built would never have been possible without the diligent efforts of Zhu Jiming, Zhu Yunfeng, Ling Qizheng, and Yao Desheng, masters of carpentry and masonry, from the region around Yin Yu Tang, who were not only superbly skilled artisans, but also patient and fine teachers to all of us yearning to understand their crafts, and appreciate their techniques which are all but lost in our culture and time.

The warm and hospitable people of Huang Cun and Huizhou region made invaluable and uncountable contributions in their willingness to answer questions, sit for long interviews and allow foreigners into their fields and their homes. I am also extremely grateful to filmmakers (and amazing purveyors) of Chinese culture, Carma Hinton and Richard Gordon, of the Long Bow Group, who not only skillfully interviewed and filmed so many of our participants, but also provided a warm and gracious face for the project in China. Many of the quotes from family members included in this text are from interviews conducted with Carma and Richard.

The expressive photography for this book, as well as for the interpretive gallery at the museum, was professionally provided by a team of artists, including Richard Howard, Marc Teatum, Jeff Dykes, Mark Sexton, Cheng Shouqi, and Olivia Parker. I am also thankful to Professor Gong Kai of Dongnan University in Nanjing and his architecture students who produced fine architectural surveys of Huang Cun village, and Ray Lum and the Harvard-Yenching Library for providing photographs for this publication.

I am extremely grateful to Feng Yu and Pauline Lin for their expert skills in deciphering and translating the many complex, and occasionally barely legible documents and letters found in Yin Yu Tang. Shen Jing at the Harvard Yenching Library was of great assistance in my investigation of the Huang family genealogies. I am additionally appreciative of the support of the Fairbanks Center for East Asian Research at Harvard University where I am a Research Associate.

In achieving the publication of this book, Ike Williams, Ashley Benning, Holger Jacobs, Lindsey Kiang, and Hope Denekamp have been wonderfully committed, conscientious, and encouraging, and I am indebted to Ed Walters for providing professional and creative assistance of the highest order.

For the past four years, Bruce MacLaren has been an indispensable Assistant Curator of Chinese Art, affably and skillfully providing research, organization, and global assistance. I am also extremely appreciative of Anne Curley, Michael Melanson, and Martha Small for essential help in this project, and Patricia Hurley, for her warm and wise guidance.

The initial stages of the project benefited greatly from the knowledge and guidance of the architects Cowley Denue Prudon and construction management of Andrew Anway and, in the latter stages, as the house rose on site, from the experience of Liberty Street Restoration.

Personally, I will always be grateful for the enthusiastic support and guidance given to me over the years by my friends, colleagues and mentors in the field of Chinese cultural studies, including Professor Ronald Knapp, Wang Shixiang, Jean Marie Simonet, Zhu Chuanrong, Zhu Jiajin, and Andre Kneib.

From the largest perspective, the entire Huang family and their ancestors have provided the world with an enthralling house and a magnificent cache of documents—letters, account books, and even poems—that has richly informed the exploration of their home. I am above all indebted to them for meticulously caring for the home for so many years and for now trusting others with their precious inheritance and history. I am daily touched by the generous friendship, time and warmth that Huang Zhenxin, Huang Binggen, and Huang Xiqi and their families have offered to me and the others working on this project. While we have all arrived at a place none of us could have dreamed of when we stood in the Yin Yu Tang courtyard so many years ago, my sincere hope is that the project has yet fulfilled some of the Huang family's wishes, though world's apart from any their ancestors could have imagined.

Finally, the unpredicted enormity and complexity of this project created a whirlwind in my own personal life. I am extremely grateful to a number of people, especially my husband, Bill Mellins, and my parents, Barney and Mim Berliner, for their constant and daily support, their humor and their encouragement during these years.

While I am deeply grateful for all the assistance I have received from everyone noted above, I, of course, take full responsibility for any unfortunate mistakes or omissions in this text.

—Nancy Berliner